VOICES IN IRELAND

A TRAVELLER'S LITERARY COMPANION

Other books by the author

POEMS
An Enchantment (1991)
Collected Poems (1992)

MEMOIR AND TRAVEL
The Perfect Stranger (1966)
Finding Connections (1990)

NOVELS
A Song and Dance (1968)
A Happy Man (1972)
People and Weather (1978)
Scarf Jack (1978)
Rebel for Good (1980)
Only by Mistake (1986)

ESSAYS
People and Places (1988)

EDITED
Collected Poems of Ivor Gurney (1982)
The Essential G. K. Chesterton (1985)
The Oxford Book of Short Poems (with James Michie, 1985)
Selected Poems of Ivor Gurney (1990)
A Book of Consolations (1992)

VOICES IN IRELAND

A Traveller's Literary Companion

P.J. Kavanagh

JOHN MURRAY

© P. J. Kavanagh 1994

First published in 1994
by John Murray (Publishers) Ltd.,
50 Albemarle Street, London W1X 4BD
Paperback edition 1995

A catalogue record for this book is available from the British Library

ISBN 0–7195–5389–X

Typeset in 12½/12½ Bembo by Colset (Private) Limited, Singapore
Printed and bound in Great Britain at the University Press, Cambridge

CONTENTS

ILLUSTRATIONS

The author and publisher would like to thank the following for permission to reproduce illustrations: 1: Rex Roberts; 2: Office of Public Works, Dublin; 3: National Museum of

Ireland; 4: Crown Copyright/MOD. Reproduced with the permission of the Controller of HMSO; 5: Northern Ireland Tourist Board; 6: Mrs Edwin Smith; 8: Maurice Craig; 9: Colin Smythe; 10: Sir Toby Coghill; 11: Bord Fáilte; 12: Mansell Collection; 14: Colin Smythe; 15: from *Elizabeth Bowen* by Victoria Glendinning. Reproduced courtesy of Wiedenfeld & Nicolson Archives; 16: *Irish Times*; 17: BBC; 18: G.A. Duncan

PREFACE

A book like this needs the help of local knowledge, and of hospitality. For both of these, special thanks are owed to Dorinda and Henry Dunleath, Victoria Glendinning and Terence de Vere White, Pearse Hutchinson, Tina and Andrew Kavanagh, Rosemarie and Sean Mulcahy, Helen and Tomás Ó Canainn, Valerie and Thomas Pakenham, Daphne and Sebastian Ryan, Janice and James Simmons, Angela and Robert Welch. With thanks also to the many others in Ireland who gave help and advice, in particular to Alan Biddle, Peggy Butler, Brian Connolly (of County Cavan library), Brian Friel, Nicholas Furlong, John Gregg (of Croom), Benedict Kiely, Jeff O'Connell (of Kinvara), Mary O'Donnell (of Glenties), Frank Ormsby, Brendan Purcell, Bruce Stewart, Art O'Sullivan (of Carnacon); and in England, to Glen Cavaliero, Ben Howard, Douglas Matthews (who compiled the index) and the staff of the London Library.

Hints have been given towards the pronunciation of Irish names, but apologies are offered in advance for any errors or inconsistencies which arise from a compromise in Irish spellings and accents. (No attempt has been made to standardize the various spellings in quotations.)

The Notes are intended to provide some extra biographical placing of Irish writers who may be less familiar or less accessible, and to indicate the connections with Ireland of writers from England and elsewhere; together with a few suggestions of paths not taken in the main text. With grateful acknowledgement to Kate Kavanagh for these, and for her path-finding, navigation and sustaining enthusiasm.

P.J. KAVANAGH

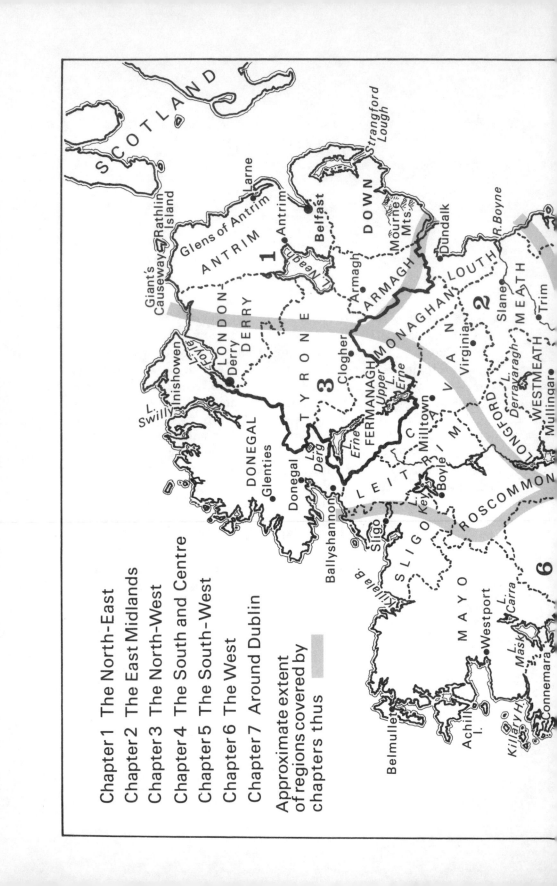

Chapter 1 The North-East
Chapter 2 The East Midlands
Chapter 3 The North-West
Chapter 4 The South and Centre
Chapter 5 The South-West
Chapter 6 The West
Chapter 7 Around Dublin

Approximate extent
of regions covered by
chapters thus

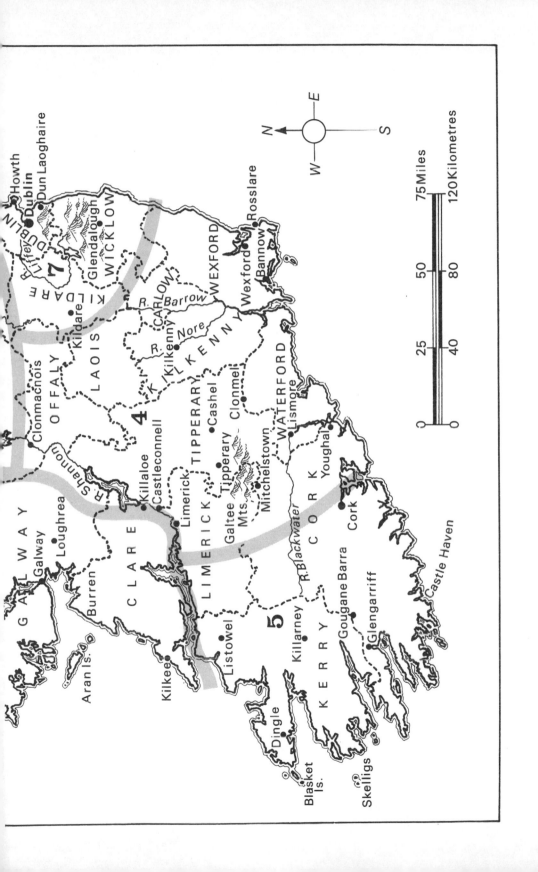

INTRODUCTION

This is a journey round the island led by the literary associations of place, and the best way for a visitor to enjoy the trip, at least for a visitor from England, like me, is to remember that Ireland has the fascination of a foreign country, with a different history; despite its close links it is not a quaint variant of England. Failure to recognize this has been the cause of many misconceptions.

The reasons for the differences of Ireland are many and ancient. The Romans with their laws and roads never reached it, and the Normans only did so long after they had conquered England, and when they came they were soon absorbed into the island (it has that power, of absorption). However, as Frank O'Connor said, 'Books about Ireland that begin with its history have a tendency to remain unread. The misunderstandings are too many.'

One way to reduce the misunderstandings is to remember that Ireland is a foreign country because, uninvaded, it was able to develop a language and a culture of its own (and a system of laws) unlike those of the rest of Romanized Europe. When these became troublesome to English government, a systematic effort was made to destroy them, to 'anglicize' Ireland. This was resisted, the language and culture were forced underground and jealously, secretly, recorded, which is why Ireland is richer in its early literature than almost any other country in Europe. This 'hidden' Ireland, tenderly guarded, unknown to its governors or ignored by them, became a part of its separate identity; as did, after the Reformation, its allegiance to unreformed Catholicism. (In fact, with Irish contrariness, this book begins in the predominantly Protestant north, but that also is a foreign country, sometimes in surprising and pleasant ways.)

The richness of Ireland's distinct tradition is proved by its Irish-language poets down the generations, many of whom are quoted here. Fortunately, there are many brilliant translators of these – among them Frank O'Connor.

There is, however, an internal twentieth-century argument in Ireland, concerned precisely with this past. The rediscovery of the vast extent of the Irish literary inheritance was largely made in Victorian times, and the excitement of its riches caused it to be exalted, waved like a flag of cultural nationhood. Later Irish writers grew impatient, they felt Ireland was looking back too much, it was time it thought about its present. In 1943 Ireland's *Taosieach*, de Valera, was publicly dreaming of a land 'bright with cosy homesteads, whose fields and villages would be joyous with the sounds of industry, with the romping of sturdy children, the contests of sturdy youths and the laughter of comely maidens'. This at a time, as Sean O'Faolain never tired of pointing out, when Ireland was run by townsmen, who knew nothing of 'fields and villages', and when 25,000 Irish men and women were being forced to emigrate every year. It is no wonder that the Irish become uneasy at any whiff of sentimentality about their past. An Irish anthologist of Irish writing complained in 1993 that the majority of such compilations still have a donkey on their cover, or a broken Celtic cross. (On his own he puts a photograph of a demure Marilyn Monroe reading *Ulysses*.)

Ireland has changed and is changing, and does not want to be lumbered with stale images of itself. A book such as this, although it comes up to the present in terms of living writers, is bound, riskily, to be concerned largely with past associations; that is its purpose. It is to be hoped that the affection the place and its writers arouse in me will not be mistaken for sentimentality.

In this book also, behind these Irish discoveries and argments, are four centuries of English voices wondering, in tones that vary from the sympathetic to the murderous, why these people on England's doorstep insist on remaining so resolutely un-English.

Perhaps the quotations included here will go some way to explaining why. They concern *Irish* doorsteps – and lanes and lakes and towns, and ideas. The Irish traditionally have, or had, an acute sense of locality. There was no Industrial Revolution to displace the population; there was instead the long-drawn-out tragedy of emigration. Those who stayed felt all the more identified with the places they lived in, and those who left tended to exaggerate their beauties from afar. This attachment to place was also a literary convention of great strength; from the earliest times, in the sagas, a story was fixed topographically, and the characters defined in terms of where they came from. More recently, there can hardly be a more pedantically 'placed' book than James Joyce's *Ulysses*.

For this reason, to have some knowledge of the associations of a place is to begin to see it as the local Irish see it themselves. The modest Hill of Ushna (Uisneach) for example, in County Westmeath, is seen differently when we learn it was the ancient crowning-place of kings, and that King Cormac, having lost an eye, wore on the Hill a new one, 'made of gold leaves, fastened with silver springs'. Instead of a gentle slope out of the plain of Meath, dotted with peaceful cows, it now puts us in mind of Agamemnon's Mycenae. When we listen to the roar of the waves on Inch Strand in the Dingle peninsula, they are further dramatized for us if we know of the great Egan O'Rahilly's full-throated defiance of them, in his lament for the fate of eighteenth-century Ireland, and the end of the bards. In a similar way, at Drumsna, in County Leitrim, a ruined farmhouse called Ballycloran looks like any other such dilapidation, until we learn that the sight of it gave Anthony Trollope the plot for his first novel, *The MacDermots of Ballycloran*.

The intention is to allow a traveller to see Ireland and Irish pre-occupations through a variety of Irish eyes, and those of non-Irish visitors; in this way to get a little under the skin of the place, through myth and saga, which were always particular as to locality, and through poems, stories, argument. Through novels too, but to a lesser extent, because fiction often conflates landscapes and settings, and may be true to atmosphere but is diminished when confined to one actual place. (When it is exact in this respect it usually arouses local ire.)

There is a second purpose which is almost incidental, and a bonus: to tempt the reader further into exploration of an extraordinary land-scape. The following of literary associations was found to lead not only into corners of the Irish mind but into corners of the island itself, often surprisingly beautiful ones now that they came to be looked at closely, even if at first they were not obviously so; an unexpected beauty, not deceptive, but subtle. Ireland is a place where nothing is quite what it says or seems; not even the landscape, in the constantly changing light. The places mentioned have been visited, to see if they have changed – many of them have hardly done so at all.

One generalization can be risked at the end of what was a fasci-nating journey. The national and historical diversity of this loquacious island – its invention, celebration, boisterousness, lament, and wit – always remains oddly and recognizably the expression of a particular people, and this is still true. It retains, in the phrase of the German novelist Heinrich Böll, who was besotted by the place, 'this utterly un-uniform unity that is Ireland'.

1

THE NORTH-EAST

ANTRIM: LARNE TO LOUGH NEAGH

From Britain, the nearest point of entry is Larne in County Antrim. So it seems reasonable for a Literary Companion to begin there, as St Patrick began his Irish experience in Antrim.[1] Patrick was a writer, even if he did not have much confidence in his Latin:

> Therefore I have long had it in mind to write but have in fact hesitated up till now, for I was afraid to expose myself to the criticism of men's tongues, because I have not studied like others.
>
> As a youth, indeed almost a boy without any beard, I was taken captive before I knew what to desire and what I ought to avoid. And so, then, today I am ashamed and terrified to expose my awkwardness, because being inarticulate, I am unable to explain briefly what I mean, as my mind and spirit long to, and the inclination of my heart dictates. . . .

Patrick was probably about sixteen years old when he was seized somewhere in Britain, between 395 and 400, and brought to Antrim. There he became a slave, and tended pigs on the slopes of Slemish, about fifteen miles from Larne. These slopes were probably wooded then, which are bare now, but the hill must have been as surprising a feature in the landscape as it is today. Among the small green fields it rises up, a mass of crystallized basalt, like a symmetrical Gibraltar; if ever a hill was sure to be considered a holy or magical place, Slemish is one.

After six years Patrick escaped back to Britain, to his family, 'who asked me earnestly not to go off anywhere and leave them this time, after the great tribulations I had been through'. But he has a vision of 'a man coming as it were from Ireland (his name was Victoricus), with countless letters, and he gave me one of them, and I read the heading of the letter: "The Voice of the Irish". . . . "We beg you, holy boy, to come and walk again among us."' So he returned, landing once more near Slemish. Patrick is careful to name the angel that appeared to him: 'Victoricus'. This particularity is a traditional feature of Irish writing and was formulated early:[2] 'The four things to be asked of every composition are place, and person, and time, and cause of invention.' It can sometimes lead to a blizzard of precise namings from which a reader has to be rescued, but also it can help to make the surprising seem less so.

As a missionary Patrick did not have an easy time of it, confronting head-on a pagan Iron Age culture, and having to endure attacks on his flock of converts, from Scotland, whither they were taken as slaves. In his furious letter to Coroticus, ruler of Strathclyde, demanding the return of his people, Patrick strikes another long-sounding Irish note, a suspicion that Ireland has been singled out for special persecution: 'It is an offence to them that we are Irish.' Of course, he found violence in Ireland, and magic, and a rich mythology glorifying both. For example, the legendary Cuchulainn ['Coohullin'],[3] who defended Ulster single-handed against the invading forces of Queen Maeve (*Medb*) from Connaught, while the rest of the men of Ulster lay under a spell. Cuchulainn's metamorphosis before battle is described in the epic 'Cattle Raid of Cooley' (*Táin Bó Cúailnge*) ['Toyn Boh Coolinger'],[4] as is his deadly effectiveness:

> He did a mad feat of turning his body around inside his skin. His feet and shins and knees turned backwards. His heels, calves, and buttocks came round to the front. His calf sinews rose on the front of his shins and each round lump of them was the size of the balled fist of a warrior. His huge head-sinews stretched down to the nape of his neck, and every immense swelling of them was as big as the head of a month-old boy. Then his face became a red cavity. One eye he sucked back into his head so that a wild crane could scarcely pluck it from the recess of his skull onto the middle of his cheek . . .
> He came across into the middle of their ranks and threw up huge ramparts of his enemies' bodies around and outside the host . . . They fell, sole of foot to sole of foot, headless neck to headless neck, such was the depth of their corpses. Three times again he circled them in this way so that he left a layer of six bodies around them, the soles of three to the necks of three all around the fort.

That is taken from a manuscript centuries later than St Patrick, but the story is much older, and gives an idea of the culture he had to face, a very considerable one, for all its almost oriental transformations and calculated barbarisms.[5] It was relinquished reluctantly, while the argument between free pagan and disciplined Christian continued for centuries, sometimes wittily, sometimes yearningly. The stories are still alive; Irish writers use these myths still, as the ancient Greeks used theirs.

James Simmons (b. 1933) fuses ancient violences with recent, less heroic ones, in a poem with bitterness in the title, 'From the Irish'. The gruesomely pretty images come straight from the *Táin*:[6]

> Most terrible was our hero in battle blows:
> hands without fingers, shorn heads and toes
> were scattered. That day there flew and fell
> from astonished victims eyebrow, bone and entrail,
> like stars in the sky, like snowflakes, like nuts in May,
> like meadows of daisies, like butts from an ashtray.
> Familiar things, you might brush against or tread
> upon in the daily round, were glistening red
> with the slaughter the hero caused, though he had gone.
> By proxy his bomb exploded, his valour shone.

Next to Larne, enclosing Larne Lough, is Islandmagee (where Simmons now lives). Along the sea-cliffs is The Gobbins, scene of a sectarian massacre of Catholics; or, as the Belfast poet John Hewitt (1907–87) more carefully puts it, site 'of the legendary and largely fictitious event which is supposed to have taken place in 1642'. Hewitt wrote a play about the massacre, called *The Bloody Brae*, and in it one of the killers asks forgiveness of the shade of a girl he slew. This is granted, in a qualified fashion: 'I have said I pardon you. But the sword's edge/is marked with blood forever. . . .'[7]

Towards the end of the sixteenth century, and during periods of the seventeenth, parts of Ireland were 'planted' with farmers from England and Scotland, and the local inhabitants dispossessed; with lasting resentments on the one hand, and guilts, however suppressed, on the other. In this region most of the planters were Scots, and Presbyterian, which obviously led to difficulties with the local Catholic Irish, and with the English, Church of Ireland, Anglicans: the tangle starts early.

Ballycarry is across the bridge at the lower end of Islandmagee. The first Presbyterian minister in Ireland was appointed there, in 1613. A hundred and fifty years later, James Orr (1770–1816),[8] 'The Bard of Ballycarry', is still defiantly celebrating this:

There thy revered forefathers heard
The first dissenters dared to tarry,
On Erin's plain, where men felt pain
For conscience' sake, in Ballycarry. . . .

There seems a contradiction here – 'on Erin's plain' sounds proud and
Irish. So indeed it is. James Orr, a weaver, son of planters, was a
United Irishman, the movement that wanted to separate Ireland from
England altogether. He, and others like him, now felt they were
Irishmen – with a difference. Orr took part in the Rising of 1798,
and only avoided the terrible reprisals that followed its suppression
by escaping to America. The sectarian strife that continues in
this part of Ireland does not seem to have been inevitable. On the
whole the planters got on reasonably well with the Irish Catholics,
up to and after 1798. Both were dissenters, excluded from power
by the Anglican ascendancy, and had this grievance in common. It
was in the nineteenth century that Catholic Emancipation and the
growth of the ultra-Protestant Orange Order complicated matters.[9]
At Ballycarry there is a monument to James Orr, sand-coloured and
masonically decorated, in the ground of the ruined church there, called
Templecorran.

Jonathan Swift (1667–1745),[10] who loathed all dissenters,
preached at Templecorran: it was one of the three parishes he was
appointed to when he was first ordained in 1695. The others, equally
isolated as far as Swift was concerned, were Kilroot and Ballinure,
in the churchyards of which the ruins of Swift's churches can still be
seen. Swift disliked preaching almost as much as he disliked dissenters,
saying of himself that he could only preach political pamphlets, or
'the idlest trifling stuff that ever was writ, calculated for a church
without a company or a roof'. He does himself an injustice, if one
of his surviving sermons is a test. His was a confident age, not given
to introspection, and in his sermon, 'The Difficulty of Knowing
Oneself', he suggests that such confidence is misplaced: 'How wild
and impertinent, how busy and incoherent a thing is the imagination,
even in the best and sanest of men; insomuch, that every man may
be said to be mad, but every man does not show it!'

Swift greatly chafed at his exile to rural Ireland, with so few
Anglican parishioners, or none. Indeed, a contemporary claimed that
at Templecorran 'all were Presbyterian save the parson and the clerk'.
It is possible that he wrote parts of his satirical *A Tale of a Tub* at
Kilroot, near the shore of Belfast Lough. (He had a parsonage there
'shaped like an egg', but that burnt down in 1959.) In *A Tale of a*

Tub he makes fun of the pride and self-delusion contained in excesses of religious dissent: 'When a man's fancy gets astride on his reason, when imagination is at cuffs with the senses, and common understanding as well as common sense is hurled out of doors; the first proselyte he makes is himself. . . . For, cant and vision are to the ear and eye, the same that tickling is to the touch.' His church at Kilroot, possibly 'roofless' then, is now certainly so, an ivy-covered set of high broken walls, dripping with melancholy. He must have been lonely there. It is reached from the Whitehead-Carrickfergus road by following a sign saying 'Salt Mines'. The church may have been nearer to the sea in his day, because there is a story that he rolled stones from the shore to the church, followed by a curious crowd. Then he clapped the door shut on a captive congregation.

Swift was a man who attracted to himself such stories. Born in Dublin, of English parents, he thought of his Irish sojourn as a banishment from the heart of affairs in London. Yet, in a later, unbuttoned letter to a correspondent unknown to him, an Irish officer, a Jacobite, serving abroad with one of the continental armies, he makes explicit the growth of his sympathy with Ireland, and his admiration (usually disguised under irascible scorn) for its people. He cannot approve of his correspondent's 'trade',

> yet I cannot but highly esteem those gentlemen of Ireland, who with all the disadvantages of being exiles and strangers, have been able to distinguish themselves by their valour and conduct in so many parts of Europe, I think above all other nations, which ought to make the English ashamed of the reproaches they cast on the ignorance, the dullness, and the want of courage, in the Irish natives. . . .
>
> I do assert that from several experiments I have made in travelling over both kingdoms, I have found the poor cottagers here, who could speak our language, to have much better natural taste for good sense, humour, and raillery, than ever I observed among people of the like sort in England. But the millions of oppressions they lie under, the tyranny of their landlords, the ridiculous zeal of their priests, and the general misery of the whole nation, have been enough to damp the best spirits under the sun.[11]

At Carrickfergus the poet Louis MacNeice (1907–63)[12] spent some of his first ten years. His father was Church of Ireland rector at

St Nicholas's church. In his autobiography MacNeice says the rectory was 'in a garden, enormously large (an acre), with a long prairie of lawn and virgin shrubberies and fierce red hens among cauliflowers run to seed, and the other side of the hedge was the cemetery, you could hear the voice of the minister tucking people into the ground'. The house behind the church has been pulled down and an old people's home built in its place ('MacNeice Fold'), but the cemetery is still there.

Sir Arthur Chichester's tomb is in St Nicholas's and it fascinated MacNeice as a child. Between the two Chichesters, 'like a roll of suet pudding, on a little marble cushion, was a little marble baby . . .'. Sir Arthur Chichester was a captain with Sir Francis Drake, sent to pacify Ulster. He is said to have reported killing 'one hundred people, sparing none what quality, age, or sex soever, besides many burned to death; we kill man, woman and child, horse, beast, whatsoever we find'.[13] In 'Carrickfergus' MacNeice remembers his childhood in

. . . smoky Carrick in County Antrim
Where the bottle-neck harbour collects the mud which jams

The little boats beneath the Norman castle,
The pier shining with lumps of crystal salt;
The Scotch Quarter was a line of residential houses
But the Irish Quarter was a slum for the blind and halt . . .

I was the rector's son, born to the anglican order,
Banned for ever from the candles of the Irish poor;
The Chichesters knelt in marble at the end of a transept
With ruffs about their necks, their portion sure.

Wristy, elegant, semi-detached, MacNeice was haunted by his Irish childhood, and returns to it often in his poems. Public school in England, his working life spent there – teaching classics in Birmingham, writing features for the BBC in London – he still never felt quite at home, although he is considered an English poet, not an Irish one. Somewhere he says, 'If only one could *live* in Ireland, or *feel oneself* in England', and this sense of a mixed and troubled identity has struck a chord among many younger Northern Ireland poets, so that they claim him for their own. His ashes are at Carrowdore, in the Ards Peninsula, placed in his mother's grave, who died when he was a child. The graveyard is at the top of a slow green swell from the sea. Derek Mahon (b. 1941) has a poem about MacNeice and his burial place; it reflects on MacNeice's humane classicism that has its roots here, in the landscape of his childhood:[14]

Maguire, I believe, suggested a blackbird
And over your grave a phrase from Euripides,
Which suits you down to the ground, like this churchyard
With its play of shadows, its humane perspective.

Locked in the winter's fist, these hills are hard
As nails, yet soft and feminine in their turn
When fingers open and the hedges burn.
This, you implied, is how we ought to live. . . .

On the tombstone at Carrowdore is written a line by MacNeice himself, 'This man with a shy smile who left behind something intact'.

West of Carrickfergus, on the road into Antrim, another influential poet is buried, Sir Samuel Ferguson (1810–86).[15] Outside a pretty church at Donegore, his entombment place, flat and gravelled and enclosed by chains, is set on a steep hillside between two ancient mounds, one below and one above, so that it has the air of a bunk lowered from the green walls of a ship's cabin. Born in Belfast, Ferguson properly belongs to Dublin, where he lived and worked. He was an early figure in the Irish literary renaissance, and his reworking, in verse, of Irish myths helped to remind Ireland of its pre-English past. W.B. Yeats, in gratitude, called him a genius. Subsequent poets and scholars have been less generous, reacting against the rather heavy Victorianism of his *Lays of the Western Gael*. Ferguson's lyrics have worn better. At least one, 'The Lark in the Clear Air', has a traditional melody, which comes across in the words:

> . . . I shall tell her all my love,
> All my soul's adoration;
> And I think she will hear me
> And will not say me nay.
> It is this that fills my soul
> With its joyous elation,
> As I hear the sweet lark sing
> In the clear air of the day.

At Antrim town, on the shores of Lough Neagh, in a little close called Pogue's Entry, Alexander Irvine was born in 1863.[16] Irvine escaped poverty and illiteracy, inspired by his mother, became a minister famed for his preaching, and a worker in the slums of New York. In 1913 he published, in honour of his mother, *My Lady of the Chimney Corner*, a book which has never been out of print. The tough-minded could suspect it of sentimentality, the reverence for the mother is so undiluted, but her spiritual strength and charm come so strongly out of the book, and it contains such an unaffected description of extreme poverty, that it is a worthy survivor.

On his last visit to his mother before her death, Irvine took her to see the Round Tower of Antrim, the best-preserved in Ireland. These strange lighthouse-like constructions, which seem to emerge from bare ground for no apparent reason, were built near the door of an abbey church, but stoutly, so that during any alarm the monks could climb inside with food and the abbey valuables and draw up the ladder behind them, to sit out the siege. The surrounding buildings would be of wood, or at any rate less well built, so now no trace of these remains, and the tower therefore stands unrelated and unexplained. They puzzled travellers; although, as the Frenchman Latocnaye noted in 1796, 'Whatever these ancient buildings may have been, the Irish have now for them the greatest possible veneration.'[17]

In Irvine's day the Antrim tower was in private ground (it is now in a public park) and when he returns home from America, now a clergyman, he realizes that his mother has never visited it, though it is not more than a mile or so from her 'chimney-corner'. So he takes her there, and she reacts like a young girl:

> 'If we lived here d'ye know what I'd like to do?' 'No.' 'Just take our boots off and play hide and go seek – wouldn't it be fun?' 'You seem bent on getting your boots off,' I said, laughingly. Her reply struck me dumb.
>
> 'Honey,' she said, so softly and looking into my eyes, 'do you realize that I have never stood on a patch of lawn in my life before?'
>
> Hand in hand we walked towards the gate, taking an occasional, wistful glance back at the glory of the few, and thinking, both of us, of the millions of tired feet that never felt the softness of a smooth green sward.

This is not a side of Ireland the visitor was likely to encounter, even the energetic and sympathetic Mrs Dinah Craik,[18] author of the enormously successful *John Halifax, Gentleman* (1857), a book without which no school library used to be complete. Indeed, in his autobiography Irvine, then a seaman, says that the first book that opened for him the world of literature was *John Halifax*. Mrs Craik visited this tower in 1886, and is shown it by the proprietor. She remarks on its 'mystery'. '"Yes, it's a fine tower, and it made once a splendid play-place for us boys," said the owner. "My father was always rather proud of it. . . ."' Mrs Craik is rather shocked at this lack of veneration, clearly not imagining that it might yet be venerated by some of the surrounding, nearly invisible, Irish.

Antrim is near, and on, Lough Neagh, 153 square miles of shallow water, the largest lake in the British Isles. As there is no horizon, no rise of land on either side, it has the aspect of an island sea, and has attracted the myth-makers: its waters are said to be able to turn wood to stone; the giant Finn MacCool scooped it out and threw what he scooped into the sea, to form the Isle of Man. Seamus Heaney (b. 1939), who was born near the head of the Lough, in County Derry, begins his 'Lough Neagh Sequence' by pulling some of its stories together:[19]

> The lough will claim a victim every year.
> It has virtue that hardens wood to stone.
> There is a town sunk beneath its water.
> It is the scar left by the Isle of Man. . . .

Mrs Craik's *John Halifax, Gentleman* concerns matters more practical, the rise in the world of a poor orphan through hard work and integrity. She would have approved of Alexander Irvine (and of his mother). Predictably, she is disturbed by the 'non-utility' of Lough Neagh, regretting that 'the glittering expanse of it is empty . . .'. She is with a friend who agrees with her: '"See how we Irish throw away our blessings," said my companion, as we stood looking at the lovely sight. "In England such a splendid sheet of water would have been utilized in many ways, and made a centre of both business and pleasure. Factories would have sprung up along its shores, yachts, steamers, fishing boats, would have covered it from end to end."' There are still no factories, but there are marinas, with pleasure-craft at anchor, and water skiers in wet-suits – moving weirdly fast as the unhindered wind streaks across the water.

BELFAST

Louis MacNeice was born in Belfast,

> Where hammers clang murderously on the girders
> Like crucifixes the gantries stand. . . .[20]

Until recently shipbuilding dominated Belfast. E.M. Forster (1879–1970),[21] steaming up the Lough in 1912, thought the gantries, and perhaps the skeletons of ships being built, looked like 'shattered cathedrals of iron'. He disliked the place: 'That chilly Presbyterian spire! The soul of Ulster, observing, but not welcoming the stranger . . .' In 1912 there was an added distaste for its politics, as Unionist Northern Ireland, fearing that a Liberal government in London would finally grant 'Home Rule' (limited self-government) to the whole of Ireland, was preparing to defy the 'principle' of law:

> We went to tea on Sunday to a pillar of the Ulster Reform Club. 'Belfast,' he told me, 'will listen to anyone except a Judas; or a turncoat.' (I glanced nervously at my own, which has been turned so often I forget which side was which originally.) Then, 'We are not acting in accordance with any principle, and we do not pretend that we are'; this very majestically. 'It just shows the uselessness of principles,' cried the exultant little wife, and passed on the glad news to the baby.

Belfast intransigence was dealt with as comedy in *The Red Hand of Ulster*, a novel published in 1912. Its author, George A. Birmingham, was the pen-name of a Church of Ireland canon, James Owen Hannay (1865–1950), born in Belfast. He was a sympathetic and impartial observer of Ulster who, in political despair, took refuge in what was almost a philosophy of the absurd. He charts the logic, dead-pan, that led Unionists to smuggle arms in order to fight against those with whom they wished to be united. His Unionist is still recognizable: 'Babberley is the most terrific of all Unionist orators. If his speeches were set to music, the orchestra would necessarily consist entirely of cornets, trumpets and drums. No one could express the spirit of Babberley's oratory on stringed instruments. Flutes would be ridiculous.' At the end of the book the British Navy lobs a shell into Belfast and only succeeds in blowing up the statue of Queen Victoria.

By the summer of 1914 things were more serious; the Ulster 'No Surrender' Volunteers (organized by Sir Edward Carson to resist Irish independence) smuggled a cargo of arms from Germany into Larne harbour. George Buchanan (1904–89) recalls menace invading the countryside around his father's rectory:

> Coming out from an amateur theatrical performance in Larne, my mother finds the main street lined with members of the volunteer force. She recognizes and questions a pedlar who has often called at the rectory. Heavy with pride in his duties, he says slowly: 'Go you home to bed, and ask no questions.' She

continues to ask him, and he concedes: 'All you need to know is that the Ulster Volunteers are doing their duty. We're out all over the country tonight.'

On her way home she passes a stream of cars and lorries, with full headlights, that are racing in the direction of the harbour. And all through the night, on the road beside the rectory, we can hear the cars and we can see the trees constantly illumined by their headlamps.

In the morning it is understood that an extraordinary event has occurred. . . . From this night the rebellion passes beyond the stage of play-acting.[22]

It is difficult to find an unbiased reaction to Belfast. G.K. Chesterton (1874–1935), visiting Ireland in 1918, faced the problem of Ulster square-on. He decided to give a heroic dimension to human peculiarity: Ulster is the home of a bigotry which is like a magnificent dream, therefore he announces, characteristically, that this dream is Ulster's distinction and glory:

A man told me in North East Ulster that he heard a mother warning her children away from some pond, or similar place of danger, 'Don't you go there; there are wee popes there. . . .'

Nobody in Manchester, however Nonconformist, tells even a child that a puddle is a kind of breeding place for Archbishops of Canterbury. . . . Wherever men are still theological there is a chance of them being logical . . . bigotry is by no means the worst thing about Belfast. I rather think it is the best.[23]

There are some things to be said in defence of the unyielding forefathers of Belfast, whose grim statues are outside the City Hall: 'In whatever way the city had been crippled by religious intolerance, the same intolerance made those men set their faces against slave markets. . . . While Liverpool, only a few miles across the water, waxed wealthy on the slave trade, as Bristol did also, Belfast stood firm in its belief. . . . No slaver ever sailed in and out of Belfast Lough.'[24]

The young V.S. Pritchett (b. 1900), on working trips to Belfast in the early 1920s when he was a journalist in Dublin, found:

One can always find the gentler and more reasonable spirits. One of these, whom I always went to see, was Forrest Reid. He was a friend of Yeats and E.M. Forster and his few novels have an element of pagan symbolism that is present also in Forster's early short stories, and reflect something of Yeats's mysticism. . . .

Reid's autobiography, *Apostate*, describes his upbringing in Belfast. It is a minor classic, and it will stand beside Gosse's *Father and Son*. He was indeed an apostate in that awful, rainy and smoky Presbyterian city: he was a genuine pagan. He stayed there as if in hiding, I used to think. He lived alone on the top floor of a sour house shaken by industrial traffic, and opposite a linen mill. The smoke hung low and blew into his windows, so that he had been obliged to bind his thousands of books in white paper covers: not very practical in that place for the smuts stood out on them. . . .

I would make for Forrest Reid's room to hear softer and more civilized accents. It was a relief after a day with a shipyard owner. There was one to whom I spoke about Forrest Reid. 'Wratin' poetry don't drave no rivets, yoong man,' he said.

All Reid's books contain a search for a lost paradise, glimpsed in moments of ecstasy through natural beauty, a beauty not hard to find in the country and seacoasts of northern Ireland. As a child he found that paradise in dreams, but even Belfast, around 1880, had a pastoral air:

My waking world, also, was gradually expanding though it still remained the very small world of a provincial town – a rather hard, unremarkable town too – devoted exclusively to money making, but a town, for all that, somehow likeable, and surrounded by as beautiful a country as one could desire. The Belfast of my childhood differed considerably from the Belfast of to-day. It was, I think, spiritually closer to that surrounding country . . . the whole town was more homely, more unpretentious. A breath of rusticity still sweetened its air; the few horse trams, their destinations indicated by the colour of their curtains, did little to disturb the quiet of the streets; the Malone Road was still almost a rural walk.[26]

The industrialization of Belfast, from its beginnings, affected visitors in different ways. John Keats, walking into Belfast from Donaghadee in 1818, was appalled: 'We heard on passing through Belfast the most disgusting of all noises . . . the sound of a shuttle.'[27] William Thackeray, however, was delighted in 1842 by the cotton and linen industry, and the girls who work in it. He visited Mulholland's mill:

There are nearly five hundred girls employed in it. They work in huge long chambers, lighted by numbers of windows, hot with steam buzzing and humming with hundreds of thousands of whirling wheels that all take their motion from a steam-engine which lives apart in a hot cast-iron temple of its own, from which it communicates with the innumerable machines that the five hundred girls preside over. They have seemingly but to take away the work when done – the enormous monster in the cast-iron room does it all. He cards the flax, and combs it, and spins it, and beats it, and twists it; the five hundred girls stand by to feed him, or take the material from him, when he has had his will of it. . . .

I have seldom, I think, seen more good looks than amongst the young women employed in this place. They work for twelve hours daily, in rooms of which the heat is intolerable to a stranger, but in spite of it they look gay, stout, and healthy; nor were their forms much concealed by the very simple clothes they wear while in the mill.[28]

Like Dublin, Belfast is finely situated, at the head of a sea-lough and in a cup of hills: the basalt of Antrim and the slatiness of Down. The centre of the city is little more than a couple of miles from the contour of green that encircles it. To those brought up in the suburbs of the town, the contrast between the rural and the urban seems sometimes to obsess. C.S. Lewis (1898–1963) takes us to a place high above Belfast and looks down:

And here we come to one of the great contrasts that have bitten deeply into my mind – Niflheim and Asgard, Britain and Logres, Handramit and Harandra, air and ether, the low world and the high.

Your horizon from here is the Antrim mountains, probably a uniform mass of greyish blue . . . here where you stand is another, sunlight and grass and dew. . . . In between them, on the flat floor of the valley at your feet, a forest of factory chimneys, gantries, giant cranes rising out of a welter of mist, lies Belfast. Noises come up from it continually. . . . And because we have heard this all our lives it does not, for us, violate the peace of the hill top; rather, it emphasizes it, enriches the contrast, sharpens the dualism.[29]

What he is saying seems hardly surprising, though obviously of esoteric importance to him; and this duality in the imagination is also strong in other Ulster writers, like Reid and Buchanan and the poet John Hewitt. These were life-long Ulstermen, whereas no one thinks of Lewis as particularly 'Irish'; nevertheless, his friend J.R.R. Tolkien said that with Lewis, 'you must always look for the *Ulsterior motive*'.[30]

Perhaps the Ulster dyes and flavours sink in unusually deep. It was (Irish) Elizabeth Bowen who remarked of Henry James that 'few of his critics have noticed that he displayed all the careful qualities of a Protestant from Lower Ulster'.[31]

A less typically 'Ulster' writer, but one who certainly felt herself to be Irish, was the medieval scholar Helen Waddell (1889–1965),[32] daughter of a Presbyterian missionary to China; she lived most of her early life in Belfast, and always considered the country of South Down to be her spiritual home. The newspapers called her 'the Darling of Ulster' for her fame and her charm. She was the best-selling author of *Peter Abelard* (1933) and, earlier, *The Wandering Scholars* (1927), an account of the monks and poets, many of them Irish, who kept poetry and learning alive in Christian Europe's early years.

There is obviously no such simple thing as 'Irishness' and 'English-ness'. But history shows that a bafflement can rise up between Ireland and the mainland, to put it calmly, which suggests that each tends to look at the world differently, though the difference is not easy to define. It is best suggested by anecdotes. For example, in 1942 six Belfast youths were sentenced to death for the murder of a policeman; as Parliament was not in session, leave to appeal to the House of Lords was refused. This struck Waddell as unjust, and she wrote to *The Times*: '. . . is the memory of a kindly Ulster policeman to become a thing of horror in men's minds . . . thanks to the savagery of his avengers?' This provoked English Dorothy L. Sayers (a writer with much in common with Waddell, which perhaps brought out their differences) to pronounce that 'no Irish person ever understood the majesty of England and lost no chance of vilifying it'. (The death sentence was commuted.)

No writer was more explicitly aware of the depth of the Ulster dye than the poet John Hewitt. It is not that he wants to escape from it, or change colour. What he is concerned with is to puzzle out the way history has formed him. It is his subject:[33]

> Kelt, Briton, Roman, Saxon, Dane and Scot,
> time and this island tied a crazy knot.

But:

> This is my country. If my people came
> from England here four centuries ago,
> the only trace that's left is in my name.

He goes into a Catholic church and thinks of adding a candle to those
already burning:

> suppressed the fancy, smiled a cynic thought,
> turned clicking heel on marble and went out.
> Not this my father's faith: their walls are bare;
> their comforts all within, if anywhere. . . .
> The years since then have proved I should have stayed
> and mercy might have touched me till I prayed.

Ulster Protestantism may reject candles and statues, but it creates
its own saints, even martyrs, of industry. Shan F. Bullock (1865–
1935)[34] in *Thomas Andrews, Shipbuilder* (1912) writes a panegyric,
almost a hagiography, of the young man who, at thirty-two, became
managing director and chief of the design department at Harland and
Wolff, on Queen's Island. The shipyard built the *Titanic*, in which
Andrews went down. From what men praise, we learn what they
and their society value: 'His job required a knowledge of its 53
branches equal to that of any of the 53 men in charge of them. . . .
One sees him, big and strong, a paint-smeared bowler hat on
his crown, grease on his boots and the pockets of his blue jacket
stuffed with plans . . . his generosity, kindliness, patience, geniality,
humour, humility, courage, that great laugh of his, the winning
smile, the fine breezy presence. . . .
   Andrews was also celebrated by the Bard of the Dockyard, Thomas
Carnduff:[35]

> A Queen's Island Trojan he worked to the last;
> Very proud we all feel of him here in Belfast;
> Our working-men knew him as one of the best –
> He stuck to his duty, and God gave him rest.

How does a writer from the south see Belfast? Kate O'Brien
(1897–1974), initially doubtful, finds it 'packed with real faces, no
two alike' and notices something that strikes any visitor to the centre
of the city: 'It is full of light. At noon in Belfast, even in bad winter,
one seems to be in the presence of the full light of the sky, and all
the inexcusable buildings around and including the City Hall stand
leisurely back from the wide, white-gleaming pavements so that you
can mock them at your ease. . . .' She walks over Queen's Bridge to
the shipyards:[36]

> I remembered the 'Titanic', pride of Queen's Island, and how
> some old crone of a myth maker had told us children after it

sank, that it had 'To hell with the Pope' stamped on its every piece of steel. That was indeed silly talk to be making up in faraway, sleepy Limerick. . . . It takes Ireland, I suppose, to have men still [in 1959] opposing each other to the points of tragedy and death on an issue of religious belief; perhaps it marks our country's unmanageable originality.

Louis MacNeice, Ireland-haunted, shows English impatience (in 1939) with the whole of Ireland:[37]

> The land of scholars and saints:
>   Scholars and saints my eye, the land of ambush,
> Purblind manifestos, never-ending complaints. . . .
> Such was my country and I thought I was well
>   Out of it, educated and domiciled in England,
> Though yet her name keeps ringing like a bell
>   In an under-water belfry.

SOUTH ANTRIM – DOWN

South of Belfast[38] – the plain of Down – is drumlin country, flat-ish but lumpy. C.S. Lewis gives a complicated recipe for a reproduction of its characteristics. This involves putting some medium-sized potatoes in a dish, lightly covering them with earth so that their shapes can still be seen, and turning the earth green. 'You have now got a picture of the "plain" of Down, which is a plain only in the sense that if you were a very large giant you would regard it as a level but very ill to walk on – like cobbles.'[39] (It seems that the very surface of Down was forcing Lewis to invent Finn MacCool.)

Jeremy Taylor (1613–1667)[40] certainly found it 'ill to walk on' when he was dropped among this lumpiness. He is described by Edmund Gosse[41] as 'of a genius comparable only with those of Shakespeare, Bacon and Milton', but this was not enough to save him from Ulster. Born in Cambridge, Taylor rose, quite young, to be chaplain to Charles I. His early book, *Liberty of Prophesying* (1647), was a plea for toleration, an urgent suggestion that Anglicans and dissenters should remember the original teachings of Christianity and stop arguing themselves towards a civil war. He first came to Ireland in 1658, and was later made bishop of Down, with responsibility for Dromore. Coleridge was a passionate admirer of Taylor's prose, which gives rise to an example of his own: 'I believe such a complete man hardly shall we see again . . . such a miraculous combination of

erudition, broad, and deep and omnigeneous, of logic subtle as well
as acute, and robust as agile. . . .'

Taylor's style was a combination of the simple and elaborate, and
sweetly musical:

> *The Practice and Acts of Patience, by way of Rule.*
> At the first address and presence of sickness, *stand still and arrest
> thy spirit.* . . .
>
> For so doth the Libyan lion, spying the fierce huntsman; he
> first beats himself with the strokes of his tail, and curls up his
> spirits, making them strong with union and recollection, till
> being struck with a Mauritanian spear, he rushes forth into his
> defence and noblest contention; and either scapes into the secrets
> of his own dwelling, or else dies the bravest of the forest.
>
> Every man when shot with an arrow from God's quiver, must
> then draw in all the auxiliaries of reason, and know that then
> is the time to try his strength, and to reduce the works of his
> religion into action. . . .[42]

Sad to think of Taylor delivering such images and cadences where
they were not wanted, to small congregations or none, in villages such
as Ballinderry, where the parishioners were largely Presbyterians who
detested his form of Anglicanism. He stayed in Ballinderry, near
Lough Neagh, at a large house called Portmore, once described as the
most magnificent mansion in Ulster. Only what look like the walls
of a huge enclosed garden still stand, and Gosse (by 'plashing about')
found a line of broken brickwork in a boggy field, which is still there.
There may have been a bridge to Ballinderry 'Lower Church', which
was Taylor's. This now stands on a small eminence, at the end of
a quiet road, a tree-surrounded ruin in an old graveyard, with that
special quality Irish ruins often have, as though they suit the landscape, living thoughtfully inside their own green silence.

Taylor took this church to pieces himself, in order to build the
'Middle Church', further back along the road. This also fell into ruin,
but was reconsecrated in 1902 and restored in the 1930s. Its small
and pleasing dimensions, and its simple furnishings, which are of
Taylor's period, with a three-tiered wooden pulpit, give some idea
of his austere but elegant Anglicanism.

Taylor was first invited to Ireland 'to keep the flickering lamp of
Anglicanism from being utterly extinguished'. He was not welcome.
Cromwell seems to have acted as some sort of shield, but when he
died Taylor's parishioners had their pastor, briefly, arrested. Life
became so impossible for him that his famed patience finally snapped;

he threw out the Presbyterian incumbents of thirty-six parishes and replaced them with English Anglicans of his own choosing. This did not go down well in his diocese, or with the king. 'He had pleased nobody, his flock was persuaded that he was cruel and unjust, and the government regarded him as dangerous and embarrassing. . . .' It is said that in the end, Taylor ordered his servant to gather up every available copy of *Liberty of Prophesying*, his plea for patience and toleration of twenty years before, and to burn them in the market-place of Dromore. 'The iron had entered his soul,' says Gosse, 'and he was no longer the Jeremy Taylor whose patient energy and active sympathy we have loved.' Shortly after that he was dead, aged fifty-four.

To Dromore, in 1783, and to the see of Connor and Down, came a bishop of an altogether more Trollopian stamp: Thomas Percy (1729–1811),[43] famous in Dublin for the splendour of his silken umbrella. Unlike most English bishops in Ireland at this time, he was at least not an absentee, but was happy to live in Dromore cultivating his garden, completing the Georgian Bishop's Palace. Percy could be said to be lacking in tact. He took down the ancient cross in the market-place of Dromore, erected by St Colman, in order to make it a decoration in his park. Detecting a hefty local resistance, he gave up the idea and on the vacant plinth erected the stocks instead. Despite all this he was on friendly terms with the local Catholic priest. In 1797, just before the Rising, Percy's agent looked out of the window and saw this man about to be hanged by a mob. The agent was shaving at the time and dashed out, razor in hand, able to cut him down before it was too late.

Percy was a friend of Johnson and Garrick. Indeed, Johnson said that he never left Percy's company without having learned something (though he was also heard to remark that Percy 'ran about with very little weight on his mind'). However that may be, Percy published a book, in 1765, from an old manuscript he said he had rescued, that was to have a significant effect on the poetry of Europe and the whole Romantic movement, *Reliques of Ancient English Poetry*: 'Wordsworth, who, through the influence of the ballads, was the first of our modern poets to return to nature and truth, declared that the poetry of England had been absolutely redeemed by Percy's *Reliques*, while that of Germany, as shown in the works of Goethe, Schiller, and Heine, was greatly influenced by that work.' Percy let no one see his source for the *Reliques*, or take notes from it, during his lifetime. This may have been because he had tidied the texts in an

unscholarly manner. In Ireland he encouraged competitions among
local poets, and was a founder member of the Royal Irish Academy;
he had been surprised that 'not a Fellow of Dublin College appeared
able to read a line in their old manuscripts'.

Percy's fascination with another eighteenth-century interest, garden
design, did not always meet with approval. Sir Walter Scott, when
he visited the Giant's Causeway in Antrim, considered taking some
of the basalt columns home to Abbotsford, but rejected the idea.
Percy had no such scruples and brought one to Dromore, six-sided,
nine feet high, which he placed in one of his 'vistas', inspiring William
Jessop, poet-clergyman at Lismore, County Cork, to complain:

> From single columns Taste withholds her praise,
> Though not unknown in Rome's Augustan days;
> Incumbent weights were columns meant to bear;
> Who wants their succour to support the air?

Jessop had further complaints (in his 'Essay on Gardens', dedicated
to Percy) about the new fashion of 'improved nature', with its romantic winding paths:

> Whene'er your walks from straight direction swerve
> Some semblance of necessity preserve
> If no such plausible pretext be found,
> We titter, as we wriggle round and round. . . .

Between Ballinderry and Dromore, now a motorway junction, is
Moira, where, in 636, was fought the famous battle of Mag Rath,
for the lordship of the whole north. Because an aristocratic poet was
wounded in the battle, called Cenn Faelad, we have an account of
what happened to him which takes us to the beginning of written
Irish literature.

Robin Flower (1881–1946), the Englishman whom the *Dictionary
of Irish Literature* calls 'the most erudite of Celtic scholars and graceful
of translators', has a rendering of the story, which tells us that Cenn
Faelad was wounded in the head so that 'his brain of forgetting was
stricken out of him'. He was carried for healing to Toomregan in
County Cavan (about sixty miles from Moira): 'And there were three
schools in that place, a school of Latin learning, a school of Irish law
and a school of Irish poetry.' As he could forget nothing, 'everything
he would hear of the recitations of the three schools every day he
would have it by heart every night. And he fitted a pattern of poetry

to these matters and wrote them on slates and tablets and put them in a vellum book.'[44]

Cenn Faelad was called a *sapiens*, and his death is recorded in the *Annals of Ulster*,[45] with the names of other learned men, *sapientes*. In England, the Venerable Bede (673–735) says there was a heavy traffic from England to Ireland in order to meet these teachers:

> At that time there were many of the English nation, both of noble and of lesser rank, who whether for divine study or to lead a more continent life, had left their native land and had withdrawn to Ireland. Certain among them gave themselves up willingly to the monastic way of life, while others rather went about from cell to cell of the teachers and took pleasure in cultivating study. And all these the Irish most freely received, and made it their study to provide them with food from day to day without any charge, with books to read and with free teaching.[46]

There was another distinguished casualty of the battle of Moira/Mag Rath, King Sweeney (*Suibhne*). He was cursed before the battle by the irascible St Ronan, whom he had provoked by complaining about his bells. He leaves the battle maddened and takes, literally, to the trees.[47] In a ninth-century poem, Sweeney turned man-bird describes his 'oratory' in a tree, one of the perching-places in his mad flight all over Ireland:[48]

> That you may be told its story, it was a craftsman who
>   made it –
> my little heart, God from Heaven, he is the thatcher who
>   thatched it.
> A house where rain does not pour, a place where spear
>   points are not dreaded,
> as bright as in a garden and with no fence about it.

The idea of the 'madness of Sweeney', with poetry attributed to him, runs through Irish literature. It is used by Flann O'Brien[49] in his comic masterpiece *At Swim-Two-Birds* (1939), where Sweeney appears (along with Finn MacCool and various other legendary and supernatural characters) in a Dublin pub. There, O'Brien translates Sweeney's poems only partly for comic effect:

> If I were to search alone
> the hills of the brown world,
> better would I like my sole hut
> in Glen Bolcain[50]. . . .

A haughty ivy
growing through a twisted tree,
myself on its true summit,
I would lothe leave it.

I flee before skylarks,
it is the tense stern-race,
I overleap the clumps
on the high hill-peaks. . . .

Seamus Heaney's version of that last verse is:

The skylarks rising
into their high space
send me pitching and tripping
over stumps on the moor. . . .

Heaney's early home at Bellaghy was on the verges of Sweeney's
kingdom (south County Antrim and north County Down), 'in sight
of some of Sweeney's places and within earshot of others'; he says
that Sweeney 'seemed to have been with me from the start':[51]

Gazing down at clean gravel,
to lean out over a cool well,
drink a mouthful of sunlit water
and gather cress by the handful. . . .

Sweeney's poems about wild nature represent a reaction against
monasticism, against ordered civilization itself; 'the wilderness versus
the cloister, the greenwood versus the garden', as Heaney has said.
Battle-of-Mag-Rath-deranged Sweeney can be thought of as the
opposite of the *sapientes* of the *Annals*, among whom Mag-Rath-
wounded memory-man Cenn Faelad has his place. Perhaps they are
the same, two sides of an Irish argument between freedom and order.

East of Belfast, two great centres of the learning mentioned by Bede
were at Bangor on the sea, and Movilla (now Newtownards) at the
head of Strangford Lough. The monastery at Bangor was founded in
555 and the one at Movilla in 540. It was from Bangor that the missionary St Columbanus went to the continent to help in the founding
of abbeys in Switzerland and Italy: Luxeuil, St Gall and Bobbio, 'the
chief centres of religion and scholarship in a Europe struggling out
of the Dark Ages'.[52]

There was plenty of darkness to come; the two Irish abbeys were
destroyed again and again in succeeding centuries, by Vikings. Never-

theless, from these abbeys the missionaries and teachers continued to go out; some of the 'Wandering Scholars' described by Waddell in her book. They did not go altogether happily, regarding their self-imposed exile as a 'white' martyrdom; not quite as bad as a 'red' one, but bad enough.[53] So, as they copied and decorated the codices in distant Europe, they sometimes wrote little nostalgic poems in the margins, in Irish: another of the beginnings of Irish literature.

Movilla and Bangor have been destroyed so often that it is difficult to get an idea of what they were like originally. But Nendrum on Mahee Island, on the west side of Strangford Lough, gives a very good idea indeed. Most holy places were used as burial grounds and this caused them constantly to be disturbed, but for some reason Nendrum never was, it was allowed to fade away (with help from raiding Vikings) and became covered over.[54] Its site was discovered only recently, the original foundations intact, and sites of the monks' small cells, Round Tower, schoolroom and so on (even a bell was discovered). It is a lovely place, green and quiet, except for the calling of the birds which haunt the lough in huge variety and numbers. A perfect place to be a monk in, except for the Vikings' raids, which made it only possible to relax when there was bad weather:

> The bitter wind is high tonight
> It lifts the white locks of the sea;
> In such wild winter storm no fright
> Of savage Viking troubles me.[55]

   That is in a ninth-century codex in St Gall in Switzerland, but almost certainly written in Ireland and taken to the continent later; 'most moving of all', says Helen Waddell, 'to one who remembers the low grey ruins on the island in Strangford Lough', are the words of a marginal gloss, 'Mahee of Nendrum'.[56] Waddell then quotes one of the most famous of Irish poems, and one of the earliest, as though she hopes it comes from this place. Robin Flower calls it 'the first example we have in manuscript of the personal poetry of the Irish', and it is his translation:

> I and Pangur Ban my cat,
> 'Tis a like task we are at:
> Hunting mice is his delight
> Hunting words I sit all night. . . .
>
> Often times a mouse will stray
> In the hero Pangur's way;

Often times my keen thought set
Takes a meaning in its net. . . .

Practice every day has made
Pangur perfect in his trade;
I get wisdom day and night
Turning darkness into light.

Bangor and Movilla were founded about a hundred years after the arrival of St Patrick. It is a tradition that Patrick's first landfall on his return to Ireland was at the lower end of Strangford Lough, at the mouth of the River Quoile, near Downpatrick. His first church was nearby, at Saul. 'Saul' means 'barn' and a barn on a hill was granted to him by one of his first converts, Dichu. On the site today is a new church in the traditional Irish style, small, with a little Round Tower, among tiny buildings that are much older. It has exactly the situation, modest, but on a prominence, that a missionary would choose. The question as to why Patrick began his mission here has been diffidently answered, but rather charmingly. When he was a slave on Slemish, his master had a daughter, Bronach. Among the first converts he made at Saul were six brothers, and these were the sons of Bronach. 'It must have been a quarter of a century since Patrick had seen her. But the idea suggests itself that here he expected to find an old friend, as evidently he did.' (Missionaries have to begin somewhere.) Nendrum was founded by one of Bronach's sons, Machaoi (anglicized to 'Mahee'), and St Patrick must surely have visited it.[57]

Sam Hanna Bell (1909–90)[58] lived as a child on a farm not far from Mahee Island, and sets his novel *December Bride* along the shores of Strangford Lough. It is filled with a precise spirit of the place, the working-rhythms of the small farms scattered there. His characters have a sort of self-imposed and taciturn inarticulateness. This Protestant family has prospered, while one of the cottages on the hill is lived in by Catholics:

'And there's the housing o' the crops,' said Sarah.
'Aye, there's the housing o' the crops. We couldna get the barn door closed on the last harvest, and the haggard's no grown any since last year.'
'Ye may clear one o' the cottages on the hill.'
Hamilton laid down his spoon and stared at her. 'In the name o' God, woman! We canna put the craturs out on the road for a wheen av bags o' corn and praties!'

'There's no talk of them going out on the road. There's more cottages nor one in the countryside.'

'We didna buy the Dineens wi' the land!' Frank burst out angrily. 'And we're no going to be held up by the likes o' them. This thing's twixt you and me,' he continued pointedly. 'And that's my say, flat and plain.'

'You've taken a very sudden scunner at the Dineens.'

'I've taken no scunner at the Dineens. But there's no good saying one thing and thinking another. We'll be looking that cottage afore the harvest, so what's the use of all this farting and fiddling around?' He paused, and then added, 'As Sarah says, there's more nor one place they can go to in the countryside.'

The three of them continued eating in silence. Not one of them honestly believed that it was necessary to turn the Dineens out. Had it been any other family the brothers would have put themselves to any inconvenience to find another storage house. Yet they, and even Sarah, liked Owen Dineen. But deep down in all three the centuries-old enmity against the papist stirred, and neighbourliness and a more ancient kinship were forgotten.

> Ah Clandeboye! Thy friendly floor
> Slieve Donard's oak shall light no more;
> The mantling brambles hide thy hearth,
> Centres of hospitable mirth,
> All undistinguished in the glade
> My sire's grand home is prostrate laid. . . .
> And now the stranger's sons enjoy
> The lovely woods of Clandeboye.

So sang Sir Walter Scott, in *Rokeby*,[59] referring to the confiscation of O'Neill estates, in 1604. Harold Nicolson (1896–1968) is loftily English about Scott's sense of history. 'The O'Neill hearth at Clandeboye may, or may not, have existed. For all I know it may have been laid prostrate.' Nicolson loved the place as it was, in his own childhood, and described it in *Helen's Tower*, his genial biography of his uncle Lord Dufferin, Viceroy of India.[60] Dufferin built the tower in 1860 as a tribute to his mother Helen (1807–67), granddaughter of the playwright Richard Brinsley Sheridan, a woman much celebrated for her beauty and goodness. She shows herself more tender to the dark history of the province than Nicolson, in her poem 'The Emigrant Ship':

Is the cabin still left standing? Has the rich man need of all?
Is the children's birthplace taken now within the new park wall?

The Tower was engraved with verses by various hands, including
Tennyson's with its fine fifth line:

> Helen's Tower, here I stand,
> Dominant over sea and land.
> Son's love built me, and I hold
> Mother's love in lettered gold.
> Love is in and out of time,
> I am mortal stone and lime. . . .

Nicolson says that in the family the Tower was treated as a sort of
shrine. A copy of it was built at Albert in northern France, as a
memorial to the Ulster dead of the 1914–18 war.

At the north-east top corner of the Ards peninsula is Donaghadee,
the old, pre-steam, pre-Larne point of arrival from Scotland. It was
here that John Keats stepped ashore, in July 1818, with his friend
Charles Brown. They had been walking in Scotland and planned this
trip as an extra excursion. It is said that they stayed at Grace O'Neill's
bar in the High Street (as on another occasion did Peter the Great
of Russia). They hoped to walk to the Giant's Causeway, but 'found
those 48 miles to be irish ones which reach to 70 english'. They also
discovered Ireland to be three times as expensive as Scotland, so they
contented themselves with walking into Belfast (where Keats was
disgusted by the sound of the weaving-shuttles) and then back to
Donaghadee. 'The dialect on the neighbouring shores of Scotland and
Ireland is much the same – yet I can perceive a great difference in the
nations from the chambermaid at this nate Inn kept by Mr Kelly. She
is fair, kind and ready to laugh, because she is out of the horrible
dominion of the Scotch Kirk.'

The squalor and poverty of Ireland disgusts Keats and excites his
sympathy. After two days' stay there and more walking in Scotland,
he permits himself some generalizations about the natives: 'It seems
to me they are both sensible of the character they hold in England
and act accordingly to Englishmen. Thus the Scotchman will become
over grave and over decent and the Irishman over impetuous. I like
the Scotchman best because he is less of a bore – I like the Irishman
best because he ought to be more comfortable.'[61]

Down – Armagh

Below Donaghadee, down the Ards Peninsula (passing Carrowdore where MacNeice's ashes are buried), a few minutes on the ferry at Strangford where the lough meets the sea (the Norse name means 'Strong Ford', and the Vikings found the current a fierce one), and you are on the road to Downpatrick, where St Patrick is supposed to be buried. Fingerposts point to the 'St Patrick Trail', which leads to the place where the saint landed, to his statue on a hill, and to Saul where he had his first church.[62]

If you continue west, above the mountains of Mourne, there appear more fingerposts, surprising ones (because the Bronte sisters were all born in England): you are now in the 'Bronte Country'. Their father, Patrick Brunty or Prunty (Pronteaigh) (1777–1861), was born here, at Ballyskeagh (the country he would have known is roughly between Loughbrickland and Rathfriland); and he cannot have felt too homesick in the part of England where he finished up, because this region has a flavour of Yorkshire, with the Mourne mountains, fell-like, always in view. Patrick began in very humble circumstances indeed, but taught himself to read and, amazingly, made his way to Cambridge University, thence (now called Brontë) to Yorkshire and Haworth Rectory, and into literary history as father of three remarkable daughters. They never came here, but when *Jane Eyre* was published, by 'Currer Bell', the Irish Bruntys heard of it, and also of the anonymous review which speculated about the identity and sex of the author: 'Whoever it be, it is a person who, with great mental power, combines total ignorance of the habits of society, a great coarseness of taste, and a heathenish doctrine of religion.' This was enough (the story goes) for Patrick's brother Hugh. He sailed to Liverpool, walked the seventy miles to Haworth, and announced to a horrified Charlotte his intention of going to London to thrash the reviewer. In London, he called on Charlotte's publishers who, clearly at a loss, vaguely gave him a ticket to the Reading Room of the British Museum. He returned to Ireland baffled and disappointed (it emerged later that the person he wanted to thrash was a woman, Lady Eastlake).[63]

This rolling landscape, the border of County Down with County Armagh, was Helen Waddell's idea of an 'earthly paradise'.[64] Waddell's great-uncle was the colourful adventurer and writer of ripping yarns, Mayne Reid (1818–63), a child of the manse at Ballyroney.[65] At Markethill, Swift stayed, and chopped down a 'fairy' thorn much treasured by local people; he celebrated this unamiable act in one of his facetious verses ('This aged, sickly, sapless Thorn/Which must alas no longer stand/Behold! the cruel Dean in scorn/ Cuts down with sacrilegious Hand . . .').

Not far north-east of Armagh there are places associated with two poets who were almost of an age, were friends, had roughly the same Protestant backgrounds, and lives and work that could hardly be more different. They can stand as a warning against generalizing about 'Ulster Protestants'; or, for that matter, 'Ulster writers'. W.R. Rodgers (1909–69)[66] was Presbyterian minister at Loughgall from 1935 to 1946. The forebears of John Hewitt (1907–87) were buried at Kilmore, a mile or two away. The poems of Rodgers delight in exaggeration, are sensuous, pyrotechnic; Hewitt's, careful and dogged, almost prosaic. Rodgers cannot describe a train without saying it 'has a screech stuck in her hair like a feather'; Hewitt is sedate and orderly, and celebrates these Planter qualities with satisfaction:[67]

> Kilmore, Armagh, no other sod can show
> the weathered stone of our first burying.
> Born in Belfast, which drew the landless in,
> that river-straddling, hill-rimmed town, I cling
> to the inflexions of my origin.

Hewitt stays in Belfast, but Rodgers gives up his ministry in 1946, goes to London, becomes an urbanite, friend and drinking-companion of Louis MacNeice, with whom he worked at the BBC. (He also writes 'Lent', one of the rare, contemporary Christian verse-meditations.)

Belfast-based Hewitt is clearly happiest (he says so) in the solitudes of the Glens of Antrim, which, for all his proud Protestantism, are predominantly Catholic; and, for all his Christianity, he has his memorial cairn erected in the Glens next to 'Ossian's Grave' – pagan Oisín, son of the great Finn, and defier of St Patrick. He finds a fitting image for these strands in Kilmore:

> When I discovered not long ago, that the Planter's Gothic of Kilmore church still encloses the stump of a Round Tower, and it was built on the site of a Culdee holy place, I felt a step nearer to that synthesis. . . . It is the best symbol I have yet found for the strange textures of my response to this island of which I am a native. I may appear Planter's Gothic, but there is a Round Tower somewhere inside and needled through every sentence that I utter.[68]

Rodgers, from his lonely parsonage at Cloven Eden in Loughgall, celebrates Armagh city itself ('Raised at a time when Reason was all the rage,/Of grey and equal stone'):[69]

> There is a through-otherness about Armagh
> Of tower and steeple,
> Up on the hill are the arguing graves of the kings,
> And below are the people. . . .
>
> Through-other is its history, of Celt and Dane,
> Norman and Saxon,
> Who ruled the place and sounded the gamut of fame
> From cow-horn to klaxon.
>
> There is a through-otherness about Armagh
> Delightful to me,
> Up on the hill are the graves of the garrulous kings
> Who at last can agree.

Armagh still has a 'through-otherness' – a local word meaning pleasant muddle; it is also still what St Patrick intended it to be, the ecclesiastical capital of Ireland. An account of how Patrick brought this about, in Muirchu's seventh-century Latin *Life of Saint Patrick*, is a typical mixture of magic, superstition and hard-headedness.[70] A rich man, Daire, gives the saint a piece of ground, though not the ground he wanted, which was on a hill. Then Daire presents the saint with 'a wonderful three-metretae bowl', for which the saint merely says 'Thanks' (*gratias agam*, which Daire hears as 'Grazacham'). This seems inadequate to Daire, so he takes the bowl back, to which the saint says 'Grazacham' again. Daire is delighted: '"*Grazacham* when you give it, *Grazacham* when you take it away: what he says is so good – his bowl will be brought back to him with these *Grazachams*." And this time Daire came personally and brought the bowl back to Patrick, saying to him: "Here, keep your bowl. For you are a firm, steadfast man. What is more, I give you, as far as it is mine to give, that piece of ground which you once requested."' So they climb the hill, and find a hind and a fawn which Patrick protects from his followers, and 'the saint himself took the fawn, carrying it on his shoulders; and the hind followed him like a very gentle, docile ewe, till he had let the fawn go free . . .'

No one underestimates the continuing power of a story, especially in Ireland, and the Catholic cathedral, a twin-spired extravaganza, was built (1840–1904) on the place where Patrick let the fawn go. The sober Church of Ireland cathedral (on the first piece of ground) has been used as a fort, wrecked, repaired, burnt and re-repaired over the centuries.

On the far side of Armagh, to the west, and worth waiting for, is 'Navan Fort',[71] the ancient *Emain Macha* ['Evin Vacha'], home of Rodgers's 'garrulous kings'. For six hundred years the kings of Ulster were crowned here, from 350 BC to AD 332. It was pillaged in the fourth century AD from Tara in Meath and, though it had been subject of many previous burnings, this time it was never rebuilt. It was not long after its end that Patrick came, to give Armagh a new kind of primacy. But Emain Macha was much more than a royal crowning-place. It is the Mycenae of Ireland, the setting of many of the pre-Christian legends and myths. Its high mound, now grass-grown and quiet, has enormous presence, as though still waiting. From the top of it you can see Patrick's Slemish, forty miles to the north-east, on the other side of Lough Neagh. It was to Emain Macha that the great half-magical hero Cuchulainn came as a boy, to receive his training. The 'Cattle Raid of Cooley' contains a description of his arrival: 'Then he turned the left side of his chariot towards Emain which was tabu for it. And Cu Chulainn said: "I swear by the god by whom Ulstermen swear that, unless some man is found to fight with me, I shall shed the blood of everyone in the fort."' King Conchobor orders the women, led by the queen, to go out to meet him with bared breasts. 'He hid his face. . . .'[72]

From the Cattle Raid, the reader 'gets a vivid picture of the life and manners of the race in one of its great strongholds, from which he may conjecture, and even assume, a good deal with regard to the others' (Douglas Hyde).[73] In this sense, ancient Ireland is very fully recorded. 'In the rest of Europe there is not a single barrow, dolmen, or cist, of which the ancient traditional history is recorded; in Ireland there is hardly one of which it is not' (Standish O'Grady).[74] In the ancient tales there is an extraordinary amount of detail, about clothing, weapons, jewellery, and, even especially, hair-styles.

Beautiful indeed was the youth who thus came to display his form to the hosts, namely Cu Chulainn mac Sualtaim. He seemed to have three kinds of hair, dark next to his skin, blood-red in the middle and hair like a crown of gold covering them outside. Fair was the arrangement of that hair with three coils in the hollow in the nape of his neck, and like gold thread was each fine hair, loose-flowing, bright-golden, excellent, long-tressed, splendid and of beautiful colour, which fell back over his shoulders. A hundred bright crimson ringlets of flaming red-gold encircled his neck. Around his head a hundred strings interspersed with carbuncle-gems. . . .[75]

Emain Macha was also the site of the death of Deirdre, heroine of another great story, connected with the *Táin*, ancient Ireland's equivalent of the tale of Tristan and Iseult: 'The Exile of the Sons of Uisneach' ['Ushna'] (also 'Uisliu' – all the names are variously spelt). The story has been much plundered by more recent Irish writers; Yeats and Synge among others wrote plays on it. They seem to fall in love with Deirdre. James Stephens wrote: 'A time comes when our hearts sink utterly,/When we remember Deirdre and her tale,/And that her lips are dust.'[76] Before her birth it is prophesied that Deirdre will become the most beautiful of all women, 'and a cause of slaughter'. King Conchobor ['Conchooer'] decides to keep her for himself, and has her brought up out of the sight of men. But she catches sight of Naisu (Naoise) ['Neeshuh']. To his initial dismay, she decides he is the man for her. Despite the force of Destiny, she is a spirited and independent young woman, as are most of the women in the old Irish stories. William Trevor calls the *Táin*, and related tales, 'a beady examination of both men and women, both sexes equally regarded, equally endowed with wit and intelligence when beset by folly and passion. They happen to be Celtic aristocrats, the cream of a remarkable race, but it's the ordinariness of their humanity that so vividly gives them life.'[77] Deirdre escapes to Scotland with Naisu and his two brothers. They are enticed back by a trick – landing in County Antrim at Fair Head, Ballycastle – and the three brothers are killed on Emain, with thousands of others. The prophecy is fulfilled. Their slaughter is stylized as though on a stage:

> The sons of Uisliu were standing in the middle of the green, and the women were sitting on the rampart of Emhain. Then Eoghan ['Owen'] went against them with his troop over the green, but the son of Ferghus came so that he was beside Noisiu. Eoghan welcomed them with a thrusting blow of a great spear into Noisiu, so that his back broke because of it. . . .
> They were killed then all over the green, so that none escaped but those who fought their way out by point of spear and edge of sword; and she was brought across to Conchobhar so that she was in his power, and her hands were bound behind her back.

In this, the older version of the story, Deirdre herself is not let off with a quick death:

'What do you see that you most hate?' said Conchobhar. 'Yourself, surely,' said she, 'and Eoghan.' 'Then you shall be a year with Eoghan,' said Conchobhar. He put her then at Eoghan's disposal.

They went the next day to the assembly of Macha. She was behind Eoghan in a chariot. She had vowed that she would not see two husbands together on earth. 'Well, Deirdriu,' said Conchobhar, 'it is the eye of a ewe between two rams that you make between me and Eoghan.' There was a great boulder of stone before her. She dashed her head on the stone so that her head was shattered, so that she died.

That is the exile of the sons of Uisliu and the exile of Ferghus and the violent death of Uisliu and of Deirdriu.[78]

Thus abruptly, almost matter-of-factly, does the great story end. Kate O'Brien justly remarks on 'the brutal, overbearing logic' of these old stories.[79]

ARMAGH – NORTH ANTRIM

Moving northwards from Armagh you pass through Moy, which could be called 'Muldoon country'. Paul Muldoon (b. 1951), younger than James Simmons, is equally conscious of violence below the apparently innocent:[80]

> The Volkswagen parked in the gap,
> But gently ticking over.
> You wonder if it's lovers
> And not men hurrying back
> Across two fields and a river.

Northwards again, west of Lough Neagh and turning north-east, through Bellaghy (Seamus Heaney country), then across the River Bann which flows north out of the Lough, and you are in County Antrim once more, between Sweeney's favourite roosting area, Glen Bolcain (Rasharkin), and St Patrick's Slemish, over the hills to the Glens of Antrim. They run down to the north-eastern coast, one of the most beautiful regions in Ireland, as the cliff-road that leads to them from the south, from Larne to Cushendall,[81] is one of the most dramatic in Europe.

The Glens contained a specifically Irish surprise for Kate O'Brien: 'When I walked into the hotel at Cushendall on a bright, cold

Wednesday afternoon, the first Wednesday in March, I was puzzled to find on each, open welcoming brow that turned towards me a central smudge of black. Schooldays, Mother Philomena, Sister Bernard – I remembered. Ah yes – Ash Wednesday! But this is Antrim! I am in the North! And so I learnt to my surprise that the population of the Glens of Antrim is almost ninety percent Roman Catholic.'

Protestant John Hewitt spent as much time as he could there, at Cushendall: 'No other area of my native province has been so nourishing to my senses, my imagination and my heart, not even the hill-hooped Belfast where I was born or the apple orchards of Armagh where my people first settled in this island.'[82] He passes a hill farm in the evening, and hears the family inside reciting the rosary:

> At each Hail Mary, Full of Grace
> I pictured every friendly face,
> clenched in devotion of a kind
> alien to my breed and mind . . .

and he wrestles, as ever, with the complexities of the province:

> This is our fate: eight hundred years' disaster
> crazily tangled as the Book of Kells;
> the dream's distortion and the land's division,
> the midnight raiders and the prison cells.
> Yet like Lir's children banished to the waters
> our hearts still listen for the landward bells.

Catholic-born Kate O'Brien also remembers Lir's children, as well as Deirdre: the myths are still at work in both writers:

When I walked alone over Ballycastle Strand towards the rocks below Fair Head, I found myself considering these so as to choose that one on to which Naisi, son of Usnagh, might have skipped with his wife Deirdre in his arms on the day when he and his brothers brought her back so happily from Scotland to meet only the old man's treachery of Conor MacNessa. These black rocks were the very ones that took part in that bright promising day of return – and with no effort at all I saw the young people landing and Fergus waving, running to them. But the story of the sons of Usnagh is one that is always crystal clear; truer and more likely than any foul play of yesterday's newspaper. Still, it was interesting to stand on those long ago important little rocks; they endeared Ballycastle to me.

And so did the near presence of grey Rathlin Island, seeming nearer than its four miles' distance across the cold silver channel. It was up and down these waters, they say, between Fair Head and Rathlin, that the four children of Lir had to sail unrestingly for centuries. . . .

She quotes Thomas Moore: 'Lir's lonely daughter told to the night star her tale of woes.' The children were turned to the shape of swans by their jealous stepmother, until a bell would break the spell. A saint's bell eventually rings

and the children at once regained human shape. But now they were old, old, old, and horrible and frightening in each other's sight. So they died at once, and Moore's Melody suggests, as far as I remember, that they had miraculous Christian deaths and went straight to Heaven – which may sound like a happy ending; but I think that after four hundred years as a swan I should have preferred, were I Finuala, to have died a swan. The moment of changing back was, as it could only be, hideous; and that it had to be undergone is an example of that brutal, overbearing logic that distinguishes Irish legends, a logic which saves them from the vapours, and makes us remember them with anxiety.[83]

On Rathlin Island in 1306 Robert the Bruce watched the patient spider 'try, try again', and was inspired to return to Scotland and the battle of Bannockburn (1314). In 1575 the Earl of Essex (the elder) brought about a slaughter there. Sorley Boy MacDonnell defied Essex from the Glens and sent his women, children and valuables to Rathlin for safe-keeping. Essex heard of this at Carrickfergus and despatched three frigates – one of them commanded by Sir Francis Drake: 'There have been slain that came out of the castle of all sorts two hundred. They be still occupied in the killing, and have slain all that they have found hidden in caves and in cliffs of the sea to the number of three hundred or four hundred more.' Thus coolly does the Lord Deputy of Ireland, Sir Henry Sidney (father of the poet Sir Philip), report the massacre, to a grateful Queen Elizabeth. An observer reported that Sorley Boy MacDonnell, hearing the gunfire, watching the burning, ran up and down on Fair Head – that beautiful cliff below which Deirdre had landed with Naisu on their way to meet treachery at Emain Macha – until 'he was like to run mad, turning and tormenting himself'.[84]

A short way to the west of Fairhead and Ballycastle is the Giant's Causeway. Two of the many nineteenth-century visitors from the mainland bring to it a trace of Sir Henry Sidney's detachment, and offer less hospitality to myth and imagination than Hewitt or O'Brien. Sir Walter Scott, on a cruise in 1814 (he was admittedly distracted by recent news of a friend's death):

> To those who have seen Staffa, the peculiar appearance of the Causeway itself will lose much of its effect. . . . The people ascribe all these wonders to Fin MacCoul whom they couple with a Scottish giant called Ben-an- something or other. The traveller is plied by guides, who make their profit by selling pieces of crystal, agate, or chalcedony, found in the interiors of the rocks. Our party brought off some curious joints of the columns, and, had I been quite as I am wont to be, I would have selected four to be capitals of a rustic porch at Abbotsford. But, alas! alas! I am much out of love with vanity at this moment.[85]

Thackeray (in 1842) could hardly wait to get out of the place: 'The savage rock sides are painted of a hundred colours. Does the sun ever shine there? When the world was moulded and fashioned out of formless chaos, this must have been *the bit over* – a remnant of chaos. Think of that! – it is a tailor's simile. Well, I am a Cockney, I wish I were in Pall Mall!' He goes off to have his dinner in the Causeway Hotel (admired by Mrs Craik in 1886 and still there), but that also appals him: 'In spite of the bright fire, and the good dinner, and the good wine, it was impossible to feel comfortable in the place, and when the car wheels were heard, I jumped up with joy to take my departure and forget this awful lonely shore, that wild, dismal, genteel inn. . . .'[86]

He escapes to Coleraine, 'famous for beautiful Kitty who must be old and ugly now, for it's a good five-and-thirty years since she broke her pitcher, according to Mr Moore's account of her'. The words of that song retain charm (though not by 'Mr Moore' but Anon):

> As beautiful Kitty one morning was tripping
> With a pitcher of milk from the fair of Coleraine,
> She saw me and stumbled, and the pitcher it tumbled,
> And all the fine buttermilk watered the plain.
> Oh, what shall I do now? 'twas looking at you now;
> Sure, sure, such a pitcher I'll ne'er meet again,

'Twas the pride of my dairy, oh, Barney McCleary,
You're sent as a plague to the girls of Coleraine. . . .

'Kitty of Coleraine' is taken from *Ulster Songs and Ballads* (1925), for
which the Ulster playwright St John Ervine (1883–1971) provides a
foreword, pugnacious in defence of his province:

> When an Englishman thinks of an Ulsterman, he thinks of a
> dour, humourless, unkindly and uncouth person, deeply
> absorbed in the making of money, and almost destitute of culture
> and charm. . . .
>   With extraordinary skill, the Southern Irishman has persuaded
> the Englishman to accept his myths as eternal truths, and has
> been assisted in his persuasions by the susceptibility of the
> Englishman to the 'charm' which is better described as hum-
> bug. . . . Already people are agreeing that there is more humour
> in Ulster than in all the other provinces of Ireland put
> together.[87]

'The Irish are a fair people – they never speak well of one another,'
said Dr Johnson; and Sean O'Faolain, having already disposed of
Ervine's native town ('one thing to be said in favour of Belfast – you
can get out of it quickly'), has his own views about Ervine's works:
'The only Belfast writer who has tried at all to bottle the "realism"
of the city . . . but he is lacking in poetry, and has only succeeded
in making it taste like re-boiled mutton gone cold.'[88] It would have
been good to have seen these two squaring up to each other. (It
is entirely possible that they were friends.) How does O'Faolain,
Ervine's 'Southern Irishman', react to Coleraine?

> Coleraine is one of the cleanest market towns in these islands,
> solid and bright and comfortable. If a Norfolk man or a Kentish
> man were dropped into it he would feel so much at home that
> not until he noted such names as McClusky or McKimmins,
> would he see anything at all unusual enough for wonder. And
> that is what this really is – a British market town, in a fine farm-
> ing centre, with a lovely setting of wood and river. I felt myself
> at a great distance from home in Coleraine.

'Apart from two songs – one about Kitty of Coleraine, and the
other about Coleraine whisky – I could remember nothing about the
town until I entered it. . . .' But then he recalls swathes of history
(the Plantations, the grants of land after the 1607 flight of the Earls)
and literature and myth ('Swift stayed here . . . King Conchobar of

the great Deirdre story is said to have come down the river . . .')
in a way northern Protestants perhaps do not, or not so readily,
because for them there is a discontinuity.

Sam Hanna Bell is quick to explain that nothing is so simple as that:

> It has been concluded by dance-band lyricists, hydroponic poets
> and writers of travel books that the traditions of Ulster can be
> found only in Catholic homes, because Catholics are more
> 'poetic', less 'materialistic'. I don't think this is so. . . .
>
> In Ulster, for reasons which you will find in history, the
> mountainsides are inhabited by Catholics and the valleys by Pro-
> testants. Understandably, the old beliefs live longer among the
> scattered cottages in the hills than in the plump lowland acres
> tilled to the hedges where the fairy thorns have been torn out
> and the souterrains filled in for the sake of a few extra buckets
> of grain.[89]

But Thackeray, impatient to get back to London from the barren-
ness of the Giant's Causeway, and even Scott observing its geology
and contemptuous of tales of giants like 'Fin McCoul' (and their later
equivalents, one may suppose), are impervious to layers of imagination
in a way that, say, O'Faolain and O'Brien are not.

Ulster legends have tended towards the large scale, with Cuchulainn's
monstrous transformations, and Finn MacCool (who in other versions
of the tales appears at least half human) as a giant scooping out Lough
Neagh. Finn MacCool is the legendary leader of the companions of
the Red Branch (O'Faolain also remembers this at Coleraine; they had
a base nearby). They are warriors and hunters, at the fringes of society
but at the service of the kings of Ireland, and their band is called the
Fianna (as in the political party Fianna Fail ['Feena Foil']). The stories
about them are called the Fenian cycle, and 'Fenian' was a name
adopted early by Irish nationalists.[90]

Around the twelfth century an attempt was made to bring together
the pagan Ireland of the Fenian cycle and the Christian Ireland of St
Patrick. Finn's son, Oisín ['Usheen'], 'Ossian',[91] was a warrior bard
who is spirited off to the Land of Youth by the fairy queen, Niamh
['Nieve']: 'As to Oisín, some say it was hundreds of years he was
in the Country of the Young, and some say it was thousands of years
he was in it; but whatever time it was, it seemed short to him.'[92]
Oisín decides to go and take one more look at Ireland and Niamh
says that will be all right, he will remain young and vigorous, so long
as he does not get off his horse. But he grows thirsty, forgets,

dismounts to drink at a spring, and is immediately, like the children of Lir, very old indeed. In this condition, having discovered that Finn and the Fianna are all long gone, he meets, to his disgust, St Patrick. Christian Ireland seems very boring to Oisín, but the interest for us is that in the argument with St Patrick, transcribed from oral tradition by monks, Oisín is allowed to get the better of it:[93]

> Patrick you chatter too loud
>   And lift your crozier too high,
> Your stick would be kindling soon
>   If my son Osgar stood by. . . .
> But how could the God you praise
>   And his mild priests singing a tune
> Be better than Fionn the swordsman,
>   Generous, faultless Fionn. . . .

That is part of a translation by Frank O'Connor, from a poem that was probably written in the sixteenth century, 'but', O'Connor says, 'it has the feeling of the eighth or ninth century'. In Lady Gregory's version Oisín is dissatisfied with St Patrick's hospitality, and says so:

'They say I am getting food, but God knows I am not, or drink; and I Oisín, son of Finn, under a yoke, drawing stones.' 'It is my opinion you are getting enough,' said St Patrick then, 'and you are getting a quarter of beef and a churn of butter and a griddle of bread every day.' 'I often saw a quarter of a blackbird bigger than your quarter of beef,' said Oisín, 'and a rowan berry as big as your churn of butter, and an ivy leaf as big as your griddle of bread.' St Patrick was vexed when he heard this, and he said to Oisín that he had told a lie.

Furious at this challenge, Oisín, old as he is, goes out and does various fierce and miraculous things, which include the killing of a giant bird, a quarter of which was indeed greater than the quarter of beef granted to him, and in its belly is the largest rowan berry ever seen, and of course a gigantic ivy leaf. These he shows to St Patrick: 'And now you know, Patrick of the Bells,' he said, 'that I told no lie; and it is what kept us all through our lifetime,' he said, 'truth that was in our hearts, and strength in our arms, and fulfilment in our tongues.' 'You told no lie indeed,' said Patrick.

There is a wild humour in the talk between the old pagan and the old priest, and a wild grief in Oisín, that rises to great eloquence. Oisín even finds it in himself to forgive Patrick's God, and with no trace of humility: 'Without the cry of the hounds or the horns, without guarding coasts, without courting courteous women; all that I have suffered by want of food, I forgive the King of Heaven in my will,' Oisín said. 'My story is sorrowful. The sound of your voice is not pleasant to me. I will cry my fill, but not for God, but because Finn and Fianna are not living.' It is a lament for pagan Ireland, and must have passed from mouth to mouth long before it came to be written down; part of the hidden life of Ireland, perhaps of Europe.

2

THE EAST MIDLANDS

LOUTH – MONAGHAN

Ever since Synge and Yeats, romance has been held to reside in the wild west of Ireland; but it is here, in the north-east midlands, good farming land and at first sight prosaic to the visitor's eye, that the action of most of the sagas and stories took place. It is now business-like, and in *An Irish Journey* (1940) Sean O'Faolain wonders if anybody in Dundalk, or in Ulster, talks about Cuchulainn and the *Táin* (the 'Cattle Raid of Cooley') these days, any more than they talk about Agamemnon in Athens. He asks a friend from the north, who says:

> I was going home to Belfast one Christmas, drinking in the dining-car with a bacon-slicer salesman who had driven me to Dublin. As we left Dundalk the Mournes pounced [*sic*] on me, as sudden and as exultant as that grand blare of brass in Beethoven's Fifth. I went mushy. I began to talk – me and the whisky – about Cuchulainn and the *Táin*. About the way I always imagined myself in the spacious savagery of pre-Christian Ireland, whenever the train went through that Gap. I enthused and enthused. The bacon-slicer man knocked back his liquor – he drank lemonade in it by the way – and pressed the bell. 'Man,' he said, '*you're* the quare boy!'[1]

The Cooley Peninsula, which is between Dundalk Bay and Carlingford Lough, is the 'Cooley' (*Culaigne*) of the famous 'Cattle Raid', the *Táin Bó Cúlaigne* ['Toyn Boh Coolinger'], where the bull was kept that Queen Maeve came to seize. Cuchulainn's native patch was Murtheimne ['Mur-hevny'], which corresponds with present-day County Louth, the plain below Cooley and the hills bordering Ulster; and this he defended against her single-handed. Cuchulainn mostly fought at fords. At Ardee (*Ath Ferdiadh*) took place the most famous of Irish single combats, and in the river. After a four-day fight, filled with end-of-the-day courtesies, Cuchulainn reluctantly slew his foster-brother Ferdia, but only after he had been run through by a sword himself. This extremity forced Cuchulainn to resort to his secret weapon, the *gae bolga*, the precise nature of which many scholars have pondered. It was magic, of course, and seems to have been something like a present-day heat-seeking missile, with many warheads, launched from underwater. Cuchulainn mourns Ferdia:

> All gaming, all sport,
> Till I met Ferdia at the ford . . .

'Well, my friend Laeg,' he says to his charioteer, 'cut open Ferdia now and take the *gae bolga* out of him, for I must not be without my weapon.'[2]

'The Cattle Raid', says Frank O'Connor, 'bears the same relation to epic that Avebury, say, does to the Parthenon, and those who can be impressed by the magnificence of Avebury may appreciate the beauty of *The Cattle Raid*.'[3] O'Connor is selling the saga short; it is more exciting than Avebury, even though (in the various versions that have come down to us) it is a great muddle. Thomas Kinsella, by conflation, has made much of this confusion clear in his fast-moving version, which brings out the mixture of the barbaric with the natural; also the variety, which enabled Yeats to say that 'not one of those fights is like another, and not one is lacking in emotion and strangeness. When we think imagination can do no more, the story of the Two Bulls, emblematic of all contests, suddenly lifts romance into prophecy.'[4] (The two bulls, the Brown and the White, fight locked together all over Ireland. The Brown – the one the Raid was about – dies last.)

'The Táin Trail' is signposted at the Cooley Peninsula, and to climb by car from the sedate seaside villas around it to the heights above is to find yourself, in a matter of minutes, among the rock-bordered fields of the west of Ireland, or the wind-swept moors of Kerry. You have moved, in moments, into what Daniel Corkery called the Hidden Ireland. This Ireland continued to have its own poets, right into the eighteenth century, when to outward appearances native culture might have been thought to be dead. With the defeat of the Irish at the battle of Kinsale, in Cork, in 1601, and the 'Flight of the Earls' from Ulster that followed soon after, the Elizabethan conquest of Ireland was completed. Within a century nearly all (85%) of Irish land was in English hands, and the old, feudal Ireland, which protected its bards, had all but disappeared. It was the end, or seemed to be the end, of literature in Irish.

Now, in their poems (they continued to write because they still had a native audience) Irish-language poets looked back to the

previous times as a golden age, or looked forward to the return of
the old ways and the old patrons, until that hope was extinguished
(nearly) by the Battle of the Boyne in 1690 and the victory of King
William. As they sank in the social scale (their new employers having
no idea how they were revered among their own people) their poems,
still in the traditional strict forms, became more personal, allusive,
more 'modern', but remained part of a continuing oral culture. There
were groups of these poets in the south and west of Ireland, and
one such group flourished in this district, south-east Ulster. They
are called the 'Oriel' poets, after the region round Mount Oriel, south-
west of Dundalk.[6]

One 'Oriel' poem is much translated. Cathal Buí Mac Giólla Gunna
(d. 1756? probably on the Cavan-Fermanagh border) was apparently
a famous drinker (he ends his lament for himself, for 'Yellow-haired
Cathal', 'I shall say in the presence of God, I am guilty, my Lord').
In his most famous poem, 'The Yellow Bittern', he laments the death
of a bird for which he has a fellow-feeling because it dies of its thirst:
trying to scoop a drink from the lough it broke its neck – the lough
was frozen.[7] The translation is by Thomas MacDonagh (1878–
1916), executed for his part in the Easter Rising.

> The yellow bittern that never broke out
>   In a drinking bout might as well have drunk;
> His bones are thrown on a naked stone
>   Where he lived alone like a hermit monk.
> O yellow bittern! I pity your lot,
>   Though they say that a sot like myself is curst –
> I was sober a while, but I'll drink and be wise,
>   For fear I should die in the end of thirst.
>
> It's not for the common birds that I'd mourn,
>   The blackbird, the corncrake or the crane,
> But for the bittern that's shy and apart
>   And drinks in the marsh from the lone bog-drain.
> Oh! if I had known you were near your death,
>   While my breath held out I'd have run to you,
> Till a splash from the Lake of the Son of the Bird
>   Your soul would have stirred and waked anew.
>
> My darling told me to drink no more
>   Or my life would be o'er in a little short while;
> But I told her 'tis drink gives me health and strength,
>   And will lengthen my road by many a mile.

You see how the bird of the long smooth neck
    Could get his death from the thirst at last –
Come, son of my soul, and drink your cup,
    For you'll get no sup when your life is past. . . .

The poem has fascinated generations of Irish poets. Here is Mac-Donagh's second verse translated by a contemporary, Tom MacIntyre (b. 1931):[8]

Heron, blackbird, thrush, you've had it too:
sorry, mates, I'm occupied,
I'm blinds down for the Yellow Bittern,
a blood relation on the mother's side;
whole-hog merchants, we lived it up,
carpe'd our *diem*, hung out our sign,
collared life's bottle disregarding the label,
angled our elbows met under the table. . . .

The rescue of the work of these poets, from oral sources and from manuscripts, has been a part of Ireland's rediscovery of itself, 'an act of repossession' as Thomas Kinsella says. Irish largely relies on verbal music; non-Irish-speakers have to take it on trust when Irish scholars and Irish-speaking poets tell us how good the poems of these centuries can be. Fortunately, there have been some brilliant translators, and the existence of this Irish-language culture cannot be forgotten. Its presence, 'underground', is what gives the special flavour even to English-speaking Ireland.

The Oriel district is 'rightly famous for Ó Doirnín's poetry, which is a delightful combination of traditional learning and passionate expressions of independence and love'. Peadar Ó Doirnín ['Padder O'Durneen'] (1704?–69)[9] was a 'hedge schoolmaster' (i.e. non-official, Catholic, teacher) at Forkhill, near Dundalk. Indeed he is said to have been found dead by his pupils outside his school there, 'sleeping in the sleep that would never be broke'. His poetry sounds rather like that of the much earlier, Welsh, Dafydd ap Gwillym, concerned with successful wooing, or with rueful accounts of being turned down by girls.

O quiet sweet-tempered lady of the pearly tresses,
Come along with me in a little while,
When the nobles, the clergy and the layfolk will be deep
Asleep under white bedclothes. . . .

He is buried at Urnea, in a tiny churchyard isolated in a field, with an old church, long roofless, whose walls have nearly sunk into the ground. Urnea is below Forkhill, almost on the border between the Republic and Northern Ireland. Forkhill (in 1992) is a fortified Army observation post; so that a visitor to his grave, with its recent commemorative stone, feels himself to be under surveillance by the present and by the past, because many of the surrounding slate gravestones have older hand-scratched lettering, in Irish, indications of past poverty, of 'secret', defiant burial.

These poets were not isolated village rhymsters, however ignorant of their existence the ruling class might have been. Ó Doirnín knew the work of his fellow Oriel poets because he makes reference to it, echoes it, in his own poems, 'in which he makes claims to be at least their equal'. A story is told about one of these, Art MacCooey (Mac Cumhaigh, 1738–73), that, lost in poetic reverie, he once carried the same load of dung up and down a hill several times, forgetting to unload. MacCooey was born near Crossmaglen, and not far south of this, at Inniskeen, was born probably the most influential of recent Irish poets, Patrick Kavanagh (1904–67), who in his youth surely drove loads of dung while lost in reverie, and wrote a poem about this, which he called simply 'Art MacCooey'.

There is a charming sense in which Irish poets make a point of acknowledging their predecessors, as though there were an unbroken tradition. In fact Kavanagh, all of whose poetry is in English, seems effortlessly to retain the tone of earlier Irish poetry, in his satires, and in his descriptions of sudden illuminations brought about by some event in nature, like a fog, or a blackbird, which have the simplicity of Irish poems written in the margins of ninth-century manuscripts.

As you approach Inniskeen (not easy, the signposts seem to have been taken down, perhaps to confuse cross-border smugglers), between Dundalk and Carrickmacross, at last there are signs and these tell you that you are entering 'Patrick Kavanagh Country'. This is true, because he recorded it in detail, with love and loathing. A sign points to his birthplace, and this only partly tells the truth; he says himself in his autobiography, *The Green Fool* (1938), that the house he was born in was knocked down when he was five years old, and the present two-storied house his father built in its place. Kavanagh has been called a 'peasant-poet' but he always denied he was a peasant. His father was a shoemaker who also farmed sixteen acres of his own, a considerable number for this region.

Kavanagh, loftily, never thought much of his neighbours:

The River Fane ran through our parish on its way to the Irish Sea. It was a clear, swift-flowing stream. Anglers came long journeys to dream and smoke tobacco on its banks. These anglers said the Fane was as good a trout-stream as there was in Ireland. I shouldn't say so – the trout in its waters took after the people of Inniskeen in being hard to catch. Like the people, they knew humbug, and were dubious-minded as a jealous husband. . . .

    The name of my birthplace was Mucker. . . . The name was a corrupted Gaelic word signifying a place where pigs were bred in abundance. Long before my arrival there was much aesthetic heart-aching among the folk who had to put up with, and up in, such a pig-named townland. In spite of all this the townland stuck to its title and it was in Mucker I was born.[10]

The work was hard. A sign directs you to a steep hill, Shancoduff, part of the acres his family owned and worked. He ends his poem of that name:

> The sleety winds fondle the rushy beards of Shancoduff
> While the cattle-drovers sheltering in the Featherna Bush
> Look up and say: 'Who owns them hungry hills
> That the water-hen and snipe must have forsaken?
> A poet? Then by heavens he must be poor.'
> I hear and is my heart not badly shaken?

The young Kavanagh found his way to Dublin, then to London where the first contact he approached did not help him, but the second one did: 'Miss Helen Waddell was in, and in to a stranded poet. She received me as the Prodigal Son was received.' It is pleasing to hear first-hand evidence that Helen Waddell deserved her sobriquet, 'The Darling of Ulster'. Of course it was not the Promised Land. His experiences in London were 'a trifle comical, the image of my soul'. Years later, in London again, now an admired poet, he was not able, perhaps had no wish, to shake himself free of Inniskeen:

Kerr's Ass

> We borrowed the loan of Kerr's big ass
> To go to Dundalk with butter,
> Brought him home the evening before the market
> An exile that night in Mucker.
>
> We heeled up the cart before the door,
> We took the harness inside –

The straw-stuffed straddle, the broken breeching
With bits of bull-wire tied;

The winkers that had no choke-band,
The collar and the reins. . . .
In Ealing Broadway, London Town
I name their several names

Until a world comes to life –
Morning, the silent bog,
And the God of imagination waking
In a Mucker fog.

MEATH

The Boyne is the sacred river of the Irish, and many things happened
in its beautiful valley, both real and imagined.[11]
　　Cuchulainn fought his first battle with the invaders from Connaught at Ath Gabla, a ford across the River Mattock that meets
the Boyne near the tumulus of Dowth. There are three of these
famous tumuli – or burial mounds, or fairy palaces – next to each
other and to the river, on its north bank between Drogheda and
Slane: Dowth, Knowth and Newgrange.[12] They are more than five
thousand years old. Their associations in Irish mythology go back
even further than Cuchulainn; they reach back to Aengus Óg,[13] the
Celtic God of love, one of the Tuatha Dé Danann ['Tooha Day
Danann'] the 'People of the Goddess Dana', who were said to have
come from Greece in 1896 BC.[14] The Tuatha Dé Danann became
the gods of ancient Ireland, and they certainly seem to exude a
Mediterranean or Aegean spirit; there is nothing dark and Nordic
about them, and when you read their stories it is hard not to believe
they were taking place under some Olympian sun, not below Ireland's
changeful skies.
　　The story of Aengus Óg's dream, the lovely *Aisling Aengusa*, was
written down in the eighth century but is much older than that.
The *aisling* ['ashling'] is one of the earliest, and longest lasting, of
Irish literary forms. It consists of a dream of an absent love: literally,
a falling in love with an absence. Later, in seventeenth- and
eighteenth-century Ireland, this absent love was a personification of
Ireland in her woes, and therefore an expression of longing for a
return of the Stuarts, or for help from abroad, and so became
political.[15] But the original *Dream of Aengus* is about a real woman

(or nearly so; Aengus discovers that she spends every other year in the form of a swan) who appears to him in a dream, and for whom he searches Ireland. After various happenings, practical and magical, she is at last found: 'She went to him. He cast his arms about her. They fell asleep in the form of two swans, and went round the lake three times, so that his promise might not be broken. They went away in the form of two white birds till they came to [the Brugh] and sang a choral song so that they put the people to sleep for three days and three nights. The girl stayed with him after that.'[16] (One of the most attractive features of these early Irish magical stories is the abrupt and matter-of-fact way that they end.)

The place that Aengus took her to, the Brugh, also called Brugh na Bóinne (Hill of Boyne), is generally identified as the mound of the chamber-tomb now known as Newgrange, thought to be the palace of the Tuatha Dé Danann and afterwards the Druidical burial-place for the ashes of the Kings of Tara. Or perhaps Aengus flew with the girl, Caer Ibormeith ('Yewberry'), to another tumulus or 'fairy palace', to Dowth nearby? George Moore (1852–1933)[17] and 'AE' – George Russell (1867–1935)[18] – appear to think so, in Moore's account of their visit to Dowth in 1901. He describes this trip in *Hail and Farewell*, one of the most entertaining books to come out of the Irish Literary Revival.

In London at the turn of the century, cosmopolitan novelist George Moore (of an old Irish family from Lough Carra in County Mayo) has become so disgusted with British Imperialism, with the Boer War and Britain's involvement in it, that he decides to quit London forever and, *boulevardier* though he is, throw in his lot with his native Ireland and the Gaelic Revival – even attempt to learn Irish. As a man of the world it seems to him therefore essential to get in touch with the Top People, which in this case are the ancient Irish Gods, the Tuatha Dé Danann. He recruits AE, mystical poet, painter, practical agricultural reformer and key figure in the Revival, to effect the introductions. AE decides to take him to the tumuli near the Boyne. The Gods are sure to be there. They go by train and then by bicycle. 'We'll seek the ancient divinities of the Gael together,' says Moore, triumphant. He clearly feels that AE is an excellent contact. On the way AE points out to Moore the monument erected in commemoration of the Battle of the Boyne. Moore is indignant. 'The beastly English won that battle. If only they'd been beaten.' They both crawl inside the tumulus at Dowth, holding candles. Moore decides it is time for AE to do his job, and introduce him to the Gods: 'AE acquiesced, and he was on the ground soon, his legs tucked under him like a Yogi, waiting for the vision, and, not knowing what else to do, I withdrew to the second chamber, and ventured to call upon Angus. . . .'

Disappointed, Moore decides to leave AE to it, and climbs out of the tumulus. He lies on the grass above while AE meditates below, and then, horror, two clergymen arrive and enter the mound:

> I leaned over the opening, listening, hoping their bellies might stick in the narrow passage; but as they seemed to have succeeded in passing through, I returned to the tumulus hopeless. The Gods will not show themselves while Presbyterian ministers are about; AE will not stay in the tomb with them; and at every moment I expected to see him rise out of the earth. But it was the ministers who appeared a few minutes afterwards, and, blowing out their candles in the blue daylight. . . .
>
> Is it a history he's brooding down there? one of them asked, laughing; and I lay down on the warm grass thinking of the pain their coarse remarks must have caused AE, who came out of the hill soon after. And it was just as I had expected. The vision was about to appear, but the clergymen had interrupted it, and when they left the mood had passed.

Outside Newgrange, AE begins to sketch the designs on the stones and the loquacious Moore, at first irritated, decides it is perhaps impossible to talk outside a building that is five thousand years old. So he surrenders himself to enjoyment of the view, but is not silent long:

> The same landscape that had astonished me at Dowth lay before me, the same green wilderness, with trees emerging like vapour, just as in AE's pastels. My eyes closed, and through the lids I began to see strange forms moving towards the altar headed by Druids. Ireland was wonderful then, said my dreams, and on opening my eyes Ireland seemed as wonderful in the blue morning, the sky hanging about her, unfolding like a great convolvulus. . . .
>
> A giant outline showed through the sun-haze miles away. Has Angus risen to greet us, or Mac Lir come up from the sea?[19] I asked, and, shading his eyes with his hand, AE studied the giant outline for a long time. It's Tara, he said, that you're looking at. On a clear evening Tara can be seen from Newgrange.

Moore now starts to enthuse about Tara, and as they bicycle off

AE tells him repressively that no Gods are to be seen there. AE is clearly getting huffy, he does not want to make the detour to Tara, but Moore eggs him on: 'We passed a girl driving her cows homeward. She drew a shawl over her head, and I said I remembered seeing her long ago in Mayo, and AE answered, "Before the tumuli she was. . . ."' Then, ' "You're punctured!" AE said', and Moore has no need to describe how triumphantly he said it.

The tunnels they entered at Dowth are now closed by gratings, though the mound is (so far) untouched. Newgrange, formerly tree-grown, has been excavated and refurbished, its front set with stones of white quartz so that it gleams from afar, and this is thought to be how it originally looked. Deep inside it are three beautiful stone bowls, said to have been for the ashes of the kings. They are now empty. Where are the ashes? A question worthy of George Moore. Vanished on visitors' feet, says the guide. (There has been a crescendo of visitors since 1700.)

On the opposite bank to the Brugh/Newgrange is Rosnaree, scene of another clash (or fusion) between paganism and Christianity.

The great king, Cormac Mac Art,[20] said to have reigned over a supposed Golden Age in the third century – though it sounds troubled enough – refused to be buried with his ancestors in Newgrange because, a century before the arrival of St Patrick, he had decided there was one God, not several, so he did not wish to be interred according to Druidical rites.

> Spread not the beds of Brugh for me
>   When restless death-bed's use is done;
> But bury me at Rosnaree,
>   And face me to the rising sun.
>
> For all the Kings who lie in Brugh
>   Put trust in gods of wood and stone;
> And 'twas at Ross that first I knew
>   One, Unseen, who is God alone. . . .

Samuel Ferguson's poem 'The Burial of King Cormac' is known to generations of Irish schoolchildren, celebrating for their edification a sense of Christianity that is deeper in the past of Ireland, even, than St Patrick. The pagan Druids did not give up without a fight. They tried three times to get Cormac's body across the Boyne, to the Brugh, but the river kept flooding:

And now they slide, and now they swim
  And now, amid the blackening squall,
Grey locks afloat, with clutching grim,
  They plunge around the floating pall;

While as a youth with practised spear
  Through jostling crowds bears off the ring,
Boyne from their shoulders caught the bier
  And proudly bore away the king.

At morning, on the grassy marge
  Of Rosnaree, the corpse was found;
And shepherds at their early charge
  Entombed it in the peaceful ground.

The poem is evidence, early in the nineteenth-century Irish Revival, of the thousand-year attempt to knit Christian Ireland to its mythical past.

Perhaps Cormac's descendants were also buried at Rosnaree. Francis Ledwidge (1897–1917)[21] dreamed of it in the trenches of 1917 Flanders:

All the dead kings came to me
At Rosnaree, while I was dreaming,
A few stars glimmered through the morn,
And down the thorn the dews came streaming. . . .

He was born opposite Rosnaree, not far from Newgrange, at Janeville, near Slane. The tiny cottage he shared with his parents and seven siblings is still there on the road from Knowth, a museum dedicated to him. Few peasants are poets, it is too time-consuming an art, but Ledwidge has a claim to be one. At the age of fourteen he was at work in other men's fields, and before he joined the army he was a roadman. By the time of the Great War he had made contact with other poets, nationalists, like Thomas MacDonagh and Padraig Pearse. (And with mystical/practical AE: 'I have not seen Ledwidge for four months because he borrowed £5 from me on promise to return it the next day. This singular silence which I have not broken by enquiry has made me think that his verse will lack something or other.')

As a nationalist, and trade-union activist, it seems surprising that Ledwidge joined up. 'I joined the British Army because she stood between Ireland and an enemy common to our civilization and I would not have her say she defended us while we did nothing but pass resolutions.' He survived Gallipoli, served in Serbia, but on his last leave home before being sent to France he confessed his disillusion. His friends MacDonagh and Pearse had been executed for their part in the Easter Rising in 1916. 'If someone were to tell me now that the Germans were coming in over our back wall, I wouldn't lift up a finger to stop them. They could come!' He was offered a chance to desert, by the nationalist underground, but he went back to France, and died there.

The poet Padraic Colum knew Ledwidge, and praises him for his response, 'not to the tumult but to the charm of life'. Poets are usually best at defining what other poets are good at:

It was his triumph that he made us know the creatures of his world as things freshly seen, surprisingly discovered. The first poem in his first volume let us know the blackbird's secret –

And wondrous impudently sweet,
Half of him passion, half conceit,
The blackbird whistles down the street. . . .[22]

It would be near Janeville that Ledwidge stood and watched, 'As raindrops pelted from a nodding rush/To give a white wink once and broken fall/Into a dark deep pool. . . .' He could be exact, and musical, and had a good ear. His 'Lament for Thomas MacDonagh' (written a week after the 1916 execution) contains a memory of Mac-Donagh's translation of the poem about the bittern:[23]

He shall not hear the bittern cry
In the wild sky, where he is lain,
Nor voices of the sweeter birds
Above the wailing of the rain. . . .

In the bar of the Conyngham Arms in Slane, Ledwidge met a local sculptor who had found a patron and advised Ledwidge to do the same. So Ledwidge sent his notebook to Lord Dunsany, who was enthusiastic. In the Ledwidge museum there is a framed newspaper cutting, headlined 'Peer discovers Poet'.

Dunsany Castle is south of Slane at Dunshaughlin (about halfway between Slane and Dublin). Ledwidge was given the run of the place. Dunsany (1878–1957) was sensitive about the effect of social position on the writer because he had suffered from it, as it were, from the other end. He ends his preface to Ledwidge's first collection, *Songs of the Fields* (1914): 'I hope that not too many will be attracted to this book on account of the author being a peasant, lest he come

to be praised by the how-interesting school; for know that neither
in any class, nor in any country, nor in any age, shall you predict
the footfall of Pegasus, who touches the earth where he pleaseth and
is bridled by whom he will.' (This sentence caused mirth in the cottage at Janeville. 'Pegasus' was the name Ledwidge and his brother
had given to their bicycles.)

Dunsany's rank gave him a varied life; he was an international
chess-player, big game hunter, crack shot. In what is considered his
best, powerfully nostalgic, novel, *The Curse of the Wise Woman*
(1935), there is a suggestion of himself as a boy: passionate about
hunting and shooting, in love with the landscape of his Irish home,
respecting what Irish people he was able to meet, but somehow, in
some essential, cut off from both, as if from an adult world, with
Ireland an extra element in this alienation. 'Laura and I understood the glory of leaf and flower, and the rejoicing symphony of
blackbirds and thrushes . . . the mention of any of these things at
Eton, or elsewhere, usually met with derision, as though there was
something evil about the song of a bird, or contemptible in a
flower. . . .'

The natural description in his writing has a closeness of detail which
is like W.H. Hudson's,[24] and rises to the level of poetry. There are
many bogs in Ireland, and Dunsany's is the way to stare into one:

> I looked and saw little beetles navigating the dark water like
> bright pellets of lead, and rather seeming to be running than
> swimming. Then an insect with four legs skipped hurriedly over
> the surface, going from island to island of scarlet grass, and a
> skylark came by singing. Above me in the mosses beyond the
> top of the bog's sheer edge the curlews were nesting, their spring
> call ringing over the pools and the heather. Beside me a patch
> of peat was touched with green as though it had gone mouldy,
> and up from it went a little forest of buds, each on its slender
> stalk, for spring had come to the moss as well as the curlews.
> In amongst the soft moss grew what looked like large leaves,
> but so fungoid was their appearance that it was hard to say
> whether they belonged to the moss, or were even vegetable at
> all: rather they seemed to haunt the boundary of the vegetable
> kingdom as ghosts haunt the boundary of man's. . . .[25]

As a peer, and a loyal British subject in Ireland, he had little in
common with most of his fellow writers and the Gaelic Revival. His
first play was commissioned by W.B. Yeats, but there was not much
sympathy between them. Dunsany's stories in *The Book of Wonder*

could be thought of as mocking the whole 'faery' aspect of the Revival, and of having a bash at Cuchulainn as well:

> When Plash-Goo came to the mountain he cast his chimahalk down (for so he named the club of his heart's desire) lest the dwarf should defy him with nimbleness; and stepped towards Lrippity-Krang with gripping hands, who stopped in his mountainous walk without a word, and swung round his hideous breadth to confront Plash-Goo.
>
> Already then Plash-Goo in the deeps of his mind had seen himself seize the dwarf in one large hand and hurl him with his beard and his hated breadth sheer down the precipice that dropped away from that very place to the Land of None's Desire. . . .[26]

Ledwidge was not the only writer Dunsany helped. Not far from Dunsany Castle, between Navan and Trim (the castle of which Dunsany at one time also owned), Mary Lavin (b. 1912) bought the Abbey Farm next to the ruined abbey at Bective, and Dunsany wrote the preface to her first book of short stories, *Tales from Bective Bridge* (1942). As a widow, Lavin had a struggle to bring up her children, run the farm and write. She described herself as a 'one-armed writer', one hand stirring the pot and the other steering the pen. Lavin's subjects are for the most part domestic (her children say she wrote while they played around her), and the 'domestic', and her personal experience, are put to powerful use. 'In the Middle of the Fields', the title story of her 1967 collection, is about a widow's aloneness and bafflement set, precisely, in the middle of the fields of Meath.

> Like a rock in the sea, she was islanded by fields, the heavy grass washing about the house, and the cattle wading in it as in water. Even their gentle stirrings were a loss when they moved away at evening to the shelter of the woods. A rainy day might strike a wet flash from a hay barn on the far side of the river. Not even a habitation! And yet she was less lonely for him here in Meath than elsewhere. Anxieties by day, and cares, and at night vaguer, nameless fears, these were the stones across the mouth of the tomb.
>
> But who understood that? They thought she hugged tight every memory she had of him. What did they know about memory? What was it but another name for dry love and barren

longing? They even tried to unload upon her their own small purposeless memories. 'I imagine I see him every time I look out there,' they would say as they glanced nervously. Oh, for God's sake! she'd think. She'd forgotten him for a minute.

The English writer T.H. White (1906–64), who came to County Meath to fish in the River Boyne and stayed for six years, describes the landscape with one of the culinary metaphors this hill-studded part of Ireland seems to inspire. 'Meath and Louth are what you might get if you brought Norfolk to the boil . . . a country of bubbles.'[27]

One of the larger bubbles, but not that much larger, only swelling to about five hundred feet, is Tara, chief capital of ancient Ireland, a seat of kings and of the High King from the earliest times to the sixth century AD. Despite its modest height you can see for miles in every direction, and from the top it is easy to understand its significance; the kings could overlook and supervise their lands. The grandeur that once was there can be deduced from early descriptions of other palaces: '. . . nine couches (or bedchambers) between hearth and wall; thirty-five feet was every façade of bronze, chased with gold. In the front part of the house was a royal couch for the king . . . above all the couches of the house, covered with carbuncles and with precious stones, and with the hue of every region, in such wise that day and night were of equal brilliance. . . .'[28]

The kings of Tara have been thought of as priest-kings, guardians of the sacred fire. Ritual fires were certainly lit on Tara, and no fire was allowed in the district until the sacred fire of the Druids had been kindled. To light one was a punishable blasphemy. St Patrick had to challenge the priest-king and so, before the fire of the vernal equinox was lit on Tara by the Druids, Patrick lit his own fire on the Hill of Slane, on 25 March 433, the date of Easter that year. As George Moore noticed, the other way round, Slane can be seen from Tara; outraged, the king and his Druids rode to Tara to punish the culprits. St Patrick, in his own simple and dignified *Confessio*, left no description of their encounter. Instead the story is told in Muirchu's *Life* of the saint in which it is mixed up with all sorts of wizardry.[29] However, it was recorded that on the Hills of Slane and Tara there took place one of the key moments in the Christianizing of Ireland, because Patrick converted the High King.

Tara was the site of at least three ecclesiastical synods,[30] and was a place for games and bardic competitions. These verse contests, in tightly controlled traditional forms, could attain great complexity.

There is nothing in Ireland that can be taken seriously (as James Stephens took its myths, and poetry, seriously) which cannot also be taken lightly:

> The Games were being played at Tara. . . . The bards were in Convention at the Well of the Elf Mound discussing if all that could be achieved by the Great Eight Line Curved Verse could not be as competently managed by the Little Eight-Line Curved Verse, and whether the Great Curving Eight-Line Return Verse was a necessity or an outrage: these holding that brevity, and those that diversity, was the chief ornament of poetry.
>
> 'Where there is only room for brevity,' quoth a young bard, 'there is no room for poetry.'
>
> A savage ancient confounded him.
>
> 'Where, sir, there is space for diversity there is place and to spare for foolishness.'
>
> 'A goat in a small plot,' cried a pastoral bard, 'starvation follows.'
>
> 'Ah!' cried another, who knew his animals, 'a goat in a large plot – extended destruction!'
>
> Love poems, war poems, place poems, histories – this would be a busy, a contentious, gathering.[31]

James Stephens (1882?–1950) was a leading figure in the Irish Revival. *Deirdre* (1920) and *In the Land of Youth* (1924) were part of a projected retelling of all the ancient tales which he never completed.

If it is true that, as Heinrich Böll said in his *Irish Journal*,[32] 'Folklore is something like innocence; when you know you have it, you no longer have it', then Stephens is the exception, the proof that by some chance of temperament, or effort of will, the past can be reinhabited. You feel if there had been no ancient literature to draw upon he could have made it up himself and got the tone of it right. Stephens found in Dunsany's stories 'great windy reaches and wild flight among stars and a very youthful laughter at the gods', and he contains such laughter himself. In his poem 'The Ancient Elf' he might be describing his own method:

> I, careless and gay,
> Never mean what I say,
> For my thoughts and my eyes
> Look the opposite way. . . .

T.H. White, author of a retelling of the King Arthur stories, *The Once and Future King*, which strongly suggests the influence of

Stephens, stayed in a farmhouse ('Doolistown', now a ruin) by the River Boyne, near Trim, not far from Tara, for six years (1939–45). He had a complicated relationship with the Irish, part awed affection, part Blimpish exasperation. He even said the rosary every evening with his landlady and her family, but, 'I have strange feelings about this. They are of love for the family but lack of communion with the thing: like somebody trying to be sick, when he has been sick.' Whenever he feels the affection for Ireland, and the exasperation, overwhelming him, he takes refuge in his Blimpish persona:

> It is not the Irish, he thought, it is the climate. It is not the fault of the race. The Irish are not lazy, not backward, not dirty, not superstitious, not cunning, not dishonest. They are as nice as anybody else. It is not them. It is the air.
>
> It is that bloody Atlantic, said Mr White, looking angrily in the direction of Mullingar: that's what does for us. It is those millions of square miles of water vapour pouring in from the south-west, supersaturated, bulging, coloured, and weighted like lead. It is like living under a pile of wet cushions: they force us to our hands and knees. . . .
>
> Why, even champagne will hardly fizz here: one might as well be living down a coal mine. I believe, he continued doubtfully, that champagne does not fizz in coal mines; but, if you take it to the top of a mountain, where the air is lighter, it fizzes so much that the whole bottle turns to froth. That is what happens if you take an Irishman away from his native hell. . . . Drop him across the channel, and immediately he boils over like a firework display. He invents quarternions or conquers Napoleon or writes *St Joan*. And the same thing happens the other way round. Leave him in England, and Swift is the master of ministers, the friend of princes, and cynosure of wit. Drag him away to the atmospheric pressure of the County Meath, and he is only a nasty-minded, complaining parson at Laracor, and finally he goes dotty altogether, and no wonder.[33]

Doolistown was a couple of miles from Laracor, south of Trim; and White's view of Swift not an unusual one. Frank O'Connor feels otherwise: 'If you share my mania for Swift, you may well aim for Laracor, but you will find it a disappointment. It contains no memories at all of the great Dean, of Stella and Dingley . . . and the other characters who grow upon you from the pages of *Journal to Stella*. "The willows by the river's side my heart is set upon . . ." but you are not likely to find them.'[34] They are now replaced by alders, and the church by the roadside which replaces Swift's has become a private house. But there is the knob of a burial mound (tree-grown) in the field by the river where his glebe house used to be, which he must have looked at often, and the friendly, intimate landscape cannot much have changed. 'Stella's Cottage' is a short way down the road towards Trim, labelled but with its walls reduced to waist height, giving it the dimensions of a largish pig-stye.

WESTMEATH – LONGFORD

North-west of Trim is the small town of Delvin, scene of a famous literary row in 1918. Brinsley MacNamara (1890–1963) – real name John Weldon, son of the town schoolmaster – in that year published *The Valley of the Squinting Windows*. It was his first book, and, drawing on his youthful experiences of Delvin, he cheerfully and wholesale maligned everybody in 'Garradrimna', which was as recognizably his native town as its natives were recognizable to themselves, and to others. There are eye-witness accounts of the local people reading the book out loud to each other (proud of their local author), laughing as they recognized their neighbours, falling silent and aghast when they recognized themselves. The postmistress, for example, is represented as in the habit of steaming open letters (the plot hangs on this); the publican's wife is described as 'the hardest woman in Garradrimna. Her childlessness had made her so. She was beginning to grow stale and withered, and anything in the nature of love and marriage, with their possible results, was to her a constant source of affliction and annoyance.' The response of the enraged publican, and his childless wife, was to grimly order drinks all round until there was soon an inflamed mob. The book was burned.

MacNamara fled. Metropolitan Ireland, having got over its delight at any sort of a rumpus, decided that the burning was symptomatic of the narrow prejudices of rural small-town life, and that MacNamara was some kind of martyr. He had to live away from Delvin for the rest of his life, which possibly he did not mind, but one consequence was more serious; the book has been suspected of inaugurating a 'squinting windows' school of writing, in which Irish small-town life is seen to contain nothing but malice, hypocrisy and frustrated lust, usually under a stream of unceasing rain. *Squinting Windows*, save for its melodramatic end, is funny. It contains what MacNamara said he wished all his work to contain, 'the long, low chuckle of the mind'.[35]

Delvin also had its bards. Bonaventura O'Hussey (O hEodhasa, *c.* 1570–1614) was trained in a traditional bardic school, went to France at the end of the sixteenth century, became a Franciscan and was one of the founders of the Irish College of St Anthony in Louvain. His poem, lamenting the death of Richard Nugent, son of his friends William and Janet Nugent, 'has the rare combination of sincere feeling and the polished language and technique of Classical Irish poetry'.[36]

> The sound of your sighs makes my ears go numb,
> The sight of your weeping drains the blood from my heart.
> I wish I could take your pain to add to my own,
> And I may be able to do this, mine is so great.
> You have lost your son, your delight (the pain of it)
> Your only one, your laughter-bringer is dead, Janet. . . .

The poem makes you realize that at least at the beginning of the seventeenth century, Delvin contained the sensitive, or even civilized, people whom MacNamara later failed to find.

In *The Absentee* (1800), Maria Edgeworth describes a 'Nugentstown' in all its terrible dilapidation. Delvin is not far from where she lived, and its connection with the Nugent family may well have suggested the invented name:[37]

> This 'town' consisted of one row of miserable huts, sunk beneath the side of the road, the mud walls crooked in every direction; some of them opening in wide cracks or zig-zag fissures, from top to bottom, as if there had just been an earthquake – all the roofs sunk in various places – thatch off, or overgrown with grass – no chimneys, the smoke making its way through a hole in the roof, or rising in clouds from the top of the open door – dung-hills before the doors, and green standing puddles. . . .

Daniel Corkery in *The Hidden Ireland* remarks that 'the appearance of the countryside changed but little in all the years of misery between 1690 and 1881'.

There were ancient glories further to the south-west, beyond Mullingar.[38] The little Hill of Uisneach ['Ushna'] probably predates Tara as a crowning-place for kings. Like Tara it is a 'bubble', gently rising to about six hundred feet, but as is so often the case with these apparently insignificant 'royal' hills, the view from it is vast. On it is the 'Cat Stone' or 'Stone of Divisions' or 'Umbilicus' which signals that it was considered the physical, as also a mystical, centre of Ireland.[39]

The Annals of Westmeath (1907)[40] is enthusiastic about Uisneach. The entertaining *Annals* is prone to nationalist excitement: it was a favourite of John Betjeman's while staying at nearby Pakenham Hall and he derived at least one poem from it. Uisneach is, in appearance, just a pretty little hill, but: 'This noble seat is sacred as the ancient meeting place of the renowned men of Ireland, the city of Laberos, mentioned by Ptolemy. The memorials of this once famous and ancient city are strewn around and over the plain. . . .'

A king was not allowed to continue as king if he became deformed or disabled. According to the *Annals* Cormac Mac Art (he of Rosnaree) found a classically stylish way round this: 'When Cormac Art was obliged to retire from the sovereignty of Ireland owing to having been deprived of one of his eyes by Aengus of the poisoned spear, Aengus was arraigned at Uisneach before a great convention of the chiefs, and himself and his tribe were banished for ever from Erin. King Cormac, who attended the convention, wore leaves of gold fastened with silver springs on his eye in order to conceal the injury.' This strikes a note 'both great-hearted and light-hearted', like James Stephens's recreations of ancient times.

On past Uisneach, a right fork towards 'Auburn', and you are at 'The Pigeons' pub, signalled to 'Goldsmith country' which is shared by counties Westmeath and Longford.

Oliver Goldsmith (1728–74)[41] spent his boyhood at Lissoy, later variously called Auburn, the name he gave it in his poem 'The Deserted Village', or The Pigeons, after the Three Pigeons inn where Tony Lumpkin caroused, in his play *She Stoops to Conquer*:

> Let schoolmasters puzzle their brain,
>   With grammar and nonsense and learning;
> Good liquor, I stoutly maintain,
>   Gives genius a better discerning.
> Let them brag of the heathenish Gods,
>   Their Lethes, their Styxes and Stygians:
> Their Quis, and their Quae, and their Quods,
>   They're all but a parcel of Pigeons.
> Toroddle, toroddle, toroll. . . .

Goldsmith could write a good drinking song, but he could write a good just-about-anything: a long poem, a play, and a novel (*The Vicar of Wakefield*); and for all of them he draws on his boyhood experiences of Lissoy, where his father was Anglican vicar. But he left Ireland early. The house he was supposed to have mistaken for an inn – thus providing himself with one of his best plots, in *She Stoops to Conquer* – still stands, in Ardagh nearby, now a convent. Not much remains of his father's vicarage. Not much remains of Lissoy, though various mildewed notices point out places mentioned in 'The Deserted Village' – the schoolhouse, the mill and so on, 'of which few traces remain'. Nationalists have sometimes been shocked that there is little specific reference to the woes of Ireland in 'The Deserted Village', but Goldsmith was trying to earn a living in London, and London has seldom been receptive of Irish woes. He was a warm-hearted man, and cared for his country. 'Why, why was I born a man, and yet see the sufferings of wretches I cannot relieve!'[42]

Although he was only ten years old when the now-famous blind harper Turlough Carolan (1670–1738) died, it is possible that Goldsmith heard him, for Carolan played at Edgeworthstown nearby, and Goldsmith wrote a short *Life*, calling Carolan 'The Last Irish Bard'.[43]

> The original natives never mention his name without rapture; both his poetry and music they have by heart. . . .
>
> His death was not more remarkable than his life. Homer was never more fond of a glass than he; he would drink whole pints of Usquebaugh, and, as he used to think, without any ill consequence. His intemperance, however, in this respect, at length brought on an incurable disorder, and when just at the point of death, he called for a cup of his beloved liquor . . . and when the bowl was brought him, attempted to drink but could not; wherefore, giving away the bowl, he observed with a smile, that it would be hard if two such friends as he and the cup should part at least without kissing; and then expired.

Goldsmith is said to have gone to school in Edgeworthstown (or Mostrim, County Longford). There, in the Big House (as such places are called in Ireland), Maria Edgeworth (1767– 1849) lived from the age of fifteen. Her first and most enduring novel, *Castle Rackrent*, was published in 1800. The intention was to give the English reading public a picture of the true state of Ireland; she attacks the irresponsibility of the landed gentry (among whom, of course, the Edgeworths belonged).[44] Her touch, in *Rackrent*, is light. She hits upon

a marvellous comic device. Her narrator is the butler, or family
steward, Thady, and he reports the chaotic and often dreadful goings-
on of successive generations of his masters with such deep respect
that even while you wince you are forced to laugh. Her popularity
was immense, so was her literary influence. Sir Walter Scott
(1771–1832) says in his preface to *Waverley* (1829) that it was after
reading her that he was inspired to become a novelist: 'I felt that
something might be attempted for my own country, of the same
kind with that which Miss Edgeworth so fortunately achieved for
Ireland – something which might introduce her natives to those of
the sister kingdom, in a more favourable light than they had been
placed hitherto, and tend to procure sympathy for their virtues and
indulgence for their foibles.'

Scott and Maria Edgeworth became friends. They shared the same
practicality and common sense. In 1825 he came to stay with her
at Edgeworthstown where, according to Scott's son-in-law and
biographer, Lockhart, her brother filled his classical mansion every
evening 'with a succession of distinguished friends, the élite of
Ireland'. Lockhart, like most nineteenth-century British visitors, exag-
gerates the popularity of the Irish Protestant gentry. The Edgeworths
had had to flee before the rebels in 1798, were nearly blown up by
an exploding ammunition cart, and Maria's father, thought to be a
spy, narrowly escaped lynching. In 1836 a visiting American writes
of Edgeworthstown: 'As we passed through the crowd to the
schoolhouse the enmity of the Papists to the Protestant landholders
was but too evident. Though Mrs Edgeworth [Maria's stepmother]
had been the Lady Bountiful of the village for many years, there were
no bows for her and her friends, no making way before her, no
touching of hats, no pleasant looks. A sullen expression and a dogged
unmovability on every side of us.'[45]

The Edgeworths were undoubtedly good landlords. Scott was
delighted with the conditions of the Edgeworth tenants, though
when they all make a journey into the west of Ireland even Lockhart
notices that his father-in-law's face is becoming sadder. Maria remarks
in a letter that Scott said to her, ' "Do explain to the public why
Pat, who gets forward so well in other countries, is so miserable
in his own." A very difficult question: I fear above my power. But
I shall think of it continually, and listen, and look and read.'

Wordsworth visited the Edgeworths in May 1829, but in his rather
stolid letters home he says little about them or the place.[46] He
refers to Maria only as 'Miss Edgeworth the authoress'. He reports
that when he is detained by rain, 'I made the best use of my time

in conversing with the people.' He finds that many he spoke to 'forbode the worst from Catholic bigotry', whereas Scott seemed to forbode the worst from the 'determined Orangemen', who reminded him 'of the Spaniard in Mexico'. But perhaps Scott had been talking to Maria's brother, because Wordsworth says, 'Mr Edgeworth whom we had left in the morning sees things from quite a different point of view – but I will not enter into particulars, it is late and I bid you all good night as I propose to be up before six to look about me'. Wordsworth's letters from Ireland are like that. 'I have no more room and the subjects before me are inexhaustible.' As for 'the authoress': 'I enjoyed the snatches of Wordsworth's conversation that I was able to have and I think I had quite as much as was good for me. . . .' (Perhaps she considers that a little sharp, and she relents.) 'He was a good, philosophical bust, a long, thin, gaunt face, much wrinkled and weather-beaten . . . with a cheerful and benevolent expression.'

Maria Edgeworth devoted her life to being happy and to being useful. She lived long enough to devote her last energies to relieving some of the effects of the Great Famine of the 1840s. Above all, she loved family life, and her home. In Paris (in 1820) she is fêted, meets everybody, but 'the constant chorus of our moral as we drive home together at night is, "How happy we are to be so fond of each other! How happy we are to be independent of all we see here! How happy that we have our dear home to return to at last!"'

The Edgeworth house is now a convent nursing home, and although the original house has been more or less preserved, the extensions and additions to it are not sensitive. Lockhart's 'classical mansion' (Maria described her father's house as 'tolerably good, old-fashioned' but that may have been before he improved it) now stands on a bald slope, the old trees cut down and few replanted, with a stark box-like extension and salt-cellar chapel.

East of Edgeworthstown, back in County Westmeath, is Lough Derravaragh, scene of one of the 'three sorrowful tales of Ireland', the 'Fate of the Children of Lir'. It takes place in the time of the Tuatha Dé Danaan. The Children are taken by their jealous step-mother to Lough Derravaragh to be drowned, but she relents and turns them into swans. The spell over them is to last for nine hundred years: for the first three hundred they live on the lake, sweetly singing, for they retain their human voice. 'From all parts of the island companies of the Danaan folk resort to Lake Derravaragh to hear this wondrous music and to converse with the swans, and during

that time a great peace and gentleness seemed to pervade the land.'
But then they have to fly to the freezing seas of the northern coast,
by Rathlin Island, for a further three hundred years; and for the last
three centuries to the wild Atlantic off the Belmullet peninsula. The
sister Fionnuala protects her three brothers throughout their ordeal.
According to T.W. Rolleston, 'in all Celtic legend there is no more
tender and beautiful tale than this'.[47]

Maria Edgeworth knew Derravaragh because it is near Pakenham
Hall (now called Tullynally), at Castlepollard, and there was much
visiting between the Pakenhams and the Edgeworths, even though
there was (and is) a bog between them. Apart from the bog there
were other hazards:

> On Friday we went to Pakenham Hall. We sat down thirty-two
> to dinner, and in the evening a party of twenty from Pakenham
> Hall went to a grand ball at Mrs Pollard's. . . . We stayed till
> between three and four in the morning. . . . The postilion had,
> it seems, amused himself at a *club* in Castle Pollard while we
> were at the ball, and he had amused himself so much that he
> did not know the ditch from the road: he was ambitious of
> passing Mr Dease's carriage – passed it: attempted to pass Mr
> Tuite's, ran the wheels on a drift of snow which overhung the
> ditch, and laid the coach fairly down on its side in the ditch.
> We were none of us hurt. . . . I never fell at all, for I clung
> like a bat to the handstring at my side, determined that I would
> not fall upon my mother and break her arm. None of us were
> even bruised . . . the gentleman hauled us out immediately.[48]

John Betjeman (1906–84)[49] knew Lough Derravaragh in the early
1930s. He came often to stay at Pakenham Hall (Tullynally) and it
was in the library there that he came across the gossipy *Annals of
Westmeath* and the story of Sir John Piers, a famous and cynical rake
who made a bet in 1807 that he could seduce the new bride of a
friend. In his poem about this, 'The Return', Betjeman has the
would-be seducer liken the eyes of his prey to the lake, and he
attempts an old Irish metre:

> I love your brown curls/black in rain, my colleen,
>   I love your grey eyes/by this verdant shore
> Two Derravaraghs/to plunge into and drown me. . . .

Betjeman calls County Westmeath 'the lake-reflected' (in 'Ireland
with Emily'). His Irish poems are among his best, he seems to have
loved the place:

O my small towns of Ireland, the raindrops caress you,
The sun sparkles bright on your field and your Square
As here on your bridge I salute you and bless you,
Your murmuring waters and turf-scented air. . . .

Betjeman's hosts were Edward and Christine Longford. Edward, Earl of Longford (1902–61), was a playwright, as was his wife, and they ran their own theatrical company.[50] To Pakenham Hall they invited other young writers; it was in the library of Pakenham Hall that Evelyn Waugh, idly spinning a globe, decided to go to Abyssinia, a journey that inspired a travel book and a novel. Longford had more money than most of his guests and had the endearing habit of making bets with them just before they left, which he was bound to lose, thereby helping them with their travel expenses.

The present owner of Tullynally is his nephew, Thomas Pakenham, the historian, himself the author of a book about travels in Abyssinia; perhaps the spun globe always stops at the same spot, like a fixed roulette-wheel. Pakenham's account of the 1798 Rising, *The Year of Liberty*, is the most factual and unbiased. (The Crown forces mobilized to put down the Rising camped on the lawns of Pakenham Hall.)

EAST CAVAN

Castles, like Pakenham Hall, and big houses, like the Edgeworths', have their own cultures, and their distinguished visitors. However remote from 'the centre' – in this case Dublin, Trinity College, and England – we are not surprised if they have literary associations; people visit them from the Centre. It is more surprising, though perhaps it should not be, to find in the eighteenth century clusters of literary folk in less grand circumstances and more out-of-the-way places, some of whom had a notable influence on the future. One such group was in the south-east corner of County Cavan, near the border with County Meath.

Thomas Sheridan the elder (1687–1738), friend of Swift, was a schoolmaster and classicist; father of Thomas Sheridan (1719–88) the actor-manager, who was father of Richard Brinsley Sheridan (1761–1816), the playwright. The older Sheridan was one of the group of valued younger-brotherish cronies (he was twenty years younger) in whose company Swift could take off his wig, amuse himself with country exercise, exchange facetious verses – and revise

Gulliver's Travels.[51] The Sheridans' house, Quilca or Cuilcagh, was a modest place, by a small lake north-east of Virginia, in pretty scenery. The successor to the original house is probably not all that different, with the mound across the road from it on which Thomas Sheridan the younger used to rehearse his theatrical troupes. Nor can the watery landscape have changed much since Richard Brinsley Sheridan spent his early childhood here. The place was sold up in 1768, when he was seven. There is a selling-up scene in *The School for Scandal*; he may have been in Quilca at the time, and remembered it.

The elder Thomas Sheridan sounds a disorganized sort of man and Swift never tires of teasing him about the discomforts of Quilca. He makes the house speak: 'Let me my properties explain/A rotten cabin, dropping rain/Chimnies with scorn rejecting smoak/Stools, tables, chairs and bed-steads broke. . . .' There is a Marie-Antoinettish quality about these eighteenth-century intellectuals enjoying their discomforts. Swift reports: 'I battle as well as I can, but in vain. . . . Our kitchen is a hundred yards from the house, but the way is soft and so fond of our shoes that it covers them with its favours.' He was there for one whole, particularly wet, summer (1725) with 'Stella' (Esther Johnson) and her companion, Rebecca Dingley. Even so, Quilca had an idyllic quality at that season. But as Swift warned Sheridan, in December 1722: 'You will find Quilca not the thing it was last August; nobody to relish the lake; nobody to ride over the downs; no trout to be caught; no dining over a well; no night heroics; no morning epics; no stolen hours when the wife is gone; no creature to call you names. Poor miserable Master Sheridan! No blind harpers! No journeys to Rantavan!' The 'blind harper' could have been Carolan, who was born near Nobber, a few miles to the east. 'Rantavan' suggests visits to the Brooke family; it was the name of their house, near Mullagh (between Virginia and Kells/Ceanannas).

The Rev. William Brooke (1680–1745) was rector of three adjacent parishes, Mullagh, Killinkere and Moybolgue. His more celebrated son, Henry Brooke (1705–83), built himself a house nearby, at Corfoddy, renamed Longfield, where in later life he lived in reduced circumstances with his daughter Charlotte (*c.* 1740–93), who put together the pioneering *Reliques of Irish Poetry*. Henry Brooke, through Swift, became a friend of Pope's in England, and his Rousseau-influenced novel, *The Fool of Quality* (1765), was greatly admired by John Wesley, who produced a successful abridged version; in the next century Charles Kingsley found in it 'more which is pure, sacred and eternal than in anything which has been published since

Spenser's Fairy Queen'.[52] The lives of the Brookes in County Cavan also seemed pure and Virgilian to outsiders. In 1804 a book was published containing anecdotes about them and their circle, *Brookiana*. This contains a kind of classical eclogue, a conversation between a Traveller who has ventured into these wilds and an Old Man who has lived all his life in a cottage adjoining the ancient ruined church at Moybolgue. What is significant is the notice taken in it of the Irish, and their language. ' "One of our best poets reposes in that corner," ' the Old Man says. ' "Let us drop a tear on his grave. . . . In what language did he write?" "In Irish, a language admirably suited to all that is tender in the human heart. . . ." ' The Old Man then translates for the Traveller an elaborate Irish poem, and the whole conversation could be taking place in the graveyard at Urnea, where Ó Doirnín is buried, which in fact is not far away. It is an unusual note to hear in a book of that time: the meeting in the Moybolgue churchyard is supposed to have taken place in 1780, when the Irish language was despised and, for public purposes, proscribed.

Moybolgue, with its ruined church and ancient graveyard that, like so many, is still used, still suits the Old Man's description ('Solitude, the companion of the wise and the good'); the remains of the Old Man's cottage are perhaps there by the wall. It overlooks the rich, lumpy Cavan countryside, like a soft swell of green waves, criss-crossed at all angles by hedges of hawthorn; in the summer a place brilliantly green and white, and soft.

The Traveller's courteous interest in the Irish language is, as has been said, unusual. Henry Brooke intended to learn it, after a man on the banks of the Shannon addressed some verses to him in Irish. He never did so but, importantly, his daughter Charlotte did. Charlotte Brooke wrote down poems and songs repeated to her by Irish-speakers in the country, and was shown manuscripts by scholars in Dublin, where literature in Irish was beginning to be studied. Inspired by Bishop Percy's *Reliques*, in 1789 she published her own *Reliques of Irish Poetry*, in a bilingual edition, the first. It is true that her English verse translations sound too much of her century to be convincing, but by printing the originals, in Gaelic script, she rescued much that could otherwise have been lost, and made herself possibly the earliest figure in the Gaelic Literary Revival.

It was not usual in English literary circles to have much regard for the weird and difficult Irish people; it was easier to dismiss them as bumpkins, and their ancient literature as crude. So when she writes in her Introduction, 'The productions of our Irish bards exhibit a glow of cultivated genius . . . totally astonishing, at a period when the rest of Europe was nearly sunk in barbarism', it was too much for her (otherwise favourable) London reviewers. No one of her kind had spoken of the Irish like that before. 'She will excuse us for sometimes smiling at the excess to which she has carried her enthusiasm.'[53] It was her 'enthusiasm', from this secluded corner of Cavan, that rescued a significant part of Ireland's past to be built on by the enthusiasts of the following century.

3

THE NORTH-WEST

ROSCOMMON

West of Edgeworthstown (which has now reverted to its old name of Mostrim), on the N5 Longford-Castlebar road,[1] is Rathcrogan, County Roscommon. As Cruachan this was the site of the royal palace of Queen Maeve, and here were sown the seeds of the *Táin*, the 'Cattle Raid of Cooley'.[2] Maeve, Queen of Connacht, and her consort, Ailill, are in bed in their palace on one of the mounds still to be seen at Rathcrogan, and he, with mixed humour and malice, muses: 'You are better off today than when I married you.'

Maeve is indignant, and responds with an account of her genealogy, her battle prowess, and the number of soldiers of her own that she had before she married Ailill. Then she seems to change tack, admitting that she had

'a strange bride-gift such as no woman before had asked of the men of Ireland, that is, a man without meanness, jealousy, or fear;'

Ailill had brought with him those gifts, he was just such a man, equal to herself in generosity and grace. One can almost see Ailill, pleased, relaxing and lowering his guard. However, Maeve continues, she had brought with her

'the breadth of your face in red gold, the weight of your left arm in bronze. So, whoever imposes shame or annoyance or trouble on you, you have no claim for compensation or honour–price other than what comes to me – for you are a man dependant on a woman.'

Ailill replies loftily that his two brothers were kings, one of Temair (Tara), the other of Leinster, and he had only decided to marry Maeve, and thus become a king himself, 'because I heard of no province in Ireland ruled by a woman save this province alone'.

Scholars have suggested that this is the mythological representation of a historical shift from matriarchy to political patriarchy, as well as from goddess to god. It may be so, but in this story Maeve is by far the more forceful of the two. She calls for their possessions to be brought in, their pots and pans and tubs, his and hers, so that their quantities can be compared. At this point the story remains on the level of a domestic tiff, but it soon becomes epic; their herds of cattle are counted, their troops of horses, their jewels. It is no use, their possessions are equal – except for one thing. There is a famous bull, which in fact belongs to Maeve, but which has attached itself to Ailill's herd, 'thinking it unworthy to be classed as "woman's property"'.

That would seem to clinch it, but Maeve is not done yet. She knows of an even better bull, in Ulster, so she sends her men there to buy it in exchange for land. But these emissaries are heard boasting about the superiority of Connachtmen, so the Ulstermen refuse to part with the bull. Maeve invades Ulster in order to get it; the 'Cattle Raid of Cooley' begins. Maeve is opposed by the Ulster hero Cuchulainn, who defends the territory single-handed, because the rest of the men of Ulster are under a spell. The Cattle Raid, therefore, started at Rathcrogan/Cruachan.

In his retelling of the old stories, James Stephens gives Maeve's court the atmosphere of a regal house-party with magic added. He is in no doubt about the fierceness of Maeve, and her royal courtesy. She implores her visitor from the Otherworld to have one for the road – '"But you do not drink!" she cried to Nera' – but no, Nera has to be back before the door in the hillside closes. '"If you must return, you must return,"' replies Maeve, and she and her retinue accompany him to the door in the hillside as though seeing him off at the station, and in some equally magical way Stephens makes it all seem perfectly likely.[3]

In the early seventeenth century, when it was feared that Irish historical records would be destroyed by the English, four scholars were deputed to travel the country collating all the various annals that had been put together over the centuries. The result of this, the *Annals of the Four Masters*,[4] contains many references to Cruachan, all bloody, severed heads delivered there, and so on. A late one, in 1546, relates that in response to an insurrection, 'The Lord Justice, Anthony St Leger, plundered and burned the country as far as Cruachan.' The last mention is in 1594, but its days as a royal enclave were long gone.

Lady Gregory's *Cuchulain* has a description of Cruachan in its heyday, the partitions 'made of red yew with carvings on it', the house itself 'made of oak, and the roof was covered with oak shingles; sixteen windows with glass there were, and shutters of bronze on them, and a bar of bronze across every shutter. There was a raised place in the middle of the house for Ailell and Maeve, with silver fronts and strips of bronze around it, and a silver rod beside it, the way Ailell and Maeve could strike the middle beam and check their people. . . .' The mounds that remain cover an area of ten miles. They are farmed now, and fenced, and it is difficult to tell which is which. In one field, surrounded by a crumbling wall, is the limestone fissure, the cave that was thought to be the entrance to the Otherworld, where live the Shí (*Sidhe*), and which could be entered at Samhain ['Savin'], our Hallowe'en.

The Four Masters were retrieving what records they could in the 1630s. In 1854, westwards along the road from Rathcrogan, was born probably the most influential retriever of all, Douglas Hyde (1860–1949), son of the rector of Tibohine, near Frenchpark. A sickly child, Hyde was educated at home, where he taught himself Irish. He was one of the founders of the Gaelic League, the aims of which were to revive the Irish language and create a modern literature in Irish. An apolitical man, he wanted to replace political Fenianism with a cultural nationalism. His famous lecture, 'The Necessity for De-Anglicizing Ireland', was delivered in 1892: '. . . not a protest against imitation of what is *best* in the English people, for that would be absurd, but rather to show the folly of neglecting what is Irish, and hastening to adopt, pell-mell and indiscriminately, everything that is English, simply because it *is* English. . . . It has always been very curious to me how Irish sentiment sticks in this halfway-house – how it continues apparently to hate the English, and at the same time continues to imitate them. . . .'[5] Hyde published the first book of folk-tales printed in Irish in 1889, and his *Love Songs of Connacht* (1893) were an instant success and deserved to be. The poet Austin Clarke (1896–1974) gives a glimpse of the man (*Casadh an tSúgáin* ['Cassa an Toogoyn'] was Hyde's play in Irish, translated by Lady Gregory as *The Twisting of the Rope*):

As an undergraduate I escaped at one step from the snobbery of school life and discovered the Love Songs of Connaught, those poems and translations which had started our Literary Revival. . . . When the future President of Eire enacted *Casadh an tSugain* for us, he took the parts of all the characters, jumping up and down from the rostrum in his excitement, and, as he unwound an imaginary straw rope at the end of the play, found himself outside the lecture room.

On the morning of our first term, he spoke of the aims and ideals of the language revival: we were all equal, all united in the Gaelic movement. There was no vulgar competition, no showing-off, no twopence-halfpenny looking down on twopence. Those plain words changed me in a few seconds. The hands of our lost despised centuries were laid on me.[6]

Hyde's translations could be wonderfully musical. In 'Ringleted youth of my love', a girl neglected by her lover is speaking:

> I thought, O my love! you were so –
>   As the moon is, or sun on a fountain,
> And I thought after that you were snow,
>   The cold snow on top of the mountain;
> And I thought after that you were more
>   Like God's lamp shining to find me,
> Or the bright star of knowledge before,
>   And the star of knowledge behind me.

In the *Love Songs* he tells the reader how he found the texts, who gave them or sang them to him, and the stories he was told about them. He does this in both Irish and English and, it is said, his translation of his own Irish keeps so closely to the rhythm and cadence of the Irish, that the English sounds like a fresh language. Indeed, though Hyde's intention was to revive *Irish*, his English gave the idea to Yeats and to others that Irish matters could be written of in a special kind of *English*.

Hyde translates the famous Connacht song, 'Una Bhán' ['Oona Vawn'],[7] and tells the story of it. Tomás Costello, 'in the time of Charles II – I think' (Hyde is always engagingly honest), fell in love with Una MacDermot, and the girl's father forbade him access to her. Because of this Una falls ill, too ill to send for Tomás. He does not know this and vows never to speak a word to Una or one of MacDermot's people unless he should be called back before he went across the ford of the little river, the Donogue, near Lough Key (Lough Cé) ['Kay']. Of course, a messenger does come from Una, but too late; Costello will not turn back, because of his vow. Una dies, is buried on an island in the lough (Castle Island?); and eventually Tomás is buried beside her 'in the same grave-yard and island in which Una was buried, and there grew an ash-tree out of Una's grave and another tree out of the grave of Costello, and they inclined towards one another, and they did not cease from growing until the two tops were met and bent upon one another in the middle of the graveyard, and people who saw them said they were that way still (but I was lately on the brink of Lough Cé and could not see them. I was not, however, on the island).'

That is the story of what Frank O'Connor, in *Kings, Lords, and Commons* (1959), called 'the greatest of Irish songs. . . . It seems to me untranslatable, but perhaps a verse of it translated into plain prose may give an idea of its quality: "Young Una, you were a rose in a garden. You were a gold candlestick on the queen's table. You were talk and music going along before me on the road. My ruin of a sad morning that I was not married to you." '[8]

It was probably when Hyde was living in his father's rectory at Frenchpark that W.B. Yeats visited him, and went in search of the graves of Una and Tomás on the island of Lough Key:

> When staying with Hyde in Roscommon, I had driven over to Lough Kay, hoping to find some local memory of the old story of Tumaus Costello. . . . I was rowed up the lake that I might find the island where he died; I had to find it from Hyde's account in the *Love-Songs of Connacht*, for when I asked the boatman, he told the story of Hero and Leander, putting Hero's house on one island, and Leander's on another.
>
> Presently we stopped to eat our sandwiches at the 'Castle Rock', an island all castle. It was not an old castle, being but the invention of some romantic man, seventy or eighty years ago. The last man who had lived there had been Dr Hyde's father, and he had but stayed a fortnight. . . . The roof was, however, still sound, and the windows unbroken. The situation in the centre of the lake, that has little wood-grown islands, and is surrounded by wood-grown hills, is romantic, and at one end, and perhaps at the other too, there is a stone platform where meditative persons might pace to and fro.
>
> I planned a mystical Order which should buy or hire the castle, and keep it as a place where its members could retire for a while for contemplation, and where we might establish mysteries like those of Eleusis and Samothrace; and for ten years to come my most important thought was a vain attempt to find philosophy and to create a ritual for that Order.[9]

Such was the influence of a song, and of Hyde.

As well as the *Love Songs* Hyde also collected and translated *The Religious Songs of Connacht* (1906). At Boyle, near Lough Key, he records 'the greatest and best religious poet that perhaps Erin has ever had', Donagh Mor O'Daly (Ó Dálaigh), said to have been abbot of Boyle. 'I have heard from old people in the County Roscommon, his own county it is believed, more than one of his pieces. He died in the year 1244.' He goes on to translate a poem believed to be by O'Daly, indicating by italics in the first verse the internal rhyming of the original:

> Mary, mother dear of *God*,
> Hear this *clod* that prayeth – I –
> Now and at the hour of *death*,
> When the *breath* is forced to fly.
>
> Pray unto Thy Son, that He
> Like to thee be minded still,
> Thy will is to succour me,
> Pray that He be of Thy will. . . .
>
> Seven deadly sins; each sin
> Lurks within my aching soul,
> All my thoughts are terror-tossed,
> I have lost my own control. . . .

Hyde was indefatigable; he says he recorded everything, good and bad, that he came across. But he was honest; an anonymous poem on death finally defeats him:

> There was I think more in this long poem, but, when we came this far, Maurteen Rua was so tired repeating it, remembering it, and going through it in his own mind, that he said suddenly that he had only that much of it, and I was so tired myself writing it down and putting questions to him, that I let this go with him, though I was sure it was not true. And though I saw him once or twice after this I did not begin at this long poem again, for we were both of us tired of it.

(It is difficult not to like Hyde.) He died in 1949, and is buried in the graveyard of the Protestant church beside the road west of French-park. There is a museum to him in the church.

The MacDermot stronghold, where Una lived, was on the shores of Lough Key near Castle Island. When the MacDermot estates were confiscated by Cromwell the first English 'grantee' was Sir John King, whose son Edward was drowned on his way to Roscommon from England: this was the Edward King of Milton's lament, *Lycidas* (1637). The King house was succeeded by other houses on the site,

one of them designed by John Nash. The last of these, Rockingham, burned down in 1957 and the whole estate now belongs to
the Irish Government, as the Lough Key National Park.[10] Someone
who knew the last house on the site, and wrote about it in his
Woodbrook (1974), was David Thomson (1914–88), who came as a
student to work for Charlie Kirkwood as tutor to the Kirkwood
daughters. The house, 'Woodbrook', still stands, next to the golf
course. Thomson, born in India, of Scottish descent, saw Ireland with
a wondering, stranger's eye, and fell in love with it, though not with
Rockingham:

> If you entered by the main gate you were in Beech Avenue
> – a tunnel of leaves in summer, a lovely long way lined by
> strong old beeches between which you saw acre upon acre of
> rich pasture wooded here and there. At the end of it Rock-
> ingham House came into view, a splendid house, built on
> rising ground beside the lake, of the most hideous architecture
> conceivable. . . .
>
> Their servants lived in what seemed to me to be a dungeon
> specially made for them. . . . It was no worse to live in than
> the attics and basements occupied by London servants but it was
> literally under ground, parts of it being roofed by lawns and
> flowerbeds.

Those curious tunnels are still there, though no trace of the house
remains. The original MacDermots were, and are, still in the neighbourhood. Thomson remembers one of them 'who came frequently
to meals at Woodbrook and at Rockingham, and had the only real
title-deeds to both estates at home, as he sat there talking. Not that
he would have wanted either back; the remnant Cromwell had
allowed his ancestors to keep had accrued debts already. He had a
mild and humorous face and I learned years later that his name, *mac
diarmuda*, means "Son of the man without envy".'

Thomson, who has fallen in love with his young pupil, Phoebe,
is drawn deeper into the mystery of Ireland, even into its
superstitions:

> There was a holy well – Saint Lasair's well – on a cliff-like bank
> that sloped steeply to the waters of Lough Key, often rough,
> often still as a mirror. Phoebe and I went there on bicycles and
> sometimes I went alone. It became holy to me, but in a private
> way. Others worshipped there together, crawling under a flat
> rock to be cured of madness or toothache or anything. It was

a tiny Lourdes once a year and they shared the same religion, not knowing that the well and rock were holy long before Christ. And we, without their community, and as ignorant as they were of the distant past, with no religious tradition of our own, were suddenly silenced when we came there.

Reading this magical book is a painless way to learn some Irish history. By 1940 the life the Kirkwoods represented was coming to an end, after 300 years.[11] Eventually they were forced to sell Woodbrook to tenants, who had worked for them, and who had always believed the place belonged to them anyway. Thomson had noticed that the Kirkwoods, although popular landlords, were not accepted with the ease and naturalness that tenants showed towards people like the MacDermots. These had somehow clung on, perhaps had been allowed to, because after all this was Connaught and Cromwell had sent the old tribal chieftains 'to Hell or Connaught'.

Even in Penal times these old Irish aristocrats managed to maintain some of their lordly ways; keeping, or at least educating, their own harper, for example. It was the MacDermots who saw the promise of the young Carolan (whom Goldsmith described), and brought him up with their own children's tutor. When he went blind at the age of eighteen, after smallpox, they gave him a guide and a horse and he set off on his wanderings to become the most famous harper in Ireland. Carolan had (and still has) star status, and became a magnet for anecdotes; in old age he came back to be looked after by Mrs MacDermot Roe at Alderford House, Ballyfarnan. That house is still there, until recently lived in by a MacDermot; it is like a large, Georgian, English rectory. Carolan, born in 1670, died in the house in 1738. His wake lasted for four days and his funeral at Kilronan was attended by ten harpers and sixty clergy.[12]

Set on a slope by the roadside, Kilronan graveyard is very tumbled down, and must always have been so, because Carolan's skull soon appeared above ground and was used as a drinking-vessel, for the cure of ailments. The graveyard must have remained in a bad state, because the children at Woodbrook found a skull there, and bones, brought them home and enacted a primitive ritual over them, witnessed by their appalled mother – one of the scenes in David Thomson's book. Carolan's remains are now safely ensconced, with a new tablet, in the neat MacDermot enclosure in the graveyard.

Leitrim – Cavan – Fermanagh

Just over the Roscommon–Leitrim border, which here is the River Shannon, is Drumsna ['Drum snor']; where in the mid-1840s the young Anthony Trollope (1815–82) found himself on Post Office business. He had been a failure in England, but in Ireland he liked his job, was good at it and liked the place: 'It was altogether a very jolly life that I led in Ireland. I was always moving about, and soon found myself to be in pecuniary circumstances which were opulent in comparison with those of my past life. The Irish people did not murder me, nor did they even break my head. I soon found them to be good-humoured, clever – the working classes very much more intelligent than those of England – economical, and hospitable.' More to the point, at Drumsna he was born as a novelist:

> . . . As we were taking a walk in that most uninteresting country, we turned up through a deserted gateway, along a weedy, grass-grown avenue, till we came to the modern ruins of a country house. It was one of the most melancholy spots I ever visited. I will not describe it here, because I have done so in the first chapter of my first novel. We wandered about the place, suggesting to each other causes of the misery we saw there, and while I was still among the ruined walls and decayed beams I fabricated the plot of *The Macdermots of Ballycloran*. As to the plot itself, I do not know that I ever made one so good – or, at any rate, one so susceptible of pathos.[13]

Trollope describes the ruin in the first chapter of his novel *The Macdermots*. He devotes three closely printed pages to it. 'Poor old Time will soon have little left him at Ballycloran. . . .' A century and a half later it is maybe a little more ruinous, patched up here and there, and with rough fences to keep out cattle, or to guide them in to shelter in what once were well-proportioned rooms. To find it you move a little along the Dublin road, take the first left fork, turn right at a new housing estate, over a small bridge, and there, about a mile and a half from Drumsna, is the ruin. It is odd to stand in front of so well documented a first inspiration of a novelist.

The *Dublin Review*, in 1872, marvels at Trollope's ability to be 'as true to the saddest and heaviest truths of Irish life, as racy of the soil, as rich with the peculiar humour, the moral features, the social oddities, the subtle individuality of the far west of Ireland, as George Eliot's novels are true to the truths of English life'.[14]

Trollope inveighs against the poverty of the district, at Mohill, east of Drumsna, owned by his fictional Lord Birmingham, an absentee landlord, but a real place mostly owned then by the notorious Earl of Leitrim.[15] Trollope employs heavy irony: Birmingham/Leitrim is a most charitable man, tireless in his support for the Poles, for indigent authors, for who-knows-what charitable cause, and

> public and private philanthropy. . . . 'Tis true he lives in England, was rarely in his life in Ireland, never in Mohill. Could he be blamed for this? Could he live in two countries at once? or would the world have been benefited had he left the Parliament and the Cabinet, to whitewash Irish cabins, and assist in the distribution of meal?
>
> This would be his own excuse, and does it not seem a valid one? Yet shall no one be blamed for the misery which belonged to him; for the squalid sources of the wealth with which Poles were fed, and literary paupers clothed?

Trollope is never sentimental. If their masters neglected them, how much more did the Irish neglect themselves. He cannot forgive his lovely Feemy, who lived at the now-ruined Ballycloran, for her slatternliness:

> Ussher would not come till the evening, and her hair was therefore in papers – and the very papers themselves looked soiled and often used. Her back hair had been hastily fastened up with a bit of old black ribbon and a comb boasting only two teeth, and the short hairs round the bottom of her well-turned head were jagged and uneven, as though bristling with anger at the want of that attention which they required. . . . There she sat, with her feet on the fender, her face on her hands, and her elbows on her knees, with her thumb-worn novel lying in her lap between them. . . . No girls know better how to dress themselves than Irish girls, or can do it with less assistance or less expense; but they are too much given to morning dishevelment.

Both Sean O'Faolain and Frank O'Connor are good on the particular qualities of the Leitrim-Cavan landscapes.[16] O'Faolain's *An Irish Journey*: 'Leitrim, like Cavan, is a watery country, but Cavan collects the water into a thousand little lakes, and Leitrim, being hilly, indeed a maze of mountains and hills, pours it all over the place. It is boggy, soggy, rushy land, full of burrowing streams, tiniest crevices of water everywhere, and this I found very affecting, as if I was travelling with a lovely but tearful woman. . . .' And O'Connor, in *Irish Miles*: '. . . a mid-Atlantic of little hills . . . sunlit green rollers, all rearing themselves on their hind legs to catch a glimpse of us. . .' It is possible that among these 'green rollers' Irish vernacular literature was born.

It was in County Down in 636, at the Battle of Moira, one of the most famous battles of the north, that Cenn Faelad, a near descendant of two high kings of Ireland, was wounded in the head. Such an important personage had to be given the best medical treatment, so he was taken to Toomregan in County Cavan, to the house of Abbot Briccíne, 'where the three streets meet between the houses of the three professors. And there were three schools in that place, a school of Latin learning, a school of Irish Law, and a school of Irish poetry.'[17] When Cenn Faelad was trepanned by Abbot Briccíne, or whatever happened, 'his brain of forgetting was stricken out of him' and he was given total recall, so that every day he learned by heart whatever had been going on in the three schools and 'fitted a pattern of poetry to these matters and wrote them on slates and tablets and set them in a vellum book'. Scholars take this seriously, because there are a number of texts attributed to Cenn Faelad which are very early indeed; he is therefore the first author in the vernacular, Irish, literature of Ireland. There is a strong tradition that the site of the schools at Toomregan is not far from Milltown, somewhere near the ruined church with its Round Tower at Drumlane, which is set between two pieces of water, two of the 'thousand little lakes' that make the map look like a watery jigsaw. It would be appropriate if this were the place of the fabulous trepanning, and the beginnings of Irish writing, because it is an exceptionally peaceful spot.

Above Belturbet the complexity of waters turns into Upper Lough Erne (County Fermanagh). On the shores and islands here the Four Masters collected material for their *Annals*. Three of the four belonged to the O'Clery family, who were hereditary *ollaves* (scholars, archivists) to the O'Donnells of Galway. The chief of them, Michael O'Clery, became a Franciscan lay brother at Louvain, in what is now Belgium, and was sent to Ireland to begin the work. He makes his purpose clear in his preface to the *Annals*: 'Because of the cloud which hangs over the Milesian race,[18] judging that should such a compilation be neglected at present, or consigned to a future time, a risk might be run that the materials for it should never again be brought together . . . this work was undertaken.' The fate of one of these four historians is recorded by the translator of their *Annals*, John O'Donovan, who found that in an inquisition of 1632, Cucogry O'Clery, 'being a meere Irishman and not of English or British descent or surname . . . he was dispossessed'. 'He had however other possessions for which the English had no covetous desire', says Stephen Gwynn, bitterly, and his will exists, bequeathing 'the property most dear to me that I ever possessed in this world, namely my books, to my two sons, Dermot and John'.[19]

WEST TYRONE – LOUGH DERG

This dispossession of O'Clery took place on the borders of the counties neighbouring Fermanagh to the north, Donegal and Tyrone. A sense of confiscation, of a language and a culture lost (the *Annals* were of course written in Irish), pervades some Irish writing still. John Montague (b. 1929), brought up in County Tyrone, makes explicit his regret in 'A Lost Tradition', by putting into English the place-names of his childhood:[20]

> All around, shards of a lost tradition:
> From the Rough Field I went to school
> In the Glen of Hazels. Close by
> Was the bishopric of the Golden Stone;
> The cairn of Carleton's homesick poem. . . .
>
> The whole landscape a manuscript
> We had lost the skill to read,
> A part of our past disinherited;
> But fumbled, like a blind man
> Along the fingertips of instinct. . . .

Another contemporary poet, Pearse Hutchinson (b. 1927), in *The Frost is All Over* (1975) – the title is the name of an Irish jig – declares 'To kill a language is to kill a people':[21]

> Is Carleton where the tenderness must hide?
> Or would they have the Gaelic words, like insects,
> Crawl up the legs of horses, and each bite,
> Or startle, be proclaimed a heritage?
> Are those who rule us, like their eager voters,

Ghosts yearning for flesh? Ghosts are cruel,
And ghosts of suicides more cruel still.
To kill a language is to kill one's self.

Both these poets, of Irish parentage, were born out of Ireland
(Montague in New York, Hutchinson in Glasgow) and are therefore a part of the Irish diaspora: in some sense physically, as well
as historically, disinherited. They both mention Carleton. William
Carleton (1794–1869) was born near Clogher, County Tyrone, and
he helps Montague to one of his references by remarking: 'The name
Clogher is, I believe, of Druidical origin, the word Clogh-air – "or"
– signifying a "golden stone".'[22] Carlton was born into a poor,
bilingual family, went to a hedge-school, and was qualified to describe
the Irish peasantry in a fashion that neither sentimentalized nor
patronized. What Hutchinson means by his question, 'Is Carleton
where the tenderness [of the Irish language] must hide?' lies in
Carleton's ability to reproduce in English the actual cadences of Irish
talkers: 'At a time when Irish was fading as a predominant language,
the people spoke English in the syntax of their native speech. . . .
Half a century before John Synge put his ear to a Wicklow floor
to catch the talk of a servant girl, Carleton caught every turn and
nuance of Irish speech.'[23]
    Anthony Cronin (b. 1926), who edited a selection of Carleton's
stories, mixes metaphors on purpose when he says Carleton 'has an
ear for dialogue that never puts a foot wrong':

William Carleton is one of the great oddities of European
literature, a writer with no ancestors and no successors. . . . The
people Carleton wrote of had up to then been almost totally
sealed off from outside and sealed off from change. Even to the
most intelligent members of the Protestant landlord class, the
Catholic peasantry were a matter of indifference or a mystery.
Their vices were well enough known: their drunkenness, their
occasional ferocity, and perhaps still more disgusting, fecundity;
but their secret mores, the corrupted but organic loyalties that
sustained them were not, nor would the grotesque caricatures
of ancient and higher ways which still lived on among them
be recognized for what they were, but regarded simply as further
proofs of barbarism. . . .
    In Carleton we enter the cabins and the hedge-school them-
selves . . . we enter in fact the dark world of which Carleton
is the solitary voice.[24]

So, to learn what Irish Ireland was like, in the early nineteenth century, you have to read *Traits and Stories of the Irish Peasantry*. Carleton's characterization is acute, his dialogue authentic, but as for his narrative, Cronin declares that 'generally speaking if you were to read him for the story you would hang yourself'. What is remarkable is the exuberant vitality of the people he describes.

Patrick Kavanagh objected to Carleton being called a peasant – 'he was no more a peasant than yours truly';[25] but the cabin Carleton grew up in at Springtown (now signposted from Clogher) is humble, even though it is in a pretty setting.

> There was one beautiful thorn-tree, at the foot of a steep piece of ground which stretched from the back of our house to the edge of the glen; on this a particular blackbird sat and sang as regularly as the evening comes. With the music of this bird I was so intensely delighted, that I used to go to bed every fine evening two hours before my usual time, for the express purpose of listening to the music. There was a back window in the bedroom where I slept; this I opened, and there I lay until I fell asleep with the melody in my ears.[26]

From Clogher, Carleton leads us back to Lough Erne,[27] and on to County Donegal, to Lough Derg, scene of the famous pilgrimage.[28] Carleton began by wishing to be a Catholic priest, but became a journalist for the violently anti-Catholic *Christian Examiner*.

> Ever since my boyhood, in consequence of legends which I had learned from my father, about the far-famed Lough Derg, or St Patrick's purgatory, I felt my imagination fired with a romantic curiosity to perform a station [stage in the ritual] at that celebrated place. I accordingly did so, and the description of that most penal performance, some years afterwards, not only constituted my debut in literature, but was also the means of preventing me from being a pleasant strong-bodied parish priest to this day; indeed it was the cause of changing the whole destiny of my subsequent life.

That is in the preface to Carleton's first story, 'The Lough Derg Pilgrim'.[29] He describes how he was invited to write it by the 'anti-Romanist' Rev. Caesar Otway,[30] 'a man from whom I have received so many acts of the warmest kindness'. He quotes Otway's own description of looking at the island in Lough Derg to which the pilgrimage is made, and the buildings on it,

> a collection of hideous slated houses and cabins, which give you an idea that they were rather erected for the purposes of toll-houses or police stations than any thing else. . . .
>
> I was certainly in an interesting position. I looked southerly towards Lough Erne, with the Protestant city of Enniskillen rising amidst its waters, like the island queen of all the loyalty, and industry, and reasonable worship that have made her sons the admiration of past and present time; and before me, to the north, Lough Derg, with its far-famed isle, reposing there as the monstrous birth of a dreary and degraded superstition. . . .

Otway clearly wants a demolition-job from his protégé and that is what he gets, shot through, occasionally, with Carleton's ambiguous feeling. It was not surprising that Carleton, having escaped from his Catholic peasant background, should turn and rend it. What is surprising, and amusing, is his vehemence, which is the more puzzling when we consider the obvious love he manifests, in his *Autobiography*, for his Catholic parents, for both of them, especially his mother: 'I remember on one occasion, when she was asked to sing the English version of that touching melody "The Red-haired Man's Wife," she replied, "I will sing it for you; but the English words and the air are like a quarrelling man and wife: *the Irish melts into the tune, but the English doesn't*" – an expression scarcely less remarkable for its beauty than its truth. She spake the words in Irish.'

'The Lough Derg Pilgrim' is lively, funny, indignant, with a large and colourful cast. On his way to the Lough he overtakes two grotesquely dressed harpies, who mistake him for a priest, and invite him to pray with them. He describes the rites of the pilgimage, which have changed little to this day, and then violently condemns it: 'When I commenced my station, I started from what is called the "Beds," and God help St Patrick if he lay upon them: they are sharp stones placed circularly in the earth, with the spike ends of them up, one circle within another. . . .' At the end of the pilgrimage the two women wash his feet; then, pretending to brush his clothes, steal them. When he gets home he tells his parish priest, 'a Reverend Father . . . seldom known to laugh at anybody's joke but his own. . . . "So," says he, "you have fallen foul of Nell M'Collum,

the most notorious shuler[31] in the province! a gipsy, a fortune-
teller, and a tinker's widow; but rest contented, you are not the first
she has guiled – but beware the next time." "There is no danger of
that," said I, with peculiar emphasis.'

Nearly a hundred and fifty years later Seamus Heaney (in 'Station
Island') makes the same pilgrimage and encounters Carleton's ghost,
at the spot where Carleton overtook the harpies, 'the Shulers'.
Carleton exclaims disgustedly, when he learns Heaney's destination,
'O holy Jesus Christ, does nothing change?' and Heaney makes
Carleton explain himself:[32]

> '. . . It is a road you travel on your own.
>
> I who learned to read in the reek of flax
> and smelled hanged bodies rotting on their gibbets
> and saw their looped slime gleaming from the sacks –
>
> hard-mouthed Ribbonmen and Orange bigots
> made me into the old fork-tongued turncoat
> who mucked the byre of their politics.
>
> If times were hard, I could be hard too.
> I made the traitor in me sink the knife.
> And maybe there's a lesson there for you,
>
> whoever you are, wherever you come out of,
> for though there's something natural in your smile
> there's something in it strikes me as defensive.'

Heaney replies, 'I have no mettle for the angry role.' Carleton did
have such mettle; so did Patrick Kavanagh, who made the pilgrimage also; but Kavanagh's ghost ('slack-shouldered and clear-eyed') is
gentle, chaffing Heaney:

> '. . . Sure I might have known
> once I had made the pad, you'd be after me
> sooner or later. Forty-two years on
> and you've got no farther! But after that again,
> where else would you go? Iceland, maybe? Maybe the
>   Dordogne?'

Kavanagh made the pilgrimage in 1942, almost exactly a hundred years after Carleton. He sent his long poem about it to Frank
O'Connor, who suggested that each new theme mentioned should
be developed and extended. It was a prose-writer's judgement.
Kavanagh felt that he had said in verse all that he intended, more

would have sounded like a social survey, but decided not to pub-
lish it, 'lest he intrude on sacred ground'. His brother kept the
manuscript and published it in 1971, four years after Kavanagh's
death.[33]

> From Cavan and from Leitrim and from Mayo,
> From all the thin-faced parishes where hills
> Are perished noses running peaty water,
> They come to Lough Derg to fast and pray and beg. . . .
> And the half-pilgrims too,
> They who are the true
> Spirit of Ireland, who joke
> Through the death-mask and take
> Virgins of heaven or flesh,
> Were on Lough Derg Island
> Wanting some half-wish. . . .

Though perhaps some of the pilgrims' prayers 'were shaped like
sonnets', most were along the lines of, 'That my husband get his
health back, That my son Joseph pass the Intermediate, That there
may be good weather for the hay':

> This was the banal
> Beggary that God heard. Was he bored
> As men are with the poor? Christ Lord
> Hears in the voices of the meanly poor
> Homeric utterances, poetry sweeping through.

Some pilgrimages were unsuccessful dry affairs. Douglas Hyde,
in *The Religious Songs of Connacht* (1906), attributes the following
poem to Donagh Mor Ó Dálaigh (O'Daly), the twelfth-century
religious poet, abbot of Boyle; another translator puts it in the seventeenth century. It could have been written at any time:[34]

> Sad my visit to Loch Dearg,
> King of churches and bells,
> mourning your cuts and wounds
> but no tear comes from my eye.
>
> My eyeballs stay dry
> when I've done what evil I could;
> my heart craves only peace,
> O King, alas, what will I do?

> Only Son of Mary, Who created all,
> Who defeated the death of the three nails,
> with my heart hard as any stone
> sad my visit to Loch Dearg.

The pilgrimage is a recurring Irish theme. Sean O'Faolain sets his story 'Lovers of the Lake' almost wholly on Station Island in the Lough.[35] A married woman decides on impulse to do the pilgrimage and asks her lover to drive her there. Like Carleton's Rev. Caesar Otway, she is appalled by her first sight of the island:

> Confused and hairy-looking clouds combed themselves on the ridges of the hills. The lake was crumpled and gray, except for those yellow worms of foam blown across it in parallel lines. To the south a cold patch of light made it all look far more dreary. She stared out towards the island and said:
> 'It's not at all like what I expected.'
> 'And what the hell did you expect? Capri?'
> 'I thought of an old island, with old gray ruins, and old holly trees and rhododendrons down to the water, a place where old monks would live.'
> They saw tall buildings like modern hotels rising by the island's shore, an octagonal basilica big enough for a city, four or five bare, slated houses, a long shed like a ballroom. There was one tree. Another bus drew up beside them and people peered out through the wiped glass.
> 'O God!' she groaned. 'I hope this isn't going to be like Lourdes.'

Then, on the island, like Hyde's poet, she feels spiritually dry, oppressed by consciousness of self. Fasting and sleeplessness and mantra-like repetition of prayers begins to take effect: 'Bit by bit the incantations drew her in. . . . She swam into an ecstasy as rare as one of those perfect dances of her youth when she used to swing in a whirl of music, a swirl of bodies, a circling of lights, floated out of her moral frame, alone in the arms that embraced her.' She discovers that her sceptical lover has followed her to the island, and is doing the pilgrimage himself, with what seems like seriousness. They are both of them Kavanagh's 'half-pilgrims', but she at least is discovering in her fellow pilgrims more than she would have guessed. She talks to a man, 'about sixty-two or three; small and tubby, his eyes perpetually wide and unfocussing behind pince-nez glasses':

'That's right,' he said, answering her question. 'I'm from
England. Liverpool. I cross by the night boat and get here the
next afternoon. Quite convenient, really. I've come here every
year for the last twenty-two years, apart from the war years.
I come on account of my wife.'

'Is she ill?'

'She died twenty-two years ago. No, it's not what you might
think – I'm not praying for her. She was a good woman, but,
well, you see, I wasn't very kind to her . . . I didn't make her
happy.'

'Isn't that,' she said, to comfort him, 'a very private feeling?
I mean, it's not in the Ten Commandments that thou shalt make
thy wife happy.'

He did not smile. He made the same faint movement with
his fingers.

'Oh, I don't know! What's love if it doesn't do that? I mean
to say, it is something godly to love another human being, isn't
it? I mean, what does "godly" mean if it doesn't mean giving
up everything for another? It isn't human to love, you know.
It's foolish, it's a folly, a divine folly. It's beyond all reason,
all limits. I didn't rise to it,' he concluded sadly.

She looked at him, and thought, 'A little fat man, a clerk
in some Liverpool office all his life, married to some mousy little
woman, thinking about love as if he were some sort of Greek
mystic'.

She and her lover complete the pilgrimage, return to the mainland, give themselves dinner in a hotel, and go dancing. As they walk
back to their hotel the lover wonders whether he will not do the
pilgrimage again next year. She is moved, they have never been closer,
something has happened.

SOUTH DONEGAL

Further into Donegal, there are many traces of the Four Masters.
Near Kinlough, inland from Bundoran, there is a bridge over the
River Drowes that has their four tiny heads set in a monument on
its parapet. They put their materials together at a vanished Franciscan
friary somewhere near Kinlough and the river.[36] Further up the
coast, near Rossnowlagh, at the tip of a foreland, are the remains
of Kilbarron Castle, built on land granted by the O'Donnells to

their hereditary historians, the O'Clerys. (Three of the Four Masters were O'Clerys.) The place gives the impression it is at the furthest edge of western Europe and therefore an appropriate birthplace – as it is said to be – for the chief of the Four Masters, Michael O'Clery, whose job it was to rescue the records of Europe's westernmost country.

Ballyshannon, on the estuary of the Erne, is a place celebrated by another preserver and recorder, the poet William Allingham (1824–89).[37] English schoolchildren used to recite, 'Up the airy mountain, down the rushy glen/We dare not go a-hunting for fear of little men. . .'; in that poem his simplicities were intentional, because he wanted to revive, in English, the traditional Irish broadsheet ballad. He too was part of the Irish cultural rescue attempt. (Irish children now recite 'Grey, grey is Abbey Assaroe, by Belashanny town'.) The Belfast poet John Hewitt describes Allingham

> picking up folksongs from the country people and either adapting or expanding what words he could overhear, or finding fresh words, if he had caught none, sympathetic to the mood of the melody. These artefacts he sent to Dublin to be printed, anonymously, in the format of the street singers' broadsheets on long strips of tinted paper, ('3 yards of songs'), with appropriate woodcut decorations top and bottom, out of the printer's stock of blocks. When the bundles came back, he gave the individual ballads away or had them sold as the genuine ha'penny ballads were sold at fairs and markets. Then, as object and reward of the exercise, he could hear them sung back to him, passing cottage doors, by folk who had no notion of the author of the words at all. In a letter . . . 17 June 1852, he wrote 'In the meantime, I have for some part of my verses, a little audience such as poets can boast of and to whom Tennyson would, likely, seem to be the name of a town.'[38]

Allingham worshipped Tennyson, and became a friend, as he did with Carlyle and Rossetti. He has been suspected of being a toady – certainly he was modest, his collected *Letters* contain none *by* him, only letters *to* him – but in his *Diary* he gives the impression of keeping his end up, and of being a tireless PR man for Ireland. He reports a conversation with Tennyson, in England:

> Speaking of the Irish agitator who said, 'I think their cattle will not much prosper' – a speech followed by the maiming of many

animals – he exclaimed, 'How I hate that man' – Ireland's a dreadful country! I heartily wish it were in the middle of the Atlantic!'

'Below the surface?' I asked.

'No, no, a thousand miles away from England. I like the Irish – I admit the charm of their manners – but they're a fearful nuisance.'

'Very troublesome,' I admitted, 'but there's some truth in the popular Irish notion that nothing can be got from England except by agitation.'

On another occasion he patiently tells Tennyson of

> . . . the Penal Laws, the deliberate destruction of their growing industry by the English Government. 'What do you say to that?'
> T. – That was brutal! Our ancestors were horrible brutes! And the Kelts are very charming and sweet and poetic. I love their Ossians and Finns and so forth. . . .
> A. – They are most unfortunate. . . .
> T. – The Kelts are so utterly unreasonable! The stupid clumsy Englishman – knock him down, kick him under the tail, kick him under the chin, do anything to him, he gets on his legs again and goes on; the Kelt rages and shrieks and tears everything to pieces!

He introduces Tennyson to the works of William Carleton, '. . . with which he is delighted. I said I knew Carleton a little. "Then you knew a man of genius," said T. He thinks C. is not appreciated. I told him that in Ireland he is, highly. Also that C., Catholic born, turned Protestant in youth, wrote the *Traits*, then returned to his old Church and wrote many stories, in which priests and other matters were handled in a different way. "Those are not so good, I should think," T. said.' (Nor is it certain that Allingham is right about Carleton's re-conversion.) Concerning the religious side of Ireland, Protestant Allingham permits himself to sigh, in his *Diaries*, perhaps briefly overcome by the 'Englishness' of his friends: 'I love Ireland: were she only not Catholic! but would she be Ireland otherwise?'

He seizes every opportunity to draw the talent of Ireland to the attention of the British literary Great. He takes Thomas Carlyle to the Temple church in London, where Carlyle had never been:

'Close by,' I said, 'is Goldsmith's grave.' 'Where is it?' said C.,
and crept slowly on my arm till we stood beside the simple but
sufficient monument, a stone about coffin length, and eighteen
inches high. I read aloud the inscriptions. C. took off his broad-
flapped black hat saying, 'A salute.' I followed his example, and
thus we stood for a few seconds. When our hats were on and
we were turning away, C. laughed and said, 'Strange times,
Mr Rigmarole!' Then, 'Poor Oliver! – he said on his deathbed,
"I am not at ease in my mind." '[39]

Allingham worked in Ballyshannon as a customs officer, and
loved the place: 'The little old town where I was born has a voice
of its own, low, solemn, persistent, humming through the air day
and night, summer and winter. Whenever I think of that town I
seem to hear the voice. The river which makes it rolls over rocky
ledges into the tide. An odd, out-of-the-way little town ours, on
the extreme western verge of Europe. . . .'[40] The town is not much
changed, and has nearly the whole cast-list of Irish mythological
figures associated with it, its island, and the Falls of Assaroe.[41] Allingham wrote an emigrant's farewell in the form of a broadsheet
ballad:

Adieu to Belashanny! where I was bred and born;
Go where I may, I'll think of you as sure as night and
    morn. . . .

To *shenachas* and wise old talk of Erin's days gone by –
Who trenched the rath on such a hill, and where the bones may
    lie
Of saint or king or warrior chief, with tales of fairy power. . . .

He has all the traditional Irish preoccupations, with locality,
history, lament:

Grey, grey is Abbey Assaroe, near Belashanny town,
It has neither door nor window, the walls are broken down;
The carven stones lie scattered in briar and nettle-bed;
The only feet are those that come at burial of the dead. . . .

Allingham's house is preserved in Ballyshannon, and he has a plaque
on the bridge. He wanted to be buried there near his favourite sights
and sounds (and sites):[42]

> The silver salmon shooting up the fall,
>> Itself at once the arrow and the bow;
> The shadow of the old quay's weedy wall
>> Cast on the shining turbulence below;
> The water-voice which ever seems to call
>> Far off out of my childhood's long-ago;
> The gentle washing of the harbour wave;
>> Be these the sights and sounds around my grave.

His ashes were brought from Hampstead to Mullinashee – *Mullagh na Sidh* ('The Hill of the Fairies') – at the back of the house where he was born. It was the seat of the fire-god, Aed Ruadh, who drowned there while admiring his image in the water that surrounds it – 'his body was born (buried) into the elf-mound there'.[43] An Episcopal church now occupies the site, with Allingham's ashes under a large stone beside it, in the 'elf-mound'.

Up the coast, north of Ballyshannon, is Donegal town, where, in the central space called 'The Diamond', is an obelisk to the Four Masters. Their *Annals* were begun and completed at the Franciscan friary at the edge of the town on the estuary of the River Eske. Michael O'Clery says so in his preface: 'On the 22nd January, 1632, this work was undertaken in the convent of Dunagall, and was finished in the same convent on the 10th of August, 1636, the eleventh year of the reign of our king Charles. . . .' The building was blown up in 1601, but the brotherhood was permitted to live in huts or cottages near the ruins. To put that vast work together, gathered from the corners of Ireland, while camped near the ruins of one of the great foundations of their order, must have given the work an extra urgency.

Apart from the fortified abbey, there was a castle in the town itself, which belonged to the O'Donnells and is said to have been blown up by them when Donegal was 'planted' by the Protestants, many of them English or Scottish, in 1607. They did not want the castle to fall into the hands of the 'Gall'. (Donegal was founded by the Vikings and means the 'Dun of the Gall', 'the Fortress of the Foreigner'.) This is the castle that James Clarence Mangan (1803–49)[44] laments in 'The Ruins of Donegal Castle'. Mangan was a Dubliner, revered in Ireland because he was the only genuine poet of his time whose fervour for the Irish cause, expressed in English, seemed to convey to the ears of his readers a genuinely Irish and traditional sound. This is not always easy for the ears of a 'Gall' to catch,

but both James Joyce and W.B. Yeats wrote of him with admiration.
He showed how Ireland could be written about in Irish terms, and
in near-Irish sounds. He continued the tradition of Gaelic lament,
and glorification of the Gaelic past:

> How often from thy turrets high,
>   Thy purple turrets, have we seen
> Long lines of glittering ships, when summer-time drew nigh,
>   With masts and sails of snow-white sheen! . . .

Mangan addresses the castle, which had to be destroyed, by the Irish,
lest,

> Shouldst yet become in saddest truth
>   A *Dún-na-Gall* – the strangers' own.
> For this cause only, stronghold of the Gaelic youth,
>   Lie thy majestic towers o'erthrown.
>
> It is a drear, a dismal sight,
>   This of thy ruin and decay,
> Now that our kings, and bards, and men of mark and might
>   Are nameless exiles far away! . . .

For more than four hundred years a famous book was guarded in
Donegal Castle, and its story is almost the story of Ireland itself.

St Columcille, or Columba, 'the Dove of the Church' (521–597),
is, after St Patrick, Ireland's most venerated male saint. He studied
under St Finian at Bangor, County Down, and, without permission,
made a copy of one of St Finian's Psalters. St Finian asked for it
back, Columcille refused, and the matter went to the High King
of Ireland. The King decided, Solomon-like, confronted by these two
fierce clerics, 'that as a calf belongs to the cow, so a copy belongs
to the book', and Columcille must return it. Again, Columcille
refused. So there was a battle (at Drumcliff, where Yeats is buried);
the O'Donnells of Donegal Castle took their kinsman Columcille's
side, and the Psalter became theirs. It was covered in silver, the silver
was covered with gold, and from then on it was borne in battle by
the O'Donnells, at the front of their war-band, whence the book
got its name, 'Cathach' ['Caha'], which means 'the Battler'.[45]

From the eleventh century it was kept in Donegal Castle. When
the O'Donnells blew up their own castle and went into exile in the
'flight of the Earls' from Lough Swilly, in 1607, they took the
Cathach with them to France. In 1700 it is known to have been

in the possession of Daniel O'Donnell, who commanded the O'Donnell regiment against Marlborough, at the battle of Malplaquet. Perhaps he decided that he and 'the Battler' were living too dangerously for the safety of the book, and he entrusted it to the Abbot of Louvain. (Louvain is where Michael O'Clery studied, chief of the Four Masters; it is named after the Celtic sun-god, Lugh, who gave his name to the Irish Pagan summer festival, Lughnasa.)

Later, an Irish abbot of Louvain decided the book ought to go back to the O'Donnell lineal descendants, who were now at Newport, County Mayo. These eventually gave it to the National Museum of Ireland, when Ireland became independent. It is one of the few bookshrines that have survived: an example of superstition, violence, and dogged persistence in a tradition. Edmund Spenser thought that the only solution was to Anglicize Ireland. It seems there was never much chance.

St Columcille (or Columba) left Ireland after the battle over the Psalter (it is said from shame at his own warlike nature) and settled in Iona, whence he christianized Scotland. He was famous as a protector of poets (*fili*) and according to tradition a poet himself. These lines from an eleventh-century manuscript are said to have been written at the time of his self-exile:[46]

> There is a blue eye which will look back at Ireland;
> Never more shall it see the men of Ireland, nor her women.

He had founded monasteries throughout the northern half of Ireland. One, still a pilgrimage site, was at Glencolumbcille, on a bay between magnificent mountains at the far end of the peninsula that extends west of Donegal. Geoffrey Grigson,[47] connoisseur of Good Places, was drawn there by the poems and diaries of Allingham, which he edited:

> High on the hill-top
> The old King sits,
> He is now so old and grey
> He's nigh lost his wits.
> With a bridge of white mist
> Columbkill he crosses,
> On his stately journeys
> From Slieveleague to Rosses. . . .

Grigson spent several summers in the 1930s in a hidden valley beyond Port, north of Glencolumbcille (bringing friends, Dylan

Thomas among them). His glen was an 'amphitheatre of desolation' below a double black lake (Lough Anaffrin):

> The farmhouse in the Glen, built over the floor of the valley, and the potato and hay fields, is the last dwelling left out of several; of the others only a few walls remain. . . . The cliffs rise eastward and westward of the Glen to some nine hundred or a thousand feet. There is no beach when the Glen meets the sea, only a bar, underneath the cliffs, of stones round and smooth as skulls. Bathe off the bar and seals stick out their heads and swim slowly and curiously round. . . .
>
> With the sea the farmer and his wife had next to no relations. He never fished in it. He had no boat – there was nowhere to keep a boat. They might have lived two thousand miles from the sea in the Middle West or in Siberia, but for going now and then down the cliff path to look for baulks of wood or planks washed in on the shingle. He disliked the sea, felt its bigness, the savagery and blackness of its junction with the land, and disregarded it, one felt, deliberately.

Mangan had done his job for his time, had sung Ireland's wrongs, but it was clearly unhealthy to blame all of these on the 'Gall'. Later Irish writers turned more and more to what was wrong with the 'Gael'. One of the most fiercely unsentimental of these, a novelist of the people, is Patrick MacGill (1891–1963).[48] He was born in a cabin that still stands in one of the glens that run out of Glenties, in the direction of Donegal. If its situation is desirable, from a contemporary car-owner's point of view, it is necessary to remember the number of people who lived in it (he was one of eleven children) and the poorness of the soil that surrounds it. MacGill left school when he was ten years old (the school house is still standing along the lane from his home) and worked in the fields. At the age of twelve he was hiring himself out at the fair of Strabane, on the border with County Tyrone, where Scottish farmers came to find labour among the poor, many of them from Donegal. Thus MacGill became a 'tattie-howker' (a potato-picker) in Scotland, one of those anonymous bands of Irish workers, some of whom did not speak English, whose strength and ignorance and, sometimes, drunkenness went to make up the British image of 'the Paddy'. These became his subject, he was one of them himself, and he called them, as he called his novel, *The Children of the Dead End* (1914).

Most of that novel concerns itself with the life of the emigrant gangs, on the railways, and in the potato-fields of the mainland. But he can turn his eye back on 'Glenmornan' – which is what he called Glenties – and, a Catholic himself, rend its superstitions and its clergy. He had a particular quarrel with the parish priest:

The six-hand reel is a favourite Glenmornan dance, but in my time a new parish priest came along who did not approve of dancing. 'The six-hand reel is a circle, the centre of which is the devil,' said he, and called a house in which a dance was held the 'Devil's Station.' He told the people to cease dancing, but they would not listen to him. 'When we get a new parish priest we don't want a new God,' they said. 'The old God who allowed dancing is good enough for us.'

The parish priest who came in his place was a little pot-bellied man with white shiny false teeth, who smoked ninepenny cigars and who always travelled first-class in a railway train. Everybody feared him because he put curses on most of the people in Glenmornan.

What MacGill could not forgive was the ignorance people were kept in, and allowed themselves to be ruled by, and even the relish some had of ignorance for its own sake:

'To think that all the people about here are such fools as to suffer a tyrant like that to rule over them! . . . Poor unhappy Ireland! If it's not the landlord who is the tyrant, it's the gombeen man, and if it's not the gombeen man, it's the priest. . . . If they were only educated, if they only read books, papers, anything.'

'That's what has put yourself wrong', said Maura the Rosses, with an air of finality. 'It was the readin' and the books. I did me best to keep ye from the readin' but ye wouldn't take heed to what I said.'

A condescending English reviewer remarked, 'MacGill has for a long time made himself the Press Agent for the human underdog.' MacGill might have settled for that as an epitaph. He died in the United States and there is now an annual MacGill Festival in Glenties.

Also in Glenties, near the enormous comprehensive school (to which MacGill would now have gone; his little school has recently been closed down) is a house called 'The Laurels' in which the playwright Brian Friel (b. 1929) imagined his play, *Dancing at Lughnasa*

(1989; dedicated 'in memory of those five brave Glenties women'). The house belonged to Friel's aunts, and he used to spend some of his school holidays there. In the play, the five sisters in the rather lonely, fairly poor farmhouse, yearn for something wild, at Lughnasa ['Loonusa'], which is the feast in August of Lug ['Lu'], the sun god. Even in this ordinary household there is a vague, but irresistible, connection with Ireland's pagan past, which may have something to do with MacGill's type of priest, his detestation of dancing: in the play the sisters suddenly burst into a wild, uncontrolled corybantic stamping, in the kitchen.

The connection with the past was made more explicit in Friel's *Translations* (1980), a play built round the anglicization of Irish place-names by the British Ordnance Survey (for whom Mangan worked), those names, the loss of which the poets Montague and Hutchinson so bitterly regret. The play is set on the far side of County Donegal, in the Inishowen peninsular; but the Ordnance work went on all over Ireland, contributing to a sense among the Irish that the Gall was bent on destroying Ireland's past, that part of it which yet remained in the sound of the names of places.

The scene of the play is the room of a hedge-school, the décor of which owes much to Carleton's descriptions. Yolland is the English officer anglicizing the names, helped by Irish-speaking Owen, son of the schoolmaster. As English Yolland becomes more and more besotted with Ireland, and with an Irish girl, so does Owen's Irishness become more and more impatient with the absurdity of their task, and the ever-present risk of sentimentality.

YOLLAND: Something is being eroded.
OWEN: Back to the romance again! Alright! Fine! Fine! Look where we've got to. . . . We've come to this crossroads. Come here and look at it, man! Look at it! And we call the crossroads Tobair Vree. And why do we call it Tobair Vree? I'll tell you why. Tobair means a well. But what does Vree mean? It's a corruption of *Brian* ['Vreean'] – an erosion of *Tobair Bhriain*. Because a hundred years ago there used to be a well there, not at the crossroads, mind you – that would be too simple – but in a field close to the crossroads. And an old man called Brían, whose face was disfigured by an enormous growth, got it into his head that the well was blessed; and every day for seven months he went there and bathed his face in it. But the growth didn't go away; and one morning Brian was found drowned in that well. And ever since that crossroads is known as Tobair

Vree – even though that well has long since dried up. I know
the story because my grandfather told it to me. But ask Doalty
– or Maire – or Bridget – even my father – even Manus – why
it's called Tobair Vree; and do you think they'll know? I know
they don't know. So the question I put to you, Lieutenant, is
this: What do we do with a name like that? Do we scrap Tobair
Vree altogether and call it – what? – The Cross? Crossroads?
Or do we keep piety with a man long dead, long forgotten,
his name 'eroded' beyond recognition, whose trivial little story
nobody in the parish remembers?
YOLLAND: Except you.
OWEN: I've left here.
YOLLAND: You remember it.
OWEN: I'm asking you: what do we write in the Name-
Book?
YOLLAND: Tobair Vree.
OWEN: Even though the well is a hundred yards from the actual
crossroads – and there's no well anyway – and what the hell does
Vree mean?
YOLLAND: Tobair Vree.
OWEN: That's what you want?
YOLLAND: Yes.

NORTH DONEGAL

In central Donegal, near Kilmacrenan,[49] north of Letterkenny, there
is a famous well of the sort relied upon by Owen's unfortunate Brían,
the Doon Well. Stephen Gwynn visited it in 1899, and saw 'an array
of crutches, left there by healed cripples, and they are all swathed
about by the rags worn in sickness. Wind and rain and sun have
wrought upon these unsightly objects till they are cleansed and
bleached and softened in a conformity of tint with the grey stones
about them. . . . What number of real cures there are I cannot say,
but faith-healing has a good chance with Irish peasants.'[50]
    English Mrs Dinah Craik was there a few years earlier (1886), and
had difficulty finding it, even on 'a perfect August day'.

No one who has not seen them can imagine the intense desolation of these Donegal moors. Not a man, not a beast, nor a
cabin was visible. 'I don't believe there's any well at all,' said
the most incredulous of us. . . . A tiny spring, half hidden by

a big stone; near it a little forest of walking-sticks, each with a rag tied on the top – votive offerings or mementoes of those who went away cured; and in front of it a small group. Four labourers, in the prime of life, but weak and wasted, and each with that most pathetic thing to see in a working man – clean, smooth, white hands – crept feebly from the cart to the well. One after the other each knelt down before it, his head level with the water, and drank, two or three times, praying between whiles with the dumb earnestness of desperate faith. . . .

Our party, whatever they thought, had the grace also to maintain a respectful silence, and shortly to move on towards a little hill, or rather a huge rock gradually covered with vegetation. . . . When they were safely disposed of, I came back to the well. The four men had never ceased praying. I touched the oldest and sickliest of them on the shoulder; he started, and looked up with an eager face, then down at the coin I put into his hand. He hesitated to take it.

'A Protestant lady gives you this, and hopes you will soon get well.'

'Thank ye, missis. A blessin' on ye,' was all he answered, and went back to his prayers.[51]

The 'little hill, or rather huge rock' near the Well is the place where the O'Donnells were proclaimed lords of Tyrconnel. The twelfth-century British historian 'Giraldus Cambrensis', who accompanied King John to Ireland, mentions the ceremony, and tells a wild story of a whole cow being boiled there, 'and a bath prepared for the new king of the broth, into which he stepped publicly, and at once bathed and fed'.[52]

The Irish seventeenth-century historian, Geoffrey Keating, will have none of that, and nothing much to do with any tales told of Ireland by English visitors, 'inasmuch as it is almost according to the fashion of the beetle they act, when writing concerning the Irish. For it is the fashion of the beetle, when it lifts its head in the summertime, to go about fluttering, and not to stoop towards any delicate flower that may be in the field, or any blossom in the garden, though they be all roses or lilies, but it keeps bustling about until it meets with the dung of a horse or a cow, and proceeds to roll itself therein.'[53]

Edmund Spenser had heard of such a ceremony, in the 1580s:

They use to place him that shall be their Captain, upon a stone always reserved for that purpose, and placed commonly upon a hill: in many of the which I have seen the foot of a man formed and engraven, which they say was the measure of their first Captain's foot, whereon he standing receiveth an oath to preserve all the former ancient customs of the country inviolable, and to deliver up the succession peaceable to his Tanistih, and then hath a wand delivered unto him by some whose proper office that is; after which, descending ftom the stone, he turneth himself round about, thrice forward, and thrice backward. . . .

I have heard that the beginning and cause of this ordinance amongst the Irish, was especially for the defence and maintenance of their lands in their posterity, and for excluding of all innovation or alienation thereof unto strangers, and specially to the English.[54]

The approach is now by road, the Well is signposted, and recently paved. People arrive by car to say their prayers and pace barefoot, anticlockwise, around it.

Stephen Gwynn (1864–1950), politician and man of letters, whose descriptions have often been quoted here, was said by Oliver St John Gogarty, in words that savour of a funeral oration, to be 'stationary, but not a recluse. Unobtrusively he lived and died, but for patriotism, scholarship and integrity he was the greatest figure in Ireland of his time.'[55] Gwynn's story of meeting a *shanachy* (story-teller and reciter) in a cabin on lonely Cark Mountain (south-west of Kilmacrenan, below Letterkenny)[56] represents the experiences of the young nationalist men and women of the period (the end of the last century) who, like Douglas Hyde, went from place to place recording a culture that they feared was on the point of extinction – as the Four Masters had done more than two centuries before.

One friend of mine lay stretched for long hours on top of a roof of sticks and peat-scraws which was propped against the wall of a ruined cabin, while within the evicted tenant, still clinging to his home as life clings to the shattered body, lay bedridden on a lair of rushes, and chanted the deeds of heroes; his voice issuing through the vent in the roof, at once window and chimney, from the kennel in which was neither room nor light for a man to sit and record the verses.

Gwynn is told of a James Kelly on Cark (and if Mrs Craik talks of the 'intense desolation' of Donegal moors, she should have seen Cark Mountain in the rain):

I pushed my bicycle through a drizzle of misty rain up the road over mountainous moor, before I saw his cottage standing trim and white under its thatch in a screen of trees, and as I was nearing it, the boy with me showed me James down in a hollow, filling a barrow with turf. He stopped work as I came down, and called off his dog, looking at me curiously enough, for, indeed, strangers were a rarity in that spot, clean off the tourist track, and away from any thoroughfare. One's presence had to be explained out of hand, and I told him exactly why I had come. He looked surprised and perhaps a little pleased, that his learning should draw students. But he made no pretence of ignorance; the only question was, how he could help me.

Gwynn finds that Kelly 'had by heart not only the Fenian cycle, but also the older Sagas of Cuchulainn':

. . . the line was unbroken from the Ireland of heroes and minstrels to the hour when he chanted over the poem that some bard in the remote ages had fashioned.
Little wonder, too, for his own way of life was close to that of the Middle Ages. Below in the valley, where the Swilly River debouches into its sea lough, was a prosperous little town with banks and railway; but to reach the bleak brown moor where James Kelly's house stood, you must climb by one of two roads, each so rough and steep that a bicycle cannot be ridden down them. Here, in a little screen of scrub alders, stands the cottage, where three generations of the family live together. His own home consisted simply of two rooms with no upper storey, but it was trim and comfortable, the dresser well filled, and the big pot over the turf fire gave out a prosperous steam.

Cark is now even more lonely than when Gwynn went there; most of the houses are in ruins. But to sit on the broken walls of just such a cabin as he describes, still with its 'little screen of scrub alders', is to share some of the excitement he felt at coming across this remnant. Cark Mountain is the sort of place you might hope to find such a man, with its sense of being miles from anywhere; it even defeated St Patrick. There is an old story that after he visited Mullinashee (at Ballyshannon, the mound where Allingham's ashes are buried), he headed north, and at the top of Cark Mountain the axle of his chariot broke; it was mended, and broke again. St Patrick gave up and headed back east, prophesying the birth of Columcille, who would look after the north for him.

On his first visit to the *shanachy*, James Kelly, Gwynn had taken down some verses of a song. An Irish scholar identified these with some verses printed in Charlotte Brooke's *Reliques of Irish Poetry*.[57] On Gwynn's second visit he showed this similarity to Kelly, but

> the old man was of another mind. 'It's the same song,' he said, 'sure enough, but there's things changed in it, and I know rightly about them. Some one was giving it the way it would be easier to understand, leaving out the old hard words. And I did that myself once or twice the last day you were here, and I was vexed after, when I would be thinking about it.'
>
> Here then was a type of the Irish illiterate. A man somewhere between fifty and sixty, at a guess; of middle height, spare and well-knit, high-nosed, fine-featured, keen-eyed; standing there on his own ground, courteous and even respectful, yet consciously a scholar . . . one who could recite without apparent effort long narrative poems in a dead literary dialect.

INISHOWEN – DERRY

Inishowen – *Innis, Inish*, 'island' – has the feel of an island, and forms the farthest north-east part of Donegal, a peninsula between Lough Swilly and Lough Foyle, above Londonderry/Derry. In it the two Irelands met, or at least co-existed – the 'natives' in the hills and glens, the settlers from eastern, Anglicized (or Scotticized) Ulster, on the lower and the seaside places. It is not as neat a division as that, but it has that kind of a feel, which makes it an ideal setting for Friel's *Translations*. (Burnfoot, another name with which his two characters struggle, is at the very beginning of the peninsula on its western side, near the border.) An example of these 'two Irelands' is at Fahan on Lough Swilly, not far from Burnfoot. Here, in the middle of the nineteenth century, William Alexander (1824–1911), later Archbishop (Primate) of Armagh, was the Protestant rector. In her life of him his daughter remarks: 'Beside the Rectory garden is the picturesque burying ground. The graves are scattered round the ruined chancel of the old church. . . . In that quiet graveyard are graves of very diverse interest. . . .'[58]

Fahan ['Fawn'] is, properly, Fahan Mura. The 'picturesque burying ground' is the site of an abbey founded by St Columcille, no less, and presided over by St Mura, or Murus. John Colgan (1592–1658), who was born in Muff, on the Lough Foyle side of the peninsula, insists that this abbey contained 'splendid relics of antiquity which were preserved until the arrival of the mad heretics who desecrated, demolished and plundered everything sacred. . .'.[59] St Mura's bell, from Fahan, eventually found itself in the Wallace Collection in London. Colgan was right about the dispersal. But the interesting question is: how much did William Alexander know about Colgan, or of Colgan's seventeenth-century indignation; how much did he know of the history of the ruin he could see from his rectory; and did he know that the Irish people around him would have known it, and would not have forgotten the fate of the 'picturesque' burying ground?

Alexander said that he had originally intended to be a poet; 'but a summons which I could not resist made me, to my surprise, a governor of the sanctuary and of the house of God. Yet even now, late in my troubled day, I look back to my former purpose.'[60] However, it is the verses of his wife, Cecil Frances Alexander, that are as well known as any lines in English, because she wrote, among other things, the hymns 'Once in royal David's city', 'All things bright and beautiful', and 'There is a green hill far away'; also a translation of 'St Patrick's Breastplate'.

One of her *Poems on Subjects in the Old Testament* – which Tennyson said he wished he had written himself – was also a favourite of Mark Twain (Samuel Clemens), as Miss Alexander relates:

The Burial of Moses, with its noble phrasing and majestic imagery, appealed strongly to Clemens, and he recited it with great power. The first stanza in particular always stirred him, and it stirred his hearers as well. . . .

With eyes half closed and chin lifted, a lighted cigar between his fingers, he would lose himself in the music of the stately lines:

> By Nebo's lonely mountain
>   On this side Jordan's wave,
> In a vale of the land of Moab
>   There lies a lonely grave.
> And no man knows that sepulchre
>   And no man saw it e'er,
> For the Angels of God upturned the sod
>   And laid the dead man there.

William Alexander and Mark Twain once met, while receiving honorary degrees at Oxford: 'They exchanged a few words and passed

like ships in the night, and never knew of the strange bond between
them. . . .'

West of Inishowen, in the waters of Lough Swilly ('Lake of
Shadows'), below Rathmullen, there took place one of the gravest
events in Irish history, the 'Flight of the Earls'. In 1607 the greatest
of the chieftains of Ulster realized that the game was up, the English
meant to suppress the old Gaelic life at any cost, and their only
recourse was to seek help, or at least exile, in Catholic Europe. 'Red
Hugh' O'Donnell had already gone, to die of poison in Spain. Now
even 'The Great O'Neill', Earl of Tyrone, who had come near to
making himself independent king of Ulster, at last despaired. No one
is sure of the reason for this sudden collapse of hope, but it was
the end of a chance of a Gaelic Ireland. The *Annals of the Four Masters*
lists those who boarded the ship on Lough Swilly:

> They took with them the Earl O'Neill (Hugh, son of Feodorcha)
> and the Earl O'Donnell, with his year-old son, and a great
> number of the chieftains of the province of Ulster. . . . This
> was a distinguished crew for one ship; for it is indeed certain
> that the sea had not supported, and the winds had not wafted
> from Ireland, in modern times, a party of one ship who would
> have been more illustrious and noble, in point of genealogy,
> or more renowned for deeds, valour, prowess, or high achieve-
> ment, than they if God had permitted them to remain in their
> patrimonies until their children should have reached the age of
> manhood. Woe to the heart that meditated, woe to the mind
> that conceived, woe to the council that decided on, the project
> of their setting out on this voyage, without knowing whether
> they should ever return to their native principalities or patri-
> monies to the end of the world.

Sir John Davies (1569–1626), solicitor-general and attorney-general
for Ireland from 1603, and author of 'Orchestra, a Poeme of Daun-
cing' (1596), saw it differently: 'As for us that are here, we are glad
to see the day wherein the countenance and majesty of the law and
civil government hath banished Tyrone out of Ireland, which the best
army in Europe, and the expense of two million of sterling pounds,
had not been able to bring to pass.'
    There was no doubt in Irish minds of the finality of this famous
'Flight'. *Bards of the Gael and the Gall*,[61] one of the first and most
influential collections from the Irish, translates a contemporary
lament. The poet knows that this event fatally affects the whole

of Ulster from (Cuchulainn's) Emain, near Armagh, to (Allingham's) Assaroe in the far west of Donegal, near Ballyshannon. The hope for a Catholic, Gaelic Ulster is at an end:

> Great the hardship! great the grief!
> Ulster wails Tirconaill's Chief,
> From Emain west to Assaroe
> Wails gallant, gentle, generous Hugh.
>
> Children's joy no more rejoices,
> Fetters silence Song's sweet voices,
> Change upon our chiefs, alas!
> Bare the altar, banned the Mass. . . .

Derry,[62] 'Daire', means 'oak-wood'. According to twelfth-century manuscripts, 'Many wonders and miracles did God work for Colum Cille in Derry. And because he loved that city greatly Colum said: "This is why I love Derry, it is so calm and bright; for it is full of white angels from one end to the other." '[63]

> Derry mine! my small oakgrove,
> Little cell, my home, my love!
> O thou Lord of lasting life,
> Woe to him who brings it strife![64]

Derry saw much strife; it was burned down many times, captured by the English in 1600, was again burned down during an insurrection. In 1608, James I gave a charter to the London Companies to rebuild it and it thus became London-derry. 'The inhabitants were Protestants, Anglosaxons. They were indeed not all of one county or of one church; but Englishmen and Scotchmen, Episcopalians, and Presbyterians, seem generally to have lived together in friendship, a friendship which is sufficiently explained by their common antipathy to the Irish race and to the Popish religion. . . .' So Thomas Babington Macaulay, in his *History of England*.[65] His account of the Siege of Londonderry became as much a part of English patriotic lore as the Flight of the Earls, and the Flight of the Wild Geese after the Siege of Limerick (when the Irish went to France to fight against England from there), are a part of Irish legend.

When James II tried to re-Catholicize Ulster in 1688, it was natural that the Londonderry Macaulay describes became alarmed: 'It was known that the aboriginal peasantry of the neighbourhood were laying in pikes and knives. . . . A regiment of 1200 Papists commanded by a Papist, Alexander MacDonnell, laid siege to it, a famous siege, that lasted a hundred and five days.' Macaulay's language is magnificent; the eloquence of his bias – heroism of the Protestants besieged, barbarism and total wrong-headedness of the papist besiegers – must have shaped generations of English, and Ulster, minds, in their attitude to the problems of the Province. It is a stirring tale of the triumph of virtue, but first he describes the sufferings inside the town:

> One of the gates was beaten in: one of the bastions was laid in ruins; but the breaches made by day were repaired by night with indefatigable activity. Every attack was still repelled. But the fighting men of the garrison were so much exhausted that they could scarcely keep their legs. . . . The people perished so fast that it was impossible for the survivors to perform the rites of sepulture. There was scarcely a cellar in which some corpse was not decaying. Such was the extremity of distress, that the rats who came to feast in those hideous dens were eagerly hunted and greedily devoured.

Mrs Alexander's 'The Siege of Derry' sees the surrounding Irish, 'fearful as a locust band, and countless as the stars'; they shoot their capitulation terms into the city wrapped round a cannon-ball:[66]

> They were soft words that they spoke, how we need not fear
>   their yoke,
> And they pleaded by our homesteads, and by our children small,
> And our women fair and tender, but we answered: 'No
>   surrender!'
> And we called on God Almighty, and we went to man the
>   wall.

Those words, taken from the Siege, 'No surrender!' are still scrawled on the city walls, and on those of Belfast; they are seen as often as the newer Protestant slogan, 'Ulster says No!'

A brave supply ship breaks through the boom across Lough Foyle, and rescue is at hand. Macaulay describes the town after it was at last relieved:

> There was little sleep on either side of the wall. The bonfires shone bright along the whole circuit of ramparts. The Irish guns continued to roar all night; and all night the bells of the rescued city made answer to the Irish guns with a peal of joyous defiance. Through the three following days the batteries of the enemy

continued to play. But, on the third night, flames were seen arising from the camp; and, when the first of August dawned, a line of smoking ruins marked the site lately occupied by the huts of the besiegers; and the citizens saw far off the long column of pikes and standards retreating up the left bank of the Foyle towards Strabane.

So ended this great siege, the most memorable in the annals of the British Isles.

Presiding over the continuing violence (and the peace), over the two shining sea-loughs, Swilly and Foyle, as well as over the tensions of Londonderry (or Derry, the two names are part of the quarrel), is Grianan Aileach, like a stone coronet on its high green hill.[67] Two thousand years old, restored in the 1870s, it is the most spectacular and least celebrated of Ireland's ancient royal places: perhaps because – unlike Tara or Emain/Navan or Cruachan/Rathcrogan – there is something actually to be seen there. The city of Derry may owe its existence to the fort. Columcille is said to have founded his first monastery there because he wanted to be under its protection. Grianan Aileach had been deserted for five hundred years by the time of the famous Siege of 1689.

Present-day poets, born in the city so long after, appalled, make what sense they can of these continuing antagonisms, whichever 'side' they find that birth and history seems to have placed them.

Seamus Deane (b. 1940) begins his poem, 'Derry':[68]

> The unemployment in our bones
> Erupting in our hands like stones;
>
> The thought of violence a relief,
> The act of violence a grief;
>
> Our bitterness and love
> Hand in glove. . . .

James Simmons could be thought to underestimate more ancient sufferings, but his title gives recent history, and one of its slogans, a reasonable twist:

> *Ulster says Yes*
>
> One Protestant Ulsterman
> wants to confess this:
> we frightened you Catholics, we gerrymandered,
> we applied injustice.

However, we weren't Nazis or Yanks,
so measure your fuss
who never suffered like Jews or Blacks,
not here, with us;

but, since we didn't reform ourselves,
since we had to be caught
red-handed, justice is something
we have to be taught.

That reference in the 'caught red-handed' is to the mythological, armorial badge of the Province, the Red Hand of Ulster.[69]

4

THE SOUTH AND CENTRE

Wexford – Waterford – east Cork

Beginning at the nearest landing-place from Wales for this part of Ireland, Wexford was the birthplace of Thomas Moore's mother – which may seem a distant literary connection, but the poet Tom Moore (1779–1852)[1] was perhaps the most famous literary lion of his time: Wexford still regrets that his mother removed to Dublin in order to give birth to him. In 1835 Moore went to see his mother's house in Wexford and a crowd immediately gathered. 'While I was looking at this locality, a few persons had begun to collect around me and some old women (entering into my feelings) ran before me as to the wretched house I was in search of (which is now a small pot-house), crying out, "Here, Sir, is the very house where your *grandmother* lived. Lord be merciful to her!" Of the grandmother I have no knowledge . . .' but, he adds in his Diary, he remembers that his mother, 'one of the noblest-minded as well as the most warm-hearted of all God's creatures, was born under this lowly roof'. The house is still a 'pot-house' – a pleasant raftered pub now called the Thomas Moore; the words about his mother are recorded on a plaque in its wall.[2]

Oscar Wilde's mother ('Speranza')[3] also came from Wexford. Jane Francesca Elgee, later Lady Wilde (*c.* 1824–96), was born near the Thomas Moore, in a vicarage by the Bull Ring (it is now part of White's Hotel). As 'Speranza' she was one of the most vehement contributors of nationalist verse to *The Nation*, mouthpiece of the Young Ireland movement. Her stuff is rousing:

> There's a proud array of soldiers – what do they round your
> door?
> 'They guard our masters' granaries from the thin hands of the
> poor.'
> Pale mothers, wherefore weeping? – 'Would to God that we
> were dead –
> Our children swoon before us, and we cannot give them
> bread. . . .'

This is more in the spirit of nineteenth-century Irish nationalism than the ballads of Tom Moore.

There is in some quarters a grudging attitude to the English success of genial, generous Moore. He, however, always believed he was advancing the cause of Ireland with his ballads, sung in the fashionable drawing-rooms of London. In print his verses can sometimes sound thin, but set to the Irish airs he borrowed for them they can be irresistible, as anyone who has heard the recording of John McCormack singing 'Oft, in the stilly night' would agree. The best of them carry their own music:

> At the mid hour of night, when stars are weeping, I fly
> To the lone vale we loved, when life shone warm in thine eye;
> And I think oft, if spirits can steal from the regions of air,
> To revisit past scenes of delight, thou wilt come to me there,
> And tell me our love is remembered, even in the sky. . . .

Of Moore's popularity in the Ireland of that time there can be no question. In his diary of 1835, when he was fifty-seven and at the height of his fame, he describes how, after he had been dragged to see his mother's house in Wexford, he drove to Bannow, a little further along the coast. It can only be described as a Triumphal Progress, preceded by a band playing his 'Irish Melodies'. We can follow his road still, a quiet, country one, and it can never have been as crowded as it was on that noisy August day:

> We came in sight of the great multitude – chiefly on foot, but as we passed along we found numbers of carriages of different kinds, filled with ladies, drawn up on each side of the road, which, after we had passed them, fell into the line and followed in procession. When we arrived at the first triumphal arch, there was the decorated car and my Nine Muses, some of them remarkably pretty girls, particularly the one who placed the crown on my head; and after we had proceeded a little way, seeing how much they were pressed by the crowd, I made her and two of her companions get up on the car behind me. . . .
>
> As we proceeded slowly along, I said to my pretty Muse, 'This is a long journey for you.' 'Oh, Sir,' she exclaimed, with a sweetness and kindness of look not to be found in more artificial life, 'I wish it was more than three hundred miles.'

It was to prove a long two days for Tom Moore. There were addresses from the local people, in this vein: 'Sir, No sooner was it known that you were coming among us, than all was instant and electric gladness. You saw as you approached our confines the Reaper fling aside his sickle. . . . If we must give utterance at an early day to the withering word Farewell – Leave with us – Bard, Scholar, Gentleman, Historian, Patriot, Friend! – Leave with us the assurance that it will not be for ever. . . .'

But Moore was not the darling of London for nothing. He soon caught the tone: 'Went through my reception of the various addresses very successfully, (as Boyse [his host] told me afterwards), spoke much louder and less *Englishly* than I did the day before. I find that the English accent (which I always had, by the by, never having, at any time in my life, spoken with much brogue) is not liked by the genuine Pats.' Then he joined enthusiastically in the dancing, but tore himself away, and went, or tried to go, for a solitary walk by the sea, 'but with my usual confusion as to localities, I missed the right way . . . felt now rather inclined to anathematize, having seldom ever thirsted more keenly for actual beverage than I did at that moment for a draught of the fresh sea air'.

Bannow is a curious place. The old settlement has been almost entirely covered by sand, no one seems to know quite when. About the new replacement Bannow nearby, Halls' *Ireland* (1841) is eloquent. Mrs Hall (1800–81), whose husband collaborated with her on that vast three-volume work, had spent her childhood there, and laments the changes: 'The good priest, who guarded every protestant of the parish during "the troubles", so that no drop of blood was shed there – gone! the rector and his stately wife and smiling lovely daughters – gone! . . . But the people – what quaint, amusing people they were; how they used to pour out their troubles, and enlarge upon their plans!'[4] The Halls were Irish-born and sympathetic to Ireland, but Anglicized and writing for English readers: the well-meaning condescension of that last sentence is typical of the period.

The idea of the comic Irishman was already ingrained, and it is to Thomas Moore's credit that he both played up to it (as 'Tom' Moore, familiarly) and yet somehow altered it. He could play the fool, play the piano, and also play the gentleman. He probably dearly loved a lord, and his delight in his own success is endearing, but he was made indignant by suggestions that he had succumbed to the English gentry (and any Irishman, successful in England, has to watch his back in this respect). When he hears an American Southerner proclaiming the value of slavery to the poet Samuel Rogers, on the grounds that 'the highest *gentlemen* are to be found in the Slave States', and Rogers argues this is disproved by the gentlemen of England, who have no slaves, Moore comments: '. . . but certainly almost all free nations had such victims to whet their noble spirits upon and keep them in good humour with themselves . . . the Spartans their Helots, the Romans their *Servi*, and the English, till of late, their Catholic Irish.'

Not far from Wexford, there are traces of the Ireland Moore felt himself to represent, and from which he had escaped. The old, bardic tradition lingered on in remote places, doubtless attenuated, but still with life in it, and its representatives are still honoured now.

Along the main road south-west, near Kilmacthomas, inside the graveyard gate at Newtown, is the gravestone, proudly inscribed in Latin and Irish, of 'Denis MacNamara the Red', Donnachdh Ruadh ['Dunnaha Rua'] Mac Con Mara (1715–1810), a jaunty, roistering poet, at least in his early days. What is remarkable about him, and others, at the fag-end of a tradition, is how learned and well-travelled they were. MacNamara certainly went to Newfoundland, 'the Land of Fish', as did many Catholics emigrating from that part of Ireland, and his most famous song, 'The Fair Hills of Ireland', was probably written (in Irish) in America. He composed a long and graceful epitaph in Latin for his fellow poet, Teague O'Sullivan (Tadhg Gaedhealach ['Tyghe Gaeloch'] Ó Súilleabháin) (d. 1795), which stands, carefully renewed, in the old graveyard at Ballylaneen (south of the main road); translated it begins:

> This is the grave of a Poet, O Wanderer glance here in sorrow,
> Famous he was and beloved, weeds shade him now and grey
>   dust. . . .

MacNamara was also memorialized in English, and his fame exaggerated, in the *Freeman's Journal*: 'Oct 6, 1810, at Newtown, near Kilmacthomas, in the 95th year of his age, Denis MacNamara, commonly known by the name Ruadh, or Red-haired, the most celebrated of the modern bards. His compositions will be received and read until the end of time with rapturous admiration and enthusiastic applause.'[5]

The point of these Irish poets, who were scattered all over Ireland, is that they remembered an older culture, and for that are remembered in their turn (as plaques, restored tombstones and signposts attest). Stephen Gwynn in *The Fair Hills of Ireland* (1906) remembers MacNamara, as 'last of the line of these Munster poets, part scholars, part pedants, part men of genius, Bohemians in the heart of rural life, often drunken, often in trouble with the priests, yet always loyal to the faith of nationalism – who, perhaps more than any other force, kept heart and brain alive in the enslaved Catholic peasantry'.[6]

Francis MacManus (1909–65) remembered MacNamara in a trilogy of novels, which has MacNamara at its centre (see below, at Ballymacoda). Brendan Behan (1923–64) remembered the subject of the epitaph, MacNamara's friend Teague O'Sullivan, a devout writer whose *Pious Miscellany* was reprinted many times. Like the outlawed priests who would say Mass on a flat rock in some secluded spot, these poets of the seventeenth and eighteenth centuries kept up a sense of nationhood. Behan said his own simple Catholicism 'went back to the Mass Rock and the poems of [Teague] O'Sullivan, not to the pious intellectualism of Newman and his ilk'.[7]

The Binding or Knot – the summing-up verse – at the end of O'Sullivan's 'Poem to the Heart of Jesus' gives some idea of his power, even in translation:[8]

O Heavenly Monarch, how sorely thy thoughts did ache
When You wandered amongst us, and watched us forsake, forsake –
You never would boast, my Christ, that the spear would break
A way to Thy heart for the whole wide world to take.

It is not as a poet that Sir Walter Ralegh (1554?–1618)[9] is remembered at Youghal ['Yawel'], further along the south coast and into County Cork, but as an 'Undertaker', part of the Elizabethan plantation of Munster. Eventually, Queen Elizabeth granted him forty thousand acres of confiscated land. One of his houses, Myrtle Grove, with the yew trees he is said to have sat under, still stands in Youghal, next to the church below the battlements.

Ralegh was probably too busy making his way to give much thought to Ireland, except in terms of pacifying it. The generally accepted method of bringing this about was simple: starvation. In a macabre sense Ralegh could be said eventually to have helped towards this. He introduced the potato (it was once thought that he planted the first one in his garden at Youghal). It was subsequent Irish reliance on the potato that made the Great Famines of the mid-nineteenth century so devastating.

On his first tour of duty in Ireland (1580) Ralegh was very much the swashbuckling Devonian: on the ford below Midleton (on the

Youghal-Cork road) holding twenty ambushers at bay, single-handed, in order to rescue a friend unhorsed in the river, until reinforcements arrived.[10] He also took part in the infamous massacre at Smerwick in Kerry. Clearly, he was courageous and willing to do the State's dirty work without flinching. This found him favour with the Queen.

When Munster was finally subdued and devastated, its lands formally confiscated by the crown (in 1586), Ralegh's forty thousand acres, which was three times the usual grant, included the fertile Blackwater valley between Youghal and Lismore. He returned (now Sir Walter) to these estates in 1588–9, which was the occasion of his visit to Edmund Spenser. Probably even then he knew that his fortunes, his favour with the Queen, were on the wane. He makes no specific mention of Ireland in his poems (unlike Spenser, whose *Faerie Queene* is filled with the sights and sounds, the rivers and hills, of east Cork), but Ralegh's poems, more abstract, are full of a wordly-wise regret:

> Like truthless dreams, so are my joys expired
> And past return are all my dandled days:
> My love misled, and fancy quite retired,
> Of all which past, the sorrow only stays. . . .

A little to the west of Youghal – 'It would not be easy to find a quieter, more hidden, more forgotten countryside than that which stretches slowly along the sea between Youghal harbour and Cork harbour'[11] – we come across another English Elizabethan connection, and stub our toe also, once more, on Bardic Ireland.

The *Shell Guide* (1962) vents its fury on the state of Kilcredan church: 'callously unroofed by the church authorities in the nineteenth century, thereby exposing and wrecking two fine Renaissance monuments, one of them the tomb of Sir Robert Tynte; one of the weepers was an effigy of his second wife, widow of the poet Edmund Spenser'.[12] It would have been interesting to know what she looked like; the 'weepers', the kneeling figures round the tomb, are headless (though they do now have a lean-to roof over them). But the church is also interesting for another reason. It was here, more than a hundred years later, and past those kneeling figures, that there came an underground leader of the resistance to all that people like Ralegh and Spenser wanted to bring about in Ireland, Pierce Fitzgerald (Piaras Mac Gearailt, 1700–91), who signed his letters 'Chief Poet

of Munster'. He came to the church to convert (or as the Irish called
it 'pervert') to Protestantism, in order to keep what little land was
left to him:[13]

> O gossip, O friend, O Barry, most cultured in behaviour,
> 'Tis sad for me to cling to Calvin or perverse Luther,
> But the weeping of my children, the spoiling them of flocks
>   and land,
> Brought streaming floods from my eyes and descent of tears.

His 'Characteristics of the Blessed Virgin' is a litany, and begins
with a prose note: 'There is a part of the Saxon, Lutheran religion
which, though not from choice, I have accepted, which I do not
like – that never a petition is addressed to Mary, the Mother of
Christ, nor honour, nor privileges, nor prayers, and yet it is my opinion that it is Mary who is –' (and he begins his litany) 'Tree of
lights and crystal of Christianity/The sunny chamber in the house
of Glory', and so on. He ends on an entirely Irish note: 'Flood of
Graces and Clíona's Wave of Mercy'.

It must have been one of the bitter pleasures of the 'hidden Ireland',
the way the Gael could elude the Gall (foreigner), by such a quick
reference to his own culture. 'Clíona's Wave' was one of the Great
Waves of Irish mythology. They answered, by roaring, when they
heard the moaning of Conchobar's magic shield, signalling that he
was in trouble and one of the Waves was bringing its powers to
his aid. Clíona's Wave was particularly associated with west Cork,
with Glandore and/or Rosscarbery Bay. Also, Clíona (Irish *Cliodhna*)
was a Celtic goddess of beauty; so with one word Fitzgerald is
appropriating the Blessed Virgin for Ireland, and connecting her with
Ireland's pagan past.

What had they been like, the Bardic Schools of which these men
made up the tattered memory?

> Poetry was an hereditary profession, and the students gathered
> in some remote place far from the resort of people, and worked
> in a large structure divided up into cubicles each furnished with
> a bed, lying upon which in complete darkness they composed
> their poems on themes set by the master. The poem composed,
> lights were brought and they wrote it down and presented it
> to the masters for criticism in the main place of assembly. For
> week-ends and holidays they were entertained by the gentlemen
> and rich farmers of the neighbourhood, who also provided the

provisions for the subsistence of the school. They worked only from Michaelmas to the first of March. . . .[14]

This account came from 'a Tipperary man who haunted Lord Harley's library in the 1720s'. The full course lasted six or seven years, 'which you will the less admire upon considering the great difficulty of the Art, the many kinds of their Poems, the Exactness and Nicety to be observed in each, which was necessary to render their numbers soft, and the Harmony agreeable and pleasing to the Ear'.[15]

Pierce Fitzgerald clearly tried to maintain some remnant of this discipline: 'As chief poet his way was to gather the singers from both sides of the Blackwater to his house twice in the year; and for fifty years he is thought to have presided over these meetings, his Staff of Office – *Bata na Bachaille* – in his right hand.'[16] Fitzgerald's house is still there – the one he saved for his family by turning Protestant – a dignified eighteenth-century building just outside Ballymacoda, set back from the road on an eminence, looking towards the Knock-mealdown Mountains across Youghal Bay.

Francis MacManus put all these poets into his trilogy of novels about MacNamara, and in the last volume of it, *Men Withering* (1939), an account of extreme old age, seen from the inside, he has Mac-Namara remember them himself:

> He found himself talking, not about the living and the dead, but of the passing of the poets and of the petty rhymers left in their stead. He thought – but the words were really lost in the flickering and guttering of his voice – that he was saying clearly: 'Isn't it a woeful night for us when there's no poet living fit to mourn in verse the man whose house was burned in a great burning and who died at the building?'
>
> 'I knew the poets. You, you have only the stories. I knew Seán O Tuama with his tavern; and I knew Piaras Mac Gearailt who had high blood in his veins; and Piaras lost his land and saved a patch by turning heretic. . . .' He winced. If Piaras had swopped a religion for a religion, had not he himself done likewise? Had he not tried to be a heretic with a heart that would not be still?
>
> The twinge that passed through his soul like the stab of an aching tooth left him hot for a second, and he lifted his voice to quell an old lurking memory. 'And I knew Tadhg; Tadhg who was my friend, and he's gone after the rest. And I, Don-nacha Ruadh Mac Conmara, an old bag of dry feeble bones, await my turn.'[17]

How good were these poets? If we have no Irish we have to take them on trust. But to know of their existence is to feel a pulse beneath the skin of Ireland. They may have had much to complain of, but complain they certainly did, and they overglorified the past. This can become irritating to Irish, as well as to English, ears. Frank O'Connor, for example, one of the best and most accessible translators of Irish poetry, dismisses nearly all of it, except that written in the far west, in Connaught, 'because that was rooted in the lives of the common people. . . . In Munster the old world died in its sleep . . . their thought is so much of the dead old world that it is as though a veil has fallen between them and reality. When they speak in English they are slaves: whining, cadging, labouring men, but behind the barrier of their own language they move with their heads in clouds of romanticism.'[18] A fine translator of the next generation, the poet Thomas Kinsella, would not agree.[19] But older writers like Frank O'Connor were raw with desperation for the new Ireland, wanted to cleanse it of self-pity. Their task was the sorting of the worthwhile from what was merely fantasy and resentment.

In 1734 the gentle philosopher George Berkeley (1685–1753),[20] an Irishman himself, was appointed to the bishopric of Cloyne. Berkeley was an 'Idealist', as opposed to the 'Materialist' philosophers of England, or at least that is how W.B. Yeats understood him. As it was the materialist cast of the English mind that put it so much in conflict with the different cast of the Irish mind (as he saw it), Yeats tried to turn Berkeley into a representative Irish figure, and attempted to rebuild a culture partly on his shoulders. In 1925 he made a speech to the Irish Literary Society:

> It is impossible to consider any modern or philosophical or political question without being influenced knowingly or unknowingly by movements of thought that originated with Berkeley, who founded the Trinity College Philosophical Society, or with Burke, who founded the Historical. . . .
> In Gaelic literature we have something that the English-speaking countries have never possessed – a great folk literature. We have in Berkeley and in Burke a philosophy on which it is possible to base the whole life of a nation. That, too, is something which England, great as she is in modern scientific thought and every kind of literature, has not, I think.
> Feed the immature imagination upon that old folk life, and the mature intellect upon Berkeley and the great modern idealist

philosophy created by his influence upon Burke, who restored
to political thought its sense of history, and Ireland is re-born,
potent, armed and wise. Berkeley proved that the world was
a vision, and Burke that the State was a tree, no mechanism
to be pulled to pieces and put up again, but an oak tree that
had grown through centuries.[21]

Apart from the cast of Berkeley's mind, which maintained that
religious faith was more a matter of feeling and of attitude than of
reason, it is easy to see how Berkeley's consideration of the state of
Ireland (together with his simple prose style) should make him a father
figure for people like Yeats:

132. Whether there be upon earth any Christian or civilized
     people so beggarly, wretched and destitute as the common
     Irish?
133. Whether, nevertheless, there is any other people whose
     wants may be more easily supplied from home?
134. Whether, if there was a wall of brass a thousand cubits
     high round this kingdom, our native might not nevertheless
     live cleanly and comfortably, till the land, and reap the fruits
     of it? . . .
176. Whether a nation might not be considered as a family?[22]

Cloyne is a pleasant little town, even though one of Berkeley's
English successors, not untypically, characterized it as 'a dirty Irish
village'; and Irish Berkeley sounds happy there: 'It was a region of
dreams and trifles of no consequence.' A magnificent alabaster effigy
of him now lies in his otherwise rather bare cathedral, its ancient
Round Tower opposite; Cloyne had long been a religious site.
   Berkeley was radical, even ecumenical, in his Anglicanism. He
agitated for Roman Catholics to be admitted to Trinity College,
Dublin, and part of his ecumenical argument makes an attractive
sister-piece to the complaints of Pierce Fitzgerald, who regretted that
in 'Saxon, Lutheran religion . . . never a petition is addressed to
Mary'. Berkeley, who presumably would not have enjoyed being
called a Lutheran, has a gently persuasive answer to such discomforts:
'In our liturgy divers prayers and hymns are omitted which are to
be found in theirs . . . what is retained they themselves approve
of. . . . May we therefore not argue with the papists so: There is
nothing in our worship which you cannot assent to, therefore you
may conform to us; but there are many things in yours which we
can by no means allow, therefore you must not expect that we can

join in your assemblies. . . .'[23] This suggests that he considered that Catholics could attend Anglican services as well as their own; perhaps in the hope that their attendance at their own would dwindle away. 'Ireland's Plato', as he has been called, ideally might have brought about the most significant union of all, that of religion. He and Pierce Fitzgerald, the reluctant 'convert', were neighbours, and it would be good to think of them discussing this, and to learn Berkeley's reaction to Fitzgerald's 'Clíona's Wave of Mercy'.

THE BLACKWATER VALLEY – NORTH-EAST CORK

At Youghal on the Blackwater estuary, the tidal river flows down from Cappoquin and Lismore. It is a rich valley, a favourite with English settlers, with Ascendancy houses and estates along its banks and on the cliffs that overhang it; 'each its neighbour's sentry', as George O'Brien (of Lismore) says of them.[24] Molly Keane, who lived near Cappoquin, calls it 'the gentry's valley'. It is lovingly described in her early 'Big House' novel, *Two Days in Aragon*: 'The river was lower now. Its mud banks wet, dark, pearly, the water and the willows parted till tomorrow, the green pallor of the spring night growing narrower every five minutes in the emptying river until it was only long and smooth as an old candle. Tall houses showed through their trees as white as geese.'[25]

Daniel O'Connell (1775–1847) stayed in one of these river-hanging houses, Dromana, which still stands (in reduced form), near Villierstown. It was during his Waterford campaign, in which the landlord candidate was unseated by an O'Connellite, marking the beginning of the most significant Irish political career of the nineteenth century. He writes excitedly to his wife (who was evidently a reader of novels; *Florence Macarthy* (1818) is one of the best of Lady Morgan's strongly pro-Irish romances):

19 June 1826

My own sweet Love,

Here I am at this lovely spot. I believe it is that which Lady Morgan makes the scene of many of the incidents in *Florence McCarthy*. It is really a beautiful situation. As to yesterday. . . . We breakfasted at Kilmacthomas, a town belonging to the Beresfords but the people belong to us. They came out to meet us with green boughs and such shouting you can have no idea of. I harangued them from the window of the inn, and we had

a good deal of laughing at the bloody Beresfords. Judge what
the popular feeling must be when in this, a Beresford town,
every man their tenant, we had such a reception. . . . We have,
I believe, completely triumphed, and I at present am convinced
we shall poll to the last man of these voters. . . .

I cannot tell you what a sweet spot this is. The tide rises
to a considerable distance away and gives this noble river a
most majestic appearance. Darling, I must give up poetic ideas
and tell you in plain prose that I do doat on you and your
children.[26]

At Cappoquin the river turns west to Lismore. Lismore Castle, once
Ralegh's, was sold, when his fortunes fell, to Richard Boyle, future
Earl of Cork; and in 1735 it passed to the Duke of Devonshire on
his marriage to a Boyle. The present castle was built by the designer
of the Crystal Palace (formerly gardener to the Dukes of Devonshire).
But a previous version of it has a claim to literary fame. 'In 1814,
during some interior alterations . . . the opening of a long built-up
passage or recess disclosed a wooden box containing Mss in loose
staves . . . much damaged by rats. These have ever since been known
as the "Book of Lismore" and it is, of course' – Standish Hayes
O'Grady feels impelled to point out – 'the property of the Dukes of
Devonshire.'[27]

It is known that Michael O'Clery, chief of the Four Masters,
transcribed from this codex, and in 1629 it was in the Franciscan
friary at Timoleague, near Kinsale, County Cork. How it came to
Lismore is unknown, but it is an example of how thin were the
threads of chance upon which the story of Ireland's past was hung.
The book is a treasure-trove of information: genealogies, hagio-
graphies, even vaudeville jokes (like the one about three penitents
who forsook the world and vowed silence. At the end of the first
year one remarked that it was a good life, at the end of the second
year one of his companions agreed with him, and at the end of the
next year the third man said that if they didn't keep quiet he was
going back to the world).

Above all it contains the stories which came to be known as the
'Colloquy of the Ancients'.[28] The son of the hero Finn MacCool
(Mac Cumhaill), Oisín, and other warriors of the ancient band, the
Fianna, now all about a hundred and fifty years old, meet St Patrick,
and he asks them what it was like in the old days, what sort of

man was Finn. He is given the now famous reply: 'Were but the brown leaf which the wood sheds from it gold – were but the white billows silver – Finn would have given it all away.' Patrick asks, therefore, how did they maintain themselves, who had so prodigally generous a master? and is given the answer: 'Truth was in our hearts, and strength was in our arms, and fulfilment in our tongues.' Patrick is delighted: 'Success and benediction attend thee, Cailte ['Keelte'],' Patrick said; 'this to me is a lightening of spirit and of mind; and now tell us another tale.' Thus encouraged, the Ancients take Patrick all over Ireland, giving him the lore of every glen and hill and rath; and the saint, clearly enjoying himself, is always eager for more. It is a courteous, highly detailed, historical and topographical conflation of the old and the new, the pagan with the Christian.

Standish Hayes O'Grady devotes a large part of his *Silva Gadelica* (1892) to translations from the Book of Lismore. O'Grady also enjoys himself in his Introduction to the *Silva*. His task is to make ancient Irish texts (after all, not long rediscovered) known to a wider public, but he cannot resist quoting the English Jesuit and martyr, Edmund Campion (1540–81)[29] on the subject of the Irish. In 1571 Campion published a politically hostile account of Ireland: 'I found a fragment of an epistle wherein a virtuous monk declareth that to him (travailing in Ulster) came a grave gentleman about Easter . . . the priest demanded him whether he were faultless in the sin of homicide? he answered that he never wist the matter to be heinous before; but being instructed thereof he confessed the murther of five.' O'Grady comments: 'Better for him he had tarried with the wild men that never harmed him, or in some of the lands which he visited after them; when he returned, his own highly civilized countrymen rewarded his John-Bullism with a degree higher than any he had taken at Oxford: in fact, on the 1st of December, 1581, they hanged and quartered him.'

From the seventh century on, Lismore was a religious centre, with a famous school that attracted scholars from all over the British Isles. This gives an opportunity to quote one of the most delightful of old Irish poems, thought to be by Mael Isu O Brolcan, the best-known religious poet of his day, who died on pilgrimage to Lismore in 1086. The novelist George Moore was impressed by the evidence of sexual activity in the poem and it inspired him to write *A Story-teller's Holiday* (1918);[30] but later scholars have shown that the priest in the poem was not addressing an old woman-love but his Psalter, as Frank O'Connor translates:

The Priest Rediscovers His Psalm-Book

How good to hear your voice again,
   Old Love, no longer young, but true,
As when in Ulster I grew up
   And we were bedmates, I and you.

When first they put us twain to bed,
   My love who speaks the tongue of Heaven,
I was a boy with no bad thoughts,
   A modest youth, and barely seven.

We wandered Ireland over then,
   Our souls and bodies free of blame,
My foolish face aglow with love,
   An idiot without fear of blame. . . .

You slept with four men after that,
   Yet never sinned in leaving me,
And now a virgin you return –
   I say but what all men can see. . . .

The novelist Elizabeth Bowen (1899–1973) lived in this part of County Cork, be-castled, fought-over, with its later Anglo-Irish towns. She knew the life of the Anglo-Irish gentry at first hand. She describes Mallow, a popular spa in the mid-eighteenth century; its absence of literary cultivation, of self-awareness:

Books, in Mallow, were heard of and even owned; they were the proper fittings of a gentleman's house. That their contents did much to aliment talk, I doubt. Opinion gave statements variety, colour, character; in a life lived at Mallow pace there was not much context for knowledge. Our self-consciousness asks for literature: Mallow was not self-conscious at this time. And what need to diversify hours that clattered past, like coaches over the stone roads from gate to gate? The Mallow gentry had no nostalgia, no wish to escape. . . . Meanwhile the Gaelic culture ran underground, with its ceaseless poetry of lament. (Gaelic was spoken in the kitchens and fields and in untouched country the settlers did not know.)

   It has taken the decline of the Anglo-Irish to open to them the poetry of regret: only dispossessed people know their land in the dark.[31]

There are two wall-plaques in Mallow which suggest a later respect for books, or at least for the literature of Irish Nationalism. One marks the birthplace of Canon Patrick Sheehan (1852–1913), whose many novels helped to give dignity to the cause. The other native-son commemorated is Thomas Davis (1814–1845),[32] founder of *The Nation* periodical, and one of the most influential spirits in the 'Young Ireland' movement, which called for separation from England, and therefore, inevitably, for the destruction of the Ireland of Bowen's ancestors.

Bowen talks of 'the ceaseless poetry of lament'. Not all disasters were man-made: in the 1740s Berkeley writes from nearby Cloyne, where pestilence has followed famine: 'The distress of the sick and poor is endless. The havoc of mankind in the Counties of Cork and adjacent places, hath been incredible. The nation will not recover this loss in a century. . . .'[33]

A hundred and fifty years before, Edmund Spenser (1552–99) witnessed the distresses of the people of Cork after the suppression of the Desmond rebellion in the 1580s, when Munster was laid waste. For which Spenser blames the Irish themselves:

> Out of every corner of the woods and glens they came creeping forth upon their hands, for their legs could not bear them; they looked like anatomies of death, they spake like ghosts crying out of their graves; they did eat of the dead carrions, happy were they if they could find them, yea, and one another soon after, insomuch as the very carcasses they spared not to scrape out of their graves; and if they found a plot of water-cresses or shamrocks, there they flocked as to a feast for the time, yet not able long to continue therewithal; that in short space there were none almost left, and a most populous and plentiful country suddenly made void of man or beast: yet sure in all that war, there perished not many by the sword, but all by the extremity of famine which they themselves had wrought.[34]

After some time in Ireland as an Elizabethan official, Spenser was granted 3,000 acres of Munster, in what is now the north of County Cork, north of Mallow and south of the Ballyhoura Mountains. His castle was called Kilcolman and his estate also included Doneraile and Doneraile Court. It was probably at Doneraile that he had his pleasant meeting with Walter Ralegh, and they read their poems to each other:

He piped, I sung; and, when he sung, I piped;
By change of turns, each making other merry;
Neither envýing other, nor envíed,
So pipéd we, until we both were weary.

Doneraile is likely to be where the two 'shepherds' – Spenser calls
Ralegh 'Shepherd of the Ocean'[35] – piped, because Spenser mentions
the 'Mulla', his name for the Awbeg river that runs through the
grounds of the Court (now a public park). In the same poem, 'Colin
Clout's Come Home Again', which is dedicated to Ralegh, he
describes how Ralegh

. . . gan to cast great liking to my lore,
And great disliking to my luckless lot:
That banished had my self, like wight forlore,
Into that waste where I was quite forgot . . .

From this it has been deduced, by Bowen and others, that Spenser
disliked Ireland. Sean O'Faolain, in *An Irish Journey*, does not care
whether he did or not:

I would not say that this countryside inspired him. I am not
much concerned whether or not this countryside gave anything
to him; all I care is that he gave a great deal to this land and
that as we drive over it, now, I see it under the imprint of
his mind.
    To-day is not a day of 'blustring stormes', or 'ever drizzling
raine upon the loft', of 'watry clouds' or 'flying heavens'; it is
rather a day of 'secret shadowes', and a 'murmuring winde
much like the sowne of summer bees'. In the sun stretch out
the 'thickest woods', north and south to the 'towring rocks that
reach unto the skie', and off, between, to County Waterford
in the east, to the great plateau that I see stretching not merely
to one horizon but to many horizons, until the last edge of
distance becomes drowned in the haze of its own replication.
One does not see Cork when one reads his poem. One may
well see his poem when one sees Cork, and find in it the excitement and dignity and sensuous beauty of his imagination of
it.[36]

Ralegh talked Spenser into accompanying him to London. There
Spenser read part of the *Faerie Queene* to Queen Elizabeth, who
granted him a pension which might have been larger, but is thought
to have been reduced by Lord Burghley, because it was 'a good
example too good to be given to a ballad-monger'.[37] Nothing else

came of his visit to the court and he returned to Ireland, to 'Arcady', to write 'Colin Clout's Come Home Again', with what sounds like relief. Rather than dislike the place, there are signs, in the *Faerie Queene* and elsewhere, that Ireland thrilled Spenser. He passed fifteen years at Kilcolman:

> And sure it is yet a most beautiful and sweet country as any is under Heaven, seamed throughout with many goodly rivers, replenished with all sorts of fish, most abundantly sprinkled with many sweet islands and goodly lakes, like little inland seas, that will carry even ships upon their waters, adorned with goodly woods fit for building of houses and ships, so commodiously, that if some princes in the world had them, they would soon hope to be lords of all the seas, and ere long of all the world; also full of good ports and havens opening upon England and Scotland, as inviting us to come to them, to see what excellent commodities that country can afford, besides the soil itself most fertile, fit to yield all kind of fruit that shall be committed thereunto. And lastly, the heavens most mild and temperate, though somewhat more moist than the part towards the West.[38]

Spenser was an Englishman of his time. He believed in the imposition of public order, of what he called 'civilitie', with any degree of rigour that was necessary. In Ireland he was of the opinion that order could only be imposed by de-Gaelicization, and he suggests ways of doing this in his *View of the Present State of Ireland*. But he is not the wholesale exterminator that Irish legend makes him. He finds much that is wrong with English administration. He admires the courage and horsemanship of Irish fighting men. He is even impressed by the zeal and devotion of the Jesuits. He took an interest in Irish poems:

> I have caused divers of them to be quoted unto me, that I might understand them, and surely they savoured of sweet wit and good invention, but skilled not of the goodly ornaments of Poetry; yet were they sprinkled with some pretty flowers of their own natural devyse, which gave good sense and comeliness unto them, the which it is a great pity to see so good an ornament abused, to the gracing of wickedness and vice, which would with good usage serve to beautify and adorn virtue.[39]

Robin Flower wonders what poems Spenser saw, and how they were Englished:

There are translations and translations. And we do not know
who served Spenser in this office. It is clear that the poems he
meant were bardic poems of the more formal sort extolling the
deeds of chiefs. Poems of our type [lyrics] perhaps never came
his way. Surely, if they had, he would have recognized a familiar
note in them. For these poems are witty and well-favoured in
a kind that was only being brought to perfection in Spenser's
own day.

> White hands of languorous grace,
> Fair feet of stately pace
> And snowy-shining knees –
> My love was made of these. . . . [40]

Spenser might well have enjoyed the anonymous fragment which
Flower translates; he wrote that sort of thing himself. He was probably married in Cork town, and his *Epithalamium* with its lovely
refrain, variations of 'That all the woods may echo and your answer
ring', surely refers to Irish woods:

> . . . Tell me ye merchants' daughters did ye see
> So fair a creature in your town before,
> So sweet, so lovely, and so mild as she,
> Adorned with beauty's grace and virtue's store;
> Her goodly eyes like sapphires shining bright,
> Her forehead ivory white,
> Her cheeks like apples which the sun hath rudded,
> Her lips like cherries charming men to bite,
> Her breast like to a bowl of cream uncrudded,
> Her paps like lyllies budded,
> Her snowy neck like to a marble tower,
> And all her body like a palace fair,
> Ascending up with many a stately stair
> To honour's seat and chastity's sweet bower.
>
> Why stand ye still ye virgins in amaze,
> Upon her so to gaze,
> Whiles ye forget your former lay to sing,
> To which the woods did answer and your echo ring. . . .

If what Spenser heard translated were bardic poems, extolling Irish
warlike deeds, he would be justified, as an English official, in thinking
they contained 'wickedness and vice'. He was in Arcady; he was also

in danger: 'He was not only living in an insecure part, on the very border of disaffection and disturbance, but like every Englishman living in Ireland, he was living amid ruins. An English home in Ireland, however fair, was a home on the side of Etna or Vesuvius; it stood where the lava flow had once passed, and upon not distant fires. . . .'[41]

Kilcolman Castle today does seem a 'fair' home. It is difficult to visit, because the lake beside it, now a marsh, has been turned into a bird sanctuary. Nevertheless, it can be reached, with difficulty, across fields, and signposts still point invitingly towards it. The tower is today perhaps much as it was when Spenser precipitately left it, when his worst fears were realized, and the Irish came down from the Ballyhoura Mountains to burn him out. Ben Jonson told Drummond of Hawthornden that a baby son of Spenser's died in the flames, but that is not certain. Spenser returned to London where, almost immediately, in 1599, he died.

It was a miserable end, to a fifteen-year sojourn, and left Kilcolman 'an intact shell, whose stairs you can still climb' in Elizabeth Bowen's phrase. There he wrote the greater part of the *Faerie Queene*, and it is not hard to imagine him doing so; from his little castle you can look out of his windows, see what he saw, seated on his stone window-seat.

Spenser evokes the landscape hereabouts, rather than describes it. Elizabeth Bowen[42] believes it ought to be first seen from an aeroplane: 'From the air you discover unknown reaches of river, chapels, schools, bridges, forlorn graveyards, interknit by a complex of travelled roads. . . . On Sundays you get an idea of the population: everybody appears. . . .'

Her account of the home of the Bowen family, *Bowen's Court*, is the history and texture of a corner of Ireland seen through generations of Ascendancy eyes, and through her own. She may want to fly over it, but even when back on the ground, her love for the place makes her again take flight:

> . . . there are marshy reaches trodden by cattle, fluttered over by poplars from the embanked lanes. Herons cross there in their leisurely flopping flight; water peppermint grows among the rushes; the orchids and yellow wild iris flower here at the beginning of June. Lonely stone bridges are come on round turns of the stream, and old keeps or watchtowers, called castles, command the valleys; some are so broken and weathered that they

look like rocks, some have been almost blotted out by the ivy; some are intact shells whose stairs you can still climb. . . .

She goes on to the landscape round Kilcolman Castle: 'The foot of the Ballyhouras is Faerie Queene country – dazzling, for all its woody shadows, and in its openness mysterious. You could not but love the Awbeg itself, even though it might flow through a hated land. It glitters with Spenser's gentler memories, and the flames of Kilcolman were never reflected there. It flows through woods and gardens, through water-meadows, under fantastic rocks into the gorge where it joins the Blackwater. . . .'

Elizabeth Bowen suggests that her Anglo-Irish forebears were too resistant to the Irish atmosphere. They were practical,

but nothing, during those years of their steady increase in property, gave the soul any chance to stand at its full height. . . .

At the same time, though one can be callous in Ireland one cannot be wholly opaque or material. . . . The light, the light-consumed distances, that air of intense existence about the empty country, the quick flux to decay in houses, cities and people, the great part played in society by the dead and by the idea of death and, above all, the recurring futilities of hope, all work for eternal against temporal things.

At the climax of the Anglo-Irish eighteenth-century prosperity and amenable forms of Reason had combined to attempt to deny sorrow and to make a social figure of God. The attempt failed, and decay was following it.

Bowen describes the village of Doneraile; its main street, 'wide, with colour-washed houses, starts uphill (as you enter from our direction) from the Awbeg bridge . . . near the bridge stands the urbane Protestant church. In the great days of the Doneraile neighbourhood the line of gentlemen's carriages outside this church used (they say) to be a mile long.' She does not mention that if you pass that way, from the Bowen's Court direction, you also pass, on the other side of a bridge, the house, now marked with a plaque, of Canon Patrick Sheehan (1852–1913), Catholic parish priest, and the novelist of what he would have been happy to call 'the carriage-less non-gentlemen'. Sheehan was parish priest of Doneraile from 1895 to his death. His novels were widely read; mostly, perhaps, by the people for whom they were intended. They can still be read with pleasure, not least *Glenanaar* (1905), which is set among the peasants of the Ballyhouras, the descendants of the men whom poor Spenser most feared. It concerns the 'Doneraile Conspiracy' of 1829, during which, says Bowen, 'four "attempts" were made on the lives of Doneraile gentlemen. Though there is now (and really was at the time) every reason to think that the shots were let off by footpads, it was felt immediately by the *élite* of Doneraile that the entire countryside was in arms and plotting to slay its betters.'

Before a packed jury in Cork, local men were condemned to death in batches, and were only saved from hanging by Daniel O'Connell after his epic night-long ride from his house at distant Derrynane in Kerry. His ride, and the flamboyant way he called for breakfast in court, and ate in his riding-clothes, is described in Sean O'Faolain's biography of O'Connell, *King of the Beggars*.

Glenanaar, a novel strongly constructed along Victorian lines, is a celebration of the local people, their contradictions, weaknesses and virtues (also their terrifyingly long memories of injustices). These were the people, Sheehan said, 'even the savage effects of Elizabethan and Cromwellian freebooters had failed to destroy'. You get some idea what Spenser was up against three hundred and fifty years before, and the Cromwellian Bowens fifty years after him. 'No Wordsworth has yet sung the praises of these Irish Dalesmen,' said Sheehan, and that is what he was trying to do.

A critic has said that he was strongest in character-drawing, 'but when Canon Sheehan the priest takes the pen away from Sheehan the novelist, characterisation begins to ring false'.[43] This is sometimes true, and perhaps inevitable, given his period and his intention. But, 'he is so good that one longs for him to be better'; and his popularity at the time is easy to understand. He was trying to explain the Irish to themselves, and he knew them well, if somewhat distantly, as a priest. He reflects on the mood that succeeded the 'Doneraile conspiracy':

Providence has balanced very lightly this airy Irish nature. It swings to a touch. Where heavier natures creep slowly up and down according to the weight of pressure of circumstances, the Celtic temperament leaps to the weight of a feather; and you have sullen depression, or irresistible gaiety, murderous disloyalty or more than feudal fealty, in swift and sudden alternation.

During these momentous trials, for instance, O'Connell thought it his duty to challenge a Protestant juror. It was reported that this man had said, after the convictions on the first trial, that there should be a gibbet at every cross-roads in the county. A wave of indignation swept over the minds of the people at this truculent, unscrupulous expression. But lo! a witness testifies that the words were used in quite a different sense, and were condemnatory of Crown methods of prosecution, and sympathetic with the prisoners. 'If this kind of thing is to go on,' he said, 'they might as well erect a gibbet at every cross-roads in the country.' Quite a different thing! And so Irish anger swept around and evaporated in a cloud of incense about the popular magistrate.

Sheehan's last novel, *The Graves at Kilmorna*, published in England in 1915, the year before the Easter Rising in Dublin, could be seen as positively seditious. Described as 'an attempt to set forth the spirit of the Fenian [ultra-nationalist] movement of 1867', it could only be interpreted as a positive attempt to rekindle it. The Fenians are seen as noble heroes, their opponents as brutes or ignoramuses, and the rebellious spirit of Ireland is described as in sad decline. It is a good, politically dangerous, book, and in view of what happened so shortly after its appearance there can be no doubt that Sheehan had an influence.

His bronze statue, complete with biretta and wire spectacles, stands outside the Catholic church in Doneraile, at the opposite end of the village from the 'urbane' Protestant one. It would be interesting to know what the inhabitants of Bowen's Court and their friends thought of him, or if they knew of him at all.

Bowen continues her almost entranced description of the neighbourhood of Bowen's Court, until she reaches her home village; and, almost modestly, the subject of her book. 'Passing straight through Kildorrery (on the road to Mallow) one drops downhill into Farahy. Tucked rather deeply into a crease of trees, this small place is unexpectedly come upon; here are a bridge over the small Farahy river, two or three shops, some yellow and pink cottages, the lower avenue gate-lodge of Bowen's Court, a Protestant rectory and a Protestant church.' Once there, she analyses the character of the house, room by room and entire: 'This is Bowen's Court as the past has left it – an isolated, partly unfinished house, grandly conceived and plainly and strongly built. Near the foot of the mountains, it has little between it and the bare fields that run up the mountainside. Larger in manner than in actual size, it stands up in Roman urbane strongness in a land on which the Romans never set foot. It is the negation of mystical Ireland: its bald walls rebut the surrounding, disturbing light.'

To Bowen's Court came, while she lived there, a long list of writers from England and America: Virginia Woolf (who called the house 'a great stone box'), Iris Murdoch, Carson McCullers, Rosamond Lehmann, Lord David Cecil; and Irish writers, like Sean O'Faolain. He admired her writing so much that he besought her to write about Ireland. Then he read her already published novel, *The Last September* (1929), and saw that it was entirely Irish – 'if that matters a damn. (We're so sick of hearing our *Nazionalists* ask for Irish literature – so thirsty for just literature.)'[44] But he feels the old class-divide. He tells her that when he was staying at another Big House he remembered his father, a constable in the Royal Irish Constabulary, who came from a small farm in the hills nearby. 'As we sat on the steps a man came sidling up with his hat in his hand, an old man with a drooping moustache. He might have been my father. The butler came out to fend him off from the lady of the house. The butler was possibly the old man's second cousin, and he might have been mine. I felt something turn over in my bowels to see the two men talk to each other in that way. . . .'

O'Faolain wanted her to write about these tensions in Ascendancy/native-Irish life; and in *Bowen's Court*, many years later and in her own way, she did. Bowen said in an interview: 'I regard myself as an Irish novelist. As long as I can remember I've been extremely conscious of being Irish. . . . I must say it's a highly disturbing emotion. It's not – I *must* emphasize – sentimentality.' She was forced to sell Bowen's Court to a neighbour in 1959, believing he would live in it, with his young family. Within a year it was demolished. Signposts in Farahy point to its 'site', but even the site is not easy to determine. She remarked that it had at least not lived to become a ruin. (She killed it, someone has said, 'as deliberately as if she had taken a beloved old pet to the vet to be put down'.)[45] She and her husband are buried outside the Protestant church at the garden-lodge gates.

Of nearby Mitchelstown the eighteenth-century English agronomist, Arthur Young,[46] was of the opinion that it had the amenities and spaciousness worthy of a capital city. This may be, or may have been, but compared to the hugger-mugger cosiness of its neighbour towns (like Mallow, or Tipperary) it has an un-Irish feel. There is a post-colonial atmosphere to the place, as though the English have imposed an abstract idea of a town on the Irish landscape, and the Irish have not yet been able to make themselves comfortable in it. This is a subjective impression, but one that might have been understood by Mary Wollstonecraft (1759–97), who went there as a governess to the children of Lord and Lady Kingsborough, in 1786. It was an unsuitable job, since she believed that 'there is not only more virtue, and most happiness, but even most true politeness, in the middle classes of life'. Author of *A Vindication of the Rights of Man* (1790) and of *A Vindication of the Rights of Woman* (1792), a sympathetic witness, at first hand, of the French Revolution, then the wife of the radical philosopher William Godwin, mother of Mary Godwin, who eloped with Shelley (and who wrote *Frankenstein*), Wollstonecraft later became a sort of holy terror to an Establishment badly rattled by the upheavals in France. Sermons were to be preached, in which Voltaire and Mrs Wollstonecraft Godwin 'were linked in infamy'. It was not surprising she did not last long at Mitchelstown.

After she had left, Bishop Percy (of the *Reliques*) spread it about that Mary had 'wanted to Discharge the Marriage Duties' with Lord Kingsborough. By the time Percy was spreading the gossip, at the height of English panic at the French Revolution, anything was useful that blackened the name of the dangerous radical Wollstonecraft. She was accused of having politically corrupted her aristocratic charges.

It seems that she was a good governess. Her older pupil, Margaret, later wrote: 'Almost the only person of superior merit with whom I had been intimate in my early days was an enthusiastic female who was my governess . . . for whom I felt an unbounded admiration because her mind appeared more noble and her understanding more cultivated than any others I had known.'[47]

Perhaps she did have an influence on Margaret, who had republican views, and abandoned her husband and children to live in Italy with her lover (where, in Pisa, she knew Shelley and his second wife, Mary Wollstonecraft's daughter). But Mary can have had little direct effect on a younger Kingsborough daughter who sensationally eloped, in 1797 (the year of Wollstonecraft's death), with the illegitimate half-brother of her mother. The young girl may not have known of this kinship, but her brother and her father did; they found them and murdered him. Conveniently, Kingsborough had just succeeded to the Earldom, so he elected to be tried by the Irish House of Lords, which acquitted him without a witness being called. It was about the last thing it did before it was abolished.

Elizabeth Bowen knew Mitchelstown Castle well, or rather, the castle that was built in its place. Kingsborough's son and successor (and his accomplice in the murder) tore down the Palladian mansion and built a sort of imitation Windsor Castle, intended for the reception of George IV, who never came. But the influences of radical Mary Wollstonecraft and her like had been burrowing for nearly fifty years, and his foundations at last gave way. There came a bye-election and his tenants did the unthinkable: they disobeyed his instructions and voted his candidate out. Bowen makes a dramatic scene from what followed (she calls him 'Big George'):

> 'You are hiding something from me,' he said, looking round at his friends. . . . He was on the road back to Mitchelstown all that night.
>
> By next night, his tenants from all three counties had been immediately summoned into his presence. They did not disobey: they came. Big George sat on a dais at the far end of the hundred-foot-long castle gallery. As more and more tenants came pressing in at the door, the front of their crowd was pressed more and more up on him. Big George did not cease to cover the mobbed perspective of gallery with his eye. That eye of his, and his dreadful continued silence, renewed the domination of centuries. But they were here to hear him: he must speak. He did not: he took the alternative and went mad. Leaping out of his seat he threw his arms wide. '*They are come to tear me to pieces; they are come to tear me, to tear me to pieces!*' Forty-eight hours later he had been taken away. . . .
>
> It was democracy, facing him in his gallery, that sent Big George mad.

There was a last garden-party at Mitchelstown Castle, on the day the First World War broke out:

> That afternoon we walked up the Castle avenue, treated by the gusty sound of a band. The hosts of the party were the late Lady Kingston's second husband Mr Willie Webber, and his companion Miss Minnie Fairholme. . . . They received their guests indoors, at the far end of Big George's gallery.
>
> People only covertly made incursions into the chain of brocade saloons. Wind raced round the Castle terraces, naked under the Galtees; grit blew into the ices, the band clung with some trouble to its exposed place. The tremendous news certainly made that party, which might have been rather flat. Almost every

one said they wondered if they really ought to have come, but they *had* come – rightly: this was a time to gather. . . . The tension of months and years – outlying tension of Europe, inner tension of Ireland – broke in a spate of words.

Big George's castle was first occupied, then blown up, by the Republicans in 1922. Now a vast blue and white creamery stands in its place, almost as large, surely, as the castle must have been. Its facing stones were taken away to help in the building of the Trappist monastery at Mount Mellaray near Lismore. The creamery looms over an elegant little square (a Kingston legacy to the town) designed as a refuge for distressed Protestant gentlefolk, 'twelve gentlemen, and eighteen ladies'.

A lighter view of Mitchelstown Castle before its extinction comes from the infant Cyril Connolly:

> It was winter and there were icicles along the lake. I wore brown gloves on week-days and white ones on Sundays and held an icicle (the first I had seen) with its mysterious purposeful pointed whiteness, in my white glove.
>
> Of the rest of the visit I remember little. Lord Kingston descendant of Milton's Lycidas had long been dead, but my grandfather was there, terrifying. 'Where is grandpapa?' I asked my nurse one morning. 'He's busy.' 'What's he doing?' 'He's doing his duty.' This answer, which would have covered the activities of all Irish landlords at that date, I took to mean that he was in the lavatory ('have you done your duty today?'), and was more frightened of him than ever except when he would come in with his gun and a huge stiff dead grasshopper two feet long in his hand, waving it at me and saying 'snipe, snipe!'
>
> This was my first visit to Ireland since babyhood and besides the love of the beautiful, it awoke in me a new passion. I became a snob. . . .[48]

Tipperary – Limerick

Edmund Spenser was fascinated by the hills and rivers of this region: the Funcheon, the Awbeg, the Bregoge, and their tributary streams; the Ballyhoura Mountains, and the Galtees, with its commanding hill, Galtymore, which Spenser calls 'Arlo'. It forms one side of the Glen of Aherlow, between Mitchelstown and Tipperary.

For the rivers Spenser weaves mythologies, marrying them to each other, or having them betray each other, as though Munster is classical Arcadia, and in the *Faerie Queene* he sets his Judgement of the Gods firmly on 'Arlo', Galtymore:[49]

> Being of old the best and fairest Hill
> That was in all this holy island's heights . . .
> When Ireland flourishéd in fame
> Of wealth and goodness far above the rest
> Of all that bear the British island's name,
> The gods then used (for pleasure and for rest)
> Oft to resort thereto, which seemed them best. . . .

Ireland, therefore, the perfect place – but in the past. These hills have now been cursed (by Diana, because Faunus spied on her while she was bathing):

> Since which, those woods and all that goodly chase
> Doth to this day with wolves and thieves abound:
> Which too-too true that land's in-dwellers since have found.

The Glen of Aherlow was a hiding place for outlaws, for men on the run, or 'on their keeping' as the Irish phrase is. The historian and poet Geoffrey Keating (Séathrún Céitinn) (1580?–1650), a Doctor of Divinity from the University of Bordeaux, was forced to hide in the Glen when driven from his parish at Tubbrid because he had accused, in church, the President of Munster's mistress of adultery.

While he was 'on his keeping' he put together, in Irish, his *A Basis of Knowledge about Ireland* – sometimes called the *History of Ireland*. It has also been called 'an able but extravagantly mad performance', because he put into it everything he heard from other scholars, fantastic or not. He says himself he inserted matter into his history, 'not with any desire that it be believed, but only for the sake of order, and out of respect to some recording of the past'.[50]

> Keating's significance is other and greater than merely as a historian. He was contemporary with the Four Masters who like him gathered and digested all that they could find in the ancient records of their country. But they, the descendants of hereditary and professed historians, maintained the professional tradition of a deliberately archaic style, which scorned popular comprehension. Keating wrote for the people in the Irish which was spoken

by educated men of his day. He is the first classic of modern Irish prose.[51]

He is said to have been killed by a Cromwellian soldier in St Nicholas's church, Clonmel. He is buried at Tubbrid, on the other side of Galtymore, south of Cahir; signposted, like other Irish literary heroes, and with a plaque set in the wall of his ruined church.

The spirit of resistance continued in the Glen. Douglas Hyde translates a satire by John Macdonnel (d. 1754), on the death of Colonel Dawson of Aherlow, a local tyrant of the fields:[52]

Squeeze down on his bones, O ye stones, in your hall of clay.
Yon reeking, gore-sprinkled boar, old Dawson the grey.
Sheathed was his sword when the foeman called to the fray,
But he cheated and sold and slowly slaughtered his prey.

The town of Tipperary has a bronze statue of the novelist and Fenian, Charles Kickham (1828–82).[53] He is said originally to have held a bronze pen, but this, unlike Canon Sheehan's wire spectacles on his statue at Doneraile, seems to have gone missing. The statue was unveiled in 1897, in anticipation of the centenary of the 1798 Rising, by John O'Leary,[54] himself a Tipperary man, friend and mentor of the young W.B. Yeats – 'Romantic Ireland's dead and gone,/It's with O'Leary in the grave.'

An earlier 'Romantic' Ireland lies to the west of the town. Knockainey, the hill of Áine, the sun-goddess, came to be associated, in ways not entirely mysterious, with the Earl of Desmond, Earl Gerald (Gearoid Iarla), 'Gerald the Rhymer' (1338–98).[55] A Norman, a Fitzgerald, he wrote poems of courtly love, in Irish, 'in which the manner of European love-poetry met the manner of Irish tradition':[56]

Speak not ill of womankind,
'Tis no wisdom if you do,
You that fault in women find,
I would not be praised of you.

Sweetly speaking, witty, clear,
Tribe most lovely to my mind,
Blame of such I hate to hear.
Speak not ill of womankind.

Bloody treason, murderous act,
    Not by women were designed,
Bells o'erthrown nor churches sacked.
    Speak not ill of womankind. . . .

When the Norman Fitzgeralds became overlords of Munster they were quick to connect themselves to the power-source of Irish myth. Gerald's father, the first Earl, was called by his bard 'Aine's king', and the story was that he had surprised the sun-goddess bathing in Lough Gur, and she had borne him a son – Gerald the Rhymer. As a consequence, so many magical and fantastic stories became associated with the Rhymer that his achievements, both private and public – he was not only an elegant poet, he was twice Chief Justice of Ireland – have been swallowed up in fairy-tale. He is said to sleep on the bottom of the (admittedly 'atmospheric') Lough Gur, rising up every seven years to ride its waters until the silver shoes of his horse are worn out.

In *The Farm by Lough Gur*, by Mary Carbery, an account of Irish farm-life in the mid-nineteenth century, Gerald has by that time been reduced, more or less, to a local spook, and the goddess Aine has shrunk to a banshee, an Irish country portent. However, some traces of the ancient sun-worship lingered: 'After breakfast we children carried a large flat milk-pan into the sunshine on the kitchen floor, filled it with water and gently shaking it made the sun dance on the ceiling. We little knew that in keeping this Easter custom of Lough Gur, we were honouring the sun exactly as pagan sun-worshippers did a thousand years ago.'[57]

Further westward, skirting Limerick city, lies the village of Croom, associated with a famous murder and the writer who fictionalized it, Gerald Griffin (1803–40).[58] In 1819 the body of a young girl, her feet weighted with a rock, was washed up on the shores of the Shannon estuary. Her name was Ellen Hanley, sixteen years old, daughter of a small farmer, and already noted for her beauty – a 'colleen bawn' (literally 'white girl', probably best translated as a 'golden' one). She had gone through a form of marriage with the well-connected John Scanlon, of Ballycahane Castle, near Croom, who fled when her body was found. He was eventually discovered hiding in a hay barn at his family house (a casually prodding bayonet caused him to cry out) and was arrested. Daniel O'Connell was hired to defend him at his trial in Limerick, and it was generally believed that no member of the gentry would be convicted of the murder of a peasant girl. However, he was found guilty, and hanged at Limerick, as later was his boatman, Sullivan, who had killed the girl on his master's instructions, after drinking a bottle of whiskey.

Griffin's novel based on the murder, *The Collegians* (1829), was highly successful; made into a play, *The Colleen Bawn*, by Dion Boucicault (1820–1860), and an opera by Jules Benedict, *The Lily of Killarney*. It is considered one of the best of the classic Irish novels.[59] Tastes change, but the writing in *The Collegians* seems hectic. Hardress (Scanlon) finds a crowd round the girl's body recovered from the river. He rides madly back to the castle, nearly bursting his horse's lungs in his haste: 'The creature presented a spectacle calculated to excite the compassion of a practised attendant upon horses. His eyes were wide and full of fire – his nostrils expanded, and red as blood. His shining coat was wet from ear to flank, and corded by numberless veins that were now swollen to the utmost by the accelerated circulation. As he panted and snorted in his excitement, he scattered the flecks of foam over the dress of the attendant.' Two servants are disgusted at his treatment of the horse: 'Dawley turned away with a harsh grunt; the groom led out the heated steed upon the lawn, and Falvey returned to make the cutlery refulgent in the kitchen.'

The young poet Aubrey de Vere was so impressed by the book – although he loathed the vulgarity of the play and the opera that were made out of it – that he and his father offered Griffin rooms in their great house, Curragh Chase, near Limerick, to write in peace.[60] Griffin declined, preferring to remain in cramped circumstances with his brother at Pallaskenry, by the Shannon. Soon he turned against fiction-writing altogether, because he had doubts about its moral value. By all accounts an unusually charming and good-looking man, he gave up writing and took up teaching, becoming a Christian Brother, dying at the age of thirty-seven.

Griffin is remembered in Croom (a poem of his, on the next village, Adare, where he spent his childhood, is a local favourite); also John O'Twomey (Seán Ó Tuama) (1706–75), whose birthplace it is. As one of a group who guarded the old traditions, in 1754 O'Twomey sent out a 'school-call' to his fellow poets of Munster: they should meet to discuss ways of preserving the Irish language. That might still be safe in high or boggy places that nobody wanted, but the land round Croom was rich, and English-speaking incomers were taking it over. 'The little that still lives of the language will soon become nothing unless some way is found to foster it,' he said in his summons.

O'Twomey was an innkeeper in Croom, also in Limerick town, later reduced to keeping hens for an incoming woman whom he satirized in Irish. Perhaps the decline in his fortunes could be attributed to the invitation on his inn-sign:

> No landless wanderer of the noble Gael,
> No brother bard, no doughty heart, and game,
> Though for this time he lack the price of ale,
> But John O'Twomey welcomes all the same.

At all events, he died poor, according to Corkery's *Hidden Ireland*.[61] But then all Corkery's poets died in want, by his account. Very likely they did, poets often do, but if anyone feels that the Irish should be protected from their own sentimentalizing – or feels he is becoming sentimental about Ireland himself – it must be remembered that the Irish are incisively good at deriding themselves. What these poets complained of were foreigners, reasonably enough, because of their sense of having been dispossessed: 'Maud and Moore and Bagwell ousting us at every step, Fowkes and Hoop and Bassett, three who left me vagrant', sang O'Twomey – but even that contemptuous listing of foreign names is an ancient alliterative device. O'Twomey, like the rest, may naturally have resented the dispossessors, but it could have been his own genial generosities that made a 'vagrant' of him, not the Hoops and Bassetts. 'The English tongue has addled us', but

> Sweeter for me the crystal clink
> Of a new-drained cup on the bar and a host
> Of friends in company who share a drink –
> And we'll crack his pate who refuses the toast!
> O Ireland, my heart, I am thinking of you.[62]

As has been said, the best of the Irish can be left to deal with national sentimentality or other shortcomings. Frank O'Connor goes round Ireland (in *Irish Miles*) in a wittily controlled rage: at the philistinism of the Church, with its curious habit of building hideous new churches when an exquisite ruin nearby only needs a roof, and at the money-grubbing ignorance and carelessness (worse, destructiveness) of his own government. He composes letters to de Valera in his head, the de Valera for whom he fought, on the Republican side against the Free State, in the Irish Civil War.[63] He is talking of a ruin in Ennis, in County Clare, but he could be anywhere. The contempt is lethal, or should have been:

Built into a modern tomb in the chancel and half eaten by rain, were the five panels of a fine fifteenth century altar-piece; a stone copy of the alabaster altar-pieces common in England at the time. It is the only example left in Ireland; possibly in the United Kingdom. I began to compose another letter to Mr de Valera in my head.

This time the line to be taken was rather different. One owned up that the infernal thing was a work of art, but suggested that it might make a pleasant decoration for a villa garden and offered to buy it. The price was a crucial question. I first thought of five shillings a panel, but then I realised that the panels of the Betrayal and Entombment were rather smaller than the others, and that it wouldn't do to overlook the fact. Yes, I thought; five shillings for the large, and three and sixpence each for the small panels will look like a reasonable offer. Otherwise one might be suspected of facetiousness.

Still skirting Limerick city, through Adare (which Frank O'Connor declared 'the most beautiful village in the county'), to the de Vere house, Curragh Chase, near Askeaton.

There are two literary Aubrey de Veres. The first, poet and friend of Wordsworth,[64] born at Curragh Chase in 1788, died 1846; and his son, poet and friend of Tennyson, born at Curragh Chase in 1814, died 1902. The second has been called a link between the Romanticism of the early nineteenth century and the Celtic Renaissance at the end of it. He was early, for example, in his rendering of the old Irish tales. His version of the 'Cattle Raid of Cooley', which he called The Foray of Queen Maeve, was published in 1882. He also retold the stories of the Sons of Uisnach (Deirdre) and of the Children of Lir.

At his first invitation to Curragh Chase, in 1842, Tennyson somehow missed de Vere in London and set off for Ireland by himself, to spend a lonely fortnight wandering from Limerick and Killarney down to Cork. Tennyson got to Curragh Chase six years later, in 1848, having previously stipulated that he would only come if he was not expected to come down to breakfast, could have half the day alone, could smoke in the house, and there should be no talk of Irish distress. (This last is reminiscent of Winston Churchill's anguished plea, 'Not Cromwell again, please Mr de Valera!')

De Vere's Recollections (1897), written late in his life, give a picture of an unusually cultivated life in a 'Big House':

I had happened to say to my father, 'I suppose every one knows that Byron is the greatest modern poet?' He answered quietly, 'I do not know it.' 'Then who is?' He replied, 'I should say Wordsworth.' 'And, pray, what are his chief merits?' He answered, 'I should say, majesty, and pathos, as, for instance, in his "Laodamia."' I read 'Laodamia,' standing, to the last line, and was converted. I seemed to have got upon a new and larger planet. . . .

Soon afterwards a present from an unknown donor was made to my sister, a copy of 'The Beauties of Shelley', with her initials glittering on its green morocco cover. She read aloud the 'Ode to a West Wind', and a few evenings later, by the last light of a summer evening, his 'Adonais'. About the same time I became acquainted also with the poetry of Keats, Landor, and Coleridge. We used to read them driving about our woods in a pony carriage. The pony soon found us out, and we had many hairbreadth escapes. Sometimes we read them by night to the sound of an Aeolian harp, still in my possession.

On one of those nights a boat lay on the lake at the bottom of the lawn; I lay down in it, allowing it to float wherever the wind blew it. Sometimes it got entangled in weeds, and sometimes it was captured by a woody bay. There I lay half asleep, till a splendid summer sunrise told me that it was time to get to bed. It was all Shelley's fault. His was a sleepless spirit – the worse for him, and probably for his poetry.[65]

The lawn and the lake at Curragh Chase are still there, well kept up, and the lake would be a perfect one to float about on. But the large house is a carefully preserved shell, burnt out by accident in 1942. The tops of its walls are sealed, as are its windows, as though it awaits a second life. The large park is open to the public.

Frank O'Connor, a Corkman, found Limerick 'the pleasantest town in Ireland' (in 1940);[66] the German novelist Heinrich Böll (c. 1955)[67] found it dreamlike:

Dark clouds came up from the Atlantic – and the streets of Limerick were dark and empty. Only the milk bottles in the doorways were white, almost too white, and the seagulls splintering the grey of the sky, clouds of white plump gulls, splinters of white that for a second or two joined to form a great patch of white. Moss shimmered green on ancient walls from the eighth, ninth, and all subsequent centuries, and the walls of the twentieth century were hardly distinguishable from those of the eighth – they too were moss-covered, they too were ruined.

He begins to find it all too much, too mysterious – 'So painfully white the milk bottles, not quite so white the seagulls'. But explanation is at hand:

In Dublin we had been told: 'Limerick is the most devout city in the world'. So we would only have had to look at the calendar to know why the streets were so deserted, the milk bottles unopened, the shops empty: Limerick was at church, at eleven o'clock on a Thursday morning. Suddenly, before we had reached the centre of modern Limerick, the church doors opened, the streets filled up, the milk bottles were removed from the doorways. It was like an invasion: the inhabitants of Limerick were occupying their town.

The novelist Kate O'Brien is another rhapsodist of the discreet charms of Limerick; she was born there.[68] She begins her book *My Ireland* with Limerick, and has to tear herself away from the place: 'But let us leave Limerick for a bit. The place grows too much my own.' She returns to it again, almost at the end of the book, still rhapsodizing, telling a story of the origin of a name still execrated in Ireland:

Limerick had its First Citizens murdered by Black and Tans. . . . Michael O'Callaghan who was Mayor in 1920 was said to have been the one who gave those 'Auxiliaries' their nickname. He by chance saw somewhere a first lorryload of them just landed, with Lloyd George's terrible instructions, and in their untidy uniform, half policeman's black, half soldier's khaki – and described them as like a famous Tipperary pack of hounds, Black and Tans.

George Clancy, who took mayoral office in 1921, had been a friend of James Joyce in University College, Dublin – and had tried to interest him (a) in the Irish language and (b) in Irish patriotism. He is called 'Davin' in *A Portrait of The Artist as A Young Man*.

Both Clancy and O'Callaghan were woken and shot dead, in their homes, by the Black and Tans. 'So in this we match Cork – that Limerick has a Mayor and Ex-Mayor to remember with mourning pride out of "The Troubles."'

Cork-man Frank O'Connor says his family came from Limerick, 'but that was in the eleventh century, and I am no believer in racial memories'. Limerick even has literary associations, he says (though not many): 'At No. 5, Clare Street, on the Kilmallock road, died Brian Merriman, the Gaelic poet. Admittedly, Merriman was a Clareman, but so are most other Limerickmen. So little does Limerick know or care about him that not even a tablet marks the house.'[69] Merriman was the author of a famous, even notorious, poem, 'The Midnight Court', a satire on the sexual inactivity of Irish men. His house in Limerick has been demolished, but perhaps times have changed; the development on its site, it is said, will be called 'Merriman Square'.

THE SHANNON

Above Limerick, where the Shannon leaves Lough Derg (or Dergderc, to distinguish it from Lough Derg of the pilgrims, in Donegal), is pretty Killaloe.

> Oh where, Kincora! is Brian the Great?
> And where is the beauty that once was thine?
> Oh where are the princes and nobles that sate
> At the feast in thy halls, and drank the red wine?
>   Where, oh Kincora?

asks nineteenth-century James Clarence Mangan longingly (claiming that his poem is 'from the Irish'). 'Brian' is Brian Boru (941–1014), Ireland's King Alfred, who fought and conquered the invading Danes, and came nearer to uniting Ireland than anyone has been able to since. 'Kincora', where he was brought up and where, later, he had his palace, *Beal Borumha*, is Killaloe.

'The most famous king for his time that ever was before him or after him of the Irish nation for manhood, fortune, manners, laws, liberties, religion and many other good parts . . .', claimed the *Annals of Clonmacnois*, in the seventeenth century, six centuries after his death. He quickly became a focus for Irish nostalgia – 'the ages have coated Brian's life and reign with an almost stifling gloss'.[70] He belonged to the tribe of the Dalcassians, which is why pubs and cafes in this region sometimes have that name:

> Oh, never again will Princes appear,
> To rival the Dalcassiáns of the Cleaving Swords!

> I can never dream of meeting afar or anear,
> In the east or the west, such heroes and lords!
>   Never, Kincora!

As well as being a successful warrior, Brian was clearly an astute politician. He had himself crowned High King at Cashel, in his own territory of Munster – it has been known ever since as 'Cashel of the Kings' – whereas the traditional place for such a coronation should have been Tara, in Meath. Instead he marched into Ulster to receive the formal homage of the northern princes (though as a sop to them he confirmed Armagh in its ecclesiastical primacy over the whole of Ireland).

As an old man he was killed by the Danes at the Battle of Clontarf (Good Friday, 1014), though he had won the battle, on the site of present-day Dublin. (Patrick Kavanagh, when asked in the 1950s for an interview by a Danish journalist, growled 'You killed my king'.)

> Oh, dear are the images my memory calls up
> Of Brian Boru! – how he never would miss
> To give me at the banquet the first bright cup!
> Ah, why did he heap on me honour like this?
>   Why, oh Kincora?

Brian built the church that is at the water's edge at Killaloe, but the site of the palace and the feasting that Mangan so yearns for is the subject of dispute. Scholars put it on a spur that juts into the Shannon, ideal for controlling river-traffic and raiders, but Stephen Gwynn (in 1906) thinks otherwise:

> For my part, I am clear that the fort was merely a kind of bar-rack; and the truth was forced in on my mind when we went back to look at the cathedral. The door was locked (after the very ungodly fashion which prevails in Ireland), though it was a Sunday; and I had to climb a steep street to look for their verger. At the top, suddenly I emerged on an open windy square crowning the top of this low hill . . . a market-place, of course, and what is a market-place to-day in an Irish country-town has been so for countless generations. Here, beyond a doubt, I think, was the abode of the kings. The place was a natural rath; and down at the foot of it, beside the river, rose the stone roof of Brian's parish church.[71]

The 'windy square' now contains the Catholic church (which has a typically jewel-toned window, with a touch of the Faery, by Harry

Clarke); and to the contemporary eye, because of its commanding height, this does seem a suitable place for Brian Boru's (and Mangan's) Kincora.

The novelist Edna O'Brien (b. 1930)[72] was born at Tuamgraney in County Clare, and 'the county remains so much in her veins that the people there continue to find themselves in her work'. The versions of herself in the books retain to a high degree the Celtic sense of locality, almost to the extent of it becoming a feared obsession:

> The towns were the colour of a creamery tank, pewter. You said their names, you knew them off by heart, that long litany of names that charted the journey from the city to where you were conceived and born: Leixlip, Mountmellick, Port Darlington, Toomevara, Cloughjordan, Borriseykeane, Kenigad, Nenagh, Portroe – towns and townlands, meadows and chieftains, raspberries on canes, sundials and hounds and hallways, and two-roomed houses with a tangle of roses and damp clay. To think of such things was balderdash.

The father in this novel, *A Pagan Place* (1970), in which almost every character is frustrated to the point of lunacy, has this sense of place to an overbearing degree:

> When the car crossed from one county to the next your father knew although it was not written up. He knew the fence or the stone wall, or the tree, or whatever it was that marked the boundary between one county and the next. If there was something in particular that he pointed to, you tried to focus it but your stomach began to sway and your head too and the sway interfered with your vision. Excitement got the better of you. Each time when he said Look, you got dizzy and couldn't see.

Brian Merriman (*c*. 1749–1805)[73] set his famous poem, *The Midnight Court*, on the shores of Lough Graney in the hills of County Clare, west of Lough Derg(derc):

> When I looked at Lough Graney my heart grew bright,
> Ploughed lands and green in the morning light,
> Mountains in rows with crimson borders
> Peering above their neighbours' shoulders. . . .

His poem is a satire on the sexual puritanism of Irish men.

> Shame on you without chick or child
> With women in thousands running wild! . . .
> The little white saint at the altar rail,
> And the proud, cold girl like a ship in sail –
> What matter to you if their beauty founder,
> Belly and breast will never be rounder,
> If, ready and glad to be mother and wife,
> They drop unplucked from the boughs of life?

The poem is amiably unbuttoned rather than obscene. Though at least one critic found its grossness utterly repellent, its 'discovery' was much enjoyed in the first decades of this century, perhaps because it mirrored the puritanism of the Ireland at that time, and possibly because the new generation, which now learned Irish at school, had not realized that such things were so enjoyably written about in that language in eighteenth/nineteenth-century Ireland. Little is known about the life of Merriman, except that he was a schoolmaster, at Feakle, near Lough Graney, and probably a teacher of mathematics. He also farmed; a local publication says that he won a prize of two spinning wheels for growing half an acre of flax at Feakle; it also says, despite his poem, that he waited till he was thirty-eight before he married. He is buried at Feakle, grave-site unknown. The placing of a plaque in his honour, on the graveyard wall, was locally opposed, as 'a dishonour to the brave men buried there'; but it was put up nevertheless.

On the eastern, County Tipperary, bank of Lough Dergderc, at Terryglass, we come to one of the earliest recorded associations with literature in Ireland:

> Life and health from Find, Bishop of Kildare, to Aed mac Crimthainn, professor of learning to the high king of the Southern Half, successor of Colum mac Crimthainn [in the abbacy of Terryglass], chief shanachie [story-teller] of Leinster in wisdom and knowledge and practice of books and learning and study. Write out for me the conclusion of this little story.
>
> > Be sure of this, keen-witted Aed,
> > Rich in the holy wealth of song,
> > Be thou long time or short away,
> > I always for thy coming long.

> Send me the songbook of Mac Lonáin that I may understand
> the meaning of the poems therein, *et vale in Christo*.[74]

This letter, from bishop to monk in the twelfth century, suggesting a high degree of cultivation and courtesy, is the only private letter in Gaelic to survive from the pre-Norman period. It also is proof that in the abbey of Terryglass, on the banks of the Shannon, the 'Book of Leinster' was being put together in the scriptorium there, and sent to the bishop of Kildare, piece by piece. Yet another compilation of the fragments of Ireland's past: this one included the *Táin* (The Cattle Raid of Cooley) with its attendant cycle of tales.

Nothing much remains of the abbey now, except some very old (cyclopean) walls that enclose an eighteenth-century graveyard with some finely lettered gravestones (walls which now have 'Paddy's Bar' cheerfully, not too obtrusively, inserted into them). Also set into the ancient walls is an old plaque, which reads: 'Fland poet of Connaught rests within. Slain 898 AD.' This is the Fland Mac Lonáin whose poems the Bishop of Kildare (d. 1160) wishes to read, 'the first professional poet of Ireland of whom we have any definite tradition'. A manuscript in the British Museum claims that he is buried at Terryglass and that he composed this quatrain, 'after his slaying':

> Under Mochaime's flags we lie,
> Six goodly warriors dead;
> Stout men were we, but that passed by,
> Above our bones men tread.

In the 'Yellow Book of Lecan', yet another monkish compilation – in view of the prevailing violence plenty of these were necessary if any was to survive – there is another story of Fland's powers after death. His fellow bards have a place-naming competition, about the high places round the Shannon, and the dead Fland visits his old harper in a dream; next day the harper is able to win the competition by naming all of them, in good verses. Robin Flower, who relates all this in *The Irish Tradition*, adds: 'Fland, it will be seen, was a great posthumous poet, and he must have practised his art under difficulties, for the poem in the Museum MS tells us that he went to Hell when he died. . . .' He also earned his place in history, in the *Annals of the Four Masters*: 'Fland Mac Lonáin, the Virgil of the Scotic race, chief poet of all the Gael, the best poet of Ireland of his time, was slain by the sons of Corr Buide. . . .'

Further up the Shannon, in County Offaly, is the small town of Banagher, where Anthony Trollope lived for a while in 1842, reorganizing the Irish postal service, and where Charlotte Bronte (1816–55) spent part of her honeymoon, in 1854. This trip must have been strange for Charlotte Bronte in all sorts of ways. She was newly married at the age of thirty-eight, it was her first visit to Ireland, and she was Irish by blood. Her Evangelical clergyman father Patrick had been born into very impoverished circumstances in Ulster, a fact he did not advertise (nor that his mother had been a Roman Catholic). Patrick Bronte disapproved of Charlotte, his last surviving child, marrying his curate, Arthur Bell Nicholls, on the grounds that he did not think him good enough for her. However, when Charlotte arrived at Banagher she discovered that her husband's family was socially distinguished. She had expected 'Irish negligence', but here was none:

> In this house Mr Nicholls was brought up by his uncle, Dr Bell. It is very large and looks externally like a gentleman's country-seat – within most of the rooms are lofty and spacious and some – the drawing-room, dining-room, etc. – handsomely and commodiously furnished. . . . The passages look desolate and bare – our bedroom, a great room on the ground-floor, would have looked gloomy when we were shown into it but for the turf-fire that was burning in the wide old chimney. . . .
>
> I must say I like my new relations. . . . My dear husband appears in a new light here in his own country. . . .[75]

Behind the house was a school, established by Royal Charter in 1638, of which Dr Bell was headmaster. William Wilde, Oscar's father, was educated there. Of the house – 'Cuba House' on the edge of the town – nothing now remains. It was taken down – 'tossed' as the Irish say – in the 1980s. Part of the school still stands, and sheep take shelter in it.

Charlotte was dead within a year of her honeymoon. Not far from Cuba House, next to the church, is Hill House where Arthur Nicholls lived when he returned to Ireland, having cared for Charlotte's father at Haworth until he died eight years later. (He brought the Brontes' dog with him; and later married one of the cousins whom Charlotte had met.) Arthur Nicholls was rector of Banagher and is buried there; there is a memorial window in his church.[76]

Thirteen years before, in 1841, Anthony Trollope arrived at Banagher by canal-boat – a 'floating prison', with disgusting food – and stayed at the hotel by the bridge. Then he moved to a cottage

next to the post office at the top of the street, on the same side
as the hotel. The post office is still in the same place but, again,
in the 1980s the cottage was pulled down (to some local dismay)
and one more or less like the old one was built in its place. Charlotte
Bronte's biographer, Winifred Gérin, remarks of the sloping main
street of Banagher that 'the stone of its eighteenth-century houses
and their close-packed continuity of front affords a strange resem-
blance to Haworth'.

Up the winding Shannon, still in County Offaly,[77] is Clonmacnois
('the meadow of the sons of Nos') which, after Armagh, was the
greatest monastic centre of Ireland, almost exactly in the middle of
the island.[78] Founded in 545 by St Kieran, it became a capital of
learning, a great place for the composition of Annals, and the burial
ground of kings. The *Shell Guide* also lists its misfortunes: 'ravaged
by fire 13 times between 722 and 1205, plundered by the Vikings
8 times between 832 and 1163, assailed by Irish enemies 27 times
between 832 and 1163, by the English 6 times between 1178 and
1204. It was finally reduced to complete ruin by the English garrison
of Athlone in 1552, when "not a bell, large or small, or an image,
or an altar, or a book, or a gem, or even glass in a window, was
left which was not carried away".'

> In a quiet watered land, a land of roses,
>   Stands Saint Kieran's city fair:
> And the warriors of Erin in their famous generations
>   Slumber there.
>
> There beneath the dewy hillside sleep the noblest
>   Of the clan of Conn,
> Each below his stone with name in branching Ogham
>   And the sacred knot thereon. . . .
>
> Many and many a son of Conn, the Hundred-Fighter,
>   In the red earth lies at rest;
> Many a blue eye of Clan Colman the turf covers,
>   Many a swan-white breast.

Everyone in Ireland knows that poem by T.W. Rolleston (1857–
1920).[79] Frank O'Connor, in the 1940s, found the place in such a
mess he was moved to parody it: 'In a smelly, weedy place, a place
of mourning,/Stand some heaps of ruined stones/Where the Irish
middle classes under massive heaps of granite/Rest their bones. . . .'
He can only conclude that 'Rolleston's greatest poem was written

in absentia'.[80] However, in 1955 the Church of Ireland presented the site to the State, which up to then had only owned the masonry of the ruins, and since O'Connor's time the place has been – even excessively – tidied up.

Kate O'Brien (1897–1974) catches the melancholy peace of the place. It is beautiful, but: 'Clonmacnois still feels austere. The young men [i.e. the scholars] must have looked about them wildly some-times, over the reedy, golden land and across the cold Shannon water.' She knows Rolleston's poem too: 'It was perverse of the poet to remember only kings and soldiers in Clonmacnois – and their lovers, "many a blue eye of Clan Colman the turf covers". Yes, but this is neither a battlefield or a pavilion of pleasure. It was a school for saints and ascetics, this "dewy hillside", beneath which so many of them sleep unmentioned.' As for those young men who 'must have looked about them wildly sometimes': 'The cry of a swan, the bark of an otter or greyhound would be all they would hear beyond the bells of the Round Towers, the voices of their lecturers and round-the-clock office intoning from seven sanctuaries. . . . And all about is silence – and coldness night and day from the flooding waters of the Shannon.'[81]

Still on the Shannon, downstream a little, between Clonmacnois and Shannonbridge, is Devenish Island, in Irish *Snámh-dá-en*, literally, 'Swim-two-birds'; one of the resting places of Mad Sweeney when, bird-like, he fluttered all over Ireland after the battle of Mag Rath (Moira). It is the surrealist-sounding title chosen by Flann O'Brien for his great comic novel, in which Sweeney appears among other phantasmagoric characters and stout-swilling Dubliners. Flann O'Brien (1911–66) (one of several pseudonyms; real name Brian O'Nolan) spent a happy part of his childhood in the flat bog-landscape of Tullamore (Offaly), not far away. It is pleasing to discover that Swim-two-birds exists in reality.[82]

AROUND KILKENNY

Taking the town of Kilkenny as the centre of a clockface, there are literary associations round its dial, starting at twelve o'clock with Castlecomer. Sean O'Faolain, writer of fictions, commissioned to write a factual travel-book about Ireland, hesitates before reaching Kilkenny. Trusting the artist in himself, giving a rest to the travel-writer, he spends the night at Castlecomer, and 'as I sat in my bedroom I began to wonder why the devil I *had* come there'. So begins a free-ranging, impressionistic, meditation on what it meant to be an Irish artist/intellectual/Catholic, after Independence, in Ireland.

Slowly he begins to understand one reason, anyway, why the devil he had instinctively come there:

> It took me a while to realize that it was for the sake of James Kildare and Leighlin (1786–1834) ['JKL'], James Warren Doyle, Augustinian priest, and Bishop. He was a great man, the scourge of his clergy. . . . His predecessor in the see of Kildare and Leighlin lived in the bog in a mud hovel. So did the church cower in the bad century, the eighteenth. Doyle was of different metal. With his long lean hands he used to tear the thatch from cabins unfit to be churches, and rip the tattered vestments in two, trying to make his clergy realize that the bad century was finished and done with. Poor men, they sometimes sewed up the vestments when he was gone. Once he took a leaking chalice and smashed it flat with a stone. . . .

There is a picture of a British soldier on the bedroom wall. It reminds him of his cousin, killed at Arras. A popular Hollywood song drifts up from the street, and he accuses himself of sentimentality, for thinking about that priest of so long ago, of being conditioned by his own and his country's past:

> Suddenly I sit up straight in bed. Somebody downstairs has turned on a radio, and from Athlone I hear a woman's voice singing *Slievenamón* in Irish. God! How lovely it is! As it rises, and fades – and swells and falls, it is like a sweet wind sighing across Ireland. That sad song came out in the bad century. That I can hear it to-night – that we have not been blotted out and lost everything, we owe to men like JKL.
>
> After three minutes I am as suddenly tired of it. That is always the way with folk-music. It is electric. But it is limited. It is lovely: but it is lovely only as a shallow pool in the sands. You can paddle in it but you cannot swim in it. If I get nothing out of Ireland but that gentle, fleeting sweetness I will get very little indeed. I lean over and cover my ear with the sheet and hope again for something complex and revealing in Kilkenny.[83]

'JKL' 's cathedral is in Carlow, completed six years before his death, next to St Patrick's diocesan seminary, a vast 'manufactory' of priests, built as early as 1793. Bishop Doyle was champion of Catholic Emancipation, but his address in 1822 'To the deluded and illegal association of Ribbonmen' – a secret organization responsible for agrarian outrages – shows how far were priests like Doyle from being centres of disaffection. It is very long, after the fashion of the time, closely reasoned, eloquent, and cannot have been delivered to a friendly audience. He speaks under various 'Heads' such as:

> *Your Distresses*: And now let me ask you, How are your wants remedied and your distress removed by these associations? Is it by the breaking of canals, by destroying cattle, by the burning of houses, corn and hay, and establishing a reign of terror throughout the entire country, that you are to obtain employment?
> *Your Hatred to Orangemen*: . . . These men, who are so very hateful in your eyes, are our brethren in Christ; they are each of them as dear to him as the apple of his eye.[84]

The priesthood was detested by the leading figures of the Young Ireland nationalist movement. The northern Protestant John Mitchel described in his *Jail Journal* 'the cowardice, the treachery, or the mere priestliness of the priests . . . when the people seemed to be gathering in force, they came whispering round, and melted off the crowds like silent thaw'. The Church was treading a difficult line, trying to help the people, while preventing them from putting their heads in the noose. There is a monument to JKL in Carlow Cathedral, and Carlow museum is filled with his memorabilia.

At Borris, east of Kilkenny, it was from the Kavanagh house in 1788 that Lady Eleanor Butler of Kilkenny Castle escaped to freedom in Wales with Sarah Ponsonby; they became the celebrated 'Ladies of Llangollen'. At an earlier, foiled, attempt, Sarah Ponsonby had climbed out of her family mansion, Woodstock, at Inistioge a few miles away, 'in male attire, carrying a pistol and her little dog, Frisk'.[85] This time they succeeded:

> After three weeks, Eleanor again absconded from the home of her sister at Borris, and was concealed by Sarah in a cupboard at Woodstock till the families reluctantly agreed to their leaving, and made some very meagre financial arrangement. Their income would be in the region of £280 a year, and for the rest of their lives they would be in constant worry about their finances.

After a tour of Wales, they rented a cottage with four acres for £22.11s a year at Llangollen and sent for the maid Mary Carryl, who had been dismissed from Woodstock for throwing a candlestick at another servant and wounding him severely. . . .

Their intention was to 'devote hearts and minds to self-improvement; to eschew the vanities of society; to beautify their surroundings and to better, in so far as they could, the lot of the poor and unfortunate. . . . In one three-month period they read (aloud) twenty-three books. . . . They mastered Italian and Spanish and Eleanor woke Sarah in the middle of the night to suggest that they should get the vicar to teach them Latin.'

Llangollen was conveniently on the route to Holyhead and the boat to Ireland. The Ladies were visited by all distinguished travellers. They were often mocked. The ineffable Lockhart, son-in-law of Sir Walter Scott, describes them in old age, in a letter to his wife on his way back with Scott from Ireland in 1825, striking a note of facetious male nervousness:

At Llangollen your papa was waylaid by the celebrated 'Ladies' – viz. Lady Eleanor Butler and the Honourable Miss Ponsonby, who having been one or both crossed in love, foreswore all dreams of matrimony in the heyday of youth, beauty, and fashion, and selected this charming spot for the repose of their now time-honoured virginity.

Imagine two women, one apparently 70, the other 65, dressed in heavy blue riding habits, enormous shoes, and men's hats, with their petticoats so tucked up, that at the first glance of them, fussing and tottering about their porch in the agony of expectation, we took them for a couple of hazy or crazy old sailors. . . . Their tables were piled with newspapers from every corner of the kingdom, and they seemed to have the deaths and marriages of the antipodes at their fingers' ends.[86]

Their life sounds admirably energetic, including the traditional Irish aristocratic pursuits, genealogy and gardening:

Much of their time was spent laying out and improving their demesne; their garden was neatness itself with forty-four different kinds of rose. They designed gothic fantasies and walks, for the Romantic was increasingly fashionable. The Ladies, by going to live together, had struck a blow for feminism, but their fame rested equally on their having chosen a simple rustic life in a cottage amongst wild and magnificent scenery.[87]

South of Borris, at St Mullin's in the Barrow valley, poor mad bird-man Sweeney finally met his end: Sweeney who may be thought to represent the life of wild nature against book-learning and civilization. Cursed by one saint, after his long wandering he is protected by another, St Moling. In the end Sweeney is killed by a jealous herds-man, and (Seamus Heaney's translation) St Moling gives him a final prayer to suit his bird-nature:[88]

> His soul roosts in the tree of love.
> His body sinks in its clay nest.

In the town of Kilkenny, the castle whose world Lady Eleanor Butler escaped from is now difficult to recognize. From 1391 to 1936 it was the chief seat of the Butler earls, subsequently Dukes of Ormonde. The building is said to have survived more or less intact until it was 'Frenchified' in the seventeenth century. (That would have been the castle she knew.) But large-scale building in the nine-teenth century has swollen it to vast proportions. Frank O'Connor thought it looks as though 'entirely restored for a Royal visit around 1910'.[89]

On the other side of the road to the castle's main gate is the building that was the Kilkenny Theatre where Thomas Moore acted, and met his wife, his beloved Bessy. At the end of the eighteenth century there was a craze for amateur theatricals, and by 1802 the craze reached Kilkenny. In 1809 Moore played the name part in *Peeping Tom*, his Lady Godiva being a Miss E. Dyke, who was fourteen years old and of striking beauty. Despite a warning from his friend Samuel Rogers, 'Don't let the Graces supplant the Muses', Moore married Elizabeth Dyke, then aged sixteen, in 1811, in London. 'She had not a penny, she was a Protestant, and Moore was twice her age. It turned out ideally; his grand London friends were soon sending Bessy their "downright, honest love".'

Kilkenny Castle towers over the Nore River, and there is a riverside walk below it, not far from the theatre. Nearly twenty years after, when they were both once more in Kilkenny, Moore wrote: 'In look-ing along the walk by the river, under the castle, my sweet Bess and I recollected the time when we were used, in our love-making days, to stroll for hours there together. We did not love half so really then as we do now.'[90]

In the grounds of the cathedral of St Canice was a famous school,[91] where George Farquhar, William Congreve, George Berkeley and Jonathan Swift were educated. The school was later moved to a site by the river and since then has moved out of Kilkenny altogether, but no other Irish town, perhaps because of the number of its ancient buildings, in the dark 'Kilkenny marble', gives so strong an impression that it ought to be a university town.

In their *Ireland* (1841) the Halls say they found the town sadly decayed: '. . . we found wretched hovels propped up by carved pillars; and in several instances discovered Gothic door-ways converted into entrances to pig-sties. . . .'[92] Not long before, the French sociologist, Alexis de Tocqueville, had noted: 'The county of Kilkenny is still at this moment (25th July 1835) subject to very rigorous exceptional measures. At a fixed hour every evening all the inhabitants must be back in their homes, and the police have the right to enter and see if this is so. . . . Numerous police force hated by the people.' He questions the Catholic Bishop of Kilkenny:

Q: I have often heard it said in England and even in Ireland that the Catholic population is half-savage. That is probably false?

A: I must admit that it is part true. . . . This people has all the virtues dear to God; it has faith; there is no better Christian than the Irishman. Their morals are pure, premeditated crime is very rare. But they basically lack the civil virtues. They have no foresight or prudence. . . .

Q: Do the Catholics of the upper classes have the same beliefs as the people?

A: Yes. Real unbelief is only to be found among some Protestants.

Q: What are the proportions of Catholics and Protestants in Ireland?

A: In the South we are twenty to one, in the North only three to one. (At this point the Bishop showed us the census tables for his diocese. In general the contrasts were most striking. In one parish there were five or six thousand Catholics and only forty Protestants; there was a church, two parsons, and the value of tithes reached 60,000 francs a year.)[93]

Kilkenny's novelist(s) of the mid-nineteenth century were the Banim brothers: John (1798–1842) and Michael (1796–1874);[94]

John being the driving force. It has often been lamented that Ireland did not have its Walter Scott, and their *Tales of the O'Hara Brothers*, published in the late 1820s, tried to create an Ireland, for English readers, in the way Scott had created an image for the history and romance of Scotland. Their books were usefully literal; an accurate account in *Father Connell* (1842) of an interior of a building in Kilkenny (near the 'Tholsel') was used in the building's restoration.

In *The Fetches* (1825), a melodramatic ghost story, the Banims describe Woodstock at Inistioge, south of Kilkenny (the house which Sarah Ponsonby stepped out from, with her dog and her pistol), and its Gothic setting, which even then was famous:

> The domain is the property of an Irish gentleman of importance. It rises from the edge of the Nore, at about thirteen miles from Kilkenny, into curves and slopes, hills and dales, piles of rock, and extensive spreads of level though high ground; hills and dales are thickly or wildly planted; and mountain streams, made rough and interesting by the stony impediments in their course, seek their way through the bending and shivered banks and fantastic wood; sometimes leaping over an unusually steep barrier. . . .
>   From a nearer point appeared the lowly village of Inistioge; a few white cottages, glinting, like white stones, at the bases, and in the mighty embrace of hills, newly planted. Its light and not inelegant bridge spanned the crystal river, groups and groups of trees massing behind it; and overall the high grounds of Woodstock rising in continued and variegated foliage.

As is the case with the Halls' *Ireland*, this description is revealingly overconscious of the 'Big House' and of an English audience. Why is Inistioge 'lowly' (apart from its site below the house)? It must always have been lovely, the way it falls down towards the Nore. And the bridge is elegant, not 'not inelegant'. It is a demonstration of the way it takes time to shake off a long-imposed sense of provincialism – thus the struggles and meditations of O'Faolain at Castlecomer.

Woodstock was indeed magnificent, its grounds now a park, the house a shell, since being used as a barracks by the Black and Tans; the name of the 'Irish gentleman of importance' mentioned by Banim was Tighe ['Tye'].[95] A hundred years later:

> The Tighes were friendly charming people who did not deserve the misfortunes that happened to them. When the war broke

out Captain Tighe took his family to London, where he met his death in an accident that has never been fully explained. I do not believe they ever returned. In the spring of 1920 the Black and Tans[96] took over Woodstock and patrolled the country at breakneck speed in their Crossley tenders. Then the Treaty came and they left as rapidly as they had come. It was an empty, undefended house that was finally destroyed.

Hubert Butler (1900–91) says in the same essay, 'Inistioge is still the most beautiful and peaceful of villages'. He lived at Bennetts-bridge, further up the valley of the river Nore, and, among other things, is the chronicler of the complexities – and sometimes the wild comedy – of Irish quarrels. He tells, for example, of Standish O'Grady (1846–1928), considered by W.B. Yeats to be one of the architects of the Irish Literary Revival, who came to Kilkenny in 1898 to edit *The Kilkenny Moderator*, and immediately began to berate his own class, the Ascendancy class, with no moderation whatsoever: 'Christ save us all! You read nothing, you know nothing. You are totally resourceless and stupid. . . . England has kept you like Strasburg geese. . . .'[97]

Hubert Butler regrets, as anyone must, the ultimate destructiveness of these quarrels. He laments the burnt-out Tighes of Woodstock; the burnt-out Cuffes of Desart Court, a few miles west of Bennetts-bridge; now gone. Iris Origo (1902–88) stayed often with her grand-parents at Desart Court, for idyllic summer holidays. She describes the ordered life there, and the confusions that political changes were causing among the Ascendancy – some going with the new, Gaelic, tide; others remaining steadfastly as they had always been, despite the growing unrest: 'Looking back upon those days, it is difficult to realize that beneath this gay and friendly surface – for every farmer and cottage-woman, too, appeared devoted to their landlord and called him "the spitting image" of his own father – so much hatred (of religion, class, and race) was stirring . . .'. Origo's mother

could not understand that her father should prefer the Ireland of 'An Irish R.M.' to that of Yeats and Synge, of A.E. and Lady Gregory, and tried hard to convert him. But he only smiled. 'I know you think me a Philistine,' he told her, 'of course there is charm in all these fancies, but sooner or later they lead to cruelty and trouble. There is danger in every denial of reason. . . .'

When Otway [Cuffe, his Theosophist brother] told my grandfather that, according to Yeats, the divulgation of Irish folk-tales among educated people and the association of literature with popular music, speech and dancing might 'so deepen the political passion of the nation that all – artists and poets, crafts-men and day-labourers – would accept a common design', he dryly replied that this was precisely what he feared.

But Otway followed his own course – wearing a highly picturesque costume which he (but no-one else) declared to be the Irish national dress, setting up workshops for wood-carvers and bookbinders in the manner of William Morris, collecting folk-stories about the 'Little People' and changelings, and encouraging the study of Erse. Of this last my grandfather dis-approved . . . he believed that all differences of language tend to divide, and that what Ireland needed was unity.

There seemed very little interest in England about Ireland, or understanding of what was going on. In 1921, the Earl, Origo's grandfather, was determined to alert England to the dangers. In London,

he was sent for by the King, and went to the Palace in the belief that he would be asked to give an account of the situation in Ireland as he had left it. But: 'Ah, Lord Desart', was his cordial greeting, 'I'm delighted to hear that you still wear nightshirts, just as I do! Can't bear those new-fangled pyjamas'. The rest of the conversation ran upon nightwear, entirely oblivious of the Irish question. I have always thought this a peculiarly English story.

The next year, 1922, Desart was burned down, by raiders from Tipperary. Ten years later the widower Earl writes to his grand-daughter, Origo, from England: 'I can't bear to think of Desart – it is sadness itself. All gone, all scattered – and we were so happy there'.[98]

The other side of the coin: on from Callan westward is Mullinahone (Tipperary), birthplace and home of the novelist, Young Irelander and Fenian, Charles Kickham (1828–82).

Kickham was arrested, as a leader of the Fenian Movement (for Land Reform), in 1865 and sentenced to fourteen years' penal ser-vitude. He served four years at Woking and at Portland and was released with his health broken. He is said to have written his novel *Sally Cavanagh* (1869) while in gaol. In his preface to that book, Kickham's relief to be back at home in his house at Mullinahone – which is still there – is understandable:

I am no longer the associate of thieves and murderers. I breathe my native air, in the midst of scenes from which nothing could have tempted me to stray, but a call, the neglect of which would have made life insupportable. I am AT HOME. Opposite my window is an old ruin, whether castle or abbey no one seems to know, but the head of a United Irishman was impaled upon it in '98, and it has almost from my infancy possessed a strange fascination for me. Beyond I have a glimpse of the hills, every foot of which is as familiar to me as the street below. I move my chair, and the chapel cross looks in upon me, and seems to point at once to the graves below and the sky above. My sister's children, whom I see at play in the garden among the budding shrubs and the spring flowers, recall me to the loving hearts still around me. Wherever I turn I am greeted with something more deep and touching than mere popularity – something that would be too great a reward for all the sacrifice that mortal man could make, and of which I will try and be more worthy if God spares me life. It is a dream too blissful for earth.

Kickham could be called sentimental (he has been), but in his work there is a wholehearted appreciation of the positive qualities of the Irish people – especially those of Tipperary – which carries conviction. His best-known book is *Knocknagow; or, The Homes of Tipperary* (1879), with its gentle giant of a hero, Mat the Thresher, always ready to do a good turn, or win a contest for his village: he is a champion thrower of the sledge-hammer, and reluctantly competes with one of the gentry. He wins, but quells the enthusiasm of the crowd – 'don't do anything that might offend the captain after comin' here among us to show you a little diversion'. . . . '"Donovan," said Captain French, "your match is not in Europe. I was never beaten before." "Well, it took a Tipperary man to beat you, Captain," returned Mat Donovan. "That's some consolation," said the captain. "I'm a Tipperary boy myself, and I'm glad you reminded me of it".'

Kickham wants to present the Irish people to themselves as they would wish to be seen, and perhaps sometimes were. Father Hannigan's sermon is touching, with its sense of being man to man, the priest at one with his congregation. He finishes his homily on the gospel and turns back to the altar, then hesitates: 'He pressed the forefinger of his left hand to his temple, as if trying to recall something that had escaped his memory. "Ay! ay! ay! d'ye give up stealing turf in the name of o' God?"'

Kickham's affection has been rewarded. His little house at Mullina-hone is a museum devoted to him. The Kickham Community Park has in front of it a panel depicting Mat throwing the hammer, and this park was opened, as the Tipperary Guide puts it, 'with exquisite appropriateness for the centenary of Kickham's death by Clonmel-resident Dr Pat O'Callaghan. He made real life as large as fiction at the 1932 Los Angeles Olympic Games when his last throw sur-passed the best of Porhola the Finn.'

A field where Kickham used to walk and look at the famous hill Slievenamon ['Sleeve-na-Mon'] is also proudly pointed out. Hubert Butler has an essay about the hill, about superstition; about an appall-ing murder that took place there, of a woman suspected of possession by a fairy and burnt to death to rid her of it. But he also muses:

> You can see Slievenaman from my fields, though it is across the Tipperary border, a pale blue hump with the soft, rounded contours of ancient hills whose roughnesses have been smoothed away by time. Starting after lunch you can climb to the tip and be back by summer daylight, though it is over 2000 feet high. It can be seen from five or six southern counties and is one of the three or four most famous of Irish hills. Finn MacCool lived there and so did Oisín and Oscar, and fifty beautiful maidens, who give it its name, the 'Mountain of Women', embroidered garments for them there, or so they say.[99]

It is also said that Finn had a competition among the princesses, the one who reached the top of Slievenamon first should be his bride. They raced up, but he had taken the precaution of putting his favourite girl up there before the race, so she was in place before them. In 1992 during the Kilkenny Festival children were playing a game based on this story, in the grounds of Kilkenny Castle. Older girls, dressed (rather well) as swans, were dancing the Story of the Children of Lir. Impossible to guess how deeply these stories still inhabit the Irish consciousness, but they do make England feel rather threadbare in this respect, with not much going back further than Lady Godiva and Robin Hood.

Set into the southern slopes of Slievenamon is a Butler Castle, Kilcash. Because it sheltered priests during the Cromwellian wars it had an Irish song written about it, and the 'lady' of the song, Margaret Butler, Viscountess Iveagh, is revered, and buried in the little church, roofless, that is next to the castle. (There are many Irish poems lamenting the loss of the forests. They were cut down by new occupiers for cash, and were also felled to prevent insurgents hiding in them.) Frank O'Connor made a famous English version of this song in which, he says, W.B. Yeats had a hand,[100] and it remained one of Yeats's favourite poems:

> What shall we do for timber?
>   The last of the woods is down
> Kilcash and the house of its glory
>   And the bell of the house are gone,
> The spot where that lady waited
>   Who shamed all women for grace
> When earls came sailing to greet her
>   And Mass was said in the place.
>
> My grief and my affliction
>   Your gates are taken away,
> Your avenue needs attention,
>   Goats in the garden stray.
> The courtyard's filled with water
>   And the great earls where are they?
> The earls, the lady, the people
>   Beaten into the clay. . . .

At Clonmel, a pleasant town, Laurence Sterne (1713–68)[101] was born, son of an impoverished infantry ensign. Brought there by his father, also a soldier, was George Borrow (1803–81);[102] he went to school for a year, in 1815, in the Tholsel on the main street. From a school companion he learned Irish because he liked 'the strangeness and singularity of its tones'. He wrote about this in some early chapters of *Lavengro*, which 'for all their intolerable covenanting cant, are still the best introduction to Tipperary itself and to that terrible Ireland of the early nineteenth century with its mad Whig Ascendancy and its brutalized peasantry. . . '.[103]

A sympathetic English resident of Clonmel was Anthony Trollope, who set up there with his new wife in 1848, on the corner of what is now O'Connell Street. His biographer, Victoria Glendinning, points out that Trollope may well have been helped to understand Ireland through a non-Irish intermediary, the Italian Charles Bianconi, passionate Irish nationalist, friend of Daniel O'Connell (friend also of the Young Irelander William Smith O'Brien, later deported to Van Diemen's Land), famous as the founder of the first Irish public transport system, by stage coach, which he worked out of Hearn's

Hotel in Clonmel. Trollope saw the value of his help in the transportation of the mail and through Bianconi he met the kind of nationalist Irish the English usually did not come across, except in conflict.[104]

The Rock of Cashel, 'Cashel of the Kings', jumps out of the Tipperary plains like an Edinburgh Castle in a sea of green. In 450 St Patrick baptized a king there (accidentally pushing his crozier into the king's foot, who did not complain because he thought it was part of the rite). Brian Boru had himself crowned there in 977, the first and last of the effective High Kings of Ireland. A little over a hundred years later the royal MacCarthys gave it to the Church; it became the seat of archbishops.

Most of the buildings on the Rock are thus ecclesiastical, though they look like a composite castle, and the west end of the church was indeed fortified. Among them is one of the most appealing buildings in Europe, 'Hiberno-Romanesque' Cormac's Chapel, built in 1134, thirty-five years before the first Normans ventured into Bannow. Its barrel-vaulted roof is still intact, though the carvings and mouldings inside it are green with the weather that beats in through the unsealed windows. In its shape and its atmosphere it is reminiscent of an anchorite's cell – St Patrick's Ireland was a long time in coming to terms with European monastic communities. The Cromwellians destroyed and desecrated the church buildings, but somehow Cormac's Chapel survived, a perfect model of a Norman church. The cathedral, which is built onto it, and seems to dominate it, has fallen in, but the chapel, like a little tug tucked into the side of a half-sunk liner, floats still.

Pádraigín Haicéad (Patrick Hackett) (1600–54) was born near Cashel and became a prior on the Rock. Though he was a priest (educated in Louvain), his poems, in Irish, are fiercely cantankerous, and his epigrams witty (even slangy, if some of his translators are to be trusted). The seventeenth-century Church became nervous about the use of Irish by clerics. Censorship in Ireland was not the invention of de Valera:[105]

Having heard that it had been ordained that brothers and friars should not compose verses or songs in Irish monasteries.

Yesterday a friendly sort told me
the latest news from the land of Ireland,
that the clergy hate the subtlety of Irish,
the elegant sweetness of our ancient freedom.

I'm not going to go for the flank of their argument
since the time is past when I could put into words
every thought that arose from the sharpness of my mind,
a time when my keen intelligence was a danger;

when it would, with no loss of subtle force,
let loose against the sides of those arrogant clergy
or down on top of their horrible balding skulls,
a fistful of sharp, well-fledged, darts.

I'll stitch up my mouth with tightened string,
and say nothing about their nasty little legalities,
just damn the narrow confining gang of them,
and the hate they have for me and for my kind.

In 1686 the cathedral was restored and used by the Church of
Ireland. In 1735 Swift's friend, Archbishop Bolton, wrote to Swift
asking his help in further restoring it: 'I design to repair a very
venerable old fabric that was built here in the time of our ignorant,
as we are pleased to call them, ancestors. I wish this age had some
of their piety. . . .' His successor (and Swift's enemy) Archbishop
Price, decided that the cathedral was inconvenient, stuck up on its
Rock so far from his Palace, so an Act of Council was passed in
1749 allowing him to have his cathedral in the town below; and
soldiers were sent to strip the roof of the old one.[106] This was the
end of fifteen hundred years of history on the Rock.

The older Aubrey de Vere of Curragh Chase (Sir Aubrey, 1788–
1846), whose sonnets on Irish themes were considered by his friend
Wordsworth 'the most perfect of our age', lamented the fate of the
Rock, setting it firmly among the vanished empires. Royal and saintly
Cashel, says de Vere, should be viewed at the close of dim autumnal
days, lit between showers by a setting sun:[107]

> . . . At such a time, methinks,
> There breathes from thy lone courts and voiceless aisles
> A melancholy moral, such as sinks
> On the lone traveller's heart, amid the piles
> Of vast Persepolis on her mountain stand,
> Or Thebes half buried in the desert sand.

5

THE SOUTH-WEST

AROUND CORK CITY

Throughout the eighteenth and nineteenth century, visitors to Ireland from Britain and the Continent were appalled at the poverty of its people, and wondered at this because so much of the land was fertile. There were many reasons for the destitution, so many that Frank O'Connor neatly sidesteps them – 'Books about a country usually begin with its history. Books about Ireland which do this tend to remain unread. The misunderstandings are too many' – but he is in little doubt of the main reason: ignorance of the true condition of Ireland, on the part of its distant government, because of the difficulties involved in visiting it: 'Ultimately, perhaps, all the misunderstandings can be traced to sixty miles of salt water which stretches between Britain and Ireland.'[1]

O'Connor was writing in the 1940s. Mr and Mrs Hall begin their vast, chatty, obsequious (to the English reader) but well-intentioned three-volume *Ireland*, a hundred years earlier (1841), with a long description of the purgatory of a pre-steam crossing to Cork. They agree with O'Connor:

> It was not alone the miserable paucity of accommodation and utter indifference to the comfort of the passengers, that made the voyage an intolerable evil. Though it usually occupied but three or four days, frequently as many weeks were expended in making it. It was once our lot to pass a month between the ports of Bristol and Cork; putting back, every now and then, to the wretched village of Pill, and not daring to leave it even for an hour, lest the wind should change and the packet weigh anchor. . . .
>
> Under such circumstances, it is not surprising that comparatively little intercourse existed between the two countries, or that England and Ireland were almost as much strangers to each other as if the channel that divided them had been actually impassable.[2]

The Halls like Cork's outer harbour, Cobh ['Cove'], when eventually they reach it. Cobh is still an attractive seaside place with hotels and restaurants and a holiday air; the Halls remember its busy past, around 1800: 'Cove was then all gaiety: the steady officers, the light-hearted and thoughtless "middies," and the "jolly Jack tars," paraded up and down at all hours. The pennant floated in the breeze, redolent with dust, pitch, whiskey, and music; the fiddle and bagpipes resounded in a district named, for what reason we know not, "the holy ground," unless that it was sacred to every species of marine frolic and dissipation. . . .' The 'holy ground', which is the quay of Cobh to the east, below where the road climbs from the harbour, got its name (it is said, and was often sung) because Irish sailors were so glad to set foot on it again; on the whole, the Irish are reluctant sailors.

In the 1930s H. V. Morton calculated that three-quarters of a million emigrants had left from Cobh since the beginning of this century.[3] A hundred years before that the Halls watch some of them:

> We stood in the month of June on the quay at Cork to see some emigrants embark in one of the steamers for Falmouth, on the way to Australia. The band of exiles amounted to two hundred, and an immense crowd had gathered to bid them a long and last adieu. The scene was touching to a degree; it was impossible to witness it without heart-pain and tears. Mothers hung upon the necks of their athletic sons; young girls clung to elder sisters; fathers – old white-headed men – fell on their knees, with arms uplifted to heaven, imploring the protecting care of the Almighty on their departing children. . . .

Spike Island, in the mouth of the harbour, was once a convict prison, and John Mitchel (1815–75)[4] had no happy memories of it. Mitchel, the son of a Presbyterian minister, was born in County Londonderry. He came under the influence of Thomas Davis, but Davis's paper, *The Nation*, soon proved insufficiently radical for him and in 1848 he founded *The United Irishman*, which advocated armed rising. For this he was arrested, convicted of treason and sentenced to fourteen years' deportation. His *Jail Journal* (1854) became almost a sacred book for Irish nationalists, remarkable for its haughty scorn of all things English (and reactionary views on most other things). He is taken to Spike Island from Dublin, and does not seem sorry to leave that town: 'Dublin city, with its bay and pleasant villas – city of bellowing slaves, villas of genteel dastards – lies now behind us'.

We came to anchor opposite Cove, and within five hundred yards of Spike Island – a rueful looking place, where I could discern, crowning the hill, the long walls of the prison, and a battery commanding the harbour. . . .

We were rowed rapidly to the island, and as we walked up the approach we met an elderly, grave-looking gentleman, who said, 'Mr Mitchel, I presume!' How the devil, thought I, did you know already that I was coming to you? – forgetting that Lord Clarendon, before I was 'tried,' made sure of my conviction. However, I bowed and then he turned and escorted us to his den, over a drawbridge, past several sentries, through several gratings and at last into a small square court. At one side of this court a door opened into a large vaulted room, furnished with a bed, table, chair, and basin-stand, and I was told that I was in my cell. The two naval officers took their leave politely, saying they hoped to meet me under happier circumstances; and they seemed really sorry. I bowed, and thanked them. . . .

There were further courtesies; but eventually my door was shut, and for the first time I was quite alone.

And now – as this is to be a faithful record of whatsoever befalls me – I do confess, and will write down the confession, that I flung myself on the bed, and broke into a raging passion of tears – tears bitter and salt – tears of wrath, pity, regret, remorse – but not of base lamentation for my own fate. . . .

It is over, and finally over. In half an hour I rose, bathed my head in water, and walked a while up and down my room. I know that all weakness is past, and that I am ready for my fourteen years' ordeal, and for whatsoever the same may bring me – toil, sickness, ignominy, death. Fate, thou art defied.

In this court nothing is to be seen but the high walls and the blue sky. And beyond these walls I know is the beautiful bay lying in the bosom of its soft green hills. If they keep me here for many years I will forget what the fair outer world is like. Gazing on grey stones, my eyes will grow stony.

Literary mention of Cork city is early: in the 'Vision of Mac Conglinne' (*Aislinge Mac Conglinne*), a satire on gluttony in a twelfth-century manuscript, but probably older than that.[5] It begins by establishing the Irish need to be specific, about time, place, and purpose of writing: 'The four things to be asked of every composition must be asked of this composition, viz., place, person, and time, and cause of invention. The place of this composition is great Cork of Munster, and its author is Aniér Mac Conglinne. . . . In the time of Cathal MacFinguine it was made. The cause of the invention was the demon of gluttony that was in the throat of Cathal MacFinguine.' Mac Conglinne decides to go and see if he can get some of MacFinguine's good food, but first the author of what Robin Flower (in *The Irish Tradition*) calls 'this amazing composition' introduces himself: 'Aniér mac Con Glinne, he was a great scholar, very knowledgeable. He was called Aniér because of his way of making panegyrics and satires. . . . The scholar conceived a great desire to take to poetry and give his studies the go-by. For he had had too much of the life of learning.'

His description of the guest accommodation of the monastery of Cork suggests what comforts a travelling scholar expected:

> The blanket of the guest house was rolled up in a bundle on its bed, and it was full of lice and fleas. That was natural, because it was never aired by day nor turned by night, since it was rarely unoccupied when it might be turned. The guest house bath had last night's water in it, and with its heating-stones was beside the doorpost.
>
> The scholar found no one to wash his feet, so he himself took off his shoes and washed his hands and feet in that dirty washing-water, and soaked his shoes in it afterwards. He hung his book-satchel on the peg in the wall, put up his shoes, and tucked his arms together into the blanket and wrapped it round his legs. But as multitudinous as the sands of the sea or as sparks of fire or as dew-drops on a May-day morning or as the stars of heaven were the lice and the fleas biting his feet, so that he grew sick of them. And no one came to visit him nor to wait on him. . . .

Robin Flower points out the sophistication of this medieval work:

> Mac Con Glinne, it will be seen, is an example of the type of truant scholar, the *scholaris vagans* of European literature, the happy-go-lucky vagabond who goes singing and swaggering through the Middle Ages until he finds his highest expression and final justification in François Villon.

The tale that follows is one long parody of the literary methods used by the clerical scholars. At every turn we recognize a motive or a phrase from the theological, the historical, and the grammatical literature. The writer makes sport of the most sacred things, not sparing even the Sacraments and Christ's crucifixion. He jests at relics, at tithes, at ascetic practices, at amulets, at the sermons and private devotions of the monks; the flying shafts of his wit spare nothing and nobody. It is little wonder that the monks were at odds with such poets as this.

Yet they were interdependent. It would have been a monk scribe who copied out the satire. The quarrel and the mockery continue in Ireland to this day, 'poet' versus 'monk', writer versus religionist; violently disagreeing yet maintaining a shared identity. Heinrich Böll calls it 'this utterly un-uniform unity which is Ireland'.[6]

Frank O'Connor and Sean O'Faolain were immediately immersed in this long quarrel: both Corkmen, contemporaries, both nationalists, born Catholics. As young men in 1920s Cork, one of them, O'Faolain, founded a newspaper and the other, O'Connor, began a dramatic society. For this he was called (his real name was Michael O'Donovan) 'Mick the Moke', by a priest, and another priest, crazed by alliteration, deplored 'the madness and melancholy of the moderns meandering in the marshes of mediocrity.'

O'Connor feels himself too close to Cork to be able to describe it:

I once travelled in the train from Kilkenny with an amiable lunatic. 'Could you tell me the name of that castle?' I asked, and he put on a grave face, scratched his head and replied slowly: 'That comes under the heading of fortification.' 'But the bridge!' I urged. 'What do you call the bridge beside it?' A look of real anguish came over the lunatic's face as he scratched his head again. 'That,' he replied, 'comes under the heading of navigation.'

Something of the same pain affects me when I turn to try and write of my native city. 'That comes under the heading of autobiography.'[7]

O'Faolain sounds a cautionary note, half-loving, half genuinely nervous:

One lives every experience, every growing-pain with the greatest possible poignancy here. One is persistently made aware of what one should experience without awareness. For as these people are full of brains and full of ideas, they are also full of alertness, shrewdness, cynicism, and bitter humour, which communicates itself. Put a flower into their hands and they will admire it with a delicate perception and a fine phrase (every Corkman has the gift of words), and then . . . you will see the eyebrows flicker, and an impish look come into the eyes, and out will come some word that crushes it in the fist.[8]

Cork delighted de Tocqueville in 1835; the behaviour of its inhabitants forced him to pay them his highest compliment:

The entry into Cork is very fine. The tradesmen's quarter is beautiful. In the suburbs are filthy houses and inhabitants who are even more frightful still and such as one could find nowhere but in Ireland. The Catholic Archbishop lives in the middle of that quarter of the town. The shepherd in the midst of his flock. . . .
   In our open diligence there were two young men both very uproariously drunk. They talked to and made jokes at almost every passer-by. All, men and women, answered with laughter and pleasantries. I thought I was in France.[9]

Thackeray is horror-struck by the poverty and the beggars, as all visitors were, but notices how even the poor talked about books and writers: 'I listened to two boys, almost in rags: they were lolling over the quay balustrade, and talking about *one of the Ptolemys*! and talking very well too. . . . I think, in walking the streets and looking at the ragged urchins crowding there, every Englishman must remark that the superiority of intelligence is here, and not with us. I never saw such a collection of bright-eyed, wild, clever, eager faces.'[10]
   The boys were talking in English in the street, otherwise Thackeray would not have understood them. Seventy-odd years later in a Cork schoolroom, a poor boy with, no doubt, a 'clever, eager face' saw two Irish words written on the blackboard by a new master – 'a small man with a limp, a small, round, rosy face, a small black moustache and a slight, harsh, staccato voice'. The young Frank O'Connor asked what the words in the strange script meant and Daniel Corkery, the new master, replied: ' "Waken your courage Ireland!" '[11]
   O'Connor was sure that his mother would know the language the words had been written in; she did not, but his grandmother did. Two generations back: it is a measure of the lapse of Irish and of the size of Corkery's task; he wanted to remind Ireland of its forgotten past. Soon, stuck up in the classroom, was a picture of a poor

Cork street (nothing to be ashamed of, that picture said, to the young O'Connor) and also a picture of a blind old man playing a fiddle, with his back to a group of country people. Under it was a poem, in a language O'Connor now knew to be Irish, which began, *Mise Rafteri an filé. . . .*

This was the Connacht poet who so excited Douglas Hyde,[12] and then Yeats, and years later O'Connor made a famous translation of the poem:

> I am Raftery the poet,
>   Full of hope and love,
> With sightless eyes
>   And undistracted calm.
>
> Going west on my journey
>   By the light of my heart,
> Weak and tired
>   To the end of my road.
>
> Look at me now!
>   My face to the wall,
> Playing music
>   To empty pockets.

The appeal of the poem was that it could not have been written by an Englishman, the poet was too poor. There was therefore no longer any need to write like an Englishman, or be ashamed, too much, of Cork slums.

Corkery's vastly influential book *The Hidden Ireland* came later, in 1924. The next generation of Irish writers admired it, loved it and writhed at it, all at once: because it was pointing Ireland towards the past, whereas they wanted to point Ireland (its courage awakened) towards its future. O'Faolain called it, diplomatically, a 'unique' book, which it is; then he goes to great lengths to show that these old Irish poets extolled by Corkery were not democrats, were in fact great snobs (which they were). O'Connor called the Munster poets (on whom Munster Corkery concentrated) 'sleep-walkers', and greatly preferred the peasant poets of Connacht. But these are family quarrels. Corkery's achievement is that he drew attention to the network of bardic schools, or remnants of such, of 'Courts of Poetry', that somehow had managed to flourish when the Irish language itself was more or less proscribed – in other words he disinterred a 'hidden' Ireland.

The old poets had managed to survive by withdrawing to high, poor ground, and one such school was in Whitechurch, which overlooks Cork. Corkery is eloquent about it:

> I raise my eyes, I peer into the shimmering distance. Along the sky-line of the far-off hills, I look for a clump of trees, gapped in the middle. . . . Hidden in that far-off clump of trees are the white walls of a tiny hamlet, Whitechurch by name. To the left, as I look, lies Blarney, and near-by runs the road to Dublin. . . . For me, to gaze thus into that trembling distance, where the little wind-swept hamlet, trees and all, fades into the light of the sky, is to sink softly, and with, perhaps, some gathering wistfulness, into the Gaelic world of the eighteenth century.

You can almost hear the writers of the new school wincing at that 'wistfulness'; it is precisely what they wanted to expunge. The poets Corkery praises were not wistful but furious: that their patrons had been exiled, or had fled, to serve the King of France or the Holy Roman Emperor. These had been replaced by a very low sort of people, in their view, from England and Scotland, who were served by an even lower sort of false poet:[13]

> What a pity I'm not an out and out lout
> (though that's a bad thing for a person to be)
> so I could be at my ease
> amongst these idiotic people.
>
> Since every thick fool is blissful in speech and doings,
> and devoid of metre, coherence, and wit in his language,
> I'm sad at what I've exhausted in mastering difficult writing
> since I was a young man, when I could have practised being
>   a lout.

That is Dáibhí ['Davy'] Ó Bruadair (c. 1625–98) lamenting the break-up of the Gaelic world, and the near-disappearance of the old, strict, Bardic Schools. James Stephens wrote of Ó Bruadair that he sent up 'an unending rebellious bawl that would be the most desolating utterance ever made by man, if it were not also the most gleeful'. He was clearly also, as O'Faolain says, a snob.

Corkery goes far, in *The Hidden Ireland*, to justify Ó Bruadair's laments, and to recreate that disappearing Gaelic world. He probably goes too far, talking of a world so inveterately static that it was bound to decay. But he has a point to make and he makes it forcefully.

He remarks that a poet of this period may often end a poem with a prayer to God and St Patrick that his soul might be saved, and that scholars picking up such an eighteenth-century manuscript – in Dublin, England, Rome, America, for they are scattered – could be forgiven for thinking the poem came from the twelfth, not the eighteenth, century, because the poets of that time had used exactly the same prayer. 'Even from this almost insignificant fact we may understand how short a distance Whitechurch had strayed from the Gaelic tradition.' But in the eighteenth century:

> Of how different a world was this Cromwellian-Williamite city of Cork, on the comfort and wealth of which the little Gaelic hamlet was forever hungrily, and, perhaps, angrily, gazing down! The alien-minded city thought much of itself, was very busy putting money in its purse; yet, now that both are such old stories, what one thinks is that it was Whitechurch rather than the city of Cork that had the seed of life within it. . . . To raise the eyes, as I do now, to that wind-swept hamlet on that far-off hillside, is to feel the heart grow warm, and the pulse quicken.

Corkery mentions Blarney and Whitechurch in the same breath, because Whitechurch was where the bardic school of Blarney removed when Blarney was taken over by the 'Gall', to become 'a dwelling place for wolves', as Egan O'Rahilly called it. It was at Blarney the great MacCarthy chieftains kept their bards in royal fashion, and Egan O'Rahilly (Aogán Ó Rathaille, 1670–1726) never ceases to lament their disappearance, and pray for the return of the Stuarts, and the old ways. Unlike Ó Bruadair, desolate but 'gleeful', there is nothing whatsoever gleeful about O'Rahilly; but for power, mellifluousness, energy, he is generally accepted as the finest of the eighteenth-century Gaelic poets. He seems to have spent much of his time round about Killarney, but he was not above accepting patronage from the supplanters of the MacCarthys of Blarney. There is evidence that one of these, Sir Nicholas Brown, helped him; but the next Brown, Valentine, was a disappointment:[14]

> That my old bitter heart was pierced in this black doom,
> That foreign devils have made our land a tomb,
> That the sun that was Munster's glory has gone down
> Has made me a beggar before you, *Valentine Brown.*

That royal Cashel is bare of house and guest,
That Brian's turreted home is the otter's nest,
That the kings of the land have neither land nor crown
Has made me a beggar before you, *Valentine Brown.* . . .

Frank O'Connor apparently exempts O'Rahilly from his charge
that these poets were 'sleepwalkers' – though no one could long for
the past more fervently than O'Rahilly – and prefaces his translation
of that piece of lip-curled contempt:

With the breaking of the Treaty of Limerick by the English
in 1691 – among other things this had promised a form of
religious toleration – the Irish Catholics descended into a slavery
worse than that experienced by Negroes in the Southern States.
(When the Irish came to America, the Negroes called them
'White Niggers'.) This period is best represented in the few
authentic poems of Egan O'Rahilly. . . .
    In this fine poem he approaches, not one of the masters he
would have approached fifty years before – the MacCarthys –
but Lord Kenmare, one of the new Anglo-Irish gentry. Hence
the bitter repetition of the fellow's name. O'Rahilly himself
would have considered 'Valentine' a ridiculous name for anyone
calling himself a gentlemen, and as for 'Brown', he would
as soon have addressed a 'Jones' or a 'Robinson'. O'Rahilly was
a snob, but one of the great snobs of literature.

The MacCarthy stronghold at Blarney is a grim enough place,
eighty-five feet high with walls in some places that are six yards
thick, but its murderous gloom has been a little lightened by the
invention of the 'Blarney Stone' which, if the visitor kisses it, peril-
ously suspended upside down from the battlements, will give him
'the gift of the gab'. It is said that the legend derives from the endless
evasions of a MacCarthy in Elizabethan times who made so many
accommodations with the Government, none of which he fulfilled,
that his protestations of loyalty came to be called 'Blarney'. More
likely it is the witty invention of an early genius in the tourist trade,
who enjoyed making fun of English visitors (and seeing them hang
upside down).
    Other attempts were made in the eighteenth century to alleviate
the brooding melancholy of the castle. Arthur Young, the English
agronomist, describes how the new owner 'has very much improved
Blarney Castle and its environs; he has formed an extensive orna-
mented ground . . . there are several very pretty sequestered spots

where covered benches are placed'.[15] These are the 'Groves of Blarney' celebrated in a queer little poem which has had a strange fate. The gardens are still there, very much in the eighteenth-century Gothick taste, with 'Witch's Caves' and 'Druid Circles' and strangely shaped stones given fanciful names. A versifier called Richard Alfred Milliken (1767–1815) decided to celebrate the Groves in a mock version of hedge-schoolmasters' English, the Irish *babu*, ornate, euphuistic, which gave evidence of the Irish love of language for its own sake, and the fact that the only schoolbooks these poor teachers could get hold of were out of date, and in the ornate language of a previous generation:

> There's gravel walks there, for speculation,
> And conversation, in sweet solitude.
> 'Tis there the lover may hear the dove, or
> The gentle plover in the afternoon;
> And if a lady would be so engaging
> As to walk alone in those shady bowers,
> 'Tis there the courtier he may transport her
> Into some fort or, all under ground.
>
> For 'tis there's a cave where no daylight enters,
> But cats and badgers are for ever bred;
> Being mossed by nature, that makes it sweeter
> Than a coach-and-six, or a feather bed.
> 'Tis there the lake is, well stored with perches,
> And comely eels in the verdant mud;
> Besides the leeches, and groves of beeches,
> Standing in order for to guard the flood. . . .

A *Memoir* of Milliken (1823) says that 'The Groves of Blarney' 'continued long the favourite of every laughter-loving party . . . of late it has been introduced on the stage, by Mathews the Comedian, and is very well received by the London audience'. It is therefore a surprise that this poem, intended for mockery of the ignorant and pretentious Irish, is a favourite of several subsequent Irish poets and writers. Whether it was by design, or unintentionally, Padraic Colum finds 'the structure and sound of Gaelic poetry are reproduced in it: the "a" sound of "Blarney" is woven through every stanza, but every word that has the sound seems to have gone into its place smilingly. . . . This is the poem which James Stephens, as he told me once, "would rather have written than anything else in an Irish anthology".'[16] The rest of Milliken's verse they dismiss as 'insipid'.

Their admiration suggests the poem contains the dancing rhythm they find in poems in Irish.

Padraic Colum (1881–1972),[17] friend of Yeats, Lady Gregory, James Stephens, Thomas MacDonagh and James Joyce, a prominent figure in the Irish literary revival, is difficult to fit in topographically anywhere, because he spent most of his working life in the United States or in France. In fact he was born in Longford and lived in Dublin, but nearly all his verse, in English, contains the indefinable flavour of the Irish-language eighteenth-century Munster poets rediscovered by Corkery and others. Colum knew Corkery, of course, and tells a story of arranging to meet him at Macroom, which he somehow conflated, or confused, with Mallow. He got out of the train at Mallow, took a look at it and decided it was too bustling and hard-edged to be suitable for a rendezvous with the author of *The Hidden Ireland*. So he consulted a map and, seduced by the lilting syllables of Macroom, decided that must be the place, went back to Cork and started again, and got it right.

Colum is admired most for his adaptations of the songs of the Gaelic countryside. The traditional air, possibly eighteenth-century, to which his 'She moved through the fair' is sung, is particularly beautiful, but even without music it remains one of the loveliest of Irish poems:

My young love said to me, 'My brothers won't mind,
And my parents won't slight you for your lack of kind.'
Then she stepped away from me, and this she did say,
'It will not be long, love, till our wedding day.'

She stepped away from me, and she moved through the fair,
And fondly I watched her go here and go there,
Then she went her way homeward with one star awake,
As the swan in the evening moves over the lake.

The people were saying no two were e'er wed
But one had a sorrow that never was said,
And I smiled as she passed with her goods and her gear,
And that was the last that I saw of my dear.

I dreamt it last night that my young love came in,
So softly she entered, her feet made no din;
She came close beside me, and this she did say,
'It will not be long, love, till our wedding day.'

Outside Cork, on the main road to Macroom, is Kilcrea Abbey where
is buried, his flat gravestone fenced with iron railings, the subject
of the best-known lament in Irish. 'Lo, Arthur Leary, Generous
Handsome Brave, Slain in his bloom lies in this humble grave. Died
May 4 1773 Aged 26 years': these are the words of the epitaph;
'Generous, Handsome, Brave', the qualities most admired in the
heroic Irish tradition.

In 1691, 14,000 of the Irish Jacobite army sailed to serve under
Louis XIV, and all through the eighteenth century the flight of Irish
Catholics, to the armies of continental Europe, continued. The King
of Spain had five Irish regiments, the Irish Brigade of France consisted
of 26,000 men. There is a story of the singer Michael Kelly, friend
of Mozart (known as 'Ochelli'), being addressed in Irish by a group
of Austrian officers, when he was in the presence of the King of
Bavaria. He was embarrassed, because he did not know Irish, and
when the King expressed astonishment, that he did not know his
own language, he blurted out that 'in Ireland only the lower classes
spoke Irish'.[18]

Not true; Eileen O'Connell, aunt of the Liberator, the great
Daniel, one of the powerful O'Connells of Kerry, certainly knew
it; and wrote – or perhaps keened, for there is something primitive, as well as traditional and controlled, in her poem – her famous
'Lament for Art O'Leary', in that language.[19] It has been called 'the
greatest poem written in these islands in the whole of the eighteenth
century'.

> My love forever!
> The day I first saw you
> At the end of the market house,
> My eye observed you,
> I fled from my father with you,
> Far from my home with you . . .

it begins; and that glimpse was in Macroom. Eileen O'Connell, a
young widow, in 1768 was staying with her sister, 'at the end of
the market house' – McSweeney's the sweetshop is pointed out as the
place – when she looked through the window and fell in love:

> My friend forever!
> My mind remembers
> That fine spring day
> How well your hat suited you,
> Bright gold banded,

> Sword silver-hilted –
> Right hand steady –
> Threatening aspect –
> Trembling terror
> On treacherous enemy –
> You poised for a canter
> On your slender bay horse. . . .

There is little doubt that Catholic O'Leary, officer in the Hungarian army, cut exactly the sort of figure the Irish would love in a fellow Irishman in those abject Penal times; he was also, surely intentionally, a walking, or rather 'cantering', provocation to all right-thinking Planters:

> Oh white-handed rider!
> How fine your brooch was
> Fastened in cambric,
> And your hat with laces.
> When you crossed the sea to us,
> They would clear the street for you,
> And not for love of you
> But for deadly hatred.

They married and lived at Raleigh House, outside Macroom. It is still there, now a riding-stables, with an Imperial Eagle open-winged on its high garden wall. The 'slender bay horse' was very fine – legend says that it was given to him by the Empress Maria Theresa herself; legends have gathered round Art. In Penal times no Catholic was allowed to have a horse worth more than five pounds. Abraham Morris, High Sheriff of Cork, offered him the five pounds for the horse and O'Leary, obviously, refused. This effectively made him an outlaw. On the run, he was shot by a soldier at Carriganimmy (five miles from Raleigh House), and the poem says that Eileen was alerted to Art's fate by the horse's return, 'the reins beneath her trailing':

> I struck my hands together
> And made the bay horse gallop
> As fast as I was able,
> Till I found you dead before me
> Beside a little furze-bush.
> Without Pope or bishop,
> Without priest or cleric
> To read the death-psalms for you,

> But a spent old woman only
> Who spread her cloak to shroud you –
> Your heart's blood was still flowing;
> I did not stay to wipe it
> But filled my hands and drank it.

It is a complex poem; Art's father is given a voice in it, so is his sister. It is filled with pride of race, and status, as well as with grief. Towards the end there is a beautiful image of a shut box, with a reference to 'the school' which any Irish listener would know meant the bardic school; now gone, but Eileen O'Connell had drawn heavily on its traditions:

> Till Art O'Leary returns
> There will be no end to the grief
> That presses down on my heart,
> Closed up tight and firm
> Like a trunk that is locked
> And the key mislaid.
>
> All you women out there weeping
> Wait a little longer;
> We'll drink to Art son of Connor
> And the souls of all the dead,
> Before he enters the school –
> Not learning wisdom or music
> But weighed down by earth and stones.

'With this poem a world ended; we had not known it had lived so long.'[20] In a sense that is true. In the next generation, Eileen's nephew, Daniel O'Connell, urged Irishmen to forget the past, to forget their language, to stand up and take part in the contemporary world. In this way he won Catholic Emancipation.

SOUTH CORK

More or less due south of Kilcrea, on the coast, is another subject for a famous lament, a place rather than a person, the ruined abbey at Timoleague. This Franciscan foundation was built among wild swans and wading-birds and seabirds on a quiet inlet of Courtmac-sherry Bay, and it may be only chance that it was chosen for particular lament, among the many affecting abbey ruins that litter Ireland. There are many versions of an earlier, Irish, poem, and James Clarence

Mangan's is the best-known of these. It was published in *The Nation*, in 1846, after Thomas Davis, the editor, had recommended contributors to look at the Ordnance Survey in order to identify place-names referred to in Irish poems. It is not at all certain that the original Irish poem by Seán Ó Coileáin is about Timoleague at all – it is called 'Musings of a Melancholy Man' – and possibly Mangan did choose the name from a map; his poem would fit almost any such ruin, and he worked in the Ordnance Survey office, involved in the anglicization of place-names. (This is the subject of Brian Friel's play, *Translations*.)

Mangan's 'translation' of Ó Coileáin's poem is called 'Lament Over the Ruins of the Abbey of Teach Molaga':

> . . . Dim in the pallid moonlight stood,
> Crumbling to slow decay, the remnant of that pile
> Within which dwelt so many saints erewhile
> In loving brotherhood! . . .
>
> Rite, incense, chant, prayer, mass, have ceased.
> All, all have ceased! Only the whitening bones half sunk
> In earth now tell that ever here dwelt monk,
> Friar, acolyte, or priest,
>
> Oh! woe, that Wrong should triumph thus!
> Woe that the olden rite, the rule and the renown
> Of the Pure-souled and Meek should thus go down
> Before the Tyrannous!
>
> Where wert thou, Justice, in that hour?
> Where was thy smiling sword? What had those good men done
> That thou shouldst tamely see them trampled on
> By brutal England's power? . . .

At this point a 'Saxon' reader, however sympathetic, is likely to break off – there are three stanzas to go – and protest: Did we not also have our Dissolution of the Monasteries, and later destructions by Cromwellian soldiers? No doubt these were even worse in Ireland, but they are not, surely, specifically Irish grievances? Samuel Ferguson in his version of the poem, which itself derives from a yet earlier version by Thomas Furlong, leaves out the reference to English tyranny altogether, and turns violently on Furlong's editor for his sectarian animus, deemed totally unnecessary after Catholic Emancipation in 1829: 'He does not bate a jot of his most indignant obstinacy, he does not expunge an expression of his most inveterate and unchangeable hatred for Clan Luther, and the Saxon, but disfigures his book and disgraces himself by flinging in the teeth of his manumission, the whole miserly hoardings of his hatred when a slave. . . .'[21]

Thus can the most apparently innocent lament for a ruined place – and for ruined innocence – be cause for the violence of a quarrel. In fact the original poem does not mention England at all:

> . . . Without abbot or rule,
> Without quiet brothers.
> All I find is a pile
> Of mouldering bones. . . .
>
> My energy is sapped,
> I am aimless and blind.
> My friends and my children
> Decay in this church.
>
> My face is grim.
> My heart is a husk.
> If death called now
> I'd gladly welcome it.

That is the end of 'Melancholy Musings' by (possibly) Seán Ó Coileáin (1754–1816),[22] known in his time, in West Cork, as the 'Silver Tongue of Munster'. He became a hedge-schoolmaster on the little peninsula of Myross, between Castlehaven and Glandore harbour, a place so eloquently melancholy itself that Corkery calls it 'one of the most secret places in Ireland, without traffic, almost without the pulse of life'. It is still like that, and on a hill above it, over the sea, is one of the most dramatically desolate graveyards in Ireland. Apparently this poet was a drinker, and an 'unhappy' one, in the Irish phrase. His first wife left him, and his second, her sister, burnt his house down, or so it is said. He died at Skibbereen, where he had done some of his drinking, the rest of it probably done at nearby Union Hall.

Swift has connections with Union Hall. He is said to have stayed in the summer of 1723 with the minister at Rock Cottage, now called Glebe House, on a hill above the village, overlooking Glandore Harbour. Definite traces of Swift are hard to come across in Ireland, but news of him somehow persists. Union Hall claims that he wrote his Latin poem *Carberiae Rupes* ('Carbery Rocks') at Glebe House; but exactly which rocks, or island, are referred to, in 'many-islanded Carbery', is more vague. (Carbery is the name for the whole jagged coast.)

1. 'Take warning wave, take warning crown of the sea . . .' The Atlantic (here at Achill, Co. Mayo), source of the magical Waves of Irish legend

2. Newgrange (Boyne Valley, Co. Meath). The entrance stone, *c.* 3000 BC. The carved 'tangles' suggest a return to the centre

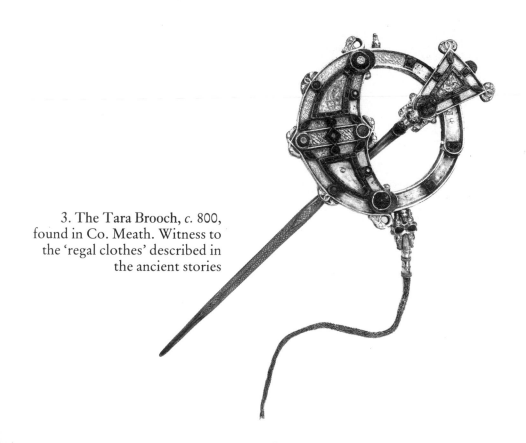

3. The Tara Brooch, *c.* 800, found in Co. Meath. Witness to the 'regal clothes' described in the ancient stories

4. Navan Fort (Co. Armagh). Emain Macha of the Cuchulainn and Deirdre legends

5. Slemish Mountain (Co. Antrim), where the young St Patrick was kept as a slave. 'If any hill was sure to be considered a holy or magical place, Slemish is one.'

6. Clonmacnois (Co. Offaly). The young scholars 'must have looked about them wildly sometimes, over the reedy, golden land and across the cold Shannon waters.'

7. Gougane Barra (Co. Cork). An early Victorian view of the place beloved of Sean
O'Faolain and Frank O'Connor – and the 'Tailor'

8. Bowen's Court in County Cork, a fairly typical house of the eighteenth-century Anglo-Irish gentry, called by Virginia Woolf 'a stone box'

9. 'Bohemian' Yeats and 'Clubman' George Moore outside Lady Gregory's Coole Park: two Masks, two performances

10. Somerville and Ross at work. 'The Cousins': Violet Martin ('Ross') on the right

11. Thoor Ballylee (Co. Galway). Yeats's Norman tower. 'I pace upon the battlements and stare . . .'

12. Augusta Gregory. At the Abbey Theatre, Sean O'Casey said, 'she acted the part of a charwoman, but one with a star on her breast.'

13. James Stephens by William Rothenstein. 'A literary acrobat, doing hair-raising swoops in the roof of the tent.'

14. The surrender of P. H. Pearse, 29 April 1916

15. Sean O'Faolain and Elizabeth Bowen at Bowen's Court. The 'new', post-Treaty, literary Ireland at ease with the 'old' Ascendancy

16. The 'new' and self-critical Ireland, at ease with each other. Brinsley Macnamara and (right) Brian O'Nolan, alias Flann O'Brien (and Myles na Gopaleen)

17. W. B. Yeats broadcasting in 1937. 'A blazing enthusiast who, well into his seventies, retained all the spontaneity and astonishment of a boy of seventeen.'

18. Frank O'Connor, who succeeded Yeats on the Board of the Abbey Theatre. 'But anyone who asks me to join the Board of another theatre will be shot on sight.'

19. The burnt-out shell of Moore Hall, Lough Carra, Co. Mayo

20. The Lake Isle of Innisfree. Yeats, homesick in London, 'saw a fountain in a
shop-window . . . and began to remember lake-water.'

Charles Smith (1715–62), the 'pioneer of Irish topography', tells us that the Dean 'often diverted himself in making little voyages on the coast, from Glandore harbour'; he identifies the Rocks as 'a stupendous arch, through which a boat may row' not far from the place where the Dean usually embarked. He also describes sea-caves 'near the west head of Castlehaven', which are low at the entrance, but grow higher within, so that 'the swell of the sea raises a boat up to the roof almost . . . which also, by turns, closes up the entrance and makes them very dark and gloomy. . . . Having made the same voyage more than once, I had the pleasure of observing that the dean's descriptions were as just as his numbers were beautiful.'[23]

Later editors have been scornful of Swift's Latin verses. In the contemporary translation they begin:

> Lo! from the Top of yonder Cliff, that shrouds
> Its airy Head amidst the azure clouds,
> Hangs a huge Fragment; destitute of props
> Prone on the Waves the rocky ruin drops.
> With hoarse Rebuff the swelling seas rebound,
> From Shore to Shore the Rocks return the Sound. . . .

Where these shores face the open sea the noise is indeed tremendous. It is possible that Swift could have been told of the mythical warning Waves that haunt so much poetry and legend in Irish, often in contradictory ways. 'Cliodhna's ['Clíona's'] Wave', for example, is called after a pre-Christian goddess of beauty, who eloped with a mortal and was reclaimed by a wave sent by her sea-god father; later she seems to have dwindled into a mermaid, drowned in Glandore harbour; whereas, as we have seen, Piaras Mac Gearailt compares the Virgin Mary herself with 'Cliodhna's Wave of Mercy'.[24]

It seems likely that Swift wrote his Latin couplets as a form of therapy. Not much is known about Swift's Dublin to Munster tour in 1723, after the death of 'Vanessa'; he wrote few letters and seemed to vanish from view. Perhaps it was then that he stayed with the Rev. Thomas Somerville, at Castlehaven Castle. This was the rectory for the little church next to it, now a ruin; nothing remains of the famously comfortable house, or of the castle itself which in 1924 slid into the sea.

By the side of the church is a little glen, overhung by trees that almost turn it into a tunnel, and a short way up the glen is the Holy Well of the local saint, St Barrahane, small tributes of rag tied to the bush that almost conceals it. The deep-sunk stream has been made into a water-garden, with grottoes and ornamental ferns. Naturally, it is said to have been a favourite walk of Swift's; and if he had walked up it a couple of centuries later, he might have encountered the sprightly, knickerbockered form of Bernard Shaw (at about the same age), coming down the glen from the new Castlehaven Rectory at the top of it, from whence he had just written to H.G. Wells that he had finished *The Doctor's Dilemma*: Shaw and his wife, related to the local Townshend family, rented the Rectory in September 1906.[25]

Further up the main inlet of Castlehaven harbour, falling towards the sea precipitately in what is more or less one long, elegant street, is that Anglo-Irish stronghold of the Somervilles, the Townshends, the Coghills, and so on – they shared a passion for genealogy and for clan intermarriage – Castletownshend. At the top of the street lived Edith Somerville, in the house called Drishane; at the bottom of it, in the church of St Barrahane (successor to the one at Castlehaven), set high on its knoll and almost entirely decorated with memorials in marble to those proud Planter families, she met her cousin from Ross in Galway, Violet Martin, in 1886, and there began the literary partnership, Somerville and Ross. At the bottom of the street, by the harbour below the church there are more traces, or rumours, of Swift. In the Castle there, in the older central portion, is a room still called 'The Dean's Room', its name painted in old letters on the door, inset, now, among later layers of paint; care has been taken not to paint it over. A ruined tower ('Swift's tower') above the house, all that remains of an older mansion, is where it is said he went to write; another candidate for the composition of *Carberiae Rupes*.

But Castletownshend's special claim to literary fame rests with Edith (E. Œ.) Somerville (1858–1949) and Violet Martin, 'Martin Ross' (1862–1915). Edith was twenty-eight and Martin (Violet) twenty-four when they met, 'hardly at the breakfast-time of life'. Edith was already making her way as an illustrator of English magazines (she trained as a painter in Paris) and she was at first uncertain when Martin suggested a literary collaboration. However, as soon as it began, it seemed to strike its individual note: flippant, bemused (at native Irish goings-on) and vigorous. By 1894 they had written their surprising masterpiece, *The Real Charlotte*, surprising because the facetiousness is now honed to a sharpness; the book is a study in malevolence, and contains more than a premonition of the decay of Anglo-Irish life, the end of the 'picnic in a foreign country' they both knew and enjoyed so much. What remains most surprising is the indistinguishable nature of the writing collaboration. They were often asked about this, but

> as a matter of fact, during our many years of collaboration, it was a point that never entered our minds to consider. To those who may be interested in an unimportant detail, I may say that our work was done conversationally. One or the other – not infrequently both, simultaneously – would state a proposition. This would be argued, combated perhaps, approved, or modified, it would then be written down by the (wholly fortuitous) holder of the pen. . . .[26]

The *Irish RM* stories followed the acerbic *The Real Charlotte* and were immensely popular. They are told in the amiably pompous and much put-upon first-person of the English Resident Magistrate, whose social certainties are constantly undercut by Irish informalities. They were written for an English market, for money to sustain their family houses, and for the authors' own independence. The social-painting sounds exact. The unfortunate magistrate is taken to meet the grandmother of his Irish (Protestant) landlord, in her castle:

> I may summarize her attire by saying that she looked as if she had robbed a scarecrow; her face was small and incongruously refined, the skinny hand that she extended to me had the grubby tan that bespoke the professional gardener, and was decorated with a magnificent diamond ring. On her head was a massive purple velvet bonnet. . . .
>
> Dinner was as incongruous as everything else. Detestable soup in a splendid old silver tureen that was nearly as dark in hue as [her servant] Robinson Crusoe's thumb; a perfect salmon, perfectly cooked, on a chipped kitchen dish; such cut glass as is not easy to find nowadays; sherry that, as Flurry subsequently remarked, would burn the shell off an egg; and a bottle of port, draped in immemorial cobwebs, wan with age, and probably priceless. Throughout the vicissitudes of the meal Mrs Knox's conversation flowed on undismayed, directed sometimes at me – she had installed me in the position of friend of her youth – and talked to me as if I were my own grandfather – sometimes at Crusoe, with whom she had several heated arguments, and sometimes she would make a statement of remarkable frankness on the subject of her horse-farming affairs to Flurry. . . .[27]

Were the stories snobbish? Perhaps inevitably they were, but Frank O'Connor, working-class Corkman, gives them full marks for authenticity:

> With Joyce's *Dubliners*, *The R.M.* is the most closely observed of all Irish story-books, but whereas Joyce observes with cruel detachment, the authors of *The Irish R.M.* observe with love and glee. 'The atmosphere of the waiting-room set at naught at a single glance the theory that there can be no smoke without fire.' Not only does that opening sentence of one story bring you straight into the waiting-room of any Irish railway station, it gives you the very accent of an Irish companion on observing it. The flick of the wit sends the phrase spinning. . . .
>
> The dialogue has the same absolute authenticity, and, with apologies to a critic who has argued that the genius of 'The R.M.' was Miss Violet Martin, I must say that the dialogue has to my ears an unmistakable ring of County Cork. As a description of a swarm of rabbits, 'I thought the face of the field was running from me' is excellent, but I cannot hear it in any but a Cork accent.[28]

O'Connor makes no mention of *The Real Charlotte*, the stature of which has only slowly come to be recognized. The authors had sharp ears for the turns of Irish speech (they used to write those down verbatim, before they forgot), and sharp eyes for landscapes also, and for gardens (the one that follows is an amalgam of Somerville's Drishane with Ross's Galway); they care for the surprising, useful word ('ingratiatingly', 'struggle') that sets a scene, and a character:[29]

> At the back of the Rosemount kitchen garden the ground rose steeply into a knoll of respectable height, where grew a tangle of lilac bushes, rhododendrons, seringas, and yellow broom. A gravel path wound ingratiatingly up through these, in curves artfully devised by Mr Lambert to make the most of the extent and the least of the hill, and near the top a garden seat was sunk in the bank, with laurels shutting it in on each side, and a laburnum 'showering golden tears' above it.
>
> Through the perfumed screen of the lilac bushes in front unromantic glimpses of the roof of the house were obtainable – eyesores to Mr Lambert, who had concentrated all his energies on hiding everything nearer than the semi-circle of lake and distant mountain held in an opening cut through the rhododendrons at the corner of the little plateau on which the seat stood.

Without the disturbance of middle distance the eye lay at ease on the far-off struggle of the Connemara mountains, and on a serene vista of Lough Moyle; a view that enticed forth, as to a playground, the wildest and most foolish imaginations, and gave them elbow room; a world so large and remote that it needed the sound of wheels on the road to recall the existence of the petty humanities of Lismoyle.

They sent an early copy of *The Real Charlotte* to their friends Sir William and Lady Gregory (who, in her widowhood, was to be the powerful patron of W.B. Yeats and the whole Irish Revival). Sir William welcomed their book 'with trumpets and shawms'. The later, older, Lady Gregory was not so sure about Somerville and Ross. O'Connor has mixed feelings: 'The terrible old lady from Coole used to say when hesitant Americans only vaguely remembered her work: "No, I am not de autor of 'The Irish R.M.'" "We work," she kept on reminding herself and others, "to add dignity to Ireland," and dignity is the thing which Anglo-Irish literature lacked before her time.' The trouble with nationalist literature, thinks O'Connor, is that it became too worthy. '"A terrible beauty was born." Also a terrible boredom. At least one is safe from that sort of thing in the pages of "The R.M."' That is the perfect example of the Irish wanting to annoy each other, because at the time O'Connor was writing it was not done to like the *Irish RM*. Although he does add, 'but old Augusta Gregory was right all the same', the irritation had already been satisfactorily aroused, as he well knew. Somerville and Ross were the last writers to make fun of, and out of, the Irish, from what could be called a 'Colonialist' point of view. From now on it had to be left to the Irish to make fun of themselves, which is what Frank O'Connor is doing. He also recognizes the dangers of this; he talks of younger writers: 'I cannot prophesy which houses they will occupy on the coast. . . . All I can prophesy is that they will be on the coast, so that, in case of necessity, they can catch the mail-boat in a hurry. An Irish writer cannot take too many precautions in the matter of keeping the mail boat in sight.'[30]

Writers who see both sides of a question – or all sides – are an embarrassment to any government, especially that of a new country, trying to find out what sort of a country it is government of. O'Connor did not want it to be a place of easy certainties. He began his career with a book of stories called *Guests of the Nation* (1931) and the title story begins:

At dusk the big Englishman, Belcher, would shift his long legs out of the ashes and say 'Well, chums, what about it?' and Noble and myself would say 'All right, chum' (for we had picked up some of their curious expressions), and the little Englishman, Hawkins, would light the lamp and bring out the cards. Sometimes Jeremiah Donovan would come up and supervise the game, and get excited over Hawkins' cards, which he always played badly, and shout at him, as if he was one of our own. 'Ah, you divil, why didn't you play the tray?'

We learn that Belcher and Hawkins are two English prisoners taken during the Irish War of Independence, being guarded by three Republican soldiers. The point is that they had all become friends, or at least are settled down domestically together. Everyone in the story, which is quite short, is given their individual humanity; even the nervy Jeremiah Donovan. News comes to the Irishmen that some Irish prisoners have been shot by the English; their orders are to shoot Belcher and Hawkins in reprisal. None of the men can quite believe it. None of them can understand what they are doing, nor do the victims quite comprehend what is being done to them. Belcher asks for the loan of a handkerchief to tie round his eyes, his own is too small. He is given one and they help him tie it.

'You understand that we're only doing our duty?' said Donovan.
Belcher's head was raised like a blind man's, so that you could only see his chin and the top of his nose in the lantern-light.
'I never could make out what duty was myself,' he said. 'I think you're all good lads, if that's what you mean. I'm not complaining.'

Sentences taken from a story that was written as carefully as a piece of music give little suggestion of its power. The three Irishmen go back to the house. The housekeeper guesses what has happened:

'Was that what ye did to them?' she asked.
Then, by God, in the very doorway, she fell on her knees and began praying, and after looking at her for a minute or two Noble did the same by the fireplace. I pushed my way out past her and left them at it. I stood at the door, watching the stars and listening to the shrieking of the birds dying out over the bogs. It is so strange what you feel at times like that that you can't describe it. Noble says he saw everything ten times the size, as though there was nothing in the whole world but

that little patch of bog with the two Englishmen stiffening into it, but with me it was as if the patch of bog where the Englishmen were was a million miles away, and even Noble and the old woman, mumbling behind me, and the birds and the bloody stars were all far away, and I was somehow very small and very lost and lonely like a child astray in the snow. And anything that happened to me afterwards, I never felt the same about again.

Sean O'Faolain also wrote a story about the brutalities attending the birth of independent Ireland. 'Midsummer Night Madness' (1932) is more operatic, set in just such a decaying Anglo-Irish house as entertained Somerville and Ross's R.M., but the mood is now infinitely blacker and more violent. The old order is finally breaking down, and the new one, in so far as it has been born, contains violence and hatreds likely to get out of control.[31]

O'Connor and O'Faolain were townsmen. When they needed the countryside they went to Gougane Barra, in the mountains, between Macroom and Bantry. It cannot have changed much since the Halls gasped at it in 1840: 'A sudden turning in the road brings the traveller within view, and almost over, the lake of Gougane Barra – a scene of more utter loneliness, stern grandeur, or savage magnificence, it is difficult to conceive; redeemed, however, as all things savage are, by one passage of gentle and inviting beauty, upon which the eye turns as to a spring-well in the desert – the little island with its group of graceful ash-trees and ruined chapel. . . .'[32]

J.J. Callanan (1795–1829)[33] wrote a poem about the place, which is now carved on a stone near St Finbar's chapel on the little island. He seems to have seen it in worse weather:

. . . And its zone of dark hills – oh! to see them all brightening,
When the tempest flings out his red banner of lightning,
And the waters come down 'mid the thunder's deep rattle,
Like clans from their hills at the voice of the battle. . . .

Sean O'Faolain set one of his stories in the hotel there, 'The Silence of the Valley':

Only in the one or two farmhouses about the lake, or in the fishing hotel at its edge – preoccupations of work and pleasure – does one ever forget the silence of the valley. Even in the winter, when the great cataracts slide down the mountain face, the echoes of falling water are fitful: the winds fetch and carry them. In the summer a fisherman will hear the tinkle of the ghost of one of those falls only if he steals among the mirrored reeds under the pent of the cliffs, and withholds the plash of his oars. These tiny muted sounds will awe and delight him by the vacancy out of which they creep, intermittently.

One May evening a relaxed group of early visitors were helping themselves to drink in the hotel bar, throwing the coins into a pint glass. There were five of them, all looking out the door at the lake, the rhododendrons on the hermit's island, the mountain towering beyond it, and the wall of blue air above the mountain line. . . .

Later in the story he mentions 'the cobbler's cottage'. Possibly he is fictionalizing the 'Tailor's' cottage.[34] With the famous 'Tailor' and his wife, Anstey (Anastasia), whom O'Faolain must have known, Frank O'Connor says he passed the happiest Christmas of his life. It was as though these two men, O'Connor and O'Faolain, and other friends from a wider world like Seamus Murphy the sculptor, young Father Traynor, and the writer Eric Cross, found in this old cottager a genuine *shanachie* (storyteller), the spirit of free Ireland perhaps (in an Ireland that was elsewhere becoming tight-lipped), or perhaps just a free spirit. He spoke a pure form of Irish, which was useful for those who wanted to perfect their own. But for Frank O'Connor: 'There are only two dialects of Irish, plain Irish and toothless Irish, and, lacking a proper acquaintance with the latter, I think I missed the cream of the old man's talk, though his English was very colourful and characteristic.'[35]

The Tailor's tales were certainly amusing enough, and far-fetched. One is about the true origin of the Rothschild family:

. . . They started in Cork. Ratschild isn't their right name at all. They are really Kellihers, but they changed that. They used to be house painters in the beginning, and one day one of the brothers was painting a house, and he was on the scaffold having a smoke for himself, when he saw a rat come out of a hole, and it had a sovereign in its mouth . . .

Kelliher went on smoking and did nothing to frighten the rat, and the rat went on carrying out sovereigns and making a pile of them. When at last he had made a good pile, Kelliher threw his paint-brush at it, and came down from the scaffold, and collected up the pile of sovereigns and counted them, and found that he had come into the way of being a rich man.

That was the beginning of the Ratschilds. They discontinued the house-painting business and started a bank and soon were in a mighty way of business, and because they had made their beginning from the money the rat had collected, they were ever afterwards called the Ratschilds, and the devil blast the lie it is.

That last expression is an insistence on the *truth* of the story.

Charm is notoriously difficult to capture on paper, and perhaps the hold the Tailor had over his visitors would have been forgotten, were it not for a judgement by the Irish Censorship Board so shocking that it remains, in O'Connor's word, 'incredible'. Eric Cross filled a book with the old man's stories, *The Tailor and Anstey* (1942). Everyone was delighted with the book, his friends, the Tailor himself, and the reviewers. In 1943 the book was banned by the Board because it was 'in its general tendency indecent'. In the Senate only one man had the courage to call this judgement nonsense, Sir John Keene, a Protestant landlord.

The verdict was no joke for the Tailor and his wife. Frank O'Connor's translation of Merriman's 'The Midnight Court' had also been banned, but that was all right: 'After all, you don't take up a dangerous trade like literature in Ireland without developing the hide of a rhinoceros. . . . What alarmed me was that the Tailor and Anstey lived in a mountain townland where people still believed in the fairies. It wasn't only an unpleasant situation; it could be a dangerous one.'[36]

Ten years later the Censorship Board ruled that the book had no such tendency. But the couple had to endure the years of ostracism, even had to be given police protection. However, when O'Connor last visited him the Tailor was talking as much and as well as ever, and later, even as he was dying, his police protector, Guard Hoare, was cycling from Ballingeary with a bottle of whiskey for him, arriving too late. (The thought of that undrunk bottle of whiskey haunted his wake.) 'Suddenly Anstey, who as usual was fussing about by the door with her broom, rested her arms on it and said, "There'll be great talk above tonight." It had suddenly dawned on her that her own loss was Heaven's happiness.'

The Tailor and Anstey are buried under a tombstone designed by Seamus Murphy in the little graveyard by the lake opposite Finbar's Island. Father Traynor who defended them is buried on the island, but no monument to him was permitted, so his friends drew his initials in the ground with pebbles.

North of Gougane Barra, Ballyvourney was a nest of Gaelic poets, and now has summer schools for the learning of Irish. In the early 1700s

> One of those Courts of Poetry was assembled in the house of Dáith Ó Iarflatha at Ballyvourney, in County Cork, when a voice was heard from outside. Catching it, Liam Ó Murchadha, poet, leaped to his feet, flung his head high, and chanted out four lines of welcoming verse, making them as he went on, not conscious of any difficulty in doing so, that single voice from the darkness having set his heart leaping and his brain alight. . . . Translation makes but poor prose of lines so skilfully woven:

> *I recognize the note of a man of true power, the witty Egan,*
> *Approaching the height, full of wisdom and respect,*
> *You have not been acquainted with the great man, nor does*
> *   he belong to your side,*
> *And with friendliness of heart I bespeak for him an hundred*
> *   of welcomes.*

> Two hundred years on from that night of living poetry amidst the mountains of West Cork, those lines were to be gathered from the lips of a peasant.[37]

'Witty Egan' is, of course, the great Egan O'Rahilly. It is easy to understand why subsequent Irish writers have flinched from pages like that one from Corkery, especially when they sense, over their shoulders, the superior smile of an English reader. In his defence it has to be remembered that the oblivion into which these writers had fallen appeared at one time to be total; remembered, too, must be the thrill Corkery will have felt when he heard, or heard some other scholar repeat, those words taken from 'the lips of a peasant'.

The old poets had not only been driven out of Irish consciousness, or nearly so, they had also in their own day been driven on to poor, unwanted land. One such place is the region of Slieve Luachra, north of Ballyvourney in the next range of hills. That is where O'Rahilly was born, within a mile of his bardic successor, Owen Roe O'Sullivan. Slieve Luachra will be reached again, from Killarney: meanwhile a circuit of the peninsulas that break up the coast of west Cork and Kerry. It was these with their harbours that brought settlers, and their beauty that attracted tourists.

WEST CORK – KERRY

Beginning at Glengarriff, and having in mind the dispossessed poets,
it is pleasant to hear Thackeray, for all his adopted 'Mr Titmarsh'
Cockney persona, taking great trouble at Glengarriff and elsewhere
to compare the native Irish favourably with some of his own countrymen. At the inn of Glengarriff a group of these, after much drinking,
decide they have been cheated by the innkeeper and threaten to report
him to his landlord, Lord Bantry. 'An Irish gentleman' intervenes
and asks them to moderate their language, saying that if men swore
and cursed like that in his house he would know how to put them
out:

> 'Put *me* out,' says one of the young men, placing himself
> before the fat old blasphemer, his relative, 'Put *me* out . . . who
> are *you*, sir? who *are* you, sir? I insist on knowing who you are.'
> 'And who are you?' asks the Irishman.
> 'Sir, I am a gentleman, and *pay my way*. . . .'

At this point Thackeray, 'like a great ass that I was', fearful that
the silent, courteous landlord might really get into trouble through
these ruffians, felt he had to intervene, and said that if they did write
such a letter he would write another to say that the landlord
'had acted throughout with extraordinary forbearance and civility'.
Whereupon he is challenged to a fight. He avoids this, and realizes
the whole incident has only furnished material for yet another Irish
anecdote; as soon as the brutes had gone, 'the first thing I heard,
was the voice of Mr Eccles repeating the story to a new cus-
tomer'.[38] Presumably nothing came of the incident, because Eccles
Hotel is still there, or a version of it, dead-centre of the two arms
of the small and beautiful bay. Bernard Shaw, who stayed at the
hotel in 1923–4, wrote *St Joan* there, or in the Italian garden of
Garinish Island, just offshore, to which he had himself rowed every
day.

That phrase, 'paying my way', seems to have obsessed Thackeray.
He is still turning it over in his mind when he reaches Killarney,
and hears a Scotchman boasting about his own country. Thackeray
wonders why the Irish are not prouder of theirs – 'so fertile and
beautiful, and has produced more than its fair proportion of men of
genius, valour, and wit. I have met more gentlemen here than in
any place I ever saw, gentlemen of high and low ranks. . . . "I am
a gentleman, and pay my way. . . ." I have not heard a sentence near
so vulgar from any man in Ireland.'

Glengarriff is at the head of the Beare (Bere, Beara) Peninsula, which pushes out between Bantry Bay and the Kenmare river.[39] Perhaps because it has more harbours, there is an even greater sense of the presence of the sea there than in the other peninsulas, and of peat-coloured streams running into it; the sounds and reflections and movements of water. One of the most famous of early Irish poems is the ninth-century 'Lament of the Old Woman of Beare' (or 'Hag' or 'Nun' of Beare, depending on the translation, and whether she is seen as a human or a symbolic woman). The sea dominates the poem, and it begins with a sea image:[40]

> Ebb tide has come for me:
> my life drifts downwards
> like a retreating sea
> with no tidal turn.

She laments her youth:

> Bony and thin
> are my hands;
> dear was the trade they practised,
> they would be around splendid kings.

The poem is realistic, harsh. She hears the warning wave, as it is so often heard in the Irish poetry of these parts, and elsewhere. 'The wave of the great sea is noisy, winter has stirred it up.' The wave may come and take her away, enter the cellar of her house, but the sea is also the will of God, so the poem rises towards its end almost to a kind of jokey blasphemy. 'Well might the Son of Mary spend the night and be under the roof-tree of my pantry; though I am unable to offer any other hospitality, I have never said "No" to anybody.' (Other translations have, 'I never said no to a man.') It ends with the sea:

> Where once was life's flood
> all is ebb.

Northwards, the next and biggest peninsula, is Iveragh (*Uíbh Ráthach*; or the Waterville Peninsula or Ring of Kerry).[41] Towards the end of its southern shore is the O'Connell fiefdom at Caherdaniel and the house at Derrynane, from which came Eileen O'Connell who married and lamented Art O'Leary, and from which her nephew, Daniel O'Connell, emerged to win Catholic Emancipation. There they lived the life of Irish chieftains. Corkery makes the observation, concerning the great, Irish, 'Lament for Art O'Leary', that Arthur Young (the English agriculturalist) could have visited Derrynane, seen the flocks and the dairy herds, suspected the smuggling, 'without suspecting that the Irish language was anything but a *patois* in which the master spoke to his herdsmen and shepherds'. He also remarks that when the O'Connells put their signatures to an official document they left out the Irish 'O', but when they went elsewhere, or rose in the outside world, they put it back: 'Of the Connells, Young could have made some report. Of the O'Connells, none.'

O'Faolain gives a picture of Daniel O'Connell at home in Kerry:

> There he was, as somebody said, like a petty German king, with his hounds, his early-morning hunting, his red-coated men with their long staves hallooing from glen to glen. One would like to dally with them there, especially where we find him seated high up the mountain-side greeting the postman from Cahir-civeen who comes clambering up with his heavy post-bag.
>
> He would breakfast on the hills, going quickly but intently through his letters, strewing the grass with *The Times*, *The Universe*, letters from France or America, reports from Dublin, the *Oxford and Cambridge* magazine that contains some article of interest to him, begging letters, appeals from his poor folk in trouble . . . while, far beneath him, all Kerry sends its hills falling to the vast sea. The day's hunt over he comes back at evening, down the slopes, followed by his shaggy dogs, his weary hunters, into the hospitable dining-room at Darrynane. . . .
>
> Even there his people drag him from retreat, and one of the most famous incidents in his career began there one autumn morning at eight o'clock as he looked out to the sound of a horse's hoofs, and saw Burke of Ballyhea staggering to the door after an all-night ride of ninety miles.[42]

Burke had come to tell him of the men condemned for the 'Doneraile Conspiracy' in County Cork (subject of Sheehan's *Glenanaar*); and O'Connell rode all day and night, breakfasted in court, took on the Crown Prosecutor and achieved a verdict of Not Guilty. From then on, he devoted himself to politics.

At the far end of the Iveragh Peninsula is Valentia Island, where Aubrey de Vere sent Tennyson to listen to the waves pounding in, promising him they would make the waves of Mablethorpe or Beachy Head sound puny.[43] Had Tennyson heard about the magic Waves of Ireland? At Valentia he said that their sound made all the revolutions of Europe dwindle into insignificance. He had also sought out waves on his previous Irish trip in 1842, when he visited the sea-caves at Ballybunion in North Kerry, and is said to have stored up an image from them:

> So dark a forethought rolled about his brain,
> As on a dull day in an Ocean cave
> The blind wave feeling round his long sea-hall
> In silence. . . .

Later in his life Tennyson tried his hand at a poem ('Tomorrow') in Irish dialect, helped by William Allingham, and getting most of his Irish vernacular from William Carleton's *Traits and Stories of the Irish Peasantry*. It is a story of the body of a young man, long dead, retrieved well-preserved from the bog, and seen by his lover, now old, who drops dead beside him at the sight. (De Vere told Tennyson the tale.) The dialect is painstaking, even if its reproduction is tiresome:

Och, Molly, we thought, machree, ye would start back agin
    into life,
Whin we laid yez, aich be aich, at yer wake like husban' an' wife.
Sorra the dhry eye thin but was wet for the frinds that was
    gone! . . .
An' now that I tould yer Honour whativer I hard an' seen,
Yer Honour 'ill give me a thrifle to dhrink yer health in potheen.

From Valentia can be seen, erupting out of the sea eight miles away, the startling needles of the Skelligs, and they can be reached, with difficulty, from Knightstown on Valentia. Settlements of anchorites lived on those precipitous crags, possibly from the sixth century, and the English poet Geoffrey Grigson (1905–85) was astonished at the state of preservation of their cells in that wind-torn place: he had expected ruins, but

. . . here on Skellig Michael all was more or less complete. The first large hut, perhaps the refectory, the common meeting-place, was perfect. Stones of white quartz let into the conical dry walling above the doorway were formed into a cross. We bent under the wide slate lintel, and went into the clean spacious interior. It was lit by window-holes above our heads, the floor was paved, pegs of slate stuck out from the walls. From these, perhaps, depended on thongs the leather 'book-cases', or satchels, in which the liturgical books were kept. A few such Irish satchels have survived . . .

I spent most of a day on Skellig Michael and came away reluctantly enough. Militant Protestants have had much to say of the selfishness and defeatism of the monastic life. I don't know. I am neither Protestant, except by upbringing, nor Catholic, but is it not moving to a degree when we think of the quiet of that selfless and hard devotion to an end which is superhuman? Moving about the coasts of Kerry afterwards, I understood what a symbol Skellig Michael must have been to those who were neither monks nor clergy, seeing it on the horizon, a single or a double peak, but always blue, always or often, with its nimbus of white cloud, its trailing coif of holiness.[44]

The next long finger of County Kerry pointing west into the Atlantic is the Dingle Peninsula, or Corcaguiney. Starting along it we again come upon Egan O'Rahilly (1670?–1726), by tradition lying sick in his sister's cottage above the huge sandbar of Inch Strand, lamenting what has happened to Ireland, to her bards, to himself. In his desperation, driven 'witless' by the relentless warning waves of Ireland, he turns fiercely on the waves themselves, warns *them* in return, threatens to strangle them.[45]

> Without flocks or cattle or the curved horns
> Of cattle, in a drenching night without sleep,
> My five wits on the famous uproar
> Of the wave toss like ships.
> And I cry for boyhood, long before
> Winkle and dogfish had defiled my lips. . . .
>
> My heart shrinks in me, my heart ails
> That every hawk and royal hawk is lost;
> From Cashel to the far sea
> Their birthright is dispersed
> Far and near, night and day, by robbery
> And ransack, every town oppressed.
>
> Take warning wave, take warning crown of the sea,
> I, O'Rahilly – witless from your discords –
> Were Spanish sails again afloat
> And rescue on your tides,

Would force this outcry down your wild throat,
Would make you swallow these Atlantic words.

At the far end of the wild peninsula, near Sybil Head, not far from
Ballyferriter, stand the remains of 'Ferriter's Castle'. Pierce Ferriter
(c.1600–53) was a Dingle chieftain of Norman descent who (as did
the earlier Norman, Gerald the Rhymer of Lough Gur) wrote poems
in Irish in the fashion of *amour courtois*:[46]

Gentlest of women, put your weapons by,
Unless you want to ruin all mankind;
Leave the assault or I must make reply,
Proclaiming that you are murderously inclined. . . .

Hide your bright eyes, your shining teeth, away;
If all our sighs and trembling and dismay
Can touch your heart or satisfy your pride,
Gentlest of women, lay your arms aside.

Ferriter (Piaras Feiritéar), like many others of families originally
Norman, joined with Ireland against England in the rising of 1641;
he led a siege against Tralee, and was hanged for this, in Killarney.
Thomas Kinsella says he is 'still a folk hero and much quoted
poet among Irish speakers in the Dingle *Gaeltacht* [Irish-speaking
region]'.

The playwright John Millington Synge (1871–1909) spent part of
the summer of 1905 in Ballyferriter, perfecting his Irish (the village
is still a centre of Gaelic studies).

I go out often in the mornings to the site of Sybil Ferriter's
Castle, on a little headland reached by a narrow strip of rocks.
As I lie there I can watch whole flights of cormorants and
choughs and seagulls that fly about under the cliffs, and beyond
them a number of niavogues that are nearly always fishing in
Ferriter's Cove. Further on there are Sybil Head and three rocky
points, the Three Sisters; then Smerwick Harbour and Brandon
far away, usually covered with white airy clouds.[47]

It was at Smerwick in 1580 that there landed an expedition of
about six hundred people, financed by the Pope, composed mainly
of Italians but with Spaniards, English and Irish among them, as well
as women and children. They occupied the Golden Fort (*Dún an Óir*)
on the headland, hoisted the Papal flag, and waited. It was the first

considerable invasion of British territory since the Norman Conquest, and was taken seriously. They were surrounded by Lord Grey's forces, surrendered and were then all slaughtered. The massacre shocked Catholic Europe. On that day Walter Ralegh was Captain of the Guard. Edmund Spenser, Lord Grey's Secretary, may also have witnessed it.

Synge's real object was to get to the Blasket Islands. The Great Blasket lies, like a wedge of green cheese, three miles off the end of the Dingle peninsula. In Blasket Sound, between the islands and Dunquin on the mainland, was enacted one of the great dramas of the wrecking of the Spanish Armada in 1588: 'A little company of ships, the chance companions of the storm, ran in upon the Kerry coast on the 11th of September. One of these was the flagship of Martinez de Recalde, Admiral of the whole Armada, who had a bitter knowledge of Corcaguiney, for he had commanded the fleet which had landed the Spanish force doomed to slaughter in the fort of Smerwick a few short years before.'

Robin Flower (1881–1946), Englishman, scholar of Gaelic, who spent many summers on the Great Blasket, imagines the scene.

> For the next few days they staggered about the sea, the uncertain wind driving them this way and that, the sick and famished crew hardly able to haul upon the ropes as the ship came about, the guns in the ballast rolling from side to side with the send of the waves, and great seas coming on board between the high castles at prow and stern. Then at last they found their way home to Spain, and Recalde took to his bed, his heart broken with the shame of that great enterprise gone awry, and in two days died in silence.
>
> It is a matter of wonder that no tradition remains among the people of this huge calamity. The galleons had ridden off the Island for days, two of them had gone down in the Sound, the cliffs were crowded with spectators looking down on the great hulks, with their patched sides and the dishonoured gilding of their stern galleries, their broken masts and tattered sails, and their spectral company eaten with disease, hollow with hunger. . . .'[48]

Perhaps there is no tradition, at least on the island itself, because it was then, as it is again now, uninhabited. The first few families settled on it in the seventeenth century. By the 1840s there were about 150 people on the island and this population remained more or less constant until after the First World War when it began to drop, until the last families left in the early 1950s, mostly settling on the mainland at places near to the Blaskets, as though they still wanted to see them.

In the early twentieth century, Gaelic intellectuals, and scholars from abroad, became fascinated by the simplicities, almost neolithic, of life on the Blaskets. The islanders were encouraged to write in Irish about the life they led, and this several of them did with great clarity, producing at least two substantial books, *The Islandman*, by Tomas O'Crohan (1856–1937); and *Twenty Years A-Growing*, by Maurice O'Sullivan (1904–50). What is astonishing about all the Blasket writers is the hardness of the lives they describe and yet, at the same time, their appreciation of the beauty of the islands and the views from them and of them. Peig Sayers (1873–1958), in *An Old Woman's Reflections*, describes rowing home after an excursion: 'It was a lovely night, the air was clean, full of brilliant stars and the moon shining on the sea. From time to time a sea-bird would give a cry. Inside in the black caves where the moon was not shining the seals were lamenting to themselves. I would hear too, the murmuring of the sea running in and out through the clefts of the stones and the music of the oars cleaving the sea. . . .'[49]

Synge was so enchanted with Blasket (he stayed with the 'king' they elected from among themselves) that he confesses he could hardly bear the thought of any other stranger going there. He sits in a pub in mainland Ballyferriter, and thinks of it:

It is evening in these four white-washed inn walls with a lamp, a book and my papers, instead of the little queen and the old king and all their company. By this time they are wandering back from the head of the cliff and are gathering in the kitchen where the little queen has sanded the floor, and filled the water crock and pushed the nets into a corner. Yet I know even while I was there I was an interloper only, a refugee in a garden between four seas.

It is curious I have a jealousy for that Island – the whole island and its people – like the jealousy of men in love. The last days I was there a stranger – a middle-aged and simple-minded man from an inland district – was staying there too, and all the time I was making arrangements to come away I was urging him, I hardly know why, to come away also. At last I was successful and he came away in the canoe beside me, but without any particular plans. . . . Then he disappeared. I made enquiries and I heard he had been seen late in the evening riding quickly towards Dunquin where one leaves for the Island. An inexplicable but fearful jealousy came over me; who was he that he should enjoy that life and quiet when I had left it? Who was he that he should sit in my place by the chimney and tell stories to the old men and boys? I was walking about my room in extravagant rage when I heard his step on the stairs, and he told me he had been out for a ride only. What mystery of attraction is in that simple life.[50]

Tomás O'Crohan was born in 1856. In *The Islandman* he talks of his young days when they used large boats; then, without explanation, they seem to be only using canoes, very light, made of wood covered with tarred fabric. Groups of them are drawn up still at the bottom of the steep cliff at Dunquin, to take summer visitors to the island. They look too flimsy to risk on even that short stretch of wild sea. Synge learned the reason for the abandonment of bigger boats, from a local:

> 'They are not better than boats,' said Maurice, 'but they are more useful. Before you get a heavy boat swimming you will be up to your waist, and then you will be sitting the whole night like that; but a canoe will swim in a handful of water, so that you can get in dry and be dry and warm the whole night. Then there will be seven men in a big boat and seven shares of the fish; but in a canoe there will be three men only and three shares of the fish, though the nets are the same in the two.'

Both O'Crohan and O'Sullivan (born nearly fifty years after O'Crohan, in 1904) knew of the legend of Pierce Ferriter, who was said to have hidden on the island in a cave when on the run from the Cromwellians. O'Sullivan, in *Twenty Years A-Growing*, is shown the cave by his grandfather:[51]

> 'Wasn't he a wonderful man?'
> 'Oh, he did great destruction on the English at that time.'
> We were down at the cave now. My grandfather crept in on all fours and I behind him, for the entrance was not more than two feet high. Once inside, there was room to stand up, for it was above seven feet. . . .
> 'Look at that stone. That's where he used to lay his head.'
> 'It was a hard pillow.'

'No doubt. Did you ever hear the verse he composed here when he was tired of the place, on a wild and stormy night? It is only a couple of words.'

His grandfather repeated the poem, checking whether his grandson now had it by heart.[52]

O God above, do you pity me now as I am,
a lonely solitary who hardly sees the day?
The drop that's high above on the top of the roofstone
falling into my ear, and the sound of the wave at my heel.

As he spoke the last words, the tears fell from the old man.

'Musha, daddo, isn't it a nice lonesome verse?'

Maurice O'Sullivan left the island to join the Civic Guard, and was drowned in a swimming accident in 1950.

O'Crohan knows that the life on the island is coming to an end. He composes a simple, clear threnody for it, and it will serve for all such endings.[53]

This is a crag in the midst of the great sea, and again and again the blown surf drives right over it before the violence of the wind, so that you daren't put your head out any more than a rabbit that crouches in his burrow in Inishvickillaun when the rain and the salt spume are flying. Often would we put to sea at the dawn of day when the weather was decent enough, and by the day's end our people on land would be keening us, so much had the weather changed for the worse. It was our business to be out in the night, and the misery of that sort of fishing is beyond telling. I count it the worst of all trades. . . .

It wasn't thirst for the drink that made us want to go where it was, but only the need to have a merry night instead of the misery that we knew only too well before. What the drop of drink did to us was to lift up the hearts in us, and we would spend a day and a night ever and again in company together when we got the chance. That's all gone by now, and the high heart and the fun are passing from the world. Then we'd take the homeward way together easy and friendly after all our revelry, like the children of one mother, none doing hurt or harm to his fellow. . . .

One day there will be none left in the Blasket of all I have mentioned in this book – and none to remember them. I am thankful to God, who has given me the chance to preserve from forgetfulness those days that I have seen with my own eyes and have borne their burden, and that when I am gone men will know what life was like in my time and the neighbours that lived with me.

AROUND KILLARNEY

Pierce Ferriter, so tenderly remembered on Blasket Island, was according to tradition given a safe-conduct after the siege of Tralee, but was nevertheless hanged by Cromwell's force, in 1643, in Killarney. He is honoured as one of the 'Four Kerry Poets', who are buried at Muckross Abbey beside the largest of the famous Killarney lakes, Lough Leane.[54]

In the eighteenth and nineteenth centuries, Killarney developed as one of the great tourist attractions of Europe, on the main route of every traveller to Ireland. Thackeray resisted the place, as well he might; it must have been full of touts and guides in 1842. What was the point of all this tourism? he asks: 'And yet, they all come hither, and go through the business regularly, and would not miss seeing every one of the lakes, and going up every one of the hills – by which circumlocution the writer wishes ingenuously to announce that he will not see any more lakes, ascend any more mountains or towers, visit any gaps of Dunloe, or any prospects whatever, except such as nature shall fling in his way in the course of a quiet, reasonable, walk.'[55]

But the Lakes of Killarney are as beautiful as everyone has said they are for two hundred years, especially if you approach them from the south, the high winding road from Kenmare; you look down on the Upper Lake, and pass a smaller lake beside the road, a perfect mirror reflecting the trees around it, the hills and the coloured clouds. That is, if you are lucky with weather. Shelley, aged twenty-one, with his even younger wife Harriet and two companions, spent two mysterious weeks in Killarney in March 1813. It was their second visit to Ireland; this time they seem to have been in hiding, after fleeing impulsively from Wales.[56] Shelley's friend Thomas Hogg, who followed them to Dublin but missed them, suggests in his bantering way that the Divine Poet had been beguiled by some 'picturesque tourist' into an irresistible delusion of Killarney as an Earthly Paradise. But back in London

he had awakened completely from his dream of fairy-land. . . .
Their wearied souls were brimful of the recollections of discomfort and miseries endured at Killarney; where, that they might
be more thoroughly wretched, they had occupied a cottage
situated upon an island in the lake. . . .

The climate is mild, but the weather rainy and stormy; beyond
belief and conception stormy. Bysshe discoursed with animation
and eloquent astonishment of the perilous navigation of the
lakes; of sudden gusts and treacherous whirlwinds. How vessels
were swamped and sunk in a moment. . . .[57]

This, of course, nine years later, was what happened to Shelley's
schooner in the Gulf of La Spezia.

From Killarney itself it is difficult to see any lake, even Lough
Leane on which the town is set. J.J. Callanan (1795–1829 – almost
a contemporary of Shelley's) has a poem 'The Outlaw of Lough Lene'.
It is a better poem than his 'Gougane Barra'; Padraic Colum says
that Callanan brought, in this one instance anyway, a recognizable
Gaelic cadence into English:

. . . Alas! on that night when the horses I drove from the field,
That I was not near, from terror my angel to shield!
She stretched forth her arms – her mantle she flung to the wind,
And swam o'er Loch Lene, her outlawed lover to find.

Oh, would that a freezing, sleet-winged tempest did sweep,
And I and my love were alone, far off on the deep!
I'd ask not a ship or a bark, or pinnace to save –
With her hand round my waist, I'd fear not the wind or the
    wave.

'Tis down by the lake where the wild tree fringes its sides,
The maid of my heart, the fair one of heaven resides:
I think, as at eve she wanders its mazes along,
The birds go to sleep by the sweet wild twist of her song.

Killarney encouraged its romantic image.[58] For this reason Gerald
Griffin rather craftily shifted much of the scene of *The Collegians*,
his fictionalized account of a real murder which took place near the
Shannon, to Killarney. This was seized upon by Dion Boucicault in
his play from the book, *The Colleen Bawn*, and the operetta by
Benedict, going one further, was called *The Lily of Killarney*. As a
result of this all sorts of places in Killarney are called things like 'the
Colleen Bawn Rock', 'the Colleen Bawn Caves', to the fury of the

Shell Guide – 'These names and the attendant tales are all bogus, for the real Colleen Bawn has no connection with Killarney.' Nevertheless, fiction had taken over from fact.

Griffin goes in for some effective scene-painting in *The Collegians*, describing the Killarney landscape. Here he is on the dramatic Gap of Dunloe, where his heroine, the hapless Eily, has been banished to a sinister cottage:

> The scenery around was solitary, gigantic, and sternly barren. The figure of some wonder-hunting tourist, with a guide-boy bearing his portfolio and umbrella, appeared at long intervals, among the lesser undulations of the mountain side and the long road which traversed the gloomy valley, dwindled to the width of a meadow foot-path. . . .
>
> Sometimes a trailing shower, of mingled mist and rain, would sweep across the intervening chasm, like the sheeted spectre of a giant, and present to the eye of the spectator that appearance which supplied the imagination of Ossian with its romantic images. The mighty gorge itself, at one end, appeared to be lost and divided amid a host of mountains tossed together in provoking gloom and misery.

It was the custom of nineteenth-century visitors to take an excursion from Killarney through the Gap of Dunloe, on horseback, until they reached the Upper Lake where boats were waiting to row them back to Killarney. It was a journey not without dangers. Charlotte Bronte took it with her husband, on her honeymoon in 1854:

> We saw and went through the Gap of Dunloe. A sudden glimpse of a very grim phantom came on us in the Gap. The guide had warned me to alight from my horse as the path was now very broken and dangerous – I did not feel afraid and declined – we passed the dangerous part – the horse trembled in every limb and slipped once but did not fall – soon after she (it was a mare) started and was unruly for a minute – however I kept my seat – my husband went to her head to lead her – suddenly without any apparent cause – she seemed to go mad – reared, plunged – I was thrown on the stones right under her – my husband did not see that I had fallen, he still held her – I saw and felt her kick, plunge, trample round me. I had my thoughts about the moment – its consequences – my husband – my father – When my plight was seen, the struggling

creature was let loose – she sprang over me. I was lifted off the stones neither bruised by the fall nor touched by the mare's hoofs. Of course the only feeling left was gratitude for more sakes than my own.[59]

In Killarney town, opposite the modem Franciscan friary, is a monument (1940) to the Four Kerry Poets, by Seamus Murphy, friend of the Tailor at Gougane Barra. Like Thackeray, the Tailor had no time for Killarney, because where he lived he was surrounded by scenery as fine. He decided that Killarney was full of giant fleas, which barked. The Four Kerry Poets on the monument are Pierce Ferriter, who was hanged nearby on the Hill of Sheep in 1643; the less famous Geoffrey O'Donoghue (d. 1677); Egan O'Rahilly (d. 1728) and Owen Roe O'Sullivan (d. 1784), both from the mountainous district of Slieve Luachra a few miles to the north-east. Three of them are said to be buried in Muckross Abbey, and Pierce Ferriter in the graveyard outside it. It is a formidable clutch of poets in one place.

O'Rahilly seems to have stayed around Killarney. Near the 'Meeting of the Waters' above Muckross Abbey is the Torc waterfall, and O'Rahilly mentions the falls in his 'Last Lines'. In his desperation he seems to have been maddened by the sound of waters, whether of the waves pounding Inch Strand or of this waterfall; he also came to see lakes and rivers ('Laune and Leine and Lee') as images of his 'lost' feudal Ireland. In the Irish poem he mentions the Torc by name, though not in Frank O'Connor's translation – he worked with Yeats on it – but O'Rahilly can be allowed his last defiant shout in that version:

I shall not call for help until they coffin me –
What good for me to call when hope of help is gone?
Princes of Munster who would have heard my cry
Will not rise from the dead because I am alone.

Mind shudders like a wave in this tempestuous mood,
My bowels and my heart are pierced and filled with pain
To see our lands, our hills, our gentle neighbourhood,
A plot where any English upstart stakes his claim.

The Shannon and the Liffey and the tuneful Lee,
The Boyne and the Blackwater a sad music sing,
The waters of the west run red into the sea –
No matter what be trumps, their knave will beat our king.

And I can never cease weeping these useless tears;
I am a man oppressed, afflicted and undone
Who where he wanders mourning no companion hears
Only some waterfall that has no cause to mourn.

Now I shall cease, death comes, and I must not delay
By Laune and Laine and Lee, diminished of their pride,
I shall go after the heroes ay, into the clay –
My fathers followed theirs before Christ was crucified.

O'Connor prefaces his translation with a note: 'Because, like himself, O'Rahilly seemed the last voice of feudalism, Yeats used the final line of this poem for one of his own.'[60]

O'Rahilly is the last of the traditional bards. He died in 1728. Twenty years later, and a mile from O'Rahilly's own birthplace, near Rathmore, was born his successor Owen Roe O'Sullivan (1748–84), whose life makes a neat representation of the fate that had befallen the Irish poets. O'Rahilly proudly looked back to the last days of the hereditary bards, supported by the clan chieftains. O'Sullivan had no such experience, he was a hedge-schoolmaster, soldier, sailor and eventually a 'spailpín' ['spalpeen'], which means a travelling labourer. A kind of bragging defiance is forced upon him, the 'heroic' becomes at times 'mock'. He writes to a smith whom he wants to mend his spade:[61]

Make me a handle as straight as the mast of a ship,
    Seumas you clever man, witty and bountiful,
Sprung through the Geraldine lords from the kings of Greece,
    And fix the treadle and send it back to me soon . . .

He then goes on to say that, if given a chance, he'll show his hirers his learning, talking of literature and history (though there is more than a suggestion that he will be given no chance) and then, having received his pay, he will 'tuck it away in a knot in my shirt to keep' and save it till they meet:

For you're a man like myself with an antique thirst,
    So need I say how we'll give the story an end?
We'll shout and rattle our cans the livelong night
    Till there isn't as much as the price of a pint to spend.

This from a man who can also write delicate, intricate *aisling* ['ashling'] (dream) poems. A poet who is still remembered: the plaque near where he died, 'in a fever hut', is pointed out in the village

of Knocknagree, in Slieve Luachra, the poor hilly distict renowned
for its refugee Irish poets.

What does it all add up to, for a non-Irish-speaker, these bards
beneath the skin of Ireland? What is clear, from the many authorities
who can read the material, is that the best of it, as in O'Rahilly
and O'Sullivan, is filled with a music that cannot truly be reproduced
in English, an intricacy of rhymes and assonances, woven through
whole stanzas, as complex as the illuminations in the Book of
Kells.

Yet, even if it cannot be entirely translated, it has affected the way
Irish poets write in English. In Newcastle West, County Limerick,
north of Slieve Luachra, a contemporary poet, Michael Hartnett
(b. 1941), decided that this had gone far enough:[62]

> Chef Yeats, that master of the use of herbs
> could raise mere stew to a glorious height,
> pinch of saga, soupçon of philosophy
> carefully stirred in to get the flavour right,
> and cook a poem around the basic verbs.
> Our commis-chefs attend and learn the trade,
> bemoan the scraps of Gaelic that they know:
> add to a simple Anglo-Saxon stock
> Cuchulainn's marrow-bones to marinate,
> a dash of Ó Rathaille simmered slow,
> a glass of University hic-haec-hoc:
> sniff and stand back and proudly offer you
> the celebrated Anglo-Irish stew.

Better, Hartnett seems to suggest, to go the whole hog and go
back to writing in Irish, which is in fact what he did, for some
years – the poem from which that verse is taken is called 'A Farewell
to English' – despite having made a considerable name as a poet in
English.

The story of the Bards is the story of Gaelic Ireland: the despair
at their ending roared by O'Rahilly, the rough fate of Owen Roe
O'Sullivan, and the straits to which he was reduced, a *spailpin*, a day-
labourer, before Irish poetry became Anglicized, as it seemed then
forever. But it survived. Hartnett translates, and preserves the
Irish form of his name, in his 'The Last Vision of Eoghan Rua Ó
Súilleabháin':

The cow of morning spurted
milk-mist on each glen
and the noise of feet came
from the hills' white sides.

I saw like phantoms
my fellow-workers
and instead of spades and shovels
they had roses on their shoulders.

6

THE WEST

What the Limerickman, Michael Hartnett, calls 'the celebrated Anglo-Irish stew' was to a large extent cooked in the West. There are many reasons why; among them the survival of the Irish language in this remote part, and the fact that many of the gentry who devoted themselves to the Irish Literary Revival – Lady Gregory, Douglas Hyde, Edward Martyn and others – lived in the West.

The Shannon is the great divide; the West begins beyond it, and one place to cross it is at O'Brien's Bridge, north of Limerick, near Castleconnel, where William Wordsworth went in 1829. Many of Wordsworth's letters from Ireland are frustrating; he says he has had an interesting time, but will tell them about it when he gets home – 'it is late, and I will not enter into particulars'. An exception is a description of his taking a boat on the rapids at Castleconnel. These are not so fierce now, because of the hydro-electric scheme up-river, but they are still turbulent enough. His party

> breakfasted at Castleconnel, a very agreeably situated village on the banks of the Shannon. . . . The Shores of the River are sprinkled with Villas and gay pleasure-boxes. On a bold limestone rock stand and lie the remains of an old Castle overgrown or richly hung with ivy – the whole landscape exceedingly pleasing.
>
> Here we took boat perhaps a little incautiously, and soon found ourselves in the noisy bed of the Shannon among water breaks and wears for the catching of salmon. We were hurried down the foaming bed of the river among waves that leapt against the stream and on one side was an eddy which would have swallowed us up had the Boatmen been wanting in skill to avoid it. But they understood their business. . . . On each side were groves and Country houses – but what were we going to see – the *falls* of Doonas – falls they scarcely are – but tremendous rapids which as we saw them today would

have swallowed up any vessel that should venture among them.

 We disembarked and walked along the margin of the magnificent stream to a limestone Rock that rises abruptly from the bed of the river and makes part of a pleasure garden. Here we stood and saw a curve of the agitated stream of at least five hundred yards. . . . From the sides of the rock grows a large Ewe tree which extends its branches some yards over the stream, and in hot weather the Salmon are accustomed to take shelter in numbers from the beams of the Sun. . . .[1]

It is unsurprising that his 'old Castle' is still there, or that he describes exactly the box-like houses near it. But a 'Ewe' tree is still there too, and among its many fallen but still vigorous boughs are the walls and parterres of the old 'pleasure garden' and a ruined, folly-like tower.

Another nineteenth-century English visitor (though with Irish blood) was Charlotte Bronte. She spent part of her honeymoon, in 1854, at Kilkee on the south-west Clare coast. It is still a popular resort and, except for a new hotel like a barracks on one side of the horseshoe bay, is not much changed from her day. The Atlantic breaks and roars on a reef at the bay's mouth, the shore at the headlands is smooth stone, gently stepped, leading to jagged cliffs, with close-cropped turf on top of them; a place of domesticated wildness.

 She and her husband had, until then, spent little time alone together:

My husband is not a poet or a poetical man – and one of my grand doubts before marriage was about 'congenial tastes and so on'. The first morning we went out on the cliffs and saw the Atlantic coming in all white foam, I did not know whether I should get leave or time to take the matter in my own way. I did not want to talk – but I *did* want to look and be silent. Having hinted a petition, licence was not refused – covered with a rug to keep off the spray I was allowed to sit where I chose – and he only interrupted me when he thought I crept too near the edge of the cliff. So far he is always good in this way – and this protection which does not interfere or pretend is I believe a thousand times better than any half sort of pseudo sympathy. I will try with God's help to be as indulgent to him whenever indulgence is needed.

It is good to learn, what she perhaps did not know, that her husband was appreciating it too. He wrote to a friend: 'Kilkee, a glorious watering-place with the finest shore I ever saw – Completely girdled with stupendous cliffs – it was most refreshing to sit on a rock and look out on the broad Atlantic boiling and foaming at our feet.' The place where you can sit and have the Atlantic 'boiling and foaming' at your feet is just round the corner from the 'West End' of Kilkee. 'Here at our Inn', writes Charlotte, 'splendidly designated "the West End Hotel" – there is a good deal to carp at – if one were in carping humour – but we laugh instead of grumbling for out of doors there is much to compensate for any indoors shortcomings; so magnificent an ocean – so bold and grand a coast – I never yet saw.'[2] The West End Hotel is now a modern building, but to the side of it are two 1850s Haworth-type houses and it seems probable that their 'inn' was like one of these.

At Ennis, on the main road through County Clare, you may wonder if literary associations drive people mad. The pleasant town doubtless has them: Sean O'Faolain was a schoolteacher there, and the Rimbaud-like prodigy Thomas Dermody (1775–1802) went off like a rocket from there, spurning Ireland – [3]

> Rank nurse of nonsense; on whose thankless coast
> The base weed thrives, the nobler bloom is lost:
> Parent of pride and poverty, where dwell
> Dullness and brogue and calumny – farewell!

– and died of drink in England, at twenty-seven. But James Joyce, in *Ulysses*, has Leopold Bloom's father commit suicide in Ennis, in the Queen's Hotel, which consequently has a Bloom Bar, a Joyce Restaurant, and a plaque in the foyer, of engraved brass, with the relevant quotation: 'In sloping upright and backhands: Queen's Hotel, Queen's Ho. . .'

North from Kilkee along the coast are the spectacular Cliffs of Moher. Anthony Trollope, stationed for a time on Post Office duty nearby at Milltown Malbay, in 1845, used the cliffs and the region around Liscannor for his late short novel (1879), *An Eye for an Eye*. The plot, a young man torn between his love for someone 'unsuitable' and his sense of his own social position, is very like that of Griffin's *The Collegians* (1829). Trollope is at first English-deprecating about these cliffs:

It may be doubted whether Lady Mary Quin was right when she called them the highest cliffs in the world, but they are undoubtedly very respectable cliffs, and run up some six hundred feet from the sea as nearly perpendicular as cliffs should be. They are beautifully coloured, streaked with yellow veins, and with great masses of dark red rock; and beneath them lies the broad and blue Atlantic. Lady Mary's exaggeration as to the comparative height is here acknowledged, but had she said that below them rolls the brightest bluest clearest water in the world she would not have been far wrong.

Trollope may tease about their height but it is on them he puts the high-point of his novel:

The peril of his position on the top of the cliff had not occurred to him – nor did it occur to him now. He had been there so often that the place gave him no sense of danger. Nor had that peril – as it was thought afterwards by those who most closely made inquiry on the matter – ever occurred to her. She had not brought him there that she might frighten him with that danger, or that she might avenge herself by the power which it gave her. But now the idea flashed across her maddened mind.

'Miscreant,' she said. And she bore him back to the very edge of the precipice.

'You'll have me over the cliff,' he exclaimed, hardly even yet putting out his strength against her. . . .

Iris Murdoch, in *The Unicorn* (1963), rather than 'brightest bluest', shows the sea below the cliffs as sinister, and the beach frightening. Her novel, filled with descriptions of the cliffs and their surroundings, also has room for a full-rigged description of something most visitors to Ireland must have wondered about: what it is like to be sucked into an Irish bog. She takes her time over it, perhaps the real time it would take, from the first observation that 'the ground had become very mushy and was coming up over his shoes', to the first fall, and first realization that he is stuck, and sinking. The effect is horrific:

At that moment something seemed to give way under his left foot, as if it had entered some watery chamber, some air bubble of the bog. He lurched, tried to take another step, and fell violently on his side. The ground gave and gurgled all round him.

He stayed still now perforce. He stayed still for several minutes with his eyes closed trying to control his mind before he was able to determine the position of his limbs. He was sitting upright with his right leg curled under him, the sticky mud gripping his knee. The other leg was stretched before him, inclining downward into a hole in which he could hear a licking lapping sound of water disturbed. He was perhaps on the brink of one of those bottomless slimy wells of the bog. He held his hands in front of his breast like two animals that he wanted to keep safe. He lifted his head slowly and saw the few stars of the night. He began to tell himself things. . . .

He still has plenty of time to do this, and we are given his thoughts. He tries to keep them practical, about search-parties, and so forth. Then comes the climax, the understanding that struggle is useless: 'There was nothing firm, his hands plunged desperately about in the mud. He became still, lifting his muddied hands to his face. He was now fixed in the bog almost to the waist and sinking faster. The final panic came. He uttered several low cries and then a loud terrified shrieking wail, the voice of total despair at last.'[4]

In contrast to this bog, the Cliffs of Moher continue northwards into a region of solid rock. The Burren, which means 'stony place', occupies most of the top western corner of County Clare, a desert which is not a desert – cattle fatten on its limy grasses, and in spring Arctic flowers jostle with Mediterranean ones, sheltered in the cracks of its limestone slabs – it is one of the strangest places in Europe.

Emily Lawless (1845–1913)[5] sets her novel *Hurrish* (1886) between Lisdoonvarna and the sea; she calls the region 'An Iron Land':

Wilder regions there are few to be found, even in the wildest west of Ireland, than that portion of north Clare known to its inhabitants as 'The Burren'. Seen from the Atlantic, which washes its western base, it presents to the eye a succession of low hills, singularly grey in tone – deepening often, towards evening, into violet or dull reddish plum colour – sometimes, after sunset, to a pale ghostly iridescence.

You picture them dotted over with flocks of sheep, which nibble the short sweet grass. . . . But these Burren hills are literally not clothed at all. They are startlingly, I may say scandalously, naked. . . .

Lawless was the daughter of Lord Cloncurry, opposed all her life to Irish nationalism, but she is sympathetic to her 'Hurrish' (Horatio), a genial giant of a small farmer, who dreams of Irish nationhood. Her characters include a 'new' type of Irish politician on the make, and an old-fashioned landowner detested by his tenants the more he tries to improve their lot. *Hurrish* has recently been reprinted in the Irish Novels series (as has Griffin's *The Collegians*).

Geoffrey Grigson (1905–85) was an enthusiast for the Burren's flora and talks of the spring gentian, 'properly an alpine, which I first saw like the flash of a sapphire ring lost in the grass as a car took me quickly along the sea road from Ballyvaughan around Black Head. Its colour is deep and clear enough for one to be able to pick it out in that way, pick out a mere single flower in the grass as one goes by at forty miles an hour.' Like Lawless, Grigson remarks how the 'battle-ship grey' of the Burren can change, particularly in low sunshine coming out under heavy cloudage, can become 'electric', and 'some evenings one experienced that strangest of effects on Burren, the limestone – plateau and hill – reflecting the pink off the clouds and becoming, suddenly, mile upon mile of pink rock'.[6]

SOUTH GALWAY

From the sea-road mentioned by Grigson, off Black Head, are seen the Aran Islands, now usually associated with John Millington Synge (1871–1909). Originally intending to be a musician, but increasingly drawn to literature, Synge first went to Aran in May 1898 as a result of a chance suggestion, made in Paris. At least, that is how W.B. Yeats remembers it:

Some one, whose name I forget, told me there was a poor Irishman at the top of the house, and presently introduced us. . . .

He told me that he had learned Irish at Trinity College, so I urged him to go to the Aran Islands and find a life that had never been expressed in literature, instead of a life where all had been expressed. I did not divine his genius, but I felt he needed something to take him out of his morbidity and melancholy. Perhaps I would have given the same advice to any young Irish writer who knew Irish, for I had been that summer upon Inishmaan and Inishmore, and was full of the subject.[7]

Synge found himself powerfully but unsentimentally drawn towards the primitive, it was part of the pagan nature-mysticism that he was constructing for himself – 'God is in the earth and not above it', he has a character say in his first play; the earthy lives of the islanders thrilled him, and the stories they told him provided the plots of two of his plays, *Riders to the Sea* and *Playboy of the Western World*. The rhythms of Irish, translated, enabled him to invent for himself what was in effect a new and heightened form of spoken English.

His account of his visits, *The Aran Islands*, written in 1901, has the detachment of an anthropologist who also happens to be a poet. Within days of his arriving at the biggest of the three islands, Inishmore, his shoes are cut to pieces by the stones:

> The family held a consultation on them last night, and in the end it was decided to make me a pair of pampooties, which I have been wearing to-day among the rocks.
>
> They consist simply of a piece of raw cow skin, with the hair outside, laced over the toe and round the heel with two ends of fishing-line that work round and are tied above the instep. In the evening, when they are taken off, they are placed in a basin of water, as the rough hide cuts the foot and stocking if it is allowed to harden. For the same reason the people often step into the surf during the day, so that their feet are continually moist.
>
> At first I threw my weight upon my heels, as one does naturally in a boot, and was a good deal bruised, but after a few hours I learned the natural walk of man, and could follow my guide in any portion of the island. In one district below the cliffs, towards the north, one goes for nearly a mile jumping from one rock to another without a single ordinary step and here I realized that toes have a natural use, for I found myself jumping towards any tiny crevice in the rock before me, and clinging with an eager grip in which all the muscles of my feet ached from their exertion.
>
> The absence of the heavy boot of Europe has preserved to these people the agile walk of the wild animal. . . .

Synge watches the islanders unblinkingly:

Although these people are kindly towards each other and to their children, they have no feeling for the sufferings of animals, and little sympathy for pain when the person who feels it is not in danger. I have sometimes seen a girl writhing and howling with toothache while her mother sat at the other side of the fireplace pointing at her and laughing at her as if amused at the sight. . . . They tie down donkeys' heads to their hoofs to keep them from straying, in a way that must cause horrible pain, and sometimes when I go into a cottage I find all the women of the place down on their knees plucking the feathers from live ducks and geese.

Emigration, the perennial tragedy of Ireland, falls most heavily on the mothers. Synge describes an old woman on the islands, keening her children in America, rocking to and fro on her stool, her shawl over her head: 'The maternal feeling is so powerful on these islands that it gives a life of torment to the women. Their sons grow up to be banished as soon as they are of age, or to live here in continual danger on the sea; their daughters go away also, or are worn out in their youth with bearing children that grow up to harass them in their own turn a little later.'

Liam O'Flaherty (1896–1984), novelist and short-story writer in English, was born, and brought up bilingually, on the largest of the Aran Islands, Inishmore. Synge was an observer, O'Flaherty an islander; his story, 'Going into Exile', is a description from the inside of the sort of leave-taking that Synge describes as a 'torment' to the mothers. With one physical, visual detail, O'Flaherty illustrates the pain. The young man is leaving his family cottage for America. 'As Michael was going out the door he picked a piece of loose whitewash from the wall and put it in his pocket.'

A candidate for the priesthood, an Irish Guardsman on the Somme, shell-shocked, a Communist, a freedom-fighter – in 1921 he led a group of unemployed dockers, seized the Rotunda in Dublin, hoisted the red flag over it and held it for several days – O'Flaherty most clearly admired the qualities of courage and endurance; and, it is evident from his stories, what he loved most was animals. His Aran peasants are usually presented with a black realism that would have made even Synge flinch.

There lived in our district an old man call Patsa. He had no doubt been one time young and innocent, but within my memory he had always been aged, wrinkled and a great scoundrel. He embodied within his stinking carcass all the vices and perversions which our ancient community has accumulated through the centuries. For that reason he was greatly feared and respected. He was also a by-word. . . .

He was extremely clever at getting money from strangers. In those days a great number of visitors came to our island. It had just been discovered by the new school of European mysticism and was considered to be the chief reserve of the gods and fairies of the Celtic Twilight. It was by exploiting these mystics that Patsa collected the golden sovereigns which are the subject of this story.

In fact he swallows them on his death-bed to keep them from his almost equally foul wife, who gives him a horse-drench until he voids them, whereupon she buys a gallon of whiskey and gives her neighbours an exhibition of her one talent, farting, while Patsa dies of rage. The visitors to the island, the 'mystics', were Yeats, Lady Gregory, the English poet Arthur Symons, assorted scholars, and John Millington Synge.

O'Flaherty is an uncategorizable member of the awkward squad who did much to liberate Irish writing from any sense of what it *ought* to be. It is not so much his subject-matter that had this influence; he also can be idyllic, about young human love, or the love between a wild drake and a domestic duck; the disgust of 'Patsa' is exceptional. A poet-critic said that to read O'Flaherty was sometimes like 'holding a robin, and feeling it quiver in your hands'.[8]

Further into Galway Bay above the Burren, still within sight of that limestone desert, is a place where something happened, quite casually, which was to have an enormous effect on the Irish Literary Revival, or 'the Celtic Twilight' as O'Flaherty sharply calls it in his story. (W.B. Yeats is to blame for the popularization of that misleading term, a 'Twilight' to which O'Flaherty did not belong, any more than did Yeats.) At a house called Durrus (variously spelt), on an inlet of the sea near Kinvarra, lived the splendidly entitled Comte Florimond de Basterot. . . .[9] It is at this point that key figures of the Revival can be mentioned in a cluster, some of them for the first time.

Late in the eighteenth century, the de Basterots of Bordeaux had married into the Frenches of Galway, and the Comte Florimond, late in the nineteenth century, still retained the small Durrus House as a shooting-lodge. In previous years most of the de Basterot estate had been sold off to neighbouring landowners, one of whom was Sir William Gregory of Coole Park, and Sir William, together with his wife Augusta, had taken to calling on Basterot when the Count was there for the shooting. Enter the great Lady Gregory, Augusta Gregory (1859–1932), future playwright, and the first genuinely popular translator of the great Irish tales, such as the 'Cattle Raid of Cooley'.[10]

In 1897 Yeats was staying with Edward Martyn (1859–1923) at his house, Tulira, at Ardrahan, not far from Coole Park. Martyn had already written two plays as his contribution to the Revival of a native literature, *The Heather Field* and *Maeve*; and Yeats had written *The Countess Cathleen*. They despaired of having their plays produced. It was at this point that Lady Gregory was taking tea with de Basterot. The story is told by Yeats, in his courteous orchestral prose, derided by some but irresistible to the present editor:

> On the sea-coast at Duras, a few miles from Coole, an old French Count, Florimond de Basterot, lived for certain months in every year. Lady Gregory and I talked over my project of an Irish Theatre, looking out upon the lawn of his house, watching a large flock of ducks that was always gathered for his arrival from Paris, and that would be a very small flock, if indeed it were a flock at all, when he set out for Rome in the autumn. I told her that I had given up my project because it was impossible to get the few pounds necessary for a start in little halls, and she promised to collect or give the money necessary. That was her first great service to the Irish intellectual movement.
>
> She reminded me the other day that when she first asked me what she could do to help our movement I suggested nothing; and, certainly, I no more foresaw her genius than I foresaw that of John Synge, nor had she herself foreseen it. Our theatre had been established before she wrote or had any ambition to write, and yet her little comedies have merriment and beauty, an unusual combination, and those two volumes where the Irish heroic tales are arranged and translated in an English so simple and so noble may do more than other books to deepen Irish imagination. They contain our ancient literature, are something better than our *Mabinogion*, are almost our *Morte d'Arthur*.
>
> It is more fitting, however, that in a book of memoirs I should speak of her personal influence, and especially as no witness is likely to arise better qualified to speak. If that influence were lacking, Ireland would be greatly impoverished, so much has been planned out in the library or among the woods at Coole

and where, but for that conversation at Florimond de Basterot's, had been the genius of Synge?[11]

That conversation at Durrus House leads us to Coole Park, home of Lady Gregory, where almost everyone connected with Irish writing stayed during the next twenty-five years. There is not much of it to see now. With indecent haste it was torn down in 1941: 'Unfortunately, Lady Gregory's house in Coole, the headquarters of the Irish Literary Theatre, was sold by Mr de Valera's Government to a Galway builder for £500 and torn down for scrap. Merely as a literary museum its value to the nation was almost incalculable; one feels they should have held out for at least £600. . . .'[12]

There were those who feared that Lady Gregory had a possessive eye, that she would take over Yeats and make him less of a poet. This did not happen, or no more than he clearly wanted it to happen:

> Lady Gregory, seeing that I was ill, brought me from cottage to cottage to gather folk-belief, tales of the faeries, and the like, and wrote down herself what we had gathered, considering that this work, in which one let others talk, and walked about the fields so much, would lie, to use a country phrase, 'very light upon the mind'. She asked me to return there the next year, and for years to come I was to spend my summers at her house.
>
> When I was in good health again, I found myself indolent, and asked her to send me to my work every day at eleven, and at some other hour to my letters, rating me with idleness if need be, and I doubt if I should have done much with my life but for her firmness and her care. After a time, though not very quickly, I recovered tolerable industry, though it has only been of late years that I have found it possible to face an hour's verse without a preliminary struggle and much putting off.[13]

Yeats loved the 'Seven Woods' of Coole ('Seven odours, seven murmurs, seven woods. . .').[14] The message he received in Inchy wood, at Coole, or after he had been there, might be hung up in every bedroom as proof against the melancholy waking in the small hours; a remedy for what Elizabeth Bowen called 'le coup de trois heures':

I was crossing a little stream near Inchy Wood and actually in
the middle of a stride from bank to bank, when an emotion
never experienced before swept down upon me. I said, 'That
is what the devout Christian feels, that is how he surrenders
his will to the will of God'. I felt an extreme surprise, for my
whole imagination was preoccupied with the pagan mythology
of ancient Ireland, I was marking in red ink, upon a large map,
every sacred mountain. The next morning I awoke near dawn,
to hear a voice saying: 'The love of God is infinite for every
human soul because every human soul is unique; no other can
satisfy the same need in God'.

Few contemporaries can be trusted on the subject of Yeats; he came
to dominate their world. George Moore certainly cannot, whom
Yeats drove nearly mad with envy. Frank O'Connor loved Yeats,
even though he worked with him for years on the board of the Abbey
Theatre. On the other hand, O'Connor thought Lady Gregory 'a
holy terror', because on first meeting her he made a joke by which,
like Queen Victoria, she was not amused.

For the rest of my life I nourished something like an inferiority
complex about the old lady until long after Yeats's death. Mrs
Yeats revealed to me that he was as terrified of her as I was.
She had always treated him as a talented but naughty child.
When at last he married and took his young wife to Coole,
he felt the time had come for him to assert his manhood.
  No animals were permitted in Coole – which, considering
what most Irish country houses are like, seems to me to be
kindness to Christians – and Yeats was fond of his cat. Now
that he was a married man, a mature man, a famous man, he
was surely entitled to his cat. So Pangur was duly bundled
up and brought to Gort. But as the outside car drove up the
avenue of Coole the married, mature, famous man grew panic-
stricken at the thought of the old lady's forbidding countenance. He bade the jarvey drive him first to the stables. There
Pangur was deposited until, everyone having gone to bed,
Yeats crept out in his slippers and brought him up to the
bedroom.
  Yet till the day she died he secretly nursed the hope of being
able to treat her as an equal. Nobody who had not been
squelched by her could realize the relief with which I heard
this.[15]

O'Connor thinks that Yeats's famous epitaph, 'Cast a cold eye/
On life, on death./Horseman, pass by!' is 'all right' as epitaphs
go, but for Yeats he finds it hard to think of anything more
inappropriate:

> There was none who cast a more eager eye on both life and
> death. He was a blazing enthusiast who, into his seventies,
> retained all the spontaneity and astonishment of a boy of seven-
> teen. The extraordinary change that came over him when he
> grew excited; the way he sat bolt upright in his chair, snorted,
> sniffed, stammered, glared, the head thrown back, while the
> whole face blazed from within. It was astonishing, because even
> in extreme old age, when he was looking most wretched and
> discontented, quite suddenly that blaze of excitement would
> suddenly sweep over his face like a glory. . . . I used to feel
> years younger after a visit to him. Disillusionment and cynicism
> simply dropped away from me when he was around.

Sir Horace Plunkett met Yeats at Coole in 1896.[16] Plunkett, a
great-uncle of Lord Dunsany, was organizing Irish farmers, newly
possessed of their own lands, into co-operatives, because they still
had no idea of how to market their produce. He was another of the
'awakeners' of end-of-the-century Ireland, and he heard that something was moving at Coole, at least on the cultural front, so he
hastened to catch up on that and take the opportunity of addressing
the local farmers. His first impresssion of Yeats was of 'a rebel and
a mystic and an ass'. A fellow-guest at Coole was Edward Martyn,
'a clever writer of a more imaginative kind'. Then Yeats addressed
the farmers himself and to Plunkett's surprise held their attention.
Plunkett, in his diary, comes up with a memorable phrase, a picture
of Yeats the public man. 'A real talent,' now decides Plunkett, 'like
a rose leaf falling among agricultural implements.'
    There was more to it than that. Yeats was shrewd, and lucky.
An organizer was needed by Plunkett to tour the West. Yeats suggested his friend AE (George Russell, 1867–1935), mystical painter,
poet and regular communer with fairies; another revered figure whose
power to influence is not easy to grasp now. Yeats knew that AE
worked successfully in the accounts department of his firm, and soon
the unlikely figure of AE was bicycling all over the West helping
farmers to become profitable, and founding agricultural banks. 'I am
devoid of anything mystical at present and know more of the price
of eggs than of what is going on behind the veil.'

That, and the quotations from Sir Horace Plunkett, are taken from Ulick O'Connor's account of the period, *Celtic Dawn*, and 'dawn' is infinitely more appropriate than the word 'twilight'.[17] There is a sense of excited beginnings, of things awakening, of men and women, in their prime, like-minded, helping each other into positions of influence in a cause greater than themselves: and somewhere near the centre is the figure of Yeats. The enthusiasm that Frank O'Connor admired could run away with him. O'Connor also accused Yeats of having fathered more bad art from his protégés than could easily be forgiven; and, later, Yeats's inclusions and exclusions of poets for his *Oxford Book of Modern Verse* (1936) were famously eccentric. But three, at least, of his geese were swans. AE became secretary of the Irish Agricultural Organization and editor of the influential co-operative magazine, *The Irish Homestead*; John Millington Synge went to Aran at Yeats's suggestion and found his own language as a playwright; Lady Gregory assembled and ordered the legends, inventing among other things her own form of Irish/English, which came to be called 'Kiltartan' after the village near Coole Park.

Of course the 'awakeners' were often at each other's throats. George Moore loathed Lady Gregory's 'Kiltartan', calling it bogus, which of course it was, and analysing it scornfully in *Hail and Farewell*:

> No light diadem of praise Yeats sets on Lady Gregory's brow when he says that she has discovered a speech, beautiful as that of Morris, and a living speech into the bargain. . . . But when we look into the beautiful speech that Lady Gregory learnt as she moved among her people, we find that it consists of no more than a dozen turns of speech, dropped into pages of English so ordinary, that redeemed from these phrases it might appear in any newspaper without attracting attention.

George Moore loved to annoy, and even if what he says – his analysis is long and detailed – contains truth, Lady Gregory was right when she described what she was attempting with the phrase (not her own): 'the talk of people who think in Irish'. As an example, pagan Oisín, son of Finn and last of the Fianna, awaits his death, maddened, as always, by St Patrick's bells; it is the farewell of paganism, bitter and defiant, and Lady Gregory gives it a *tune*:

> It is long the clouds are over me to-night. It is long last night was; although this day is long, yesterday was longer again to me; every day that comes is long to me!

That is not the way I used to be, without fighting, without battles, without learning feats, without young girls, without music, without harps, without bruising bones, without great deeds; without increase of learning, without generosity, without drinking at feasts, without courting, without hunting, the two trades I was used to; without going out to battle Ochone! the want of them is sorrowful to me. . . .

There is no one at all in the world the way I am: it is a pity the way I am; an old man dragging stones; it is long the clouds are over me to-night!

I am the last of the Fianna, great Oisín, son of Finn, listening to the voice of bells; it is long the clouds are over me to-night![18]

Between Coole and Ardrahan is a house that played its part slightly earlier in the chronology of the Revival, Tulira Castle, home of Edward Martyn (1859–1923). Martyn is unique among the writers of this period of the Revival in being both a wealthy landowner and an unbendingly devout Catholic. He was also a devout disciple of the realism of the Norwegian playwright Henrik Ibsen. Yeats was as passionately anti-realistic and specifically, determinedly, 'Irish'. So the rift was there before the theatre even started, and Martyn drifted away. He continued to write plays, and in one of the last of them, *Romulus and Remus* (1916), 'Yeats is portrayed as an extravagant poseur, George Moore as an egotistical hack writer, and Lady Gregory as a sensible person mesmerized into silliness by Yeats'.[19]

Martyn was a confirmed celibate. His forceful mother clung for a time to the hope that he would provide her with a grandchild, and to this end made him build a new house on the site of the old one. He retained, however, the ancient tower. George Moore was Martyn's older cousin, and cannot resist teasing:

The furniture which had been made for his sitting-room filled her, I could see, with dread. A less intelligent woman would have drawn no conclusions from the fact that a table taken from a design by Albert Durer, and six oaken stools with terrifying edges, were to be the furniture of the turret chamber, reached by cold, moist, winding stairs, and that his bedroom, too, was to be among the ancient walls. Look at his bed, she said, as narrow as a monk's; and the walls whitewashed like a cell, and

nothing upon them but a crucifix. He speaks of his aversion
from upholstery, and he can't abide a cushion.

Martyn came to detest 'peasant' plays, and Celtic romanticism,
though he remained an ardent nationalist. From 1904 to 1908 he
was president of Sinn Fein ('Our Selves') – which is a reminder of
the surprising people who were in at the beginning of the Irish
nationalist movement – and in 1914 he founded his own Irish
Theatre, with Thomas McDonagh and Joseph Plunkett, both poets
and both executed after the Rising of 1916. He also devoted himself
to the improvement of ecclesiastical art in Ireland, its music and above
all, its stained glass.

Perhaps the reclusive Martyn was entitled to his revenge (in
Romulus and Remus), since George Moore spends most of his vast
and frequently comic masterpiece, *Hail and Farewell* (1911–14), trying to make an ass of him. It is a devious and subtle work – Moore
claims that not he wrote it, but Ireland, or rather, 'Banba', which
is Druidical Ireland – and it becomes clear to the reader (to Moore?)
that if Moore loves anyone it is Martyn. It is as though Martyn is
some massively constructed Norman keep, defiant and unshakeable
in his convictions and solitary rectitude, to which Moore draws up
his battering rams and siege guns and is secretly relieved to see his
assaults bounce off and leave the edifice intact.

The attack begins in the first paragraph of *Hail and Farewell*, but
in the course of it Martyn gives Moore an idea. In 1884 they both
have apartments in London, in the Temple, where late of nights
Moore seeks out Martyn,

sure of finding him seated in his high, canonical chair, sheltered
by a screen, reading his book, his glass of grog beside him, his
long clay pipe in his hand; and we used to talk literature and
drama until two or three in the morning.

I wish I knew enough Irish to write my plays in Irish, he
said one night, speaking out of himself suddenly.

You'd like to write your plays in Irish! I exclaimed. I thought
nobody did anything in Irish except bring turf from the bog
and say prayers.

Edward did not answer, and when I pressed him he said:
You've always lived in France and England, and have forgotten
Ireland.

You're wrong: I remember the boatmen speaking to each
other in Irish on Lough Carra! And Father James Browne

preaching in Irish in Carnacun! But I've never heard of anybody wanting to write in it . . . and plays, too!

Everything is different now; a new literature is springing up.

In Irish? I said; and my brain fluttered with ideas regarding the relation of the poem to the language in which it is born.

A new language to enwomb new thoughts, I cried out to Edward.

Moore is a magpie for material and this is his first inkling that something is stirring in his native Ireland, that there was what he came to call 'a glimmer' in the air of the place. In England he is already a well-known writer, and it is not long before Yeats and Martyn turn to him for help in the direction and casting of those first two plays, and involve him in the Irish Revival, with all the absurdities, quarrels, flouncings-out, that accompanied everything Moore did. Moore enjoyed such things, and wondered if it came from his peculiar appearance, and his childhood: 'I do not doubt that my parents loved their little boy, but their love did not prevent their laughing at him and persuading him that he was inherently absurd.'

Perhaps he continued to enjoy being laughed at, and ensured that it went on happening by making himself a byword, purposely infuriating people to the point of apoplexy, until they preferred laughter. In *A Drama in Muslin* (1887) he vents an almost Swiftian disgust for Irish life, that of the peasant and the gentry, both, which was bound to madden his fellow countrymen; he even describes Mass at Edward's beloved church at Ardrahan: 'The mumbled Latin, the by-play with the wine and water, the mumming of the uplifted hands, were so appallingly trivial. . . . The peasantry filled the body of the church. They prayed coarsely, ignorantly, with the same brutality as they lived.'

The wonder was that Martyn ever spoke to Moore again, but Martyn attempts his revenge at Tulira. (Moore's non-use of quotation marks is at first confusing, but adds to the realism.)

As I was finishing breakfast, he had the face to ask me to get ready for to go to Mass.

But, Edward, I don't believe in the Mass. My presence will be only – Will you hold your tongue, George . . .? and not give scandal, he answered, his voice trembling with emotion. Everybody knows that I don't believe in the Mass.

If you aren't Catholic, why don't you become a Protestant? And he began pushing me from behind. I have told you before that one may become a Catholic, but one discovers oneself a Protestant. But why am I going to Gort? Because you had the bad taste to describe our church in *A Drama in Muslin* – and to make such remarks about our parish priest that he said, if you showed your self in Ardrahan again, he'd throw dirty water over you. . . . Will you not be delaying? . . .

Moore is bundled into the carriage, but detects a fellow dissident in the coachman, and later spends the Mass hour at Coole Park, where he saw 'Yeats standing lost in meditation before a white congregation of swans assembled on the lake, looking himself in his old cloak like a huge umbrella left behind by some picnic-party'.

Yeats married in 1917, when he was fifty-two. For thirty-five pounds he bought a ruined Norman tower, almost at the gates of Coole Park, Thoor Ballylee, and did it up for his family, to spend summers in:[20]

> I, the poet William Yeats
> With old mill-boards and sea-green slates,
> And smithy work from the Gort forge,
> Restored this tower for my wife George;
> And may these characters remain
> When all is ruin once again.

He called the tower a 'powerful emblem'.[21] As so often, he was lucky; the place was not only evocative in itself, it had associations: with the blind poet Raftery who sang of a famous beauty from Ballylee, Mary Hynes; and with the French family, local land-owners – he remembers that too, and the eighteenth-century land-owners' autocratic power. He uses the old castle like a theatrical property:[22]

> I pace upon the battlements and stare. . . .
>
> Beyond that ridge lived Mrs French, and once
> When every silver candlestick or sconce
> Lit up the dark mahogany and the wine,
> A serving man that could divine
> That most respected lady's every wish,
> Ran and with the garden shears
> Clipped an insolent farmer's ears
> And brought them in a little covered dish.

Some few remembered when I was young
A peasant girl commended by a song
Who'd lived somewhere upon that rocky place,
And praised the colour of her face,
And had the greater joy in praising her,
Remembering that, if walked she there,
Farmers jostled at the fair,
So great a glory did the song confer. . . .

Strange, but the man who made the song was blind. . . .

While Yeats owned the tower Ireland became a battlefield. At first
in 1919 it was the 'Black and Tans' and other crown forces, and
then came the civil war of the Republicans, or Irregulars, against
the forces of the Irish Free State.[23]

An affable Irregular,
A heavily built Falstaffian man,
Comes cracking jokes of civil war
As though to die by gunshot were
The finest play under the sun.

A brown Lieutenant and his men,
Half dressed in national uniform,
Stand at my door, and I complain
Of the foul weather, hail and rain,
A pear-tree broken by the storm.

I count the feathered balls of soot
The moor-hen guides upon the stream,
To silence the envy in my thought;
And turn towards my chamber, caught
In the cold snows of a dream.

In another poem he wonders if he should have been a poet at all,
whether a life of action might not have been better. Again he begins
with the tower, 'I climb to the tower-top and lean upon broken
stone', and after four verses of image-filled meditation, ends:[24]

I turn away and shut the door, and on the stair
Wonder how many times I could have proved my worth
In something that all others understand or share;
But O! ambitious heart, had such a proof drawn forth
A company of friends, a conscience set at ease,
It had but made us pine the more. The abstract joy,

The half-read wisdom of daemonic images,
Suffice the ageing man as once the growing boy.

That is from 'Meditation In Time of Civil War', which Yeats
dated 1923, in the book he called *The Tower*. By 1929 he had left
the place and, when we came upon it in 1957, it was a windowless
ruin:[25]

> The roof, the floors, are gone.
> Stolen your sea-green slates
> And smith-work from Gort.
> Your blue distempers run
> In cobalt-coloured rain. . . .

In the 1960s it was neatly restored and is now used for a Yeats
Summer School.

The blind poet Yeats mentioned in his poem was Anthony Raftery
(1784?–1835),[26] and in the account by Douglas Hyde of the hunt
for, and discovery of, what remained of Raftery's poetry in manuscript or in the minds of local Irish speakers there is much of the
excitement that filled literary nationalists at the end of last century.
It was Rafterys poem, 'I am Raftery the poet/Full of hope and love',
that Daniel Corkery wrote up on the schoolroom blackboard in Cork,
the first words of Irish that Frank O'Connor had seen. That must
have been about ten years after Hyde published it in his *Songs of Connacht* (1893).

The point for Hyde about near-contemporary Raftery was that
he was a genuinely popular poet, as no English-language poet had
been for centuries, with the possible exception of Burns. There is
a sense in Douglas Hyde's description and in Lady Gregory's enthusiasm (for she soon took up the hunt) that they at last felt connected
with the Gaelic past; they could reach out and touch it, it was so
recent.

Mary Hynes, the famous beauty of Ballylee celebrated by Raftery,
has, like Raftery, played her part in the Irish imagination ever since
– 'So great a glory did the song confer'. Hyde renders the beginning
of the song with the words containing the vowel-rhymes in capital
letters. (Of another Raftery poem, 'The Catholic Rent', Hyde notes
'It is entirely built upon the ae and o sounds. There are 128 rhymes
on the ae sound and 32 on the o, and no others.' It was important
for him to make it clear that Raftery was no street-balladeer, but
a descendant of the bards, with a strict discipline.)[27]

Mary Hynes, or The Posy Bright

Going to Mass of me, God was GRACIOUS,
　　The day came RAINY and the wind did blow,
And near Kiltartan I met a MAIDEN
　　Whose love ENSLAVED me and left me low.
I spoke to her gently, the courteous MAIDEN,
　　And gently and GAILY she answered so:
'Come, Raftery, with me, and let me TAKE you
　　To Ballylee, where I have to go. . . .'

In the eighteenth century the *aisling* ['ashling'] (vision poem) became a convention in which the poet is visited by a 'sky-woman' who is the personification of Ireland. That is not how the *aisling* was originally, the sky-woman was a dream of physical love, and Mary Hynes also is reassuringly flesh-and-blood. 'I never saw a woman as handsome as she, and I never shall till I die,' said an old woman to Lady Gregory. An old fiddler who remembered her said:

> Mary Hynes was the finest thing that was ever shaped. There usen't to be a hurling match in the county that she wouldn't be at it, and a white dress on her always. Eleven men asked her in marriage in one single day, but she would not marry any one of them. There were a number of young men sitting up drinking one night, and they fell to talking of Mary Hynes, and a man of them stole away to go to Ballylee to see her, and when he came to the Bog of Cloone he fell into the water and was drowned.[28]

> . . . And certain men, being maddened by those rhymes,
> Or else by toasting her a score of times,
> Rose from the table and declared it right
> To test their fancy by their sight;
> But they mistook the brightness of the moon
> For the prosaic light of day –
> Music had driven their wits astray –
> And one was drowned in the great bog of Cloone.[29]

People have tracked the observations of Dorothy Wordsworth to the poems of her brother, William; that is an example of Yeats feeding on the cottage-visiting of Lady Gregory.

Mary Hynes must have been kind, as well as beautiful, to greet so gaily a poor, blind, poet. Others, Hyde was told, would not even give Raftery their names, fearful he might put them in a rhyme, which was considered bad luck, and could give them an early death. It seems that is what happened to Mary Hynes. 'Alas!' says Hyde, 'a great gentleman who was in that county fell in love with her. She was left, and died in poverty, a short time before the Famine.' He does not say who told him this. It is so much what might be feared to have happened, perhaps he presumed it.

Because of Mary Hynes, Raftery is connected with Ballylee, but from his poems he seems to have spent much time further east in Galway, at Loughrea. At St Brendan's Cathedral in Loughrea can be seen some of the results of Edward Martyn's encouragement of the ecclesiastical arts: windows by Sarah Purser, Patrick Pye, Evie Hone, that 'admirably illustrate the beginnings and development of the Dublin School of Stained Glass'[30] (founded by Edward Martyn); and there are embroideries to designs by Jack Yeats, the poet's brother.

All this, at least partly, is the doing of a novelist, Gerald O'Donovan (1871–1942), whose life makes painful reading. He was the priest at Loughrea under a friendly bishop, who looked kindly on his artistic 'modernism'. He worked with Edward Martyn and AE in the Irish Agricultural Organization Society, invited the Yeats/Martyn/Gregory theatre-company (soon to become the Abbey Theatre) to Loughrea; brought the young tenor John McCormack down to sing in the cathedral, and so on. Then his bishop was changed (it was said that the Vatican opposed the idea that O'Donovan himself should be bishop). The Church was turning against Modernism – condemned by the Pope in 1907 as 'synthesis of all heresies' – but before that O'Donovan had left Loughrea and left the priesthood.

O'Donovan's novel about this rejection of liberalism, and the consequent agonies of a young priest, *Father Ralph* (1913), caused a sensation. The priest in the novel, refusing to accept the new censorship, is suspended by his bishop, disowned by his mother, and, on the station platform, is quietly hissed by a group of men he has known for years: 'Ralph was alone in the compartment. He sat still for awhile, his eyes fixed on the bay, along which the train skirted, and the mountains rising sheer on the far side. The throbbing of the engine seemed to prolong the hiss. He stood up and stretched his limbs. If that scene on the platform represented his country, and with a pang he felt that it did, he was without a country. . . .'

Perhaps if O'Donovan had become an influential bishop he might have helped to save Ireland from the reactionary censorship that poisoned the next decades. During the years that followed his daughter remembers him, in London, 'lying on the sofa all afternoon reading his way through the *Cambridge Ancient History* and endless detective stories, one a day. He rarely mentioned Ireland. . . .' He was an intimate friend of the English novelist Rose Macaulay, who ended her anonymous obituary of him in *The Times*, 'To know him was to love him.'

GALWAY – CONNEMARA

Ireland became philistine. Most countries are, but Ireland became so on purpose. Of course her writers and artists fought back (with 'one eye on the mail-boat'). Austin Clarke (1896–1974) excoriates the ugliness of Galway's new cathedral:[31]

> Here is the very spirit
> Of hard-drinking, sea-mouldering Galway:
> A building ugly as sin
> To prove the Boys sincere
> And still a decent crowd:
> Another thorn for the Crown
> Of Thorns, a large gall
> In the Sponge on Spear.

Reactions to Galway city, and the country that lies around it and to the west of it (Connemara), are various but passionate. 'If we should encounter a wilder barbarism in remote places, it will, at least, not be jumbled together with an advanced civilization' – pronounced Harriet Martineau, in 1857. She is horrified by the Claddagh, the fisherman's quarter of the town, now demolished:

The rest of the verdure is on the roofs. Nettles, docks, and grass grow to the height of two feet, and the thistle and ragwort shed their seeds into the thatch. Where the thatch has tumbled in, the holes are covered with matting, kept down by large stones, which make new holes in the rotten mass. The once white walls are mossy and mouldy. The sordidness is indescribable. But infinitely worse is the inside. . . . We saw, kneeling at a bench a mother and daughter, whose faces haunt us. The mother's eyes were bleared, and her hair staring like a patient's in Bedlam.[32]

Sir William Wilde, in 1871, is hearty and alliterative: 'Westward, ho! Let us rise with the sun and be off to the land of the West. . . . We have nothing to say about priests or patterns; politics, peelers, or parsons; soldiers, soupers, or sauggarths. . . . There is still plenty of fun, frolic, and folk-lore in the West; but, for the present, we have no stories to relate about friars or fairies. . . .'[33]

Padraic Colum, in 1926, is defensive about cabin life: 'On the outside walls where the thatch drips down you see the green of the damp. But inside, with the pile of burning turf on the hearth, everything is dry and warm. . . . The family sit about the fire, and at the end of the room the horse stands as quiet and as well-behaved as a guest could be.'[34]

Sean O'Faolain considers Galway the most foreign town in Ireland – 'meaning thereby that it is barbarically native. It has no veneer, unless rust is a veneer. . . .'[35] That was written before the Second World War. In 1953 the Italian novelist Ignazio Silone stayed with Kate O'Brien at Roundstone, and on his departure she took him to Galway station, in terrible rain:

> The usually tranquil old station was in a sudden chaos of 'renovation'. Cement, mud and drain-pipes heaped about for us to leap over; tarpaulins spread, and tea-pots and old Guinness bottles wherever they should not be; bad language and a cold wind and a smeared-looking train; rain thudding without mercy. . . .
>
> Silone looked smiling around, and turned up the collar of his overcoat.
>
> 'You've given us fourteen days in a Japanese paradise,' he said to me, 'and we say goodbye to you at a junction in Central Poland.'
>
> Accurate and gracious observation; Galway *has* its Central Poland days. . . .[36]

It also has now a famous theatrical company and the best bookshop in Ireland.[37]

Near the 'usually tranquil' station is Eyre Square, and on one side of it sits, in bronze, his billycock on the back of his head, Padraic O Conaire (1882–1928), the nearest thing to a shanachy (teller of stories in Irish) that the Irish literary revival could show. O Conaire is part of the contradiction – or the surprise – that lies behind so many of the revivers of a peasant tradition. His stories come convincingly from the heart of Irish country life, but he was a well-educated man, who spent many years in London in the Civil Service. The

stories are, in the main, grim and convincing, though the best-loved
of them, 'My little black ass', is cheerful. A newly-bought donkey
would not budge unless it was under trees. In the end the new owner
solves this by cutting some branches and tying them round the
donkey's neck. 'Poor animal! He went at an incredible rate. He
imagined from the music in his ears that he was still in the
wood. . . .':

> I still have the little black ass and will till he dies. We have
> gone many a long while together in rain and drizzle, frost and
> snow. He has lost some of his bad habits in the course of
> time – something I failed to do myself. And I think my little
> black ass knows that as well as anyone.
>   But he is as proud as punch since I bought him the little
> bright green cart. Getting younger he is, poor beast![38]

This conscious 'peasantry' was a deliberate attempt to revive written Irish as a vehicle for contemporary stories, about the lives of the
people who could read them. Patrick Pearse (1879–1916) was editing
the Gaelic League weekly when he wrote, 'a living modern literature
cannot be built up on the folk-tale . . . no literature can take root
which is not of the twentieth century'. Padraic O Conaire said the
same thing – 'we live in a more complex world and new methods
and new metaphysic are needed to explore it'. The Irish language,
they hoped, was to be brought into the European mainstream.[39]

O Conaire was born in Galway city, but was brought up at Rosmuck,
west of Galway, near Kilkieran Bay. Pearse had a cottage near there
overlooking the water, a sea-inlet – bird-haunted, green slopes
behind, an 'ideal' Ireland. Sean O'Faolain is made almost light-headed
by 'the calm and hidden refuge of this peninsula. . . . The lyrical note
which, here, rises sweetly over the rough and stern undertones of
Connemara'. He can understand how Pearse was moved by this to
form 'the gentle conception of the West' that he gives us in stories
such as 'Iosagán' ['Yssagaun'] (a fable of the Child Jesus). 'How
various men are! O Conaire inspired by Galway, writing in a wild
mixture of fantasy and realism. . . . Pearse idealizing everything, finding in the morning and evening light over Kilkieran the inspiration
to die for a country so lovely though so poor.'[40] Pearse exhorted
writers in Irish to deal with 'the loves and hates and desires of modern
man and woman', but it was O Conaire who attempted this, not
Pearse. Pearse's stories are like classical fables, deriving from his love
for the people and landscape round Rosmuck.

Martin O Cadhain (1906–70) was born at Spiddal, along the coast
from Galway (about halfway between Galway and Rosmuck), and
perhaps he had greater claim to a genuinely country background than
had Pearse (who was half-English) or O Conaire, the British Civil
Servant; paradoxically, his Irish is more coloured and complex in an
effort to widen the resources of Gaelic and make it more contemporary. A story such as 'The Road to Brightcity' is about a young
peasant-woman walking to town to sell butter and eggs:

> She unwrapped the eggs from their straw and paper and counted
> them again, yes, three score, scoured clean and pure, white,
> brown, pale blue. In no particular order, yet she knew the egg
> of each and every hen – the little grey pullet's, the speckled hen's
> one white with hardly the breath of a shell, and those of the
> crested hen brown and big as duck eggs. . . .
>   Though she understood the ideas 'luck', 'bad luck', 'misfor-
> tune', well enough, she was unable to give any precise sense
> to the notions of 'pleasure', 'joy of life'. . . .

but she knows it is hard, to walk nine miles there, nine miles back,
'again, and again and again . . . till her jawbones showed bleak, her
limbs weathered, the hard look came into her eyes. But she had done
them for today and that was something. Her pulse throbbed, her
heart sang. . . . She was ready again to take up the burden of life.
She gripped the strap of the butter creel.'[41]
   Whether the story in Irish has succeeded in making Irish a live
language, as it hoped to do, is uncertain. A poet of the younger
generation, Aidan Carl Mathews (b. 1956) seems to doubt it:[42]

> The tide gone out for good,
> Thirty-one words for seaweed
> Whiten on the foreshore.

But the loss of those thirty-one words would be grievous. The
discovery of this richness was one of the things that excited the Gaelic
revival.
   Of course there was a political element in that revival of the
language, in rescue of the old stories, and the making of new ones.
But they were not 'fake', these men and women. To entertain a
dream, and follow it through, when you know it will lead to being
put up against a wall in the Stonebreakers' Yard of Kilmainham
Gaol, is, whatever else it may be, not fake. Pearse translated his
own poem: 'I am Ireland: I am older than the Old Woman of Beare
. . .' He knew his likely fate, and foretold it, in a poem translated

by Thomas MacDonagh, who was executed with him. The title is
'Ideal'.[43]

> Naked I saw thee,
> O beauty of beauty!
> And I blinded my eyes
> For fear I should flinch.
>
> I heard thy music,
> O sweetness of sweetness!
> And I shut my ears
> For fear I should fail. . . .
>
> I set my face
> To the road here before me,
> To the work that I see,
> To the death that I shall meet.

Rosmuck and Spiddal have led along the lower, coastal, road from
Galway city. But for many generations of mainly English-speaking
travellers, the main road out of the city towards Connemara is the
one inland, leading to Maam Cross and Clifden. On this road, not
far from Galway, beside Ross Lake is Ross House, family home of
Violet Martin (1862–1915), the 'Martin Ross' of Somerville and Ross.
The house, built in 1777, was already in decline when she was a
girl. She was born in 1862, and by 1872 'rabbits would be seen running on the great steps before the front door'; the Martin tenants
had voted Nationalist, and it was as though the Martins 'felt their
"people" had no more powers of memory than the rabbits on the
front steps of Ross'.[44]

One of the reasons Violet Martin became a writer was to earn
money to keep the decaying place together. It was a struggle, she
was often ill, and at such times she felt herself curiously 'outside
space'. She wrote to her cousin Edith Somerville about her troubles,
in the bantering tone they shared; telling her in 1895 how 'the cat,
being in labour, selected as her refuge the old oven in the corner
of the kitchen, a brick cavern, warm, lofty and secluded'. Martin
had ordered the flues to be cleaned and had not realized they connected with this oven: 'I was fortunately pervading space that day,
and came in time to see a dense black cloud issuing from the oven's
mouth into the kitchen. I yelled to a vague assembly of Bridgets in the
servants' hall, all of whom were sufficiently dirty to bear a little

more without injury. . . . For the rest of the day Jubilee cleaned
herself and her children in the coldest parts of the house with ostentatious fury.' She seems to know the name of the cat better than
the names of the servants, but that is part of the Somerville and Ross
tone, laughing at the Irish while insisting on their own Irishness.
Violet Martin died in 1915. By 1905 Ross House was in a bad way,
and in 1924 it was sold. It has been given another lease of life in
private hands (and can on occasions be visited).

In 1893 the cousins, Somerville and Ross, published *Through Connemara in a Governess-cart*, an account of their travels in these parts,
on which they took with them a spirit-lamp, a rubber bath, Bovril
and a revolver. They have the gusto of heroines in a play by Shaw,
their pose is to be as near free spirits as corsets and feminine bowler-
hats allow them, constantly teasing each other, themselves, and
Ireland: 'Every road we have seen in Connemara makes for water
like an otter and finds it with seeming ease, sometimes even succeeding in getting into it. . . .' They arrive at Oughterard:

> 'This is the best village for its size this side of Galway,' said
> my cousin with a languid indifference that, as I well knew,
> masked the seething self-satisfaction of the resident in the neigh-
> bourhood. 'And the place has improved so wonderfully. For
> instance, there's the Widows' Almshouse. It isn't so very long
> ago that an old woman said to my grandmother, "That's the
> Widdies Almshouse, and sorra widdy in it but one little owld
> man", and now it's simply bursting with widows – at least, I
> mean – '
> This remarkable illustration of the prosperity of Oughterard
> was suddenly interrupted. . . .

Somerville and Ross were on their way, among other places, to
Ballinahinch Castle, west of Maam Cross, one-time stronghold of
the legendary Martins, 'Kings' of Connemara, most of which the
Martins owned – the house was said to have the longest drive of a
private house in the kingdom, fifty miles, from Galway, all Martin
land – and over which they ruled like feudal princes. One of the
most notable of Martins was Richard (1754–1834) who began life
as 'Hair-trigger Dick' because of his partiality for duelling, and ended
it as 'Humanity Dick', because of his long campaign against cruelty
to animals which led to the foundation of what became the RSPCA.
The ever-cheerful refugee from the French Revolution, the Chevalier

de Latocnaye, his possessions on his shoulder, tied in a bundle on a stick like Dick Whittington, called on him. 'I have never in my life been in the house of a rich man who appeared to care so little for the things of this world as Richard Martin.' De Latocnaye also observes his extravagance. Martin had begun 'a superb mansion on the borders of a pretty little lake at the foot of Leitrig mountain', but had to abandon it, as too costly. 'A palace would certainly seem an extraordinary thing in the middle of these mosses.'[45] In the midst of 'mosses' (and now, rhododendrons) Ballinahinch remains.

Thackeray stayed at the house in the 1842, in comfort, remarking on the breakfasts, and noting that 'the dinners were just as good'. The service was if anything excessive:

> There may be many comparisons drawn between English and Irish gentlemen's houses; but perhaps the most striking point of difference between the two is the immense following of the Irish house, such as would make an English housekeeper crazy almost. Three comfortable, well-clothed, good-humoured fellows walked down with me from the car, persisting in carrying one a bag, another a sketching-stool, and so on: walking about the premises in the morning, sundry others were visible in the courtyard and near the kitchen-door. . . . As for maids, there were half a score of them skurrying about the house; and I am not ashamed to confess that some of them were extremely good looking. . . .

The best description of a visit to Ballinahinch is by Maria Edgeworth (1767–1849), who in 1833 stayed with Humanity Dick's son, Thomas – for three weeks, one of her travelling-party had fallen ill – and became fascinated by his extraordinary daughter, Mary:[47] 'Now do think of a girl of seventeen, in the wilds of Connemara, intimately acquainted with Aeschylus and Euripides, and having them as part of her daily thoughts. . . .' Maria Edgeworth hears Mary rumbling whole stanzas of Scott or Byron during dinner, 'without any desire to attract attention to herself'. Unsurprisingly, the sturdy Sir Culling Smith, one of the Edgeworth travelling-party, could not stand this blue-stocking slip of a girl. After visiting the Martins' marble quarries, he asks Mary to put a question to one of her people. 'When the question had been put and answered, Sir Culling objected: "But, Miss Martin, you did not ask the question exactly as I requested you to state it." "No," said she, with colour raised and head thrown back, "no, because I knew how to put it that our people might understand it. *Je sais mon métier de reine*" '.[46]

For years afterwards Maria Edgeworth kept her ears open for news of this remarkable young woman, this 'queen'. Mary confided to Maria that she was expected to make a rich marriage, because the estate was in debt, and Maria (unmarried herself) counselled her not to: 'Never, for your father or for any human being, consent to marry a man you don't love, much less to marry one man while you prefer another . . . it would not do for you, Mary.' There were many 'suitable' matches possible, but in the end, she married her land-agent, a cousin. Her father, who died in 1847, left the estate to her, mortgaged to the Law Life Assurance Society. She could not keep up the interest payments, was sued for default, and the vast estate was sold. She emigrated to America with her husband, gave birth to a child during the voyage, and died shortly after landing.

She was made the heroine of *The Martins of Cro-Martin* (1856) by Charles Lever, a popular novel for which Somerville and Ross have little time. They describe the appearance of Ballinahinch as it was (and is) after the insurance company had had their way with it: 'As we drove along the high ground beyond, Ballinahinch came slowly into sight; a long lake in a valley, a long line of wood skirting it, and finally, on a wooded height, the Castle, as it is called, a large modern house with a battlemented top, very gentlemanlike, and even handsome, but in no other way remarkable.'[48] In 1926 the house was bought by Ranjitsinjhi, the great Indian cricketer, who treated the neighbourhood with Martin-like generosity. Each year, when he came for the fishing, he bought several cars, which he gave away to locals when he left. Ballinahinch is now a hotel, with photographs of a portly 'Ranji' on its walls, admiring a suffocated salmon.

Connemara, on a good day – and the weather from the Atlantic is so quickly changeable, few days are wholly bad – arouses an unlikely enthusiasm in some visitors. 'Cockney' Thackeray, for example, wonders why the English went anywhere else for their holidays, and Harriet Martineau, before she goes on to deplore the superstitions of the Catholic peasants, and admire the industry of the Protestants, allows herself to admit, in 1852, 'There are few things in the world more delightful than a drive at sunset, in a bright autumn evening, among the mountains and lakes of Connemara. A friend of ours describes the air of his favourite place by saying it is like breathing champagne. The air here, on such an evening, is like breathing cream.'

Kate O'Brien (1897–1974), Limerick-born, lived for many years at Roundstone, south of Ballinahinch, at the Fort overlooking the charming harbour, and for her it is not so much the air, but the light, that enchants:

> Winter and spring are Roundstone's times. Nights of fair and cool December, April mornings, wet February days – I had a good largesse of those in that place, and so I have them now until I die.
>
> The whole of South Connemara, shelving out from the hills to the sea, is silvery, level, water-striped and overflowing with light. . . . About Roundstone, over the water of Inishnee, to Cashel and Glinsk, there is often an illusion that all is afloat, an uncertainty between hill and sky, an interchange of water and stone which the indescribably clear light seems paradoxically to exaggerate.

North-west of Clifden, at Cleggan, the poet Richard Murphy (b. 1927) built himself a house, and found himself soon confronted with Ireland's past, the weight of it.[49]

> Slate I picked from a nettlebed
> Had history, my neighbour said.
>
> To quarry it, men had to row
> Five miles, twelve centuries ago. . . .

He then tells us (or is told) more of the history of the slates, and ends, perhaps defiantly, because the past can be burdensome:

> This week I paved my garden path
> With slate St Colman nailed on lath.

Possibly to make sense of Irish history, of one key moment in it, Murphy's most extended poem is on the Battle of Aughrim, fought in 1691, near Ballinasloe (east Galway), the last decisive battle between Jacobite Catholic forces, paid for by Louis XIV, mostly native Irish, and a Williamite army composed mostly of foreign mercenaries. The great Irish hero, Patrick Sarsfield, was replaced in his command by a Frenchman, St Ruth, who decided to make a final stand at Aughrim, and was killed almost at once. Sarsfield could do no more than cover the retreat. At the surrender of Limerick, the treaty Sarsfield signed was a fair one for Catholics but it was soon revoked. Meanwhile Sarsfield had left for France, and for generations afterwards, Irish Catholic soldiers, the 'Wild Geese', would be fighting on the other side, any side, against England. Sarsfield was killed fighting for France against the same William of Orange, 'King Billy':[50]

> We loved you, horseman of the white cockade,
> Above all, for your last words, 'Would to God
> This wound had been for Ireland'. Cavalier,
> You feathered with the wild geese our despair.

On the next promontory northwards from Cleggan, at the end of the farthest reach of Connemara, is Renvyle. The neighbours of the Martins of Ballinahinch, and almost as great potentates, were the Blakes, who built themselves a 'long, sea-grey house' between the lake and the shore at Renvyle. Maria Edgeworth in 1833 went there after her prolonged stay at Ballinahinch, and found it an improvement. 'We could not help sighing with the wish that our late hospitable host had half these comforts of life.' By the time 'The Cousins' (Somerville and Ross) stayed there in 1890, Renvyle was a hotel.

> We spent the morning in making a final tour of the house, up and down the long passages, and in and out of the innumerable charming panelled rooms. We have left the library to the last, and now that we are face to face with the serious business of description, our consciences tell us that we are not competent to pronounce on ancient editions and choice bindings. It seems to us that every book in the tall mahogany cases that stood like screens about the room was old and respectable enough to have been our great grandfather; we certainly had in our hands a contemporary edition of Sir Walter Raleigh's 'History of the World,' not to mention an awful sixteenth century treatise on tortures, with illustrations that are still good, handy, reliable nightmares when the ordinary stock runs short.[51]

Kate O'Brien rightly draws attention to the beach at Renvyle, which has stones of smooth marble, most dark, many pure white, some with coloured veins in them: 'Amid those coloured pebbles and having looked awhile over the wide water, and northward to Achill, having listened to the collected sounds of silence . . . on the shore of Renvyle all that is most majestical and innocent of earth encompasses us. . . .'

This is presumably why restless, witty, Oliver St John Gogarty (1878–1957) bought the place. A successful surgeon in Dublin; Senator, athlete, friend of James Joyce and of nearly everyone else (though the friendship with Joyce cooled after Gogarty appeared in *Ulysses* as 'Buck Mulligan'); he had most of the accomplishments and tells you about them amusingly, in *As I was going down Sackville Street* (1937) and other books of highly coloured reminiscences. He tells of Renvyle also, between the lake and the sea, where

> water-lilies meet the golden sea-weed. . . . Behind me a wing of the long sea-grey house stretches for forty yards. In the evening the lake will send the westering sun dancing on the dining-room panels, the oak of which sun and age have reddened until it looks like the mahogany of a later day.
>
> The sun is shining up at me from the lake and down on me from the sky. We have not long to live in the sun; and here even the sunlight is not assured.[52]

He did not only mean the weather. It was the time of the Civil War, between the new Irish Free State (led by Michael Collins) and the Republican rebels, the 'Irregulars' (led by de Valera). Gogarty was a Free Stater. His remark, that 'Dev' 'looked like a cross between a corpse and a cormorant', cannot have helped. In Dublin he was kidnapped and nearly shot, escaping by swimming the Liffey (to which he donated two swans, for his deliverance). Then a heartbroken chapter begins, 'Renvyle is burned by the I.R.A.':

> The long, long house in the ultimate land of the undiscovered West. Why should they burn my house? Because I am not an Irishman? Because I do not flatter fools? If the only Irishman who is to be allowed to live in Ireland must be a bog-trotter, then I am not an Irishman. And I object to the bog-trotter being the ideal exemplar of all Irishmen. I refuse to conform to that type.
>
> So Renvyle House, with its irreplaceable oaken panelling, is burned down. They say it took a week to burn. Blue china fused like solder. . . .

Gone also were the books that alarmed the Cousins, and the contemporary edition of Ralegh's *History of the World*.

Soon Gogarty recovers his spirits, or affects to, and is discussing ghosts of the past, the guests at Renvyle; and 'real' ghosts, apparitions that were firmly rebuked by one of the guests, 'Archimandrite Yeats' – 'You must desist from frightening the children in their early sleep. You must cease to moan about the chimneys', and so on – it seemed to work, Gogarty can be relied upon for a good story. But even his spirit sinks again, and he ends the chapter, 'Books, pictures, all consumed: for what? Nothing left but a charred oak beam quenched in the well beneath the house. And ten tall square towers, chimneys, stand bare on Europe's extreme verge.' The house was rebuilt, again as a hotel, and Gogarty stayed for a time on the Island in the lake behind it. He left Ireland for America in 1939.

The coast road from Renvyle to Lenane skirts the deep fiord, Killary Harbour. It passes the fishing village (near Salrock) where Ludwig Wittgenstein (1889–1951) spent several summers in the 1940s (he complained of earwigs and lack of the right kind of detective fiction in the village shop); farther on it runs beside dark Lough Fee, where on a wooded promontory the Wilde family had a fishing lodge.[53] At Lenane, the roads continue to Westport, or cross Killary into higher mountains northwards, past the aptly named scooped hill at 'Delphi'. To the east, through the hills of 'Joyce Country', is Lough Mask; and, above it, Lough Carra.

South Mayo

> When Patrick, glorious in grace, was suffering on goodly Cruach – an anxious toilsome time for him, the protector of lay men and women –
> God sent to comfort him a flock of spotless angelic birds; over the clear lake without fail they would sing in chorus their gentle proclamation.
> And thus they called, auspiciously: 'Patrick, arise and come! Shield of the Gael, in pure glory, illustrious golden spark of fire.'
> The whole host struck the lake with their smooth and shadowy wings, so that its chilly waters became like a silver sheen.
> Hence comes the bright name *The White Lake of Carra* of the contests; I tell you this triumphant meaning as I have heard it in every church.

That is from an eleventh-century poem.[54] 'Cruach' is Croagh Patrick, where the saint is said to have spent forty days in meditation, a symmetrical eminence which can be glimpsed (weather permitting) from all over south-west Mayo. The 'white lake of Carra' is Lough Carra, a smaller lake, rather secret, reedy, actually more greenish than white, lying at the northern end of the much larger Loughs Corrib and Mask which separate Connemara from the rest of Galway and Mayo. Lough Carra is the scene of George Moore's novel, *The Lake* (1905), and Moore was brought up on its shores, at Moore Hall.[55] Moore's father had endeared himself to his tenants, during the Famine, by pulling off a betting-coup on one of his own horses, and with the proceeds chartering a ship to bring in 4,000 tons of maize, which saved many lives. Yet his son, George, with his usual perversity, doubtless intending to shock, chooses to present both his father and himself as the worst sort of landlord barbarians:

> Until the 'seventies Ireland was feudal, and we looked upon our tenants as animals that lived in hovels round the bogs, whence they came twice a year with their rent. . . . And if they failed to pay their rents, the cabins they had built with their own hands were thrown down, for there was no pity for a man who failed to pay his rent. And if we thought that bullocks would pay us better we ridded our lands of them; cleaned our lands of tenants, is an expression I once heard, and I remember how they used to go away by train from Claremorris in great batches bawling like animals.[56]

The Lake is a subtle study of a priest, who dismisses a schoolteacher from his parish because she has an affair, and then slowly discovers that he is in love with her himself. It is said that the fate of Gerald O'Donovan gave Moore the idea. But even here Moore cannot resist a tease; he calls the priest – who leaves his clerical clothes on the bank and swims across the lake to secular freedom – 'Oliver Gogarty'. Gogarty's Catholic mother was appalled, and implored Moore to change the name: 'But, Madam, if you can supply a name with two such joyous dactyls, I will change it.'

There are signs of final impatience with Moore in Frank O'Connor, who says he began by thinking *The Lake* the best of Irish novels and ended up thinking it 'maundering'. 'The maundering style which he invented for "The Lake" he applied to a score of other subjects, including the life of Christ. "You will like this better than any of my books," wrote Moore, sending AE a copy of "The Brook Kerith." "On the contrary," replied AE, "I like it less than any other of your books. Jesus converted the world; your Jesus wouldn't convert an Irish county council." '[57]

It appears that Moore spent little or no time at Moore Hall after his boyhood. Yet he must have looked about him when a boy. His priest in *The Lake*, Father Gogarty, loves the place:

> The beautiful motion and variety of the hills delighted him, and there was as much various colour as there were many dips and curves, for the hills were not far enough away to dwindle to one blue tint; they were blue, but the pink heather showed through the blue, and the clouds continued to fold and unfold, so that neither the colour nor the lines were ever the same. The retreating and advancing of the great masses and the delicate illumination of the crests could be watched without weariness. It was like listening to music.

The gradual evolvement of the priest's self-awareness, his slow discovery of his true motives, is a fine piece of psychological storytelling. And the shores, and the lake itself, are presences.

If Moore despised his family, his family had a kind of revenge. Moore died in London in 1933. He wanted his ashes scattered on Hampstead Heath. (When Moore Hall was burnt down he remarked that he had always known 'Ireland was no place for a gentleman'.) But his family brought his ashes back to Ireland and had them buried on Castle Island opposite Moore Hall – one of the staging-posts of Father Gogarty on his swim 'to freedom' – under a carefully phrased epitaph.

> He forsook his family and his friends
> for his art
> But because he was faithful
> to his art
> His family and friends
> Recovered his ashes for Ireland
> Vale

Oliver St John Gogarty claims that he rowed the burial party out to the island.[58] It was said that had George Moore's brother 'the Colonel' been in the house at the time local people would have prevented it from being burned, he was so well-loved. It is an attractive piece of late eighteenth-century architecture, roofless, buried in conifer plantation, but the walls are in good condition, and there is talk of its restoration.

Dominating Westport (County Mayo) and beautiful Clew Bay, and its dozens of green-topped islands, all sloped on one side, like scones half-risen, is 'goodly Cruach', Croagh Patrick, St Patrick's Mountain; a place of pilgrimage for generations. On top of it St Patrick fasted for forty days, and from it banished snakes from Ireland. George Moore, as usual, chooses to be provocative on the subject of this holy mountain: 'I had once thought that with five hundred tons of dynamite the regularity of the peak might be undone, but today it seems to me the peak is all right in its landscape.'[59]

It is unlikely that George Moore climbed the mountain he had been tempted to rearrange, but, in the 1940s, with all his English hesitations, T.H. White did, and it had an unexpected effect:

> As we moved round and round so strangely, with the three hundred and sixty-five islands of the bay like toys at our feet, and Clare Island a peep-show and the White Cow island beyond – with Corslieve fifty miles to the north, and Achill hinting a shoulder, and the universal sea about, it was only possible to hold out the tragic filth of the human race for God to see – not feeling contempt for them, nor expecting anything to be done for them – without petition or sarcasm or confusion of mind.[60]

Thomas De Quincey came to Westport in 1800, aged fifteen, with the young Lord Westport, and stayed in elegant Westport House, seat of the Marquess of Sligo. It was two years before the experiences of his *Confessions of an English Opium Eater*. He explored Croagh Patrick, and it was in Ireland that his life was changed, by the kindness of a young woman with whom he discussed literature. 'When the ideal of womanhood, in all its total loveliness and purity, dawns like some vast aurora on the mind, boyhood has ended. . . .'[61]

A writer who innocently managed to antagonize both sides of Ireland was 'George A. Birmingham': Canon James Hannay (1865–1950), Rector of Holy Trinity Church at Westport from 1892 to 1913. Born in Belfast, educated at an English public school, perhaps he was too 'Englished' not to stand at an intellectual distance from Irish squabbles, which although he understood them, constantly astonished and amused him in a way that others found infuriating. To be the friend of Douglas Hyde, to be elected to the governing body of Hyde's Gaelic League (which wanted to revive Irish as the spoken language of the people) was unlikely to endear him to his Protestant parishioners. But when he published his first novel, *The Seething Pot*, in 1905, the Catholic parish priest of Westport thought himself caricatured (Hannay had not met him) and there were near-riots in the town.

Benedict Kavanagh (1907) is a defence of the Gaelic League, of Ireland's sense of itself as an oppressed nation; and when it is slow it is because of the earnestness of its plea for tolerance from the Ascendancy class. Hannay/Birmingham puts his finger on something rarely admitted, the social foundation of the religious quarrel:

> In Ireland a curious national history has created a class distinction which almost exactly corresponds to the lines of religious and political cleavage. Men of one particular creed and party claim – have indeed been almost forced to claim – a position of social superiority to everybody else in the country. The bitterness born of this claim is more potent in reality than either religious or political differences to keep Irishmen estranged from each other. It is possible to forgive a man for believing or not believing in the infallibility of the Pope. It does not seem possible to think kindly of him when he assumes that he is a gentleman and you are not. Unfortunately, the example set by one class has been imitated by every other.

After this the prolific Birmingham turned more and more to humour, as though he recognized the near-impossibility of reconciliation; Graham Greene found Birmingham, with W.W. Jacobs, 'the two funniest writers of the Edwardian period'. Even when he wrote a farce, its performance in Westport caused riots. *General John Regan* is a story of a bogus hero and of Irish gullibility. For the London production the designer had asked for 'authentic' Irish clothes, so Birmingham's wife collected second-hand clothes from the locals of Westport. The play was a success in London and New York, and when photographs of the production appeared in the papers, people could say, 'There's Tommy's coat', 'There's Molly's petticoat'. As a result, when the play came to Westport and, as they are in farces, the characters were ridiculous, local people took it personally. Some of them invaded the stage, knocked out one of the actors, who was playing a comic priest, and outside the theatre (in the town's charming 'Octagon') it took five baton charges by the police to disperse the crowd.[62]

Hannay now left Westport for a distant parish, and though over-age volunteered later for chaplain service with the Army in France during the First World War; later he settled in England. His pretty rectory in Westport, where he wrote so much in apparent innocence that caused so much trouble, is opposite the Holy Trinity Church.

In 1851 Harriet Martineau bustles into Westport, delighted at the good works of the Marquess of Sligo, but as soon as she leaves the place she becomes angry again. She is on her way to Achill Island, and 'after Westport, for some miles on the road to Newport and beyond it, the aspect of things is more dreary than anything that had met our eyes before in Ireland. We need not describe it. Those soaked and perished, and foul moorlands; those hamlets of unroofed houses . . . these features of a lapsed country are understood at a glance; and here we found them. But presently we met a gentleman. . . .'[63] To be fair to Harriet Martineau, she wanted the place better farmed by the people, so that the conditions of the people would be improved, but she seems to pay little attention to their actual circumstances, famine, rents, despair. Also, when she meets 'a gentleman' he is of course English, an excellent farmer and 'much beloved'. Perhaps he is, but the tone is unsympathetic. In contrast, the tone of Louis MacNeice is a relief:

> In doggerel and stout let me honour this country
> Though the air is so soft it smudges the words
> And herds of great clouds find the gaps in the fences
> Of chance preconceptions and foam-quoits on rock points
> At once hit and miss, hit and miss. . . .[64]

When cross Harriet Martineau reaches Achill, an island MacNeice knew well, she assures us that now English Protestants have taken Achill over, 'in half a century there may be woods clothing the bases of the magnificent hills of Achill, sheltering its valleys, and imparting an air of civilization to the wildest shores the most romantic traveller could wish to see'. There are still not many trees. In the 1830s, Achill was the subject of a concerted attempt to convert the Irish-speaking inhabitants to Protestantism, using the Irish language for their instruction. The Church Missionary Society leased the island and founded schools, a newspaper, an orphanage, and a village below Slievemore mountain, at Doogort.

Heinrich Böll came upon a deserted village in Achill in the 1950s, and it struck him with awe. It could have been the one near Doogort, which is unlike other deserted Irish villages because the houses, on the lower slopes of Slievemore, are built in a straight line. There is a cemetery at one end, and the ridges of the lazybeds, for potatoes, are still visible like ribs from this un-Irish straight terrace of ruin:

The skeleton of a village, cruelly distinct in its structure, neatly laid out on the sombre slope as if for an anatomy lesson. . . . The main street, a little crooked like the spine of a labourer. . . . Everything not made of stone gnawed away by rain, sun, and wind – and time, which patiently trickles over everything; twenty-four great drops of time a day, the acid that eats everything away as imperceptibly as resignation. . . .

No bombed city, no artillery-raked village ever looked like this. In limitless patience time and the elements have eaten away everything not made of stone, and from the earth have sprouted cushions on which these bones lie like relics, cushions of moss and grass.[65]

It would be good to have known the Anglican Bishop MacNeice's thoughts about the Missionary Society, about Doogort and these ruins, when he was a widower holidaying on Achill with his son,[66]

> . . . Carrying his boots and paddling like a child,
> A square black figure whom the horizon understood –
>
> My father. Who for all his responsibly compiled
> Account books of a devout, precise routine
> Kept something in him solitary and wild,
>
> So loved the western sea and no tree's green
> Fulfilled him like these contours of Slievemore
> Menaun and Croaghaun and the bogs between.
>
> Sixty-odd years behind him and twelve before,
> Eyeing the flange of steel in the turning belt of brine
> It was sixteen years ago he walked this shore
>
> And the mirror caught his shape which catches mine
> But then as now the floor-mop of the foam
> Blotted the bright reflections – and no sign
>
> Remains of face or feet when visitors have gone home.

NORTH MAYO

T.H. White, in Ireland on a fishing trip in County Meath at the outbreak of war in 1939, seems to have caught the urge (strong in Ireland, for visitors) to go further and further West. North Mayo is almost all bog, and White rented a shooting-lodge, Sheskin, slap in the middle of it. Admittedly there are (and must then have been) trees round the house, rare in that landscape. Many of those are now dead, and the lodge a ruin; the bog is partly scraped black to fuel a power station, the mountain slopes planted with conifers.

In 1939, White fished in the Oweniny and exulted in the landscape:

> The river, shallow with summer, rippled in herring-bone patterns like the roof of your mouth, the colour of weak beer, cutting its winding way six feet below the level of the bog. And the bog stretched flat for miles and miles, a landscape out of Browning's *Childe Roland*. Round the rim of the saucer, there were the mountains, as bare, calm and empty as the bog. . . .
>
> There was a minute waterfall or glide of water. The soft, tart, ale-coloured stream slid over the smooth stones from step to step, cool and glistening. . . .[67]

'Soft, tart, ale-coloured': White was receptive to the beauties of even the barrenest part of Ireland. As was MacNeice:[68]

> And when the night came down upon the bogland
>   With all-enveloping wings
> The coal-black turf stacks rose against the darkness
>   Like the tombs of nameless kings.

White was better with animals than with people, and at times seems barely to distinguish between them: 'The rare, crafty and ancient grouse used to hobble about on crutches or sit before their heather cottages smoking clay pipes, with steel-rimmed spectacles over their rheumy eyes, spitting in the turf ashes and exchanging folklore about Niall of the Nine Hostages. . . .'

White stayed for a while at the Western Strands Hotel in the main street of Belmullet, one of the remotest towns of Ireland. He wrote about the district and its people in *The Godstone and the Blackymor*, more fantasy than fact, but as a consequence he is still regarded in that place, fifty years later, with less than affection by the people who were kind to him and did not like to see their characters and confidences printed in a book. They particularly remember his Jaguar motor car, which must then have represented riches unimaginable.

White was filled with enthusiasms. He was convinced he had discovered a connection between ancient fertility cults and the legend of *Tir na nOg*, the Country of the Young, in the islands off the

Mullet. He was well aware of being an alien: 'It had dawned on me that we could not get much farther by questioning the old people ourselves. I was too strange for them, too dangerous, too mixed with the tradition of oppressors, and my car was much too grand. Their tender, primitive, suspicious minds were unhappy in forthright cross-examination. They were not suspicious in a mean way. They were like antelopes in the presence of some other animal, possibly carnivorous.'

It was on the stretch of water between the mainland and the islands that the Children of Lir spent the last three hundred years of their spell as swans. It was here that they heard the bell of the monk, disciple of St Patrick, sent to find them, 'and the brothers started up with fright when they heard it. "We do not know," they said, "what is that weak unpleasing voice we hear." "That is the voice of the bell of Mochaomog," said Fionnuala; "and it is through that bell," she said, "you will be set free from pain and from misery." '[69]

One of the attractions of the Lir story is the care Fionnuala takes of her younger brothers. The monk finds them at last, and protects them, as swans; they have answered his bell. A chieftain comes, to drag the famous swan-children away, to make them a present to his wife. As soon as he lays hands on them they are turned back into humans, but nine-hundred-year-old humans, withered, quickly to die (with that brutal realism Kate O'Brien finds characteristic of the old Irish stories) and they beg to be baptized at once, before it is too late; this is done, and Fionnuala asks to be buried with a brother on each side of her and one in her arms, 'And a stone was put over them, and their names were written in Ogham, and they were keened there, and heaven was gained for their souls.'

T.H. White (who does not mention the Lir story) goes to the island of Inishkea, having convinced himself it is the Land of Youth, looking for the supposed 'Godstone', a fertility symbol. But when he reaches the island (it was inhabited until 1927) a change comes over him, like the one that came upon him on Croagh Patrick. He finds many ancient remains on 'this small area of desertion. . . . The force of history hit me in the face.' Then, near 'the etiolated, clean relics' of a monastery which had perhaps been founded by a disciple of St Columba, he finds a skull; and immediately 'the peace and cleanliness of desertion had been replenished, had been filled to the brim with calm. . . . With a tranquillity about saints who to me no longer seemed to need to be connected with fertility gods or phallic symbols . . .' they climb back into their motor-boat: 'we spluttered home to the real world.' (He is not the first English traveller to find himself inadvertently silenced, by the bell-tones from Ireland's past, and then impelled to reject them, on pragmatic, no-nonsense, grounds.)

At Cross Point on the outer, Atlantic, coast of the Mullet, among sand-dunes with thin grasses on them, is an ancient burying-gound. Part of its protective wall has been swept away by the sea, so that white bones stick out of the sandbank which has been revealed, and lie among the stones of the beach. The burial-ground looks across to Inishglora and Inishkea, wave-lashed – even on a calm evening the waves can be seen climbing, white, above the low shores of the islands.

In Munster it had been difficult to move without coming across traces of poets in Irish; bards, or the rakish inheritors of the bardic role. In Connaught there seemed to be none, but in answer to a question asked near Lough Carra a local scholar had said, 'Riocard Bairéad', helpfully translated as 'Richard Barrett'. In the burial ground at Cross Point, part of which had been broken into by the sea, is a much heavier slab, safely inland, of what looks like granite, with *File* (poet) written on it. It is Barrett's, who was born and died in Belmullet (1739–1819). He is famous for a drinking song, apparently of great metrical complexity, four lines of which, in Irish, are on his stone:[70]

> Why spend your leisure bereft of pleasure
>   Amassing treasure? Why scrape and save?
> Why look so canny at every penny?
>   You'll take no money into the grave.

It is the metre used in English by Richard Milliken for his humorous poem, 'The Groves of Blarney', in which both Frank O'Connor and Padraic Colum (despite Millikens's burlesque intention) detected an approach to the true dancing lilt of the Irish.

Sligo

From Belmullet to Sligo, the coast road passes through Killala, where the French landed in 1798;[71] and where, earlier that century, Mrs Delany (1700–88) in her *Letters* describes staying with the Bishop, and watching the peasants run races on the beach. Nearer Sligo, the future Lady Morgan (Sydney Owenson, 1776–1859) wrote her first best-seller, *The Wild Irish Girl* (1806), while living at Longford

House, near Beltra (the wildly romantic castle in the book may have been inspired by the rock-stack at Downpatrick Head). At Collooney and Ballysadare we are into Yeats territory.

Sligo, the town and its surroundings, is now dyed forever with the colours W.B. Yeats gave to it; and the literal colours his painter-brother gave to it:

> Jack B. Yeats once, half in fun, told a friend of mine that he learned to paint by leaning over (he may even have said spitting over) the Garravogue bridge: the second bridge, that is, in the centre of Sligo town and the last before the water turns salt: the bridge that has the cataract and the music of falling water to mock the grunts and belches of the traffic. When the river is at the top of its form it's quite easy to see what the painter meant. The smooth black water turns the corner, holds its breath for a while and hesitates when it realizes what's in store for it, then takes the plunge: breaking up into all shapes and patterns and colours, revealing in a moment all the beauty it had stored up during its long reverie two miles upstream in Lough Gill.[72]

The poet Yeats was born in Dublin (in 1865), but his first memories are of Sligo, when he was three, and of his grandparents, the Pollexfens. (They were a Sligo family, of Cornish origins, so, naturally, Oliver St John Gogarty called Ireland-obsessed Yeats 'the Cornishman'.) Sligo town is dominated to the west by Knocknarea at Strandhill, which has a mound on the top traditionally thought to be the burial-place of the warrior Queen Maeve. Yeats mentions the mountain in his first published poem, 'The Wanderings of Oisin', which he began in 1886; Finn MacCool and his Fianna

> Came to the cairn-shaped grassy hill
> Where passionate Maeve is stony-still . . .

and mentions it in one of his last, despairing, defiant poems, 'Man and Echo' (1938):

> In a cleft that is christened Alt
> Under a broken stone I halt
> At the bottom of a pit
> That broad noon has never lit,
> And shout a secret to the stone.
> All that I have said and done,

> Now that I am old and ill,
> Turns into a question till
> I lie awake night after night
> And never get the answers right.
> Did that play of mine send out
> Certain men the English shot? . . .

Yeats means his play, *Cathleen ni Houlihan*,[73] and Alt is a deep
cleft in the side of Knocknarea. It is possible that Yeats knew little
of Maeve, or of Cruachan (Rathcrogan) in Roscommon whence she
set off on the 'Cattle Raid of Cooley' because, in 1902, in his
Introduction to Lady Gregory's *Cuchulain of Muirthemne*, he laments
his one-time ignorance: 'When I was a child I had only to climb
the hill behind the house to see long, blue, ragged hills flowing along
the southern horizon. What beauty was lost to me, what depth of
emotion is still lacking in me, because nobody told me, not even
the merchant captains who knew everything, that Cruachan of the
Enchantments lay behind those long, blue, ragged hills!' Even when
he was writing 'The Wanderings of Oisin' he perhaps did not know
the richness of the legends his childhood paradise was surrounded by.
This is why he shocked George Moore by praising Lady Gregory's
book so extravagantly, because she had made some of these stories
easily available for the first time: 'I think this book is the best that
has come out of Ireland in my time. Perhaps I should say that it
is the best book that has ever come out of Ireland; for the stories
which it tells are the chief part of Ireland's gift to the imagination
of the world. . . .'

When sent to school in London, Yeats 'longed for a sod of earth
from some field I knew, something of Sligo to hold in my hand'.
His best-known poem (and its fame came to irritate him), 'The
Lake Isle of Innisfree' – 'I will arise and go now, and go to Innisfree
. . . Nine bean-rows will I have there . . .' and so on, is pure
nostalgia. It came to him when he was poor and depressed in
London:

> My father had read to me some passage out of *Walden*, and I
> planned to live some day in a cottage on a little island called
> Innisfree. . . . I thought that having conquered bodily desire and
> the inclination of my mind towards women and love, I should
> live, as Thoreau lived, seeking wisdom. . . .
>   I had still the ambition, formed in Sligo in my teens, of living
> in imitation of Thoreau on Innisfree, a little island in Lough

Gill, and when walking through Fleet Street very homesick I heard a little tinkle of water and saw a fountain in a shop-window which balanced a little ball upon its jet, and began to remember lake water. From the sudden remembrance came my poem *Innisfree*, my first lyric with anything in its rhythm of my own music.[74]

Yeats tells the story of how, in his teens, he decided to sleep in Slish Wood (now renamed, alas, 'Lough Gill Forest') opposite the island:

I set out from Sligo about six in the evening, walking slowly, for it was an evening of great beauty; but though I was well into Slish Wood by bedtime, I could not sleep, not from the discomfort of the dry rock I had chosen for my bed, but from my fear of the wood ranger. Somebody had told me, though I do not think it could have been true, that he went his round at some unknown hour. I kept going over what I should say if found and could not think of anything he would believe. However, I could watch my island in the early dawn and notice the order of the cries of the birds.

Loneliness, fear of his grandfather, fear of gamekeepers, his own internal struggles notwithstanding, it does seem that Yeats had a childhood that was almost ideal for a poet, or, perhaps more to the point, he made it so. Above all, he had Rosses Point to go to, a family house there, by the harbour, called 'Elsinore', which had belonged to a smuggler and was said to be haunted. (The house, sadly huddled in its little hollow, looking out on the water, is being allowed to fall into a ruin.) It looks an ideal spot for an imaginative boy to spend holidays, within sight of the steamers coming and going, within earshot of the talk of sailors (the 'merchant captains who knew everything') and the wide turfy 'storm-bitten' spaces that point their green fingers into the sea, dominated on one side by Maeve's Knocknarea, and on the other by the prognathous profile of Ben Bulben: 'When I look at my brother's picture, *Memory Harbour* – houses and anchored ship and distant lighthouse all set close together as in some old map – I recognize in the blue-coated man with the mass of white shirt the pilot I went fishing with, and I am full of disquiet and excitement, and I am melancholy because I have not made more and better verses. I have walked on Sinbad's yellow shore and never shall another's hit my fancy.'

A local author who knew Rosses Point well had no difficulty with
two striking Yeats images from famous poems, 'Byzantium' and 'Sailing to Byzantium': 'When the bell buoy is being lashed about in
a storm, every Rosses Point man will know "the gong-tormented
sea", which becomes a "mackerel crowded sea", when the silver shoals
appear in the bay.'[75]

Yeats describes 'Elsinore' directly in *Last Poems*: he is still thinking
of the house in 1939, the year of his death:[76]

> My name is Henry Middleton,
> I have a small demesne,
> A small forgotten house that's set
> On a storm-bitten green. . . .

Round Rosses Point, below Ben Bulben, nestling in its woods by
the shore is Lissadell, where the grown-up Yeats stayed with his
friends the Gore-Booths. But Lissadell has much earlier associations
with a poet, of the thirteenth century, Muireadhach Ó Dálaigh
[roughly, 'Murray O'Daly'], brother of the saintly Donnachadh Mor
Ó Dálaigh, who is buried at Boyle Abbey (not so far away, near
those 'blue, ragged hills'); whom Douglas Hyde – and the Four
Masters – considered Ireland's greatest religious poet. The brother,
Muireadhach, seems to have been of a different temperament. A tax-
inspector came to Lissadell (the Four Masters put the date at 1213)
and insulted the poet, so the poet hit him with an axe. The Four
Masters report that it was an unusually sharp axe, enough to account
for the tax-inspector. Even in the thirteenth century this behaviour
was frowned on, so the poet made himself scarce for a while, though
he seems to think that everyone is taking it far too seriously:[77]

> What reason for such wrath can be?
> The rascal bandied words with me.
> I took an axe and hewed him down –
> Small matter for a prince's frown.

Eventually he had to flee to Scotland, and went to the Near East,
possibly joining the Fifth Crusade. Robin Flower says 'it is a thrilling
thought' that when St Francis came to the European camp, trying
to make peace between the warring parties, they may have met: 'the
Irish poet may have seen the great founder of the Order which was
later to have so profound an effect on Irish literature: the kinsman
of the greatest religious poet of Ireland and the Tuscan saint. . .'.

Ó Dálaigh wrote a lovely poem, 'On the death of his wife':

> I parted from my life last night,
>   A woman's body sunk in clay:
> The tender bosom that I loved
>   Wrapped in a sheet they took away. . . .
>
> The face that was like hawthorn bloom
>   Was my right foot and my right side;
> And my right hand and my right eye
>   Were no more mine than hers that died.
>
> Poor is the share of me that's left
>   Since half of me died with my wife;
> I shudder at the words I speak;
>   Dear God, that girl was half my life. . . .

The version is by Frank O'Connor,[78] and the ease of it is extraordinary because, when it is compared with a word-for-word translation, it barely departs from the original. Few have dared to compete with O'Connor since, in the matter of rhymed translations. To say that Yeats may have had a hand in them is to take nothing from O'Connor because he admits this, with loving exasperation, himself. 'He published two volumes of my translations from the Irish, and did it with such enthusiasm that he practically rewrote the lot.' (Gogarty, says O'Connor, had the same experience; he sent some of his poems to Yeats and remarked, 'Yeats is writing a couple of little lyrics for me, so I'd better drop in and see how he's getting on.')[79]

In *The Winding Stair* (1933) Yeats remembers the Gore-Booth sisters, Eva and Constance, of Lissadell. Constance, as the Countess Markiewicz, took part in the Rising of 1916 and was condemned to death, her sentence commuted to life imprisonment. She was elected the first woman Member of the House Commons, but never took her seat. Yeats remembers their beauty and grace, particularly that of Eva, and deplores their involvement in politics, as he so often deplores his own:[80]

> The light of evening, Lissadell,
> Great windows opening to the south,
> Two girls in silk kimonos, both
> Beautiful, one a gazelle.
> But a raving autumn shears
> Blossom from the summer's wreath. . . .

Dear shadows, now you know it all,
All the folly of a fight
With a common wrong or right.
The innocent and the beautiful
Have no enemy but time. . . .

Lissadell is 'under bare Ben Bulben's head' and it is on that mountain
that the long elopement of Diarmaid and Grainne (Dermot and
Graunia) is said to have come to an end, with Diarmaid's death. It
is one of the best-known of the stories of the 'Fenian cycle' and is
briefly this. Grainne is the coquettish daughter of the great king,
Cormac Mac Airt (Art) (the king who refused to be buried in New
Grange, and chose Rosnaree instead). She has been married to the
elderly hero, Finn MacCool, but runs off with Diarmaid, who is not
only handsome, but has a 'love-spot' which makes him irresistible to women. He is at first reluctant, they live as brother and sister,
but eventually he falls in love with her and they travel, fleeing
from Finn, all over Ireland: there are prehistoric dolmens everywhere
which are called their 'bed'. They patch up a truce with Finn, and
settle at Keshcorran, near Ballymore, in south Sligo. But eventually
Diarmaid, having forgotten his magic spear, is gored by a boar on
Ben Bulben, and when Finn sees Diarmaid dying, he fails in his
usual courtesy: ' "I like to see you like that, Diarmaid," said he, "and
I regret that all the women of Ireland are not looking at you now,
for your beauty is turned to ugliness and your good form to defor-
mity." '
    Diarmaid begs a drink from him, for a drink taken from Finn's
hands would be magical. Finn refuses; Diarmaid gives a long list of
all he has done for Finn in the past, the Fianna beg Finn to give
him the drink, and Finn rather sulkily says there is no spring on
Ben Bulben. Diarmaid tells him there is one not nine paces away,
'the most truly beautiful, pure-watered well in the whole world'.
Finn takes a drink to him, but allows it to trickle through his fingers,
twice; and his Fianna, for once, grows mutinous. So he does finally
take the water, and Diarmaid is already dead. One of the outraged
band makes to strike off Finn's head but is stopped by Finn's son,
Oisín – 'It is true that he has deserved that of you and of all the
Fianna of Ireland through not helping Diarmaid, but do not cause
two sorrows in the one day for us. . . .'[81]
    Below Ben Bulben is Drumcliff, site of the famous battle where
the O'Donnells of Donegal helped St Columcille keep his copy of

the psalter of St Finian, which later came to be called the 'Cathach' ['Caha'], 'the Battler', as it was carried at the head of their troops.[82] Another saint, Molaise, suggested that Columcille go into exile as penance for causing a battle over such a sacred matter, and the penitent Columcille went to Iona and founded the monastery there.

One of Yeats's ancestors was Church of Ireland rector at Drumcliff and there Yeats is buried:

> Under bare Ben Bulben's head
> In Drumcliff churchyard, Yeats is laid. . .

under his own famous epitaph – 'Cast a cold eye/On life, on death./ Horseman, pass by' – which O'Connor, who made the funeral oration in 1948, thought so unsuitable for the enthusiastic Yeats.[83]

The next stop up the coast from Sligo, the next poet, is William Allingham, at Ballyshannon in Donegal. It was Allingham 'who inspired Yeats as a young man to study the country beliefs and prehistoric traditions of Sligo, and to express the modest wish of doing for Sligo what William Allingham had done for Ballyshannon'. Later, Yeats compared Allingham with the Young Irelander Thomas Davis, whose verse was entirely political, and again seems to regret the way he, Yeats, had been drawn into politics: 'In Allingham I find the entire emotion of the place one grew up in which I felt as a child. Davis on the the other hand was concerned with ideas of Ireland, with conscious patriotism.' He sums up in favour of Allingham: 'This love was instinctive and left the soul free. If I could have kept it and yet never felt the influence of Young Ireland I had given a more profound picture of Ireland in my work.'[84]

There is now a 'Yeats Trail' in Sligo, with signs bearing a quill in an inkwell, which from a distance looks like steam coming off a cup of tea, or froth from a pint of stout. The Trail was foreseen fifty years ago by Yeats's sister Lily, who wrote that at Innisfree there would be signs: 'The beans must not be eaten. They are the property of the Land Commission.' (Nine bean-rows will I have there, and a hive for the honey-bee, And live alone in a bee-loud glade.)

AROUND DUBLIN

HILL OF ALLEN AND KILDARE

The network of the legends spreads all over Ireland. Finn MacCool
came upon the dying Diarmaid on Ben Bulben in Sligo, in the west,
and scooped out Lough Neagh in the far north; but his main *dún*,
or fort, was on the Hill of Allen, in Kildare. It was from there he
sent his men to Tara, to ask for Grainne as a wife for him (who
later famously ran off with Diarmaid, which was the cause of all
the trouble).[1] With this story in mind Yeats climbed the Hill. So
did Sean O'Faolain at the beginning of *An Irish Journey*. His book
was intended to be a full circuit of Ireland, and perhaps he was overcome at the thought:

> I feel obliged to confess that I retired to the tip-top of the Hill
> of Allen, and lay down there among the deep, wild, rank, golden
> furze, and presently fell sound asleep. It is a grand place from
> which to see the configuration of the country you may be about
> to explore, and though that immense bog beneath it, vacant,
> brown and purple, unbroken by anything except the blue smoke
> of turf-cutters' fires rising to the sky, is a mere fieldeen of a
> place compared with the true Bog of Allen, it gives one a great
> sense of the dignity of the flat land that from there begins to
> stretch half-way across Ireland.
>
> Some monstrous tower desecrates the top of the hill. I believe
> it is there to remind us that this is one of the forts of the Kings
> of Leinster. It is better seen from miles and miles away, when
> the dome of the hill is round and nippled, and this solitary break
> in the plain is lonely as a stranded bottle on a beach. You get
> to the hill top from Newbridge.[2]

In fact (1993) it is difficult to find a way to get to the hill top
because it is fenced, part of it has become a quarry, and the Hill
is being eaten away. It is also a forestry plantation, so no longer
is its dome 'round and nippled', unless the nipple is the tower, about
which O'Faolain is less than fair. It was put up in 1859, 'in thankful

memory of God's mercies, many and great' and, what is unusual in such private extravagances of landlords, the names of the men who built it are inscribed in each of its steps.[3]

In Irish the Hill is called *Cnoc Almhaine*, which Lady Gregory renders 'Almhuin'. The elderly Finn is gloomy up there:

> Finn rose up one morning early in Almhuin of Leinster, and he sat out alone on the green lawn without a boy or a servant being with him. And Oisín followed him there. 'What is the cause of your early rising, Finn?' said Oisín. 'It is not without cause, indeed, I rise early,' said Finn, 'for I am without a wife or a companion. . . .' 'Why would you be like that?' said Oisín, 'for there is not a woman in all green Ireland you would throw a look on but we would bring her to you, willing or unwilling.'

Oisín (who is Finn's son) suggests young Grainne ['Graunia'], daughter of the High King of Ireland, and old Finn approves the idea, sends Oisín to ask for her hand, and so the story begins.

It is on the Hill of Allen that Finn, on request, describes his code, an exposition of pagan, feudal morality. His list ends with an image so homely, that one understands why Yeats liked the Finn stories, 'although the impossible has thrust its proud finger into them all':[4]

> If you have a mind to be a good champion, be quiet in a great man's house; be surly in the narrow pass. Do not beat your hound without a cause; do not bring a charge against your wife without having knowledge of her guilt; do not hurt a fool in fighting, for he is without his wits. Do not find fault with high-up persons; do not stand up to take part in a quarrel; have no dealings with a bad man or a foolish man.
>
> Let two-thirds of your gentleness be showed to women and to little children that are creeping on the floor, and to men of learning that make the poems, and do not be rough with the common people. . . .
>
> That was good advice Finn gave, and he was well able to do that; for it was said of him that he had all the wisdom of a little child that is busy about the house, and the mother herself not understanding what he is doing; and that is the time she has most pride in him.[5]

Oisín later laments his father's death, describes his palace on the Hill, and the generous life they all lived:

Seven sides Finn's house had, and seven score shields on every
side. Fifty fighting men he had about him having woollen cloaks;
ten bright drinking-cups in his hall; ten blue vessels, ten golden
horns.

It is a good household Finn had, without grudging, without
lust, without vain boasting, without chattering, without any
slur on any one of the Fianna.

Finn never refused any man; he never put away any one that
came to his house. If the brown leaves falling in the woods were
gold, if the white waves were silver, Finn would have given
away the whole of it.[6]

Yeats clearly had to visit the place, and in 1904 he looks out on
what Sean O'Faolain described in 1940:

A few months ago I was on the bare Hill of Allen, 'wide
Almhuin of Leinster', where Finn and the Fianna lived, according to the stories, although there are no earthen mounds there
like those that mark the sites of old buildings on so many hills.
A hot sun beat down upon flowering gorse and flowerless
heather; and on every side except the east, where there were
green trees and distant hills, one saw a level horizon and brown
bog lands with a few green places and here and there the glitter
of water.

One could imagine that had it been twilight and not early
afternoon, and had there been vapours drifting and frothing
where there were now but shadows of clouds, it would have
set stirring in one, as few places even in Ireland can, a thought
that is peculiar to Celtic romance, as I think, a thought of
mystery coming not as with Gothic nations out of the pressure
of darkness, but out of great space and windy light. . . .

When I asked the little boy who had shown me the pathway
up the Hill of Allen if he knew stories of Finn and Oisín, he
said he did not, but that he had often heard his grandfather telling them to his mother in Irish.

The boy does not know Irish, but is learning it at school, and
'in a little while he will know enough stories to tell them to his
children some day'. It is the non-Irish speakers, like himself, whom
Yeats thinks of as deprived: 'But now they can read Lady Gregory's
book to their children, and it will make Slieve-na-man, Allen, and
Ben Bulben, the great mountain that showed itself before me every
day through all my childhood and was yet unpeopled, and half the

country-sides of the south and west, populous with memories.' Yeats goes on to imagine parents, in future years, taking their children to some place made famous by the stories, and saying to them, ' "This land where your fathers lived proudly and finely should be dear and dear and again dear"; and perhaps when many names have grown musical to their ears, a more imaginative love will have taught them a better service.'[7] These were early days, before Yeats became maddened by 'the seeming needs of my fool-driven land',[8] but he never became wholly disillusioned.

Oisín came back from the Land of the Young to berate St Patrick, and the Fianna returned to tell the saint of their exploits; and Patrick seems to enjoy their stories, always asking for more. This melding together of the pagan and Christian is even more startling in the person of Ireland's other great saint, St Brigit of Kildare (c. 450–523).[9] By tradition she was the daughter of a Druid, and was herself perhaps originally a Druid priestess.

Brigit founded an Abbey for women in the present town of Kildare:

> There can be scarcely any doubt that there was here, from prehistoric times, a sanctuary of a fire-goddess *Brigindo*, *Brigit*, whose cult is found over the whole Celtic area. There was a sacred oak, still commemorated in the name of the place ('Cell of the Oak': Kil-dare). We may presume that the sanctuary was tended by a college of priestesses, whose leader was regarded as an incarnation, and officially bore the name, of the goddess.
> The last of this succession accepted the teaching of Christianity. In her new enthusiasm, she accomplished the tremendous feat of transforming the pagan sanctuary into a Christian shrine – a feat for which she will be held in everlasting honour, and one incomparably more marvellous than the pointless juggleries (such as hanging her cloak on a sunbeam!) with which her medieval panegyrists insult her memory and our intelligence.[10]

There is no doubt that she founded her Christian community of women where the present Church of Ireland cathedral church of St Brigit now stands, on its little hill. However, her feast day, 1st February, is also the day of the pagan Imbolc, the Spring and Fire festival.[11] After the Reformation this whiff of paganism proved too strong for Reformed nostrils and the abbey fell into neglect (the church was restored in the nineteenth century).

Brigit's foundation became a seat of learning, home to scholars like Sedulius Scotus (d. 858), who wrote a Life of St Brigit in Latin hexameters. His charm is evident in his short Latin poem called 'Apologia pro Vita Sua', translated by 'Ulster's Darling', Helen Waddell:[12]

> I read or write, I teach or wonder what is truth,
>   I call upon my God by night and day.
> I eat and freely drink, I make my rhymes,
>   And snoring sleep, or vigil keep and pray.
> And very ware of all my shames I am;
>   O Mary, Christ, have mercy on your man.

Poems attributed to Brigit have charm also, and mention simple things:[13]

> I would like to have a great lake of beer
> for Christ the King.
> I'd like to be watching the heavenly family
> drinking it down through all eternity. . . .

'The art of synthesis, upon which myth-making depends, is still common practice in Ireland,' says Michael Dames in *Mythic Ireland*. Through the fusion of St Brigit with Brigit the Fire-Goddess, guardian of the hearth, who survives in many folk-customs, the ceremonies of ordinary homes 'are seen to flare on the hearthstone of infinity'.

Kildare was an important place of pilgrimage in medieval times, because of the fame of St Brigit; for this reason an unusual number of roads converge on the little square, below the cathedral which was once the site of her abbey. There is a ninth-century Christian triumphalist poem called the *Calendar of Oengus*, in which the 'Culdee' ('Companion of God')[14] Oengus celebrates the new holy places, including Brigit's Kildare; and the destruction of the old pagan ones, among them Finn's *dún* on the Hill of Allen ('Aillin' in the poem). He also mentions Cruachan (Rathcrogan, home of Maeve and her consort Ailill), Clonmacnois and Emain Macha ('Navan Fort' outside Armagh):[15]

> The faith has spread
> and will live to the Day of Judgement;
> wicked pagans are carried off,
> their fortresses unoccupied.

The fortress of Cruachan has vanished
with Ailill, victory's child;
a fair dignity greater than kingdoms
is in the city of Clonmacnois. . . .

The proud settlement of Aillin
has died with its boasting hosts;
great is victorious Brigit
and lovely her thronged sanctuary.

The fort of Emain Machae
has melted away, all but its stones;
thronged Glendalough
is the sanctuary of the western world. . . .

GLENDALOUGH AND WICKLOW MOUNTAINS

Glendalough, in County Wicklow, was the site of St Kevin's hermi-
tage, and, when his fame grew, of another ecclesiastical and scholastic
centre. Its situation is reminiscent of Gougane Barra, in County Cork;
the same dark, wind-swept lakes, the same steep hillsides rising from
them. 'Kevin's Bed' is a little cave in one of these. In 1825 Sir Walter
Scott crawled into this – as his son-in-law Lockhart loftily describes
to his wife, Scott's daughter – quoting Tom Moore, 'By that lake
whose gloomy shore / Skylark never warbles o'er': 'It is a hole in
the sheer surface of the rock, in which two or three people might
sit. The difficulty of getting into this place has been exaggerated,
as also the danger, for it would only be falling thirty or forty feet
into very deep water. Yet I never was more pained than when your
papa, in spite of all remonstrances, would make his way to it, crawl-
ing along the precipice. He succeeded and got in – the first lame man
that ever tried it.'[16]
    Between the two lakes, a little above them and in a less wild place,
a ring of stones on a small plateau marks the reputed site of St Kevin's
beehive hut. It is curiously moving, in its small dimensions, in its
charming siting, and looking around one can understand why he came
here, to be alone. It is a place for shepherds and saints, according
to Padraic Colum; but Kevin's fame spread, others came to join him,
and so he was forced to found a monastery: 'They were shepherds
who discovered Kevin; he was living in a hollow tree, a young
anchoret. The monastery that he founded had its great period at the
beginning of the tenth century – now the Round Tower, the ruins

of little churches, are all that remain of the establishment. The Round
Tower is over a hundred feet high. But one does not think of it
as really high – everything here has to be on a companionable level.
It looks like a high candle.'[17]

Because the place is wild, and not far from Dublin, it has since
become a tourist attraction, but it is still wild enough; the steep hills
and lakes channel the wind, and there is a rim of white foam round
the lake, a frame round a dark picture. All looks nearly as ruined
now as 'Cruachan's high *rath*' and 'the proud palace of Aillin'. It must
always have been a stark place.

> The wind over the Hog's Back moans,
> It takes the trees and lays them low.
> And shivering monks o'er frozen stones
> To the twain hours of night-time go. . . .[18]

Later, on the feast day of St Kevin there was a pilgrimage accompanied by a fair, with drinking afterwards, so that the pilgrimage
dissolved into those terrible 'faction fights' between feuding families,
in which the Irish vented their frustrations on each other. The night
before,

> an immense crowd usually had bivouacked, or were putting up
> tents and booths, or cooking their evening meal, gipsy-wise,
> throughout the space of the sacred enclosure. As soon as day-
> light dawned, the tumbling torrent over the rocks and stones
> of the Glendassan river to the north of 'The Churches' became
> crowded with penitents wading, walking and kneeling up 'St
> Kevin's Keeve', many of them holding little children in their
> arms. . . .
>
> Towards evening the fun became 'fast and furious'; the
> pilgrimages ceased, the dancing was arrested, the pipers and
> fiddlers escaped to places of security, the keepers of tents
> and booths looked to their gear – the crowd thickened, the
> brandishing of sticks, the 'hoshings' and 'wheelings' and 'hieings'
> for their respective parties showed that the faction fight was
> about to commence among the tombstones and monuments,
> and all religious observances, even refreshments, were at an
> end. . . .[19]

Sir William Wilde, revisiting Glendalough in 1873, says this sort
of behaviour has now been stopped. But the ruins are decaying fast:
'the wild desolation of the scene of the valley of Glendalough is passing away'.

W.B. Yeats stayed at the Royal Hotel, Glendalough, in June 1932, and while he was there wrote his 'Stream and Sun at Glendalough', which begins:[20]

> Through intricate motions ran
> Stream and gliding sun
> And all my heart seemed gay:
> Some stupid thing that I had done
> Made my attention stray.
>
> Repentance keeps my heart impure;
> But what am I that dare
> Fancy that I can
> Better conduct myself or have more
> Sense than a common man? . . .

He was there to attempt to sort out some domestic trouble that had arisen between Maud Gonne MacBride's daughter, Iseult, and her husband, Francis Stuart (b. 1902), the future novelist. Whether Yeats was thinking that his earlier proposal to Iseult, daughter of his great love, was the 'stupid thing', is hardly the point, what matters is that he has the proud humility to forgive himself. The couple were living at Laragh Castle nearby, but he declined their invitation to stay with them: 'I should bore them and talk myself stupid', he wrote to his wife George, 'We have not enough in common to give back a splash when I drop a stone. . . .'[21]

The Stuarts' relation with these Wicklow Hills is entangled with the near past of the Irish Revival. Their first house was in the next valley south of Glendalough, Glenmalure, and was called 'Barravore'. It is, according to Synge's stage-direction, 'The last cottage at the head of a long glen in County Wicklow'; the setting for his play *The Shadow of the Glen*.[22] The play is a one-acter, the scene 'a lonely cottage', and a woman is sitting by the body of her supposedly dead husband. The widow is overcome by the loneliness of these hills. 'When you do be sitting looking out from a door the like of that door, and seeing nothing but the mists rolling down the bog, and the mists again, and they rolling up the bog, and hearing nothing but the wind crying out in the bits of broken trees left from the great storm, and the streams roaring with the rain. . . .'

A tramp has called and tells her this is no place for her, she should come on the roads with him, and she agrees. Her 'dead' husband sits up and protests, but she has no sympathy with this trick; she has decided. 'You've a fine bit of talk, stranger, and it's with yourself I'll go.'

The audience was uneasy before the play even began; they suspected that satires on 'peasants' were Anglo-Irish condescension. Maud Gonne MacBride walked out of its first night in 1903, as a protest 'against the intrusion of decadence'. Nevertheless, eventually she came to own the house in Glenmalure, and her daughter and son-in-law came to live in it; and the 'mists rolling down the bog, and the mists again, and they rolling up the bog' proved too much for the young Stuart; he broke down, and that was when Yeats was summoned to Laragh.

Stuart accepted a lectureship in English and Irish literature at the University of Berlin, and he was there for most of the Second World War. During his absence from Ireland, and because of contacts he made in Berlin, there occurred a bizarre event in 1940. He had met a man in Germany, Hermann Goertz, who was training to parachute into Ireland to make contact with the IRA. Stuart casually told him to call at Laragh Castle if he got into trouble. Goertz was dropped in Westmeath, his radio was lost, dropped elsewhere, he did not know what to do, so he walked the seventy miles to Laragh and knocked on the door. It had taken him four days; and a glance at the mountainous, broken and boggy landscape suggests that he must have been a tough man, if not a very competent spy. Iseult concealed him; she and her mother – Maud Gonne, the old Fenian Rebel – shopped for clothes for him in Dublin; and (to cut an extraordinary story short) Iseult, who had meanwhile fallen in love with Goertz, was arrested, put in Mountjoy Jail but later released; and the unfortunate Goertz was discovered and jailed for the duration of the war.

In his novels, Stuart explores his conviction that a first-hand knowledge of violence in the world can sometimes lead to depths of spiritual understanding. He worries at complacence: this is the theme of *Redemption* (1949): 'We dare not be given too much security,' says one of his characters:

That's our great genius, to tame! We have our tame God and our tame art; and it's only when the days of vengeance come that there's a flutter round the pond. . . .
'There are two faces to reality, and I have seen them both. There was the bloody face of the Sister as I saw her a little later, one of all the faces of the raped, the dying, the horror-

stricken, and the other face, the face of "Not a sparrow falls
without the Father –", and whoever has seen these two faces
as one is finally delivered and at peace. But I haven't. And now
I never shall.'

For George Darley (1795–1846) the Wicklow mountains represented
the ideal landscape; he loved the details, the streams, the mosses, the
waterfalls, here described as in a heat-wave:[23]

> . . . The glittering fountains seemed to pour
> Steep downward rills of molten ore,
> Glassily tinkling smooth between
> Broom-shaded banks of golden green. . . .
> With golden lip and glistening bell
> Burned every bee-cup on the fell,
> Whate'er its native unsunned hue
> Snow-white or crimson or cold blue. . . .
> The singed mosses curling here,
> A golden fleece too short to shear!

The River Liffey rises up there, on the plateau of bare bogland,
which is so surprisingly near to Dublin. James Joyce celebrates the
young Anna Livia as lushly as Darley:[24] 'Of meadow grass and river
flags, the bulrush and waterweed, and of fallen griefs of weeping
willow. Then she made her bracelets and her anklets and her armlets
and a jetty amulet for necklace of clicking cobbles and pattering
pebbles and rumbledown rubble, richmond and rehr, of Irish
rhunerhinerstones and shellmarble bangles. . . .'

Oliver St John Gogarty invites his friends to a pastoral-fabulous
picnic, beside Lower Lough Bray, steel-grey in its green volcanic
cup – 'our very table tricked out with mica':

Not far from where we sat the Liffey sprang to birth from the
streamy mosses of Kippure – gathering water from that many-
fountained hill before it could risk a long journey without being
foiled by the flatness of its moors. For sixty miles it would wind
through the loveliest valleys in the world. . . .

We were on a high and pleasant shelf. To see the valley it
would be necessary to walk a hundred yards to the road: whence
to the south-east stood the peaks of the Golden Spears, the Head
of Bray, and beyond, a floor of shining sea. Some miles behind,
a point might be reached from which Dublin could be seen

smoke-veiled in its plain: St Patrick's Cathedral seemingly still
its highest and greyest mass beneath a pall of smoke, though
Christ Church is higher. The dear and fog-crowned Athens of
my youth![25]

The view that Gogarty surveys, after his picnic in the Wicklow
Mountains, suggests how beautifully Dublin is situated. Hills can be
seen to the south from the end of almost every street, and their
presence felt in the city; and the wide sweep of Dublin Bay makes
the sea a near-presence also (you can hear someone say, in the centre
of Dublin, 'I think I'll take a walk by the sea').

Frank O'Connor is a self-confessed literary pilgrim ('a great man
goes off like a rocket . . . Thomas Hardy has stamped himself upon
the landscape of Dorset like a phase of history') but he regrets (in
the 1940s) that most Irish rockets have gone off elsewhere – Goldsmith, Sheridan, Wilde, Shaw; it is a long list:

> When I ask myself what are the things which endear to me
> this particular portion of the world where I spend my days, I
> find them pitiably few. I write this in a room which looks
> towards Dunleary (Dun Laoghaire or Kingstown) across the
> wide reaches of Merrion Strand, and I remember that it is the
> strand where in the eighth-century saga of 'Da Dearga's Hostel'
> the British outlaws land . . . 'and its firelight shone through
> the spokes of the chariot wheels outside it.'
>   I remember that Stephen Daedalus in 'Ulysses' walked here,
> as did Mr Bloom; and that on Dalkey Hill above it another boy
> called George Bernard Shaw suddenly asked himself why he went
> on saying his prayers.[26]

O'Connor regrets the emigrants, but a glance through his window
shows up enough associations to be going on with. The 'Fate of Da
Dearga's Hostel', part of one of the longest of the Irish sagas, is
described in a ninth-century manuscript in the Book of Lismore (the
one found in the nineteenth century hidden in the walls of Lismore
Castle). The supposed site of the 'Hostel' is below Lough Bray where
Gogarty had his picnic, at the foot of the hills where Synge discovered
his version of Ireland; the hills where Yeats and 'AE', as art students,
used to walk and await visions.

In *More Pricks than Kicks* (1934) Samuel Beckett (1906–89) describes
his characters climbing the mountains outside Dublin: 'The first thing
that they had to do when they reached the top was admire the view,
with special reference to Dun Laoghaire framed to perfection in the

shoulders of Three Rocks and Kilmashogue, the long arms of the
harbour like an entreaty in the blue sea.' (It was on the eastern of
these arms that Beckett received the inspiration that was to transfom
his writing career. He realized that henceforth his subject must be
himself, in all its forms.) On the hills, Beckett's Belacqua runs his
eyes ('unruly members') to the slopes of Glendow, 'mottled like a
leopard'; thinks of Synge who haunted this region, and recovers his
spirits.[27]

DUBLIN BAY

Frank O'Connor looks out from the hills towards the bay. George
Moore looks at Dublin Bay from the sea, returning from London
at the beginning of this century, filled with plans for the Irish Literary
Revival. He nervously wonders if he will find Ireland as intolerable
as he found it before, and looks for a portent in the shapes of the
hills seen from on deck, '. . . on the left, rough and uncomely as
a drove of pigs running down a lane, with one tall hill very like
the peasant whom I used to see in childhood, an old man that wore
a tall hat, knee-breeches, worsted stockings, and brogues. Like a pig's
back Ireland has appeared to me, I said; but soon after on my right
a lovely hill came into view, shapen like a piece of sculpture, and
I said: Perhaps I am going to see Ireland as an enchanted isle after
all.'[28] Moore's lovely hill, 'like a piece of sculpture', is the island-
like Hill of Howth ['Hoath']. It is as though these writers circle
Dublin warily, before they immerse themselves in it, because they
know that once they do that nothing will be as simple again.
    V.S. Pritchett (b. 1900) celebrates the whole wide sweep of the
coastline, as far as Dalkey at its south end; relishing

> the colours of the delightful, hilly Dublin suburbs along the ten
> miles or more of the Bay. Here terraces and graceful country
> houses, and the charming single-storey cottages built on the
> principle of the cabin – the single Irish contribution to architec-
> ture – give the coast a sparkle. . . . The sea brings its sting to
> the air; the green and the blue water burns. At Blackrock, at
> Bullock Harbour, Sea Point and Dalkey, all shaded by wind-
> blown beeches and the ash, the leaves of which have the dark
> polish of sea-light on them, the sight bemuses and is
> delectable.[29]

The beautiful cliffside village of Dalkey is below Dun Leary, the southern point of the bay.[30] Flann O'Brien put it into the title of one of his books, *The Dalkey Archive* (1964). He calls Dalkey 'an unlikely town', and it does seem precariously perched, with 'a mighty shoulder of granite' climbing behind it. He scorns to compare the beautiful bay beneath it (as many do) to the Bay of Naples, because that would have 'no soft Irish skies, no little breezes that feel almost coloured'. However:

> At a great distance ahead and up, one could see a remote little obelisk surmounting some steps where one can sit and contemplate all this scene: the sea, the peninsula of Howth across the bay and distantly, to the right, the dim outline of the Wicklow mountains, blue or grey. Was the monument erected to honour the creator of all this splendour? No. Perhaps in remembrance of a fine Irish person He once made – Johannes Scotus Erigena, perhaps, or possibly Parnell? No indeed: Queen Victoria. . . .

It must have been the view from around here (it is the sort of thing Joyce scholars debate) that Joyce described at the beginning of *Ulysses*, when Stephen Dedalus (young Joyce) and Buck Mulligan (Oliver St John Gogarty), on the roof of their Martello tower, look 'towards the blunt cape of Bray Head that lay on the waters like the snout of a sleeping whale'. Stephen remembers his mother's painful death, and thinks of the bay as 'a bowl of bitter waters'. ('Dubhlinn' – Dublin – means 'dark pool'.) The Martello tower, now a Joyce museum and known as Joyce's Tower, was in fact rented by Gogarty, and Joyce spent only a few days in it, in August 1904. (Every line in *Ulysses* has been annotated, and there is a helpful *Ulysses Guide* to every precise location.)[31]

The tower is at Sandycove next to Dun Laoghaire (Dunleary, Kingstown), the harbour where most visitors arrived until recently. Dunleary still has a nineteenth-century air. In 1842 Thackeray seems ready to be impressed by it; his attention chiefly caught by the liveliness – and its contrast: 'the beach and piers swarming with spectators, the bay full of small yachts, and innumerable row-boats, and in the midst of the assemblage a convict-ship, lying ready for sail, with a black mass of poor wretches on her deck, who too were eager for pleasure. Who is not, in this country?'[32]

Sailing to Ireland from England in the mid-1950s, the German novelist Heinrich Böll feels he has crossed a frontier as soon as he boards the steamer, and seems to fall in love with Ireland, where

'trouser creases had lost their sharp edge, and the safety-pin, that
ancient Celtic clasp, had come into its own again'. He watches an
old priest sighing, as he listens to a girl who has lost her faith amid
the hardships of London. All he says is, 'My child . . .'. At last she
sleeps; the priest turns up his coat collar, and

> there were four safety pins on the underside as a reserve; four,
> hanging from a fifth that was stuck at right angles, swinging
> from side to side. . . .
>   A cup of tea, at dawn, while standing shivering in the west
> wind, the isle of saints still hiding from the sun in the morning
> mist; here on this island, then, live the only people in Europe
> that never set out to conquer, although they were conquered
> several times, by Danes, Normans, Englishmen – all they sent
> out was priests, monks, missionaries who, by way of this strange
> detour via Ireland, brought the spirit of Thebaic asceticism to
> Europe; here, more than a thousand years ago, so far from the
> centre of things, as if it had slipped way out into the Atlantic,
> lay the glowing heart of Europe. . . .[33]

Iris Murdoch (b. 1919) in her novel *The Red and the Green* (1965,
set at the time of the Easter Rising in 1916) describes the shoreline
and the harbour piers of Dunleary in remembered detail; she spent
holidays here as a child. One of her characters, Barney, is thinking
of hiding a rifle among the rocks along the pier wall. The shelters
on the pier promenade (still to be seen) were 'hollow and majestic
as Egyptian temples to the eyes of the child'; and Barney

> looked back for a moment as a touch of sun illumined the multi-
> coloured stucco fronts of the marine terraces, and behind them
> the two rival spires of Kingstown, Catholic and Protestant,
> shifting constantly in their relation to each other except when
> from the Martello tower at Sandycove they could be seen
> superimposed.
>   The pier itself, upon which he now set foot, had always
> seemed to Barney an object ancient and numinous, like some
> old terraced Ziggurat, composed of immense rocks of yellow
> granite and scarcely raised by human labour: something 'built
> by the hands of giants for god-like kings of old'. Its two great
> arms, ending in lighthouse fortresses, enclosed a vast space of
> gently rolling indigo water and a miscellany of craft riding at
> anchor. The inner side of the pier was terraced and decorated
> at intervals by strange stone edifices, wind towers and obelisks

and great cubes with doors, which made it seem all the more like some pagan religious monument.

Flying solo over Dublin around 1930, Gogarty sees 'the roof-like, flat, floating island of smoke which, seen sidelong, looks as opaque as plank or a piece of plate-glass. . . . Swinging to the east, the bright buff-coloured Hill of Howth. . . . The Danes "took a great prey of women from Howth" somewhere in the tenth century.'[34] 'A great prey of women . . .', Gogarty repeats, relishing the phrase from an old chronicle; probably because he wrote a poem about it in his youth:[35]

> . . . The chronicles say
> That the Danes in their day
> Took a very great prey
> Of women from Howth.
> They seem to imply
> That the women were shy,
> That the women were loath
> To be taken from Howth.
> From bushy and thrushy
> Sequestering Howth. . . .

Gogarty is making a point. Most of the 'Celtic Revival' writers in Ireland were Protestant, Anglo-Irish. The two undergraduate mockers, Joyce and Gogarty, were of Catholic background and felt themselves to be more rootedly Irish. In order to escape the 'Celtic' label (seen as a creation of the Protestant Ascendancy) they wanted to emphasize their Scandinavian, Viking, past; as a contemporary of theirs said, 'If Ireland is to become truly Irish she must first become European.' *Ulysses* (and *Finnegan's Wake*) has many references to the Danish founders of Dublin. (Bushy and thrushy sequestering Howth was a popular outing for Dublin couples, like Leopold and Molly Bloom – *Ulysses* begins at one end of Dublin Bay and ends at the other.)

Gogarty goes early-morning riding on horseback on Merrion Strand. Like Iris Murdoch, he notices the two steeples at the far end of the bay:

Far away, twin steeples catch the light at Kingstown. . . . The uncontaminated breezes flow in with the gentle tide, and Howth is amethystine yet. . . . You must not think that Merrion is like this every morning at the beginning of the year; certainly not, but I have seen it thus on occasions when beauty reigned in the air and made it receptive. All we have to do is to dwell on such moments of beauty. The other moments matter little, and should be dismissed as interlopers and of evil origin.

He was sure of being alone as he rode on the sands at dawn. Dean Swift two hundred years before was not so fortunate. There was 'no place so convenient for riding, as the Strand towards Howth', but he found himself being ridden down. He drew up a petition to the House of Lords (calling himself the Petitioner abbreviated to 'Petr'). Riding on the strand, he had been pursued by two 'gentlemen' in a chaise, so that his servant was in danger of his life:

> Whereupon Your Petr. made what speed he could, riding to the right and left above fifty yards to the full extent of the sd. road. But the two Gentlemen driving a light chaise drawn by fleet horses, and intent upon mischief, turned faster than your Petr., endeavouring to overthrow him. That by great Accident Your Petr. got to the side of a ditch, where the chaise could not safely pursue, and the two Gentlemen stopping their carriere, Your Petr. mildly expostulated with them. Whereupon one of the Gentlemen said: Damn you is not the road free for us as for You? and calling to his servant who rode behind, sd, Tom (or some such name) is the Pistol loaden with ball? To which the Servant answered, Yes, My Lord, and gave him the pistol. Your Petr. then Sd to the Gentleman, pray Sr do not shoot, for my horse is apt to start, by which I shall endanger my life. . . .

Swift had discovered that the bravo is Lord Blayney; and says he must now go armed, in case the same or worse should happen again, 'for the consequences of which he cannot answer'. Swift's biographer grimly remarks that 'Blayney did not have to trouble himself about consequences. The men in power would hardly have touched him if he had carried his infantile exercise a stage further.'[36]

On the Hill of Howth, in the demesne of Howth Castle, is a massive dolmen, known as Aideen's Grave. Aideen was the wife of Oscar (or Osgar), son of Oisín (Ossian, the poet of the Fianna), therefore the grandson of Finn MacCool himself. The story is that when Oscar was killed, with many of the rest of Finn's warriors (the Fianna), Aideen died of grief. Sir Samuel Ferguson (1810–86) celebrates the place. He lived on the Hill of Howth the last part of his life.

> They heaved the stone; they heap'd the cairn:
>   Said Ossian, 'In a queenly grave
> We leave her, 'mong her fields of fern,
>   Between the cliff and wave.
>
> The cliff behind stands clear and bare,
>   And bare, above, the heathery steep
> Scales the clear heaven's expanse, to where
>   The Danann Druids sleep.
>
> And all the sands that, left and right,
>   The grassy isthmus-ridge confine,
> In yellow bars lie bare and bright
>   Amid the sparkling brine. . . .

Ferguson was one of the earliest to rescue the Irish myths and put them into accessible verse, and take them seriously. His influence in this respect, on the next generation of nationalist writers – though he himself was a staunch Unionist, born in Belfast and buried near Antrim – was profound: on W.B. Yeats, for example, who also lived on Howth, as a young man.

CIRCLING THE CITY

From Howth, taking a circuit around Dublin anticlockwise, you come to Glasnevin, and the cemetery for many of the heroes of the Irish 'resistance', in all its many forms. Yeats's Maud Gonne is there, the political leader Charles Stewart Parnell; the remains of Sir Roger Casement, executed in England, were recently brought to Glasnevin. Daniel O'Connell, 'the Liberator', has an ostentatious mausoleum, complete with imitation Round Tower.

Near that Tower is the square enclosure of the burial place for the Society of Jesus. There are two hundred names on the plaque and among them is 'P.GERARDUS HOPKINS OBIIT Jun. 8 1889'. Gerard Manley Hopkins spent four years teaching classics at University College in the centre of Dublin, where he died. 'The plot is like a religious community with a vengeance, created from the bodies pressed upon each other. It seems oddly fitting for Hopkins, who was so essentially private in his life at the very time he felt it his duty to be part of the community: it is easy to imagine him passing eternity in suppressing his unworthy disinclination to share his last resting place as if it were the Great Bed of Ware.'[37]

A little to the east of Glasnevin is the Observatory at Dunsink, now in a maze of roads, or roads in the building (1993). In 1829 William Wordsworth stayed there with William Rowan Hamilton, the young professor of astronomy at Trinity College. Hamilton's sister described Wordsworth reading his 'The Excursion' very gravely (Wordsworth was much mocked), and decided at the end, 'I think it would be impossible for anyone who has been in Wordsworth's company ever again to think anything he has written silly'. Hamilton found that some lines in 'The Excursion' showed slight respect for science, 'Viewing all objects unremittingly/In disconnection dead and spiritless . . .'. 'Wordsworth first finished the passage, in a very low impressive tone, moving his finger under every line as he went along and seeming as he read to be quite rapt out of this world. He then defended himself, with a beautiful mixture of warmth and temperateness, from the accusation of any want of reverence for science, in the proper sense of the word – on the contrary he venerated it "when legitimately pursued for the elevation of the mind to God".'[38]

Padraic Colum tells a story about Dunsink and the playwright Sean O'Casey (1880–1964):

> Sean O'Casey has worked at nearly all the casual jobs that fall to the lot of the unskilled, uncollared worker in Dublin: he has been a dock labourer, a hod-carrier, a stone-breaker on the roads; as a boy he worked in Dublin's big news-agency for nine shillings per week; he had to be on the job at four o'clock in the mornings to get the newspapers folded and addressed for the early trains, and he was dismissed from his job for not holding his cap in his hand while his pay was being given him.

Colum goes on to say that O'Casey is a Socialist, a Gaelic-speaker who learned Irish in Dublin. This learning of Irish could be, for some of the urban workers, a liberating education: 'Once he took a party of young working men who belonged to his branch of the Gaelic League to visit the Observatory at Dunsink. He wanted to look and to have them look through the Observatory telescope. I have never looked through an observatory telescope myself, but as Sean O'Casey told me of it I knew it as a memorable experience. The sight he dwelt upon was the bright, bright crescent of Venus swimming into sight.'[39]

Gogarty flying over Dublin looks down on the winding Liffey ('if it ran straight it could reach the sea in ten miles, and it takes seventy-three') and its castles and houses: Castletown, reputed the largest private house in Ireland, pride of the Georgian Society; Lyons House ('there Lord Cloncurry's daughter, Emily Lawless [author of *Hurrish*], lived . . .'); and takes us to Celbridge ['Selbridge'], site of a famous, or legendary, scene in the life of Dean Swift. 'The mill-race runs through Celbridge Abbey. . . . In those stables Dean Swift tethered his horse before his brutal interview with Vanessa. Under the Abbey's embattled roof her heart broke and she died. What was the matter with the Dean?'[40]

'Vanessa' was Esther (or Hester) Vanhomrigh ['Vanumry'] (1690–1723), daughter of a Dutch merchant who had provisioned the troops in Ireland of William of Orange. She had met Swift in London in 1708, and moved to Ireland when she inherited Celbridge Abbey. There has been endless speculation, books, plays, on the subject of Swift's relations with her and with the other Esther, 'Stella' (Esther Johnson, 1681–1728), his recognized protégée and closest friend. The 'brutal interview' is supposed to have happened in 1723, after Vanessa finally wrote to Stella, asking whether she and the Dean were in fact married, as many thought; thus breaking his inflexible rules of decorum and privacy. Swift is supposed to have flung the letter down without a word and never spoken to her again. Vanessa died soon after, having changed her will in favour of the future Bishop Berkeley (whom she hardly knew). Stella left Dublin for a long visit to the country. Swift departed on his long trip alone round the South of Ireland.

Everyone has always loved and admired 'Stella'; her epitaph by Swift in St Patrick's Cathedral, his prayers written for her, the tribute to her life that he began after she died, have seemed no less than her due. 'Vanessa' in contrast has tended to be seen as tiresome and embarrassing, pursuing the Dean in unseemly fashion, even taking to drink. She has also had her sympathizers. The legends about her gained ground with the many *Lives* of Swift that appeared through the rest of the eighteenth century. Sir Walter Scott, who edited Swift, visited Celbridge when he came to Ireland in 1825, and talked to the son of a gardener who recalled Vanessa planting a laurel bush to commemorate each of the Dean's (too few) days there.

Vanessa also directed in her will that Swift's long witty poem to her, 'Cadenus and Vanessa', and their letters, should be published. Her letters are sometimes anguished, begging for more of his time; his are chatty, full of private jokes and complaints, a mixture of admiration and briskness to cheer her out of her boredom, and 'spleen' (which they shared) at the stupidity of the social world: 'When you are melancholy, read diverting or amusing books: it is my receipt, and seldom fails. Health, good humour and fortune are all that is valuable in this life, and the last contributes to the two former.'

The poem 'Cadenus and Vanessa', which was published as Vanessa directed, reveals a teasing, mutually admiring relationship; 'Cadenus' (anagram of 'Decanus', dean) is surprised and flattered by 'Vanessa's devotion but can offer only friendship:

> . . . Nature in him had Merit placed,
> In her, a most judicious Taste.

> Love, hitherto a transient Guest,
> Ne'er held Possession of his Breast;
> So, long attending at the Gate,
> Disdained to enter in so late. . . .

> But Friendship in its greatest Height,
> A constant, rational Delight,
> On Virtue's Basis fixed to last,
> When Love's Allurements long are past;
> Which gently warms, but cannot burn
> He gladly offers in return. . . .

> But what success Vanessa met,
> Is to the world a secret yet. . . .

Gogarty, who presents himself as taking a clinical line on such matters (he was a surgeon), says that he suggested to a friend of Sigmund Freud that Freud might give an opinion on the mystery of Swift's libido. There are many theories why Swift did not marry; perhaps it was that Stella and Swift were illegitimately related; it could have been his social unease; or his fears of inherited disease, or of madness; or of his own increasing disgust at the 'Yahoo' side of humanity, which forced him to separate life into compartments.[41]

'Stella', meanwhile, left a few accomplished verses, one poem entitled 'Jealousy':[42]

Oh, shield me from his rage, celestial Powers!
This tyrant that embitters all my hours.
Ah! Love, you've poorly played the monarch's part:
You conquered, but you can't defend, my heart.
So blessed was I throughout thy happy reign,
I thought this monster banished from thy train;
But you would raise him to support your throne,
And now he claims your empire as his own:
Or tell me, tyrants, have you both agreed
That where one reigns the other shall succeed?

From Celbridge,[43] the road into Dublin passes Kilmainham Gaol, where the leaders of the Rising of 1916 went before a firing-squad, in the stone-breakers' yard, not overlooked from the prison. They died against a wall on the other side of which the traffic goes in and out of the city. The shots must have been heard by passers-by and by people living in the houses round the gaol. James Stephens said, 'it was like watching blood oozing from under a shut door'.[44] They were a mixed bunch of men who were shot: politicians, trade unionists, Maud Gonne's soldier husband, MacBride; Constance Markiewicz was reprieved. At least three were poets: Patrick Pearse; the scholarly Thomas MacDonagh (who had suggested, shortly before, that the young Austin Clarke 'write a thesis on the influence of lute-music in the shaping the Tudor lyric'); and Joseph Mary Plunkett ('thin, bespectacled, as emaciated as the Spanish Saint in his prison cell in Toledo'), who was married in the prison chapel a few hours before his execution.[45]

Kilmainham is now a museum. The interpretative film for tourists relies considerably on quoting Yeats – 'a terrible beauty is born'; 'Too long a sacrifice makes a stone of the heart'. It is a complex subject: across the road from Kilmainham gaol is the stately Garden of Remembrance laid out by Lutyens, which commemorates the 49,000 Irishmen who died fighting in the British Army during the First World War.

South of the city, towards the Wicklow hills, is Rathfarnham. Gogarty looks down on it from his plane – it is 'where Yeats lives. I will look him up this evening.' It is also where Patrick Pearse had his school, St Enda's, called after the first Irish monk to retire into solitude, on the Aran Islands. Pearse's views on education, part of his attempt to rebuild Ireland, are remarkably similar to those widely held in England today. Greater contact between teacher and pupil, scope for individuality, less prescriptive teaching. Simply to teach a child in order to increase the child's earning capacity, no more implies 'a sacred relationship [between teacher and pupil] than do the rendering and acceptance of the services of a dentist or a chiropodist'. The old Irish system, pagan and Christian, possessed what was most needful, 'an adequate inspiration. . . . We must recreate the knightly tradition of Cuchulainn, "better is a short life with honour, than long life with dishonour", and the Christ-like tradition of Colmcille, "if I die it shall be of the excess of love I bear the Gael".'[46]

It is sometimes forgotten that the man in the bush-hat who finally surrendered outside the Post Office in Sackville Street (now O'Connell Street) was not only a poet and revolutionary, he was also a progressive headmaster. St Enda's, a fine building, now has a museum devoted to Patrick Pearse, and to his brother who was also executed.

DUBLIN CENTRE

The 1916 Rising takes us into the centre of Dublin.

Sean O'Casey did not take part in the Rising; he was already under arrest as a known member of the Citizen Army. *Drums under the Window* (1945), one of his six volumes of autobiography, George Orwell found distressingly anti-English, but he seems to miss O'Casey's own anger, who thought the tactics and the timing utterly mistaken. St John Ervine, the Belfast playwright, called O'Casey's style 'a mixture of Jimmy O'Dea and Tommy Handley' (and as this compiler knew and loved the Irish comedian Jimmy O'Dea, and his own father wrote the words for Tommy Handley, he wonders if this might not be a recommendation). Certainly O'Casey goes in for coinages, wordplays – 'Whoremony' for the ceremony (of Easter), 'Sacredary' for Secretary – after the manner of James Joyce (or of 'ITMA'); although in fact it goes back much further, Gaelic poetry is full of it. O'Casey's description of the final act of the Rising (in what is now O'Connell Street) is noble, partisan, and fairly restrained:

> Here comes Paudrig Pearse down the silent street, two elegant British officers waiting for him. . . . His men have been beaten; the cordon of flame has burnt out their last fading hope. *The struggle is over, our boys are defeated, and Ireland's surrounded with*

silence and gloom: the old ballad is singing in his ears. . . . His
eyes droop, for he hasn't slept for days. He has lain down, but
not to sleep. Soon he will sleep long and well. He feels this
is no defeat; that to stand up in an armed fight against subjection
is a victory for Ireland. So he stands silently, and listens to the
elegant British officer demanding unconditional surrender. The
fools, the fools!

O'Casey knows, as Pearse knew, that his execution would act
more potently on the Irish imagination than anything he could do
in life:

The listening people heard the quick, short sharp steps over the
stony square of Kilmainham. There is the squad waiting, khaki-
clad, motionless, not knowing the argument. . . .
    Then another came forth to die, with head, usually bent, now
held high, for Pearse has bidden farewell to the world: farewell
to St Enda's, its toil, its joy, its golden brood of boys; farewell to the azure sky, the brown bog, the purple heather of
Connemara. . . . Oh farewell. The moments have grown bigger
than the years.
    The face of Ireland twitches when the guns again sing, but
she stands ready, waiting to fasten around her white neck this
jewelled string of death. . . . And the Castle is alert and confident; files all correct, and dossiers signed and sealed for the
last time. Now the Irish may be quiet, and quit their moan,
for nothing is whole that could be broken. And the glasses are
full of wine, and cigar-smoke incenses the satisfaction.
    But Cathleen, the daughter of Houlihan, walks firm now,
a flush on her haughty cheek. She hears the murmur in the people's hearts. Her lovers are gathering around her, for things are
changing, changed utterly: A terrible beauty is born
    Poor, dear, dead men; poor W.B. Yeats.[47]

James Stephens was an eye-witness of the 1916 Rising, as surprised
and bewildered by it as were most Dubliners. He was Registrar of
the National Gallery at the time and his work took him past the
Shelbourne Hotel which looks out on St Stephen's Green. The
Volunteers (the Irish Republicans) had taken over the Green and
ordered everyone who passed with a cart or a car to add it to a barricade they had built across the road. People just stood about, wondering, watching, as did Stephens on his way to work. In this way

he witnesses what may have been one of the first deaths of the Rising. A man's cart had been put in the barricade. He arrives and starts to take it out. The Volunteers on the Green, behind the railings, tell him to leave it where it is. He carries on, and they fire shots over his head:

> The man walked directly towards the Volunteers, who, to the number of about ten, were lining the railings. He walked slowly, bent a little forward, with one hand raised and one finger up as though he were going to make a speech. Ten guns were point-ing at him, and a voice repeated many times: 'Go and put back that cart or you are a dead man. Go before I count four. One, two, three, four – '
>
> A rifle spat at him, and in two undulating movements the man sank on himself and sagged to the ground. . . . There was a hole in the top of his head, and one does not know how ugly blood can look until it has been seen clotted in hair. . . . At that moment the Volunteers were hated.

Rumours multiplied in the city and each evening – *The Insurrection in Dublin* is a journal he kept at the time – Stephens (who was learning the dulcimer from a book) found himself pacing his room, 'amazed, expectant, inquiet; turning my ear to the shots'. He meets Douglas Hyde in the street. 'His chief emotion is one of astonishment at the organizing powers displayed by the Volunteers.' They had clearly for some months been learning how to move about on Dublin rooftops.

> Those of the leaders whom I knew were not great men nor brilliant – that is they were more scholars than thinkers, and more thinkers than men of action. . . . But in my definition they were good men – men, that is, who willed no evil. No person living is the worse off for having known Thomas MacDonagh. . . .
>
> As to Pearse I do not know how to place him, nor what to say of him. If there was an idealist among the men concerned in this insurrection it was he . . . and if there was any person less fitted to head an insurrection it was he also. Pearse was less magnetic than any of the others. Yet it was to him and around him they clung.
>
> He had a power; men who came into intimate contact with him began to act differently to their own desires and interests. His school masters did not always receive their salaries with

regularity. The reason he did not pay them was the simple one that he had no money. Given by another man this explanation would be uneconomic, but from him it was so logical that even a child could comprehend it. These masters did not always leave him. They remained, marvelling perhaps, and accepting, even with stupefaction, the theory that children must be taught, but that no such urgency is due to the payment of wages. One of his boys said there was no fun in telling lies to Mr Pearse, for, however outrageous the lie, he always believed it.[48]

Of the writers of the Revival Stephens has the steadiest observing eye. (That hand and one finger raised by the unfortunate carter, and the two undulating movements with which he 'sank on himself'.) Yet he is generally known only for *The Crock of Gold*, if for that; whereas his *The Demigods* (1914) contains so well-judged a blend of realism and magic that it is unforgettable. If he is remembered in anthologies it is the puckish, whimsical side of him that is featured; and this can be funny, and loveable. But he also wrote a story like 'Hunger' – which is about just that, a family slowly starving; cool and unbearable. He said of it, 'The story is a true one, and would have killed me but that I got it out of my system this way.'

George Moore lived at Upper Ely Place off Stephen's Green, and Stephens uses his late, leprechaun manner to demolish him. (It is taken from a BBC radio broadcast of 1949, a year before Stephens's death.) Moore visits Stephens in his office at the National Gallery (Kildare Street) and straight away begins pulling rank. He looks at the pictures on the walls, 'Ah, copies, I presume.' They were not, but no matter. Stephens calls him 'Moore'. 'Here he broke in, "Don't you think, Stephens, that I have come to the years in which younger men should address me as Mr Moore?" "Certainly, Mr Moore."' (Stephens now calls him 'Sir', for good measure.) He knows that Moore is likely to be most ridiculous on the subject of social etiquette and sex, so Stephens humbly admits that he is going to his first dinner party, and what should he say to the unknown ladies on his left and his right? Moore makes some suggestions, and then becomes Moore-ish as Stephens must have known that he would:

> He enlarged on this matter; 'You may talk to them about their hair and their eyes and their noses, but,' he interrupted hastily, 'don't say anything whatever about their knees.'
> 'I will not, Mr Moore,' said I fervently.

'In especial, Stephens, do not touch their knees under any circumstances.'

'I will not, Mr Moore.'

'Restraint at a formal dinner party, Stephens, is absolutely necessary.'

'I quite understand, sir.'. . .

'When a woman's knee is touched, Stephens, however delicately, the lady knows infallibly whether the gentleman is really caressing her or whether is only wiping his greasy fingers on her stocking. But formal dinner parties are disgusting entertainments anyhow. Goodbye, Stephens.'[49]

At number 86 St Stephen's Green (the opposite side from the Shelbourne), Gerard Manley Hopkins (1844–89) spent his last five years, as Professor of Greek at University College. This Catholic University, founded by Cardinal Newman, in opposition to the (then) Protestant Trinity College, was an attempt to increase the number of Catholics admitted to the professions. Hopkins was completely out of sympathy with the nationalist and ecclesiastical politics of his Irish colleagues, who had not wanted him, an Englishman, anyway; though his salary was useful because, as a Jesuit, he had to surrender it. In 1884 he wrote to Robert Bridges: 'I have a salary of £400 a year, but when I first contemplated the six examinations I have yearly to conduct, the 750 candidates, I thought that Stephen's Green (the biggest square in Europe) paved with gold would not pay for it. . . . 331 accounts of the First Punic War with trimmings have sweated me down to nearer my lees and usual alluvial low water mudflats, groans, despair, and yearnings.' He allows his despair to show, in another letter to Bridges, in which this meticulous and devotedly conscientious man suddenly breaks into desperate capital letters: 'AND WHAT DOES ANYTHING AT ALL MATTER?' A year later, again to Bridges, he writes, 'I think that my fits of sadness, though they do not affect my judgement, resemble madness. . . . I have after long silence written two sonnets, which I am touching: if anything was written in blood one of these was.'[50]

His room was at the back of the house, overlooking a garden, and with a sight of the roof of the charming neo-Byzantine church that Newman had built next door. It has now been returned to the state and the furnishing that he would have known. It was here that he may have written what came to be known as the 'Terrible Sonnets', in which his voice rises clear of all constraints of his time, and has no match anywhere, not since the 'Metaphysical' poets two centuries before. Perhaps it was in this room he woke to 'feel the fell of dark':

I wake and feel the fell of dark, not day.
What hours, O what black hours we have spent
This night! what sights you, heart, saw; ways you went!
And more must, in yet longer light's delay.

With witness I speak this. But where I say
Hours I mean years, mean life. And my lament
Is cries countless, cries like dead letters sent
To dearest him that lives alas! away.

I am gall, I am heartburn. God's most deep decree
Bitter would have me taste: my taste was me;
Bones built in me, flesh filled, blood brimmed the curse.

Selfyeast of spirit a dull dough sours. I see
The lost are like this, and their scourge to be
As I am mine, their sweating selves; but worse.

In *Hail and Farewell* Moore devotes many pages to proving that there is no such thing as a good Catholic writer. Less than twenty years before, Hopkins had been a near neighbour.

James Joyce knew number 86 well, as a student, and in *Portrait of the Artist as a Young Man* (1916) he enters it with a disagreeable sensation that Hopkins might have recognized: 'But the trees in Stephen's Green were fragrant of rain and the rain sodden earth gave forth its mortal odour, a faint incense rising upward through the mould from many hearts. The soul of the gallant venal city which his elders had told him of had shrunk with time to a faint mortal odour rising from the earth.'[51]

About the time that Joyce is entering number 86 on the south side of the Green (to discuss Thomas Aquinas with the Dean of Studies; Joyce showed early his gift for pedantry), George Moore was setting up house in Upper Ely Place off the east side, determined to have as much fun *with* Dublin, as well as *in* Dublin, as he could.[52] AE found the house for him; AE, that extraordinary man. Poet, mystic, theosophist, pagan, disciple of Madame Blavatsky and the *The Secret Doctrine*, who later did as much as anyone to form the consciousness of Catholic Ireland when it became a nation. He seems also to have been a man of legendary *practical* powers, which is why Moore asked him to find him a house; 'Ireland thrives in

her belief in you – perhaps I shall,' said Moore. Within three days
AE had come up with No. 4, Upper Ely Place:

> I should have tramped round Dublin for a month without find-
> ing anything, and in three days you have found the house that
> suits me. Tell me how you did it. . . .
>   Number 3 was the home of the Theosophical Society, and
> I remember, while editing the *Review*, I used to envy those that
> had the right to walk in the orchard.
>   And now you can walk there whenever you please, and dine
> with me under that apple tree, AE, if the Irish summer is warm
> enough.

The orchard is now the site of an art gallery. Moore knew how
much Dublin relished a 'character' and started as he meant to go on.
All the front doors in Ely Place were white so he painted his a brilliant
patriotic green. The neighbours threatened a law-suit. Moore reta-
liated by rattling his stick along the railings at night, arousing all
the neighbourhood dogs. The neighbours riposted by hiring an organ-
grinder to play under his window when he was working (and posting
a copy of his *Esther Waters* through his letterbox, torn into fragments,
with a note, 'Too filthy to read'). Moore called a constable to arrest
his cook because of her inadequate omelette. . . . He sometimes
puzzled himself: 'In my novels I can only write tragedy, and in life
play nothing but light comedy, and the one explanation that occurs
to me of this dual personality is that I write according to my soul
and act according to my appearance.'[53]
    Perhaps more interesting than Moore's japes is the way AE found
him a house – because of AE's membership of the Theosophical
Society, hardly the most predictable route towards becoming an estate
agent. AE hypnotized his generation in a way that seems to have
been wholly for the good. Later, Lloyd George consulted him, the
US Secretary of Commerce sent for him; Michael Collins, head of
the Irish Free State, sought his advice at the height of the Civil War,
in Gogarty's house. (Gogarty also lived in Ely Place – could he and
Joyce have had a hand in the organ-grinder joke? It has been suggested.) Admittedly, after listening to him for a while Collins pulled
a notebook and pencil from his pocket and inquired sharply, 'Your
point, Mr Russell?'; but Gogarty was horror-struck at this *lèse
majesté*.
    Glimpses of these figures fill the accounts of this time; they were
a source of literature in others. Kate O'Brien sees Maud Gonne walking along the Green – 'dark veils flying, rain beating foolishly against

the prow-like face, and her two wolf-hounds profiling as low as to the curve of her great draped knees'. Yeats always walked 'as though through empty space'.[54]

The Yeats whom Gogarty looks down on from his aeroplane at Rathfarnham was nearing the end of his life. V.S. Pritchett catches him earlier, when he lived in Merrion Square, now a Senator with an armed guard during the Civil War (1921) – to whom Yeats sometimes read detective novels, 'to train him in his profession':

> What did he say? I have scarcely any recollection at all. I have a memory of high windows, tall candles, books, and of a bullet hole in the window. I heard a deliberate, fervent, intoning voice which flowed over me as he walked up and down. We were in the middle of the Celtic revival. Suddenly he remembered tea. He had already had tea, but now he must make a new pot. The problem was where to empty the old tea leaves. It was a beautiful pot and he walked about the room with his short, aesthete's steps, carrying it in his hand. It came spout foremost towards me, retired to the book cases, waved in the air. I invented the belief that it was Rockingham and I was alarmed for it. Suddenly he went to the Georgian window, opened it and swooshed the tea leaves into Merrion Square, for all I knew on the heads of Gogarty, AE, Lady Gregory, James Stephens – who might have popped over from the Library or the Museum. They were China tea leaves, scented.

Pritchett mentions Shaw. 'The effect on Yeats was splendid. He stopped with the tea-pot now full, waving it with indignation and contempt. "Shaw had no principles, Socialist or otherwise. He was a destroyer."' Once or twice, says Pritchett, 'I was allowed to sit with him and AE, drinking a large goblet full of vermouth and hearing them wrangle about Fascism. AE had a way of lifting a poker and scraping the soot off Yeats's fireplace as he argued.'[55]

Outside, of course, the younger generation mocked this older one, which had changed the face of Ireland. In *Ulysses* (1922), Buck Mulligan (Gogarty) has a go at Yeats and Lady Gregory with Joycean buckshot:

> – Longworth is awfully sick he said, after what you wrote about that old hake Gregory. O you inquisitional drunken jew jesuit! She gets you a job on the paper and then you go and slate her drivel to Jaysus. Couldn't you do the Yeats touch?

He went on and down, mopping, chanting with waving graceful arms:
– 'The most beautiful book that has come out of our country in my time. One thinks of Homer. . . .'[56]

– which is what Yeats did say about Lady Gregory's renderings of the old stories. (He did not say she was as good as Homer, only that she was about the same task.)

All generations mock the previous one. Denis Johnston (1901–84), playwright, author of an intriguing book on Jonathan Swift, has a go at Joyce: 'Sometimes I wonder whether in days to come there will be anything left of Shaw except his explanations of himself. Joyce, on the other hand, says little or nothing about himself. . . . He even goes so far as to delete the chapter headings from his work, so as to make us find them out for ourselves. If this makes us suspicious, it also has the effect of making him God's gift to the English departments. . . .'

Gogarty, who disliked de Valera's Ireland, went to live in New York and Johnston came across him there, watches him becoming maddened by yet another article analysing *Ulysses* and some remark he had made himself to Joyce all those years ago, exasperated almost beyond endurance by the Joyce 'industry', pronouncing that *Finnegans Wake* was 'a colossal hoax, with no other purpose than to pull the academic leg of the entire world'. 'All his life, Gogarty has been a celebrated wit in his own right, but now in his riper years he finds himself being regarded, more and more, merely as a character in the book of an early hanger-on whom he never liked. Would any man of spirit not be entitled to lose his temper, just a little, at being forced into such a role? What more degrading fate could befall anybody?'[57]

The debunking continued. Denis Johnston wrote an expressionist play called initially 'Shadowdance' in which almost every idea that Ireland had about itself is mocked, in rhetoric (as Johnston said) 'taken almost entirely from Mangan, Moore, Ferguson, Kickham . . . and the romantic school of nineteenth-century Irish poets'. When Lady Gregory, unsurprisingly, turned down the play for the Abbey Theatre, he re-entitled it *The Old Lady Says 'No!'* It is almost as though, for a while, Ireland became culturally self-sufficient, it had so much of its own past to digest. This could become an inward-looking isolation of the kind deplored by O'Connor and O'Faolain. They sensed a repressed and philistine Ireland growing up around them, and raged at it, until in time it became their turn to be mocked: 'Puritan Ireland's dead and gone, / A myth of O'Connor and O'Faolain. . . .'[58]

Frank O'Connor, after its great days, was on the Board of the Abbey Theatre and was forced, impotently, to watch its decline: 'The most famous building in the heart of Dublin is the architecturally undistinguished Abbey Theatre, once the city morgue and now entirely restored to its original purpose.'[59] (It was burned down in 1951.)

The seed planted at Durrus House, Kinvarra, at the beginning of the century, grew into what O'Connor called 'probably the most famous theatre in the world', because of Yeats, because of Lady Gregory, because of the sudden emergence of Synge; and, later, it was saved by the plays of Sean O'Casey. From the beginning there were rows. In 1899 Yeats's *The Countess Cathleen* was interrupted by rowdies who thought that Yeats had not understood Irish Catholicism – which he had not. In that play, which Yeats dedicated to her and probably wrote for her, Maud Gonne played the Countess, who represented the spirit of Ireland.

But Maud Gonne walked out of Synge's *The Shadow of the Glen* in 1903, because of what she called its 'decadence' – Irish peasant women did not leave their husbands and go off with tramps – and the whole audience erupted in 1907 during the famous row over his *Playboy of the Western World* – Irish men did not kill their fathers, Irish girls did not behave as Synge made them behave, or mention things like 'shifts'. The last row was at the production of *The Plough and the Stars* in 1926 because O'Casey allowed the national flag to be taken into a public house. On this occasion the performers did battle with the violent audience and Yeats famously strode on to the stage and faced the howling mob: 'You have disgraced yourselves again.' Superb, says Kate O'Brien, 'because so economical and so sickeningly true'.[60]

The distinction of the Abbey came not only from its playwrights, but from its style of acting 'in the old Senecan convention. . . . Everything was sacrificed to the words. Nobody spoke while moving, and while one actor spoke nobody else moved. The words were delivered in the same simple, almost monotonous way – "Homer's way" according to Yeats. (When an American lady asked how he knew this was Homer's way, he replied, "The ability of the man justifies the assumption.")'[61] By the time O'Connor was manager Synge was dead, Lady Gregory was dead, and Yeats was hopelessly at sea with the realistic theatre. Also, the actors had got beyond themselves: 'It wasn't only that the Connemara girls in *The Playboy*

of the Western World had permanent waves . . . the actors had gone
to seed and had shot up to several times their natural height. . . .
Then, as time passed, Pantomime with lyrics like "Chattanooga Choo
Choo" translated into Irish took the place of plays by Yeats and
Synge. . . . Anyone who calls me to join the Board of another theatre
will be shot on sight.'

Perhaps in the early days Yeats (b. 1865) was tempted to use the
Abbey as a private theatre. Austin Clarke (b. 1896) almost suggests
as much, but Clarke did not always see eye to eye with the older
man so perhaps his description is partly mocking.

> The plays of Yeats were a deeply imaginative experience, and,
> as the poet put on his own plays as often as possible, the
> experience was a constant one. On such occasions the theatre
> was almost empty. There were a few people in the stalls,
> including Lady Gregory, and just after the last gong had
> sounded, Yeats would dramatically appear at the top of the steps
> leading down into the auditorium.
>
> Perhaps the actors spoke the lyric lines in tones that had
> become hollow-sounding with time, borrowing the archaic voice
> which is normally reserved for religious services. It seemed right
> that the poetic mysteries should be celebrated reverently and
> with decorum. Moreover, the presence of the poet himself in
> the theatre was a clear proof that all was well.
>
> Scarcely had the desultory clapping ceased, when Yeats would
> appear outside the stage curtain, a dim figure against the foot-
> lights. He swayed and waved rhythmically, telling humbly of
> his 'little play', how he had written it and what he meant to
> convey by its lines.[62]

A playwright and Dublin 'character' more recent, whom it would
be difficult not to mention in an account of the city, is Brendan Behan
(1923–64). He had been imprisoned when he was sixteen for
Republican activities in England and his account of that time, *Borstal
Boy* (1958), which has been described as a 'Portrait of the Artist as
a Young Prisoner', reads, surprisingly, like an advertisement for the
Borstal system, in which 'he came face to face with the old enemy
and found much to love and admire in him'. The production of
his plays *The Quare Fellow* and *The Hostage*, based on his prison
experiences (he went to gaol again for shooting at a policeman) in
London in the 1950s, gave him such celebrity there that he became
almost as much of a London 'character', larger than life, as he was
a Dublin one. Then came a decline – Dublin and London pub-life

has its casualties – recounted by Anthony Cronin in *Dead as Doornails* (1975); but Cronin also suggests how entertaining Behan could be as a young man in the late 1940s: ' "Maud Gonne at the Microphone" was usually performed with a towel over the head by way of a veil and it consisted of fruity recollections of Yeats in a quavering, aged, but, of certain undertones, deeply expressive voice.'

Another writer who accumulated legends about himself in the Dublin of the late 1940s and 50s was Monaghan-born Patrick Kavanagh.[63] After an operation in the 1950s he took to lying on the banks of the canal, near Baggot Street Bridge, and his poetry had a kind of second birth; he returned, almost, to his country childhood:

> Leafy-with-love banks and the green waters of the canal
> Pouring redemption for me, that I do
> The will of God, wallow in the habitual, the banal,
> Grow with nature again as before I grew. . . .

Another poem begins, 'O commemorate me where there is water', and he has been taken at his word. There is now a Kavanagh seat by the canal, a celebration of him there every St Patrick's Day; and opposite it, on the other bank, himself in life-size bronze relaxes on yet another seat. Perhaps not the least of the appeals of Patrick Kavanagh's poetry is that, unusually, it leans hardly at all on the Irish past, is not laden with references to other writers and other times. Even at its most truculent it sounds fresh, and at its best it contains an achieved innocence, strong, because it has been re-won.

Pubs are Dublin's speciality, and stories of memorable drinkers (like Kavanagh and Behan) are recycled in memoirs until they attain the proportions of sagas – and in much the same way as the ancient manuscripts recorded older stories and were elaborated in turn. Flann O'Brien (1911–66)[64] makes this point, as well as defusing the cultural self-involvement, in *At Swim-Two-Birds* (1939), a post-Joycean, post-James Stephens, piece of fiction in which ancient heroes, fairies and very ordinary Dubliners mix with no heavier satiric message, it would seem, than absurdity. They meet in the 'Red Swan' pub in Lower Leeson Street.

In dialogue of masterly banality, they converse about their ailments, cowboy fiction (in which some of them take living parts), interesting pieces of popular science, and of course 'poetry'. In the background, meanwhile, a literally ancient Finn MacCool keeps up a recitation: of his former prowess, and of the wanderings and laments of the

legendary Mad King Sweeney, doomed by the curse of a provoked
saint to flutter all over Ireland in the form of a bird, roosting in
trees and feeding on watercress. The title of the book, presumably
chosen for its surrealist ring, and its associations with lunacy, was
the name of one of Sweeney's roosting-places (actually an island on
the Shannon).

In the course of the book, Sweeney in person (much the worse
for wear) falls out of a tree, and joins the group playing poker; but
O'Brien's translations of the ancient Sweeney poems, on the delights
and pains of living in the wild, are faithful as well as lunatic,
partly affectionate parodies (with over-literal renderings of Irish) but
genuinely noble and simple. The pub characters listen to them
indulgently, but are more interested in the verses of Jem Casey, the
'Poet of the Pick', author of the immortal refrain, *A Pint of Plain
Is Your Only Man* ['There's nothing like a glass of beer'].

Now listen, said Shanahan clearing the way with small
coughs. Listen now.

He arose holding out his hand and bending his knee beneath
him on the chair.

'When things go wrong and will not come right,
Though you do the best you can,
When life looks black as the hour of night –
A PINT OF PLAIN IS YOUR ONLY MAN.'

By God there's a lilt in that, said Lamont.

Very good indeed, said Furriskey. Very nice.

I'm telling you it's the business, said Shanahan. Listen
now. . . .

Did you ever hear anything like it in your life, said Furriskey.
A pint of plain, by God, what! Oh I'm telling you, Casey was
a man in twenty thousand, there's no doubt about that. He knew
what he was at, too true he did. If he knew nothing else, he
knew how to write a pome. A pint of plain is your only
man.

Didn't I tell you he was good? said Shanahan. Oh by Gorrah
you can't cod me.

There's one thing in that pome, *permanence*, if you know what
I mean. That pome, I mean to say, is a pome that'll be heard
wherever the Irish race is wont to gather, it'll live as long as
there's a hard root of an Irishman left by the Almighty on this
planet, mark my words. What do you think, Mr Shanahan?

It'll live, Mr Lamont, it'll live.

I'm bloody sure it will, said Lamont.

A pint of plain, by God, eh? said Furriskey.

Tell us, my Old Timer, said Lamont benignly, what do you think of it?

Furriskey rapped Finn about the knees. Wake up!

And Sweeney continued, said corn-yellow Finn, at the recital of these staves:

> If I were to search alone
> the hills of the brown world,
> better would I like my sole hut
> in Glen Bolcain.
>
> Good its water greenish-green,
> good its clean strong wind,
> good its cress-green cresses,
> best its branching brooklime.

Quick march again, said Lamont. It'll be a good man that'll put a stop to that man's tongue. More of your fancy kiss-my-hand by God.

Let him talk, said Furriskey, it'll do him good. It has to come out somewhere.

Behan with his imitations of Maud Gonne, Denis Johnston in *The Old Lady says 'No'* bringing in Robert Emmet, Wolfe Tone, Lord Edward Fitzgerald, heroes of earlier suppressed Rebellions; O'Brien with Finn and Sweeney – there was a danger that the new Ireland could suffocate itself in an orgy of self-reference. Ireland, of course, knew this.

Sean O'Faolain suggests how unendurably heavy the sense of the past could become, in his story *Discord*. He conveys an underlying sense of Dublin's huddled streets and roofs, all of them smoking with history. A young couple, married the day before, have been looking over the old part of the town from an attic window, in the company of a priest-friend, who lives there:

He jumped out of his settee and picked out a volume.

'This *Life of Mangan* reminds me. This room is full of associations. Mangan wrote most of his poetry here: he and Davis and the rest of the writers of the *Nation* used to come here and talk and argue into the dawn. . . .'

'Is that a fact?' cried the youth. 'James Clarence Mangan in this room?'

'Surely Wolfe Tone was born somewhere hereabouts?' He pointed. 'And Lord Edward Fitzgerald, where did he live?'

His hands seemed to grope with his memory.

'Why man,' cried Father Peter, 'Thomas Street is just behind us. Emmet had his depot for making bombs a stone's throw away. They hanged him in the street. . . .'

'Mangan!' said the young man.

There is much quoting of Mangan, then the priest takes them to a cellar where coffined corpses are preserved by the damp air. It is too much; they return to their hotel room and begin to laugh. 'They undressed hastily. They lay beside one another in the dark and their passion was wild in its unrestraint.'[65]

James Clarence Mangan (1803–49) occupies a special place in the Irish literary memory. He was also in the tradition of the old Bards, because of his interest in technique; he experimented with stanza forms and sound-effects that brought him close to the Gaelic, although he wrote in English. His biographer, Louise Imogen Guiney, said of him in 1897:

It may be unjust to lend him the epitaph of defeat, for he never strove at all. One can think of no other, in the long disastrous annals of English literature, cursed with so monotonous a misery, so much hopelessness and stagnant grief. He had no public; he was poor, infirm, homeless, loveless . . . morbid fancies mastered him as a rider his horse; the demon of opium, then the demon of alcohol, pulled him under, body and soul, despite a persistent and heart-rending struggle, and he perished ignobly in his prime.

There are signs that Joyce identified his own poverty, obscurity and self-sacrifice for his art, with Mangan: 'When he was carried to the hospital, a few coins and a worn book of German poetry were found in his pocket. When he died, his miserable body made the attendants shudder. . . . So lived and died the man I consider the most significant poet of the modern Celtic world.'[66]

Mangan is here being elevated into a symbol of a defeated, heroic Ireland. His larger than life-sized bust is on St Stephen's Green (as is Joyce's, smaller than life-sized); and in 1917 G.K. Chesterton noticed that Mangan's was not far from an equestrian statue of a Hanoverian king, which looked unwanted (it is no longer there): 'The fine falcon face of the poet Mangan who dreamed and drank and died. . . . What we were told all Irishmen were, hopeless, heedless, irresponsible, impossible, a tragedy of failure. And yet it seemed to be his head that was lifted, the gay flowers showed him up, as the green leaves shut out the other [the Hanoverian statue]. It was almost certain that if his monument fell down it really would be put up again.'[67]

Mangan offered his services to Thomas Davis's paper, *The Nation*, as a writer of patriotic verse, but he had no gift for it (Oscar Wilde's mother, 'Speranza', was better able to thump the tub). Mangan's gift was for regret (and a little wishful thinking):[68]

> Wifeless, friendless, flagonless, alone,
>   Not quite bookless, though, unless I chuse,
> Left with naught to do except to groan,
>   Not a soul to woo, except the Muse –
> O! this, this is hard for *me* to bear,
>   Me, who whilome lived so much *en haut*,
> Me, who broke all hearts like chinaware
>   Twenty golden years ago. . . .

A writer for *The Nation*, the leading Young Irelander, John Mitchel, caught an astonished glimpse of Mangan in Trinity College Library:

> Having occasion for a book in that gloomy apartment called the Fagel Library, which is the innermost recess of the stately building, an acquaintance pointed out to me a man perched on the top of a ladder, with the whispered information that the figure was Clarence Mangan.
>
>   It was an unearthly and ghostly figure, in a brown garment: the same garment, to all appearance, which lasted till the day of his death; the blanched hair was totally unkempt, the corpse-like features still as marble; a large book was in his arms, and all his soul was in the book.
>
>   I had never heard of Clarence Mangan before, and knew not for what he was celebrated, whether as magician, a poet, or a murderer: yet I took a volume and spread it on the table, not to read, but, with pretence of reading, to gaze on the spectral person upon the ladder.[69]

In his life, and in his indignation at Ireland's woes, there is more than a touch of pathos in Mangan. It is perhaps the absence of this pathos – whatever the horrors of his last years, when his mind broke – that makes so strong a presence of the personality of Jonathan Swift. His indignation was real enough – in St Patrick's Cathedral his epitaph, composed by himself ('the greatest in history', said Yeats) claims that he has gone 'where fierce indignation can no longer lacerate the heart' – but it was an indignation tempered with a discipline the 'Saxon and the Norman' tend to think is their own. He could put forward 'A Modest Proposal' that the English eat the babies of the Irish poor, as a reasoned economic scheme. He was famous for his alms-giving, but even that he performed with rigour. Laetitia Pilkington (1712–50) saw him surrounded by the poor outside St Patrick's, 'to all of whom he gave charity, excepting one old woman, who held out a very dirty hand to him: he told her very gravely: "That though she was a beggar, water was not so scarce but she might have washed her hands."'

Pilkington was a young beauty of about seventeen; she and her husband had dinner with Swift at his Deanery next to the cathedral, and her account of it allows us to glimpse what a tricky, dangerous, flirtatious, *orderly* man he was, and a tease; a kind of benign bully; one can understand his attraction for women.

He sat opposite a mirror, so that he could see what the servants were up to. He spots the butler helping himself to a glass of beer, and docks two shillings off his wages – 'for I scorn to be outdone in anything, even in cheating'. He sends the meat back because it is overdone and asks for it to be done less. When the cook said she cannot do this he asks, 'Why, what sort of a creature are you, to commit a fault which cannot be amended?' He then confides to his guests that in this way, 'as the cook was a woman of genius', he hoped that in about a year's time she would get the idea that it is better not to overcook things. At the end of dinner he makes the coffee himself:

> but, the fire scorching his hand, he called me to reach him his glove, and changing the coffee-pot to his left hand, held out his right one, ordered me to put his glove on it, which accordingly I did; when, taking up part of his gown to fan himself with, and acting in character of a prudish lady, he said: 'Well, I do not know what to think. Women may be honest that do such things, but, for my part, I never could bear to touch any man's flesh except my husband's, whom perhaps', says he, 'she wished at the Devil.'[70]

About three years after the dinner described by Laetitia Pilkington,

Swift's Stella (Esther Johnson) died.[71] With his usual firmness of purpose the heart-broken Swift sat down at once to write a memorial of her, *On the Death of Mrs Johnson*: 'This day, being Sunday, January 28th, 1727–8, about eight o'clock at night a servant brought me a note, with an account of the death of the truest, most virtuous, and valuable friend, that I or perhaps any other person ever was blessed with. She expired about six in the evening of this day; and, as soon as I am left alone, which is about eleven at night, I resolve, for my own satisfaction, to say something of her life and character.' He continues in this vein in his stately but surprisingly modern prose (and the seriousness with which Swift regarded serious women made him an early champion of their rights); then he breaks down.

> January 29. My head aches, and I can write no more.
> January 30, Tuesday. This is the night of the funeral, which my sickness will not suffer me to attend. It is now nine at night, and I am removed into another apartment, that I may not see the light in the church, which is just over against the window of my bed chamber.

He carries on with her praise when he is stronger, and towards the end says, 'She loved Ireland much better than the generality of those who owe both their birth and their riches to it. . . . She detested the tyranny and injustice of England, in their treatment of this kingdom.' It is easy to see why Swift has been revered in Ireland.[72]

Swift's St Patrick's left Heinrich Böll cold: 'At Swift's tomb my heart had caught a chill, so clean was St Patrick's Cathedral, so empty of people and so full of patriotic marble figures, so deep under the cold stone did the desperate Dean seem to lie, Stella beside him: two square brass plates, burnished as if by the hand of a German housewife. . . . Regimental banners hung side by side, half-lowered: did they really smell of gunpowder?'[73]

Cosy and intimate is Marsh's Library, nestling at the Cathedral's end; the first public library in Ireland (1707), which looks now much as it must have done in Swift's day. He was one of its governors and kept there is his copy of Clarendon's *History of the Rebellion* with his annotations about the Scots, 'mostly insulting'. The poet Thomas Moore used to have himself locked in there, because he wanted to work longer than the opening hours permitted. William Carleton wondered at the place, 'how such an incredible number of books could be read'; and Mangan used the library when he was working as a copyist for the Ordnance Survey.[74]

Wandering round the poor streets near the Cathedral, Böll looks at the row of little houses, 'two-storied, poor; petty bourgeois, stuffy, depressing is what the incorrigible aesthete would call it (but watch out, aesthete: in one of these houses James Joyce was born, in another Sean O'Casey)'.

Literary ghosts fill the mind of this German visitor. There are many others in Dublin: the young Shelley and Harriet dropping pamphlets out of their window in O'Connell (then Sackville) Street;[75] Walter Scott, and Tom Moore, mobbed as they walked the streets.[76] At the top of O'Connell Street is the Municipal Gallery, with portraits of many of the people mentioned here, and of Yeats's friends, so that in 1937 he is overcome,[77]

> And I am in despair that time may bring
> Approved patterns of women or of men
> But not that selfsame excellence again . . .

(he adds, 'My medieval knees lack health until they bend . . .').

There are older ghosts, very much older; in the Treasury of the National Museum are golden torques and collars and wrist-bands, cloak-fastenings and sumptuous brooches, that make one realize the descriptions of regal clothes in the tales of the 'Cattle Raid', and of Deirdre, were hardly exaggerations. From the early Christian period there are crozier-heads and book-shrines, and there is even St Patrick's bell, which so maddened Oisín, and its elegant, almost severe, housing, or shrine.

In the Royal Irish Academy is the original of the *Annals of the Four Masters* and, much earlier than that, the *Cathach*, the 'Battler' carried in fights by the O'Donnells, the copy of St Finian's Psalter illicitly made by St Columba (and that he indeed wrote it 'is actually within the bounds of palaeographical possibility').[78]

In the magnificent eighteenth-century library of Trinity College, on display, is the eighth-century Book of Kells, a Latin copy of the Gospels which, because of its decorations, has been called 'the most beautiful book in the world'. A technical account of where the monk-scribes found their colours for it is an indication of how European eighth-century Ireland was, and more than European:

> The painters of Kells used reds from red lead and kermes, made from the pregnant body of a Mediterranean insect (*Kermococcus vermilio*); yellow from orpiment (yellow arsenic sulphide, which served as a substitute for gold), ox gall and yellow ochre; purples, mauves and maroons from a Mediterranean plant

(*Crozophora tinctoria*); white from white lead; bright green from verdigris and an olive shade produced by mixing it with orpiment; a blue from either the oriental plant indigo or the north European plant woad, and most extravagantly several other shades of blue from lapis lazuli, a stone which ranked in the middle ages with gold in value. Lapis had to be brought via merchants of many nationalities from mines in the Badakshan district of Afghanistan in the foothills of the Himalayas.

Ireland is once more a European country. Always a reluctant dependency of England – with a surprising respect and affection for it, in view of the troubled history of the relationship – Irish writers, for political and religious reasons, mentally looked across England towards the Continent, and felt themselves European. Mangan said, 'There's wine from the royal Pope / Upon the ocean green / And Spanish ale shall give you hope / My Dark Rosaleen!'[79] Whether Irish writing will retain its 'Irishness', derived from its past, cannot yet be known. Younger writers show signs of having no need to refer back to Cuchulainn, or Frank O'Connor, or 'the Old Lady', or even to scandalize their pious parents; but feel themselves quite comfortably international.

> Culture is always something that was,
> Something that pedants can measure:
> Skull of a bard, thigh of a chief,
> Depth of a dried-up river.
> Shall we be thus forever?
> Shall we be thus forever?

There are signs that a tentative answer to Patrick Kavanagh's question could be, No, not any more.[80] This book has been a chart, on the whole, of 'something that was'; an attempt at a journey round the Irish imagination, that long-lasting and potent presence which has emanated from a small, poor island on the further edge of Europe. With the usual Irish dislike of stating the obvious, Irish writers seldom go on about the extraordinary beauty of their island. It is like a shared secret that they keep, to which others are welcome, but they must find it out for themselves; just as others must find the heart of Ireland, hidden, but not concealed, in its writing.

BOOKS AND ABBREVIATIONS

BOOKS

A selection from reference books, anthologies and personal views of Ireland, with abbreviations (used in Notes) for those most frequently quoted. Books dealing with particular regions or writers are mentioned in the appropriate sections and their notes.

The Field Day Anthology of Irish Writing, general ed. Seamus Deane (1991): 3 vols; a comprehensive historical literary encyclopaedia for both languages; extracts and translations from early texts, and translations from Irish. [Abbreviated *FDA*]

[Macmillan] Dictionary of Irish Literature, ed. Robert Hogan (1979, USA; British ed., 1980): critical biographies and bibliographies for 500 English-language writers, with separate long essay on Gaelic Literature. [Abbreviated *DIL*]

The Shell Guide to Ireland, ed. Killanin and Duignan (1962; rev. ed., ed. Peter Harbison, 1989): gazetteer with references to historical, archaeological and literary associations for both languages (the revised edition has less esoteric entries but an essential index). [Abbreviated *SG*]

The Oxford Book of Irish Verse (1958), ed. Donagh MacDonagh and Lennox Robinson: poems in English from the 17th century on. [Abbreviated *Oxford 1958*]

The New Oxford Book of Irish Verse, ed., with translations, by Thomas Kinsella (1986): 6th century to present day. [Abbreviated *New Oxford*]

The Penguin Book of Irish Verse, ed. Brendan Kennelly (1970): all periods, both traditions. [Abbreviated *Penguin*]

The Faber Book of Irish Verse, ed. John Montague (1974): all periods, both traditions. [Abbreviated *Faber*]

The Penguin Book of Contemporary Irish Poetry, ed. Peter Fallon and Derek Mahon (1990). [Abbreviated *Penguin Contemp.*]

Kings, Lords, and Commons, Irish poems from the seventh century to the nineteenth century (including 'The Midnight Court'), translated with a preface by Frank O'Connor (1959, reprinted). [Abbreviated *KLC*]

An Duanaire 1600–1900: Poems of the Dispossessed, ed. Seán Ó Tuama and Thomas Kinsella (1981).

The Táin, translated from the Irish epic *Táin Bó Cuailnge* by Thomas Kinsella (1969); with brush drawings by Louis Le Brocquy.

Lady Gregory, *Cuchulain of Muirthemne* (1902). [Abbreviated *CM*]

Lady Gregory, *Gods and Fighting Men* (1904). [Abbreviated *GFM*]

Daniel Corkery, *The Hidden Ireland* (1925). [Abbreviated *THI*]

Robin Flower, *The Irish Tradition*: essays on the early literature (1947).

K.H. Jackson, *A Celtic Miscellany*: translations from the Celtic Literatures (1951, reprinted).

Michael Dames, *Mythic Ireland* (1992): the prehistoric legacy in places and language.

Daragh Smyth, *A Guide to Irish Mythology* (paperback, 1988).

Mr and Mrs S.C. Hall, *Ireland: Its Scenery, Character, Etc.* (3 vols, 1841).

William Thackeray, *The Irish Sketchbook* (1842).

Mrs [Dinah] Craik, *An Unknown Country* (1887).

Ulick O'Connor, *Celtic Dawn: A Portrait of the Irish Literary Renaissance* (1984, reprinted).

George Moore, *Hail and Farewell* (*Ave, Salve*, and *Vale*, 1911–14): one-volume ed., ed. Richard Allen Cave (paperback, 1985). [Abbreviated *HF*]

Padraic Colum, *The Road Round Ireland* (1926). [Abbreviated *RRI*]

Oliver St John Gogarty, *As I Was Going Down Sackville Street* (1936); omnibus edition, *Sackville Street*, 1988 (paperback), also containing *Rolling Down the Lea* (1950) and *It Isn't This Time of Year At All!* (1954). [Abbreviated *Sackville Street*]

Sean O'Faolain, *An Irish Journey* (1940). [Abbreviated *IJ*]

Frank O'Connor, *Leinster, Munster and Connaught* (c. 1945? 'County Books' series). [Abbreviated *LMC*]

Kate O'Brien, *My Ireland* (1962). [Abbreviated *MI*]

Elizabeth Bowen, *Bowen's Court* (1942, 1964) and *Seven Winters* (1942; joint paperback ed., 1984).

Heinrich Böll, *Irish Journal* (*Irisches Tagebuch*, 1957) translated by Leila Vennewitz (1967, English edition 1983).

William Trevor, *A Writer's Ireland: Landscape in Literature* (1984): illustrated anthology arranged by theme.

Peter Somerville-Large, *The Grand Irish Tour* (1982): follows the routes of earlier travellers and their memoirs.

Caroline Walsh, *The Homes of Irish Writers* (1982): details and photographs of houses with comments from writers' autobiographies.

Marie Heaney, *Over Nine Waves*; *A Book of Irish Legends* (1994): a 'colloquial retelling' of the best known tales.

ABBREVIATIONS

CM	Lady Gregory, *Cuchulain of Muirthemne*.
DIL	*Dictionary of Irish Literature*.
Faber	*The Faber Book of Irish Verse*.
FDA	*The Field Day Anthology of Irish Writing*.
Golden Treasury	*A Golden Treasury of Irish Poetry AD 600–1200*.
GFM	Lady Gregory, *Gods and Fighting Men*.
HF	George Moore, *Hail and Farewell*.
IJ	Sean O'Faolain, *An Irish Journey*.
KLC	*Kings, Lords, and Commons*.
LMC	Frank O'Connor, *Leinster, Munster and Connaught*.
MI	Kate O'Brien, *My Ireland*.
New Oxford	*The New Oxford Book of Irish Verse*.

Oxford 1958	*The Oxford Book of Irish Verse.*
Penguin	*The Penguin Book of Irish Verse.*
Penguin Contemp.	*The Penguin Book of Contemporary Irish Poetry*
RRI	Padraic Colum, *The Road Round Ireland.*
Sackville Street	Oliver St John Gogarty, *As I Was Going Down Sackville Street.*
SG	*The Shell Guide to Ireland.*
Taisce Duan	*Taisce Duan: A Treasury of Irish Poems.*
THI	Daniel Corkery, *The Hidden Ireland.*

NOTES

Chapter 1: The North-East

1. St Patrick: b. 385(?) somewhere near the west coast of Britain, returned to Ireland in 432 (traditional date), died at Saul, Co. Antrim, 461(?). *Confessio* and *Letter to Coroticus* translated by A.B.E. Hood (1979, Phillimore, USA). Christianity was already in Ireland, but Patrick first created an organized Church.
2. In *The Vision of Mac Conglinne* (see Cork [4]).
3. The name means 'Culinn's Hound' (as a child the hero took the place of a giant watchdog); he is often called 'the Hound (Cú) of Ulster'.
4. 'Cattle Raid': the central story of the 'Ulster Cycle' in ancient Irish heroic literature. Other Tales, such as that of Deirdre, are linked to the Cattle Raid. The earliest surviving form of the story is thought to be in language of the 8th century, copied in later manuscripts. A more coherent 12th-century version of the story was used by Lady Gregory in her *Cuchulain of Muirthemne* (1902), hence by Yeats as source for his plays on Cuchulainn themes. Description of the 'warp-spasm' from unpub. trans. ('Book of Leinster' version).
5. It is similar to the pre-Roman ('La Tène') culture of Gaul and Britain which, since Ireland was not invaded by the Romans, may have survived there until the 5th century and the introduction of Christianity.
6. James Simmons: 'From the Irish' from book of the same name (1985). Lady Gregory's *Cuchulain* has: '. . . and Cuchulain came against them in his chariot, doing his three thunder feats, and he used his spear and his sword in such a way, that their heads, and their hands, and their feet, and their bones, were scattered through the plain of Muirthemne, like the sands on the shore, like the stars in the sky, like the dew in May, like snow-flakes and hailstones, like leaves of the trees, like buttercups in a meadow, like grass under the feet of cattle on a fine summer day. It is red that plain was with the slaughter Cuchulain made when he came crashing over it.' James Simmons's own version of the *Táin* is published as a play for schools (*The Cattle Rustling*, Fortnight Educational Trust, 1991).
7. *The Collected Poems of John Hewitt*, ed. Frank Ormsby (1991): *The Bloody Brae* written 1936.
8. John Hewitt, *The Rhyming Weavers and Other Country Poets of Antrim and Down* (1974).
9. Robin Bryans, *Ulster* (1964) gives a clear account of the history of this

region. George Buchanan (see Belfast, below) in *Green Sea-Coast* (1959), describes childhood in the vicarage at Kilwaughter (north of Larne-Ballymena road).

10. There is some doubt about who Swift's natural father may really have been. He was educated at Kilkenny and Trinity College; left for England in 1688, and was secretary to the statesman and writer Sir William Temple. Esther Johnson ('Stella', 1681–1728) also lived in the household (she may have been Sir William's daughter, or his niece). In 1694, Swift left the Temples for Dublin and was ordained. After little more than a year at Kilroot he returned to Sir William, acting as his literary executor when he died in 1699. Swift then came back to Ireland and received the living of Laracor near Trim, Co. Meath, but spent most of his time in England until he became Dean of St Patrick's, Dublin, in 1713.

Swift was a powerful force in the politics of Queen Anne's reign, though the Queen did not favour him. He published anonymously (the authorship guessed); campaigned increasingly for Irish political rights, and was hailed as a hero in Dublin in the 1720s, after the success of his 'Drapier's Letters' (ridiculing a proposed introduction of debased currency to Ireland). He travelled widely in Ireland, staying with friends often for weeks at a time. Many of the houses he stayed at (often replaced or rebuilt) cherish their associations with him: e.g. Markethill (Armagh) and Castletownshend (Cork).

Quotations from *Sermons and Tale of a Tub* from Evelyn Hardy, *Selected Writings of Jonathan Swift* (1950). 'The idlest trifling stuff': letter to Rev. Winder, Jan. 1699. 'All were presbyterian': quoted in Louis A. Landa, *Swift and the Church of Ireland* (1954; the ruined churches and tiny congregations nevertheless produced a substantial income in tithes, collected from everyone and source of much ill-feeling). 'Shaped like an egg': quoted (from Ball's *Life*) in Evelyn Hardy, *The Conjured Spirit* (1949).

The only surviving letter written by Swift from Kilroot is a proposal of marriage (refused) to 'Varina' (Jane Waring, sister of a college friend). *A Tale of a Tub*, pub. (anonymous) 1704; Scott in his *Life* says that Swift later exclaimed, 'Good God, what a genius I had when I wrote that book!'

11. Letter to Sir Charles Wogan (1732), in *FDA*.

12. His father was the Rev. J.F. MacNeice, later Bishop of Down and Connor. *The Strings Are False* (autobiography) and *Collected Poems*, both 1966. 'Carrickfergus', 1936–8.

13. Sir Arthur Chichester (1563–1625), Lord Deputy of Ireland, head of a dynasty of Governors of Carrickfergus; quoted in Robin Bryans, *Ulster*. Sean O'Faolain's *The Great O'Neill* (1942) describes Ulster in the time of Queen Elizabeth.

14. Derek Mahon (b. 1941), 'In Carrowdore Churchyard', *Selected Poems* (1991).

15. Samuel Ferguson: lawyer and antiquary, Keeper of the Records of Ireland; knighted 1878. *Lays of the Western Gael*, pub. 1865. Padraic Colum, in *Selected Poems of Samuel Ferguson* (1922), comments 'he took the trouble to learn Irish, and when he translated the words of Irish folklore to the music they were

sung to, he created in half a dozen instances, poems that have a racial distinctiveness' (unlike, he adds, Thomas Moore's). Other successes he cites are 'Dark Head' and 'Cashel of Munster', frequent anthology pieces.

16. Irvine died in 1941, in California. The cottage in 'Pogue's Entry' is now a museum.

17. Chevalier de Latocnaye, *A Frenchman's Walk Through Ireland*, trans. John Stevenson, 1917 (reprinted). A refugee from the French Revolution, he also wrote travel books on England and Scandinavia.

18. Mrs Craik (Dinah Mulock), 1826–87: author of novels, children's and religious books. Quotations from *An Unknown Country* (1887), on a tour of Northern Ireland in 1886. She says of the Round Tower: 'Strange to see it in this pretty modern garden, and think of the hands that built it – the long dead hands of an altogether vanished race. . . .'

19. Seamus Heaney, 'Lough Neagh Sequence', from *Door into the Dark* (1969). Thomas Moore (in 'Let Erin remember . . .') notes the legend that the Lough was formed by a sudden, Atlantis-like, flood.

20. Louis MacNeice, from 'Belfast' (Sept. 1931).

21. P.N. Furbank, *E.M. Forster: A Life* (1977), quoting Forster's Journals. 'We went to tea': *Selected Letters*, ed. Lago and Furbank, 1983. He came to Belfast in 'disconsolate but diagnostic mood' (Furbank), to visit a friend who had married. While there he met Forrest Reid (see below), whose first novel he had admired. ('A nice and very ugly man', Forster wrote to his mother. 'The University always declares there are no literary people in Belfast, & I have routed them out.') Forster returned to visit Reid, and Reid visited Forster on his yearly trips to croquet championships in England. There are essays by Forster on Reid in *Abinger Harvest* (1936) and *Two Cheers for Democracy* (1951).

22. George Buchanan, *Green Seacoast* (1959; see note at Larne, above). He worked mainly as a journalist in England. Poems in *Poets of the North of Ireland*, ed. Frank Ormsby (1990).

23. G.K. Chesterton (1874–1936), *Irish Impressions* (1919). C.S. Lewis also recorded this piece of Ulster folklore ('wee popes' = tadpoles = black and wriggly = Jesuits??). Chesterton visited Belfast on his Irish tour in 1918, 'during the dark days of the last year of the war . . . at the request of Irish friends who were working warmly for the Allied cause'; 'with a profound conviction that if Prussia won, Europe must perish, and that if Europe perished, England and Ireland must perish together.' His task, it seems, was to attempt to explain the 1916 Rising to the English, and England's threatened conscription of Irish men into the British army, to the Irish.

24. Robin Bryans (Robert Harbinson, b. 1928), *Ulster* (1964).

25. V.S. Pritchett (Sir Victor), *Midnight Oil* (1971).

26. Forrest Reid (1875–1947), *Apostate* (1926). Reid lived almost all his life in Belfast, latterly in a suburban council semi-, 12 Orminston Crescent (off the Newtownards Road); there is a plaque to him). A biography is Brian Taylor's *The Green Avenue* (1980). Reid's novels are set in Belfast and the country

near it, in an indeterminate Edwardian era of comfortable middle-class Protestant houses, from which his boy heroes escape; several also set in seaside resorts: in Newcastle (Down) below the Mourne mountains (*Following Darkness*, 1912, rewritten as *Peter Waring*, 1937); Ballycastle, north Antrim (*Brian Westby*, 1934); and Greencastle on Lough Foyle, Donegal (*The Retreat*, 1934).

27. John Keats (1795–1821), from a letter (see also Donaghadee, below).
28. William Thackeray (1811–63), *The Irish Sketchbook* (1843) by 'M.A. Titmarsh' (with a preface in Thackeray's own name). It was written at an unhappy time in his life, after his wife's mental breakdown. He takes a jaunty 'Cockney' (i.e. townee) attitude throughout. All subsequent quotations from this.
29. C.S. Lewis, *Surprised by Joy* (1955). He grew up first in the northern suburbs of the city, looking across the bay to 'what we called the Green Hills . . . not very far off but . . . to children, quite unattainable. They taught me longing. . . .' Later the family moved to the east side of the city, near the view he describes, 'over wide fields to Belfast Lough and across it to the long mountain line of the Antrim shore'. He was sent to school in England and lived there all his adult life, returning most years to visit his father.
30. J.R.R. Tolkien (1892–1973), quoted in *Life* of C.S. Lewis by A.N. Wilson (1986). Tolkien's own mythologizing has the same kind of homely-village/ 'satanic-mills' dualism. Lewis's *Pilgrim's Regress* presents the Ulster scene in allegory as 'Puritania'.
31. Elizabeth Bowen quoted in Benedict Kiely's memoirs, *Drink to the Bird* (1991).
32. Waddell lived in Belfast from the age of 9 to 30; then in Oxford and London, but frequently returned to visit her sister in Co. Down. She was an academic star at Victoria College and Queen's University; the press invented 'Ulster's Darling' when she returned to Belfast for an honorary degree in 1934. Her brother Sam was the playwright 'Rutherford Mayne' (1878–1967). The D.L. Sayers incident is quoted in the biography by D. Felicitas Corrigan (1986). One of her translations quoted at Kildare [7].
33. John Hewitt, *Collected Poems* (1991): lines from 'Ulsterman'; 'An Ulsterman'; and 'Freehold'.
34. The memoir was commissioned shortly after the *Titanic* tragedy in 1911. Bullock grew up as son of a landowner's agent in semifeudal Co. Fermanagh (the future Border); he set several novels there, sympathetic to both sides.
35. Also known as the 'Island' poet (i.e. Queen's Island, the shipyards).
36. Kate O'Brien, *My Ireland* (1962; all subsequent quotations from this). She is discussing Sam Thompson's play *Over the Bridge* (1960), which deals with confrontations in the shipyards; comparing it with an earlier play on the problems of Ulster, *Mixed Marriage* (1911) by St John Ervine.
37. Louis MacNeice, *Autumn Journal* (1938).
38. Among novels set in Belfast are those by Michael MacLaverty (1907–1992); *Odd Man Out* (1945) by F.L. Green (1902–53), better known for the film (1946); and the early novels of Brian Moore (b. 1921). A good journalist's account of Belfast in the 1980s is *The Crack* by Sally Belfrage.
39. C.S. Lewis, *Surprised by Joy*.

40. There is a memorial to Taylor in Lisburn Cathedral. The works Taylor is thought to have written while in Ireland are *Ductor Dubitantium* (on problems of moral theology) and *The Worthy Communicant*, both 1660.

41. (Sir) Edmund Gosse (1849–1928), *Life* of Jeremy Taylor (1904, 'English Men of Letters' series). Author of the classic *Father and Son* (on his own curious religious upbringing). *Life* of Edmund Gosse by Ann Thwaite (1984). S.T. Coleridge (1772–1834) quoted by Gosse.

42. Jeremy Taylor, *Holy Dying* (1651).

43. All quotations from Alice C.C. Gaussens, *Percy: Prelate and Poet* (1908). He was a member (the longest surviving) of the 'Club' in London started by Dr Johnson and Joshua Reynolds. At Dromore Percy enlarged Taylor's church, which became a cathedral in 1808. He also saved the ruined castle from demolition, and gave a plot of land for a Catholic chapel. The modest Bishops' Palace which he completed was sold in 1842 to a Jesuit community. He is commemorated by a memorial in the cathedral, a statue, and the 'Regent Bridge', built in 1811.

44. Robin Flower, *The Irish Tradition* (1947). Toomregan: see Drumlane, Cavan.

45. Annals: the writing of Irish history (and legendary history), mainly by clerics in the chief monastic centres, is said to have begun at Bangor (see below) in the 7th century. These books were valued as supreme treasures. Later Annals collated older texts and oral traditions; the 'Annals of Ulster' (not only of Ulster) were collected on Upper Lough Erne (Fermanagh) through the 16th century. The last and most famous Annals, of the 'Four Masters', which draw on all the rest, was made in the mid-17th century, when it was feared all Irish records might be lost.

46. Bede, *Historia Ecclesiastica Gentis Anglorum* (III, xxvii), written at Jarrow (Durham) in 731. Cenn Faelad *sapiens* was a cousin of King Oswiu of Northumbria, who was one of those who had come to Ireland to study.

47. Sweeney had also flung the saint's Psalter into a lake, from which it was miraculously rescued by an otter. There is a tradition in Irish literature of pagans being maddened by Christian bells (Oisín is always complaining about St Patrick's).

48. Trans. Frank O'Connor, as 'The Pity of Nature' in *A Golden Treasury of Irish Poetry AD 600–1200* (bilingual), ed. and with translations by David Greene and Frank O'Connor (1967, reprint 1990). 'This little lyric is all that remains of a ninth-century version of the story of Suibne'. It comes from the same manuscript as 'Pangur Ban' (Nendrum, below).

49. Flann O'Brien (Brian O'Nolan, 1911–66): after *At Swim-Two-Birds* (quoted at Dublin [7]) he was chiefly known for his long-running, multilingual, humorous column in the *Irish Times* under the name Myles na Gopaleen.

50. Glen Bolcain: one of Sweeney's favourite roosting-places, identified as Rasharkin, Co. Antrim (north of Bellaghy).

51. Seamus Heaney, from introduction to *Sweeney Astray* (1983, rev. 1992, in *Sweeney's Flight* (1992), with photographs by Rachel Giese). 'Sweeney's places': see above.

52. Some easily confused saints are: St Columba or Columcille or Colmcille, c. 521 (Donegal)–597 (Iona, Scotland): after founding many monasteries he went as missionary to northern Britain. St Columban or Columbanus, c. 540 (Leinster)–615 (Bobbio, Italy): 'the greatest and most influential of the monks from Ireland' (Robin Flower); his 'defiant adherence to Irish ecclesiastical customs' aroused criticism in Europe.

The monastery school is said to have been situated on 'Cranny island' (*crannog*, a man-made island) in Strangford Lough, and the earliest historical chronicle composed there. The early Irish monasteries were renowned for their scholarship – i.e. of Latin texts, but this was 'in no way inimical to the development of a written literature in the Gaelic vernacular . . . the monks adapted the Latin alphabet and Latin verse-forms to Gaelic requirements . . .' (introduction, *SG*). St Finian, founder of Movilla, introduced the Latin Bible (Vulgate) to Ireland; Columba/Columcille trained there, and it was his copy made of St Finian's Psalter that led to a battle for its possession, after which he left for Iona in remorse (see 'Cathach').

53. The third, 'green', martyrdom was that of the solitary hermits or anchorites.
54. H. Lawlor, in *Ulster, its Archaeology and Antiquities* (1928) says the site owed its rediscovery partly to the references to it in manuscript jottings.
55. Trans. Robin Flower in *The Irish Tradition*; also 'Pangur Ban'.
56. Helen Waddell, *The Wandering Scholars*.
57. *I Follow St Patrick* by Oliver St John Gogarty charts the movements of the saint.
58. He was sent as a child to live with his mother's family at Raffrey. *December Bride* (1951) has been made into a film. *Erin's Orange Lily* (1956; see Coleraine, below) is a collection of pieces (originally broadcasts) on traditions of the region.
59. 'Rokeby': a narrative poem pub. 1813. Slieve Donard: chief of the Mourne mountains.
60. Harold Nicolson, *Helen's Tower* (1937). He spent holidays as a child at Clandeboye. Lord Dufferin's *Songs, Poems and Verses by Helen, Lady Dufferin* (1894) contains a memorial of her and an account of the numerous literary figures in the Blackwood and Sheridan families. Browning also contributed to the Tower.

Caroline Blackwood (b. 1931) is said to draw on her childhood at Clandeboye in *Great Granny Webster* (1977) and *For All That I Found There* (stories, 1974); the characters in these assume an almost mythological monstrosity.

61. John Keats (1795–1821): from nos. 75 and 77 in *Letters*, ed. Forman (1947). He and Charles Brown (the friend whose house in Hampstead Keats later lived in) walked through the Lake District and Burns Country before sailing from Port Patrick (on the seaward side of the Stranraer peninsula) to 'Little Ireland' (Ards). After the brief Irish excursion they continued to Ayr, Glasgow, Iona and the Highlands, before Keats became ill and returned to London by sea.

62. There is a St Patrick Room in the museum next to Downpatrick (Church of Ireland) cathedral, where a stone marks the saint's supposed burial place. Also near Downpatrick and connected with the saint are the small stone buildings of the Struell Wells. These were described in 1515 by Francesco Chiericati, b. 1479 (Vicenza, Italy): a priest, humanist scholar (correspondent of Erasmus), later cardinal, in his *Letter to Isabella d'Este* (trans. Mary Purcell, private ed., Armagh). Chiericati was Nuncio (papal ambassador) to the court of the young Henry VIII; he was making a sightseeing pilgrimage (a hazardous one, 'beset with robbers and ruffians') to Lough Derg in Donegal.

63. W. Wright, *The Brontes in Ireland* (1894) gives the tale of Hugh and other anecdotes; he says that Patrick's father was a 'shanachy' or story-teller. Philip Henderson, in his introduction to *Selected Poems of Emily Bronte* (1947), calls Wright's book 'a highly coloured and romantic account', but comments: 'The important thing to remember about the Brontes is that they were three parts Irish – only one remove from Irish peasants . . . and they all spoke with a touch of the brogue.' Currer Bell: by coincidence, Bell was the name of Charlotte's husband's relations (see Banagher, [4]).

64. Helen Waddell: letters and poems in Corrigan's biography. An uncle's house was at Ballygowan, west of the Mourne mountains; her sister Margaret's at Kilmacrew near Banbridge.

65. Mayne Reid ran away to America aged 20 ('And I must leave thee, Erin! 'tis my fate . . . I love thee, though I could not live with thee!' – 'The Land of Inisfail'). A colourful character, friend of Poe in New Orleans, war correspondent in Mexico, magazine editor and author of over sixty tales of romance, adventure and natural history, said to have influenced Baden Powell. He revisited Ballyroney and wrote one of his bestsellers there (*The Scalp Hunters*, 1851). *Captain Mayne Reid: His Life and Adventures*, by Elizabeth Reid with C.H. Coe (1900).

66. W.R. Rodgers (1909–69; d. in Los Angeles, buried at Loughgall). Line from 'The Train'.

67. John Hewitt: from 'An Ulsterman': *Collected Poems*, ed. Frank Ormsby.

68. Hewitt, from 'Planter's Gothic', autobiographical essay quoted by Ormsby. Culdee: the *céle Dé* movement, a reaction against secularization in the early monasteries, to purer asceticism, often as solitary anchorites.

69. W.R. Rodgers, 'Armagh'.

70. Translation of Muirchu's (Muirchú moccu Machthéni, late 7th century) *Life of St Patrick* by A.B.E. Hood (1978): 'a polished work, based on written sources and oral tradition, reinforcing Patrick's role as national reformer'. By the next (8th) century, Latin and written Irish were equal in importance. There was a cathedral college at Armagh up to the Norman invasions.

71. 'Navan' from *an* (= the) *emain* ['evin'] – 'Emania' in Latin; 'Isamium' in the 2nd-century 'Geography' of Ptolemy. Its fame endured: in 1387 the King of Ulster built a house there 'to entertain the literati of Ireland' (*SG*).

72. The 'Cattle Raid' (*Táin*) trans. Cecile O'Rahilly (1976) in *FDA*. Cuchulainn is a complex character, young and sensitive as well as flamboyant and superhuman. His youthful exploits form 'pre-tales' of the main story.

73. Douglas Hyde (1860–1949; scholar, translator, President, founder of the Gaelic League to revive Irish as a national language – see Frenchpark [3]): from *The Story of Early Gaelic Literature* (1895), written as 'an answer to those who still repeated the popular fallacy that there was no literature in Irish'.

74. Standish O'Grady (1846–1928, novelist and popular historian, one of the first to retell the ancient heroic tales): from *Early Bardic Literature* (1879).

75. Trans. O'Rahilly, as above.

76. James Stephens (1880–1950), from 'Deirdre', in W.B. Yeats's *The Oxford Book of Modern Verse, 1892–1935* (1936).

77. William Trevor, *A Writer's Ireland* (1984).

78. Trans. (also previous passages) by Vernon Hull (1949) in *A Celtic Miscellany*. The 'Exile of the Sons of Uisneach' is one of the 'pre-tales' of the main 'Cattle Raid' story; it explains why Fergus (who was bound by oath to protect Deirdre and Naoise, but tricked by Conchobar into abandoning them) has left Ulster and joined the Connacht side. Among the works inspired by Deirdre are Samuel Ferguson's verse drama (1880, Victorian-Shakespearean); Yeats's short play (1907, balletic, exotic); Synge's *Deirdre of the Sorrows* (1910, intensely lyrical, stressing the love-interest); and James Stephens's novel (1923, naturalistic, stressing motivation). Most retellings use the alternative ending, of Deirdre's suicide over Naoise's grave.

79. Kate O'Brien: at Rathlin Island, below.

80. Paul Muldoon, from 'Ireland', in *Penguin Contemporary*. Beyond Moy, the road west to Fivemiletown passes through Clogher [3], birthplace of William Carleton. The road north (Dungannon – Cookstown – Bellaghy) is through mixed-tradition country, source of many troubles; Polly Devlin's *All Of Us There* (1983) describes a childhood here.

81. Moira O'Neill (1870?–1951), author of the very popular *Songs of the Glens of Antrim* (and mother of M.J. Farrell/Molly Keane), lived near Cushendall. She also lived in Canada; her most quoted poem is the expatriate's 'Lookin' Back':

> Antrim hills and the wet rain fallin'
> Whiles ye are nearer than snow-tops keen:
> Dreams o' the night and a night-wind callin',
> What is the half o' the world between?

82. John Hewitt, *Collected Poems*, ed. Ormsby: from introduction; 'The Hill-Farm'; and 'An Irishman in Coventry'.

83. 'These black rocks': 'Carraig Uisneach' below Fair Head is supposed to be where Deirdre and Naoise landed (Deirdre, in fact, was filled with forebodings). 'Lir's lonely daughter . . .': from 'The Song of Fionnuala' ('Silent, oh Moyle, be the roar of thy water . . .') by Thomas Moore. See Lough Derravaragh [2].

84. Sir Henry Sidney quoted in Stephen Gwynn, *Irish Books and Irish People* (1921). The Earl of Essex (father of Queen Elizabeth's favourite) was recalled after this massacre but reinstated; later mysteriously poisoned in Dublin. His son, sent to subdue the 'Great O'Neill', earl of Tyrone, made a treaty with him which was construed as treason, for which he was executed.

Michael McLaverty's *Call My Brother Back* (1939) is set largely on Rathlin Island.

85. Sir Walter Scott (1771-1832): excerpts from his diary, 3-5 Sept. 1814, in Lockhart's *Life* (1838). He was on a cruise of the Hebrides, and had just heard of the death of the Duchess of Buccleuch, a close friend, when they landed at Portrush ('I have waked the whole night. . . . Go ashore with a heavy heart'). They visited Dunluce castle, and (as it was calm) several of the Causeway sea-caves. They rowed past the basaltic pillars, but Scott did not go ashore. See also note at Lough Foyle [3]. Scott visited Ireland again in 1825.

86. *Irish Sketchbook*. Mrs Craik (in 1886) thought the hotel would be a cosy place to spend Christmas, but was told the windows had to be boarded over in winter.

87. *Ulster Songs and Ballads*, ed. H.R. Hayward, 1925. St John Ervine: playwright and manager of the Abbey Theatre, Dublin.

88. Sean O'Faolain (1900-91), *IJ* (1940); also below.

89. Sam Hanna Bell, *Erin's Orange Lily* (1956).

90. Finn MacCool (Fionn mac Cumhaill) ['mac Cooel']: the 'Fenian Cycle' of heroic tales (like the 'Ulster Cycle' with Cuchulainn as its hero) is one of the main groups of ancient Irish literature. Lady Gregory's retelling of this group, quoted here, is *Gods and Fighting Men* (1904). [GFM]

91. The immensely influential poems of 'Ossian', published in the 1760s by James Macpherson (1736-96), purported to be translations of ancient Gaelic texts collected in Scotland. They introduce the Irish legendary characters (Fingal = Finn; Ossian = Oisín).

92. Gregory, *GFM*. The 'Country of the Young' or 'Land of Youth': *Tír na nÓg*, the Faery paradise, part of the parallel world of the Shee (*Sidhe*). It had a different timescale, a day there equalling a year here, and so on.

93. From 'The Praise of Fionn' in *Penguin Book*.

Chapter 2: The East Midlands

1. Sean O'Faolain (1900-91), *An Irish Journey* (1940). Note on Cuchulainn at Slemish [1].
2. Unpub. trans.
3. O'Connor, *LMC*.
4. W.B. Yeats, introduction to Lady Gregory's *Cuchulain* (1902).
5. Sean O'Faolain's *The Great O'Neill* (1940) gives a powerful account of this 'watershed' battle.

6. Mount Oriel is west of the Ardee Slane road. The province of Ulster traditionally includes the 'Six Counties' of present-day Northern Ireland (Down, Antrim, Derry, Tyrone, Fermanagh, Armagh) with Donegal, Cavan and Monaghan; historically it often extended further south-east.

7. 'Yellow-Haired Cathal', i.e. *Cathal Buí* [Cahal Bwee]. The 'Bittern' lake is claimed by Lough Macnean, on the Cavan-Leitrim-Fermanagh borders. There is a monument to Cathal Buí on the shore by Termon, near Blacklion (Cavan). He is said to have composed the 'Lament' as he was dying destitute in a ruined cottage; a mysterious messenger calls a priest for him. Daniel Corkery (who wrote a play on this) says that his verses were recited as prayers by country people.

8. Tom MacIntyre's version in *Penguin Contemp*.

9. Peadar Ó Doirnín: comment, and trans. quoted, by Seamus O'Neill in *DIL* (Gaelic Literature). The story of Ó Doirnín's death is told by the Donegal (Gaelic) writer Seosamh Mac Grianna (quoted in *FDA*). Examples of Dafydd ap Gwilym (*c.* 1325–80) are in *A Celtic Miscellany*.

10. Patrick Kavanagh: all prose quotations from *The Green Fool*.

11. As well as the legends and prehistory, this stretch of the river (between Drogheda and Slane) contains a concentration of historical sites. The Battle of the Boyne (1690, when the troops of William III beat James II and his allies) took place near Cuchulainn's ford.

12. ['Dowth' and 'Knowth' rhyme with 'mouth'.] Newgrange (constructed *c.* 3100 BC) has the most prominent site among the tumuli, which made it a focus of legends. Its interior, with the mysterious circled patterns and stone bowls, was rediscovered in the 1690s. It was covered with trees before the restoration in the 1960s. Like other prehistoric buildings, its entrance passage is aligned to a significant solar date; as this is sunrise at the winter solstice, Newgrange is associated with rebirth and renewal.

13. Aengus (Oenghus) Óg ['Oghe'] (= young) is the son of Boann, goddess of the Boyne river. He is friend to lovers as well as a lover himself as here. Birds flutter round his head; 'Angus of the Birds' was a nickname for the young Yeats.

14. In the chronicles, the Tuatha come in one of the successive Invasions of Ireland. They fought the previous inhabitants, the Firbolgs, and the more monstrous Formorians from the western seas, in two decisive battles both confusingly called 'Moytura' (possibly near Lough Arrow, Sligo-Roscommon). The Tuatha in turn were defeated by the next invaders, the Milesians (Celts); the Tuatha retreated to areas with invisible boundaries, which became a separate Otherworld, the Faery paradise, the Country of the Young (*Tír na nÓg*). They became Immortals, the Shee (*Sidhe*), who lived inside mysterious hills; and eventually dwindled into Little People, leprechauns.

15. Ferguson's 'Lark in the Clear Air' (Donegore [1]) has been interpreted as being addressed to Ireland, in the *aisling* tradition.

16. Trans. F. Shaw in *A Celtic Miscellany*. James Stephens retells these stories in *In the Land of Youth*.

17. George Moore: see Ardrahan (Galway) and Lough Carra (Mayo) [6].
18. George Russell was born in Lurgan (Armagh), lived in Dublin from 1878, was an art student and Theosophist with Yeats. The pen-name 'AE' came from a printer querying the diphthong in 'Aeon' ('age-old').
19. Manannán ['Mannanaun'] mac Lir (= 'son of the Sea'), the sea-god.
20. Cormac Mac Art: a more or less mythical King who appears in the 'Fenian' stories as well as the chronicles.
21. Alice Curtayne, *Francis Ledwidge: A Life of the Poet* (1972) and ed., *Complete Poems* (1974).
22. Colum, *RRI*.
23. 'The Yellow Bittern': see above (Dundalk).
24. W.H. Hudson (1841–1922): author of books on nature and of *Far Away and Long Ago* (1918), another famous account of boyhood.
25. Lord Dunsany, *The Curse of the Wise Woman* (1935). In the novel, the great bog stretches to a lost paradise in the west (*Tír na nÓg*, Land of the Young, Land of Heart's Desire).
26. 'How Plash-Goo came to the Land of None's Desire' from *Tales of Wonder* (1916). Dunsany present these stories as escapes from the 'world of blood and mud and khaki' of the War.
27. Letter quoted by Sylvia Townsend Warner in *T.H. White: A Biography* (1967).
28. From 'The Feast of Bricriú', one of the 'Ulster Cycle' (Cuchulainn) tales; quoted by R.A.S. Macalister (1870–1950, author of *The Archaeology of Ireland*, 1927) in *Tara* (1931).
29. See note at Armagh [1]. Muirchu treats the saint as 'a hero capable of standing beside those of secular saga', and compares Tara and its king to Nebuchadnezzar's wicked Babylon in the book of Daniel.
30. At these meetings rulings were made to revise pagan laws in the light of Christianity. Rulings continued to be made on the privileges of Bards, whether they should be obliged to fight, entitled to free hospitality, etc. (if refused, they revenged themselves with satires). St Columba (Columcille) 'may be regarded as a kind of patron of poets'; when one assembly threatened to abolish their privileges he hastened all the way from Iona to defend them (Stephen Gwynn: *Highways and Byways in Donegal and Antrim*, 1899).
31. James Stephens, *In The Land of Youth* (1924). His mixing of realism with fantasy produces 'humour of a strange kind not easy to define' (Stephen J. Brown, S.J., *Ireland in Fiction*, 1919). Stephens was a close friend of Joyce, who suggested he might complete *Finnegans Wake*.
32. Heinrich Böll (1917–85; German novelist and Nobel prize-winner), *Irish Journal*.
33. T.H. White (1906–64), *The Elephant and the Kangaroo* (1948; a fable about a second Flood, with an apocalyptic ending in the manner of James Stephens, as the survivors float through Dublin). Other quotations from journals and letters in the biography of White by Sylvia Townsend Warner (1967). White's teasing attitude to Ireland, and the descriptions of the people he stayed with, caused offence. See also Belmullet [6].

34. O'Connor, *LMC*. In the 'Journal to Stella' (written from London 1710–13), Swift often refers to Laracor, how he misses the river and planting trees.
35. *The Burning of Brinsley MacNamara* by Padraic O'Farrell (1990). MacNamara (John Weldon) was a playwright, actor and director at the Abbey Theatre.
36. Version by PJK.
37. The heroine of *The Absentee* is called Grace Nugent; one of the best-known songs of the harper Carolan is 'Gracey Nugent'. The novel ridicules the pretensions of irresponsible Irish landlords living off their rents in London society, abandoning their estates to often crooked agents – unlike the Edgeworths, who lived chiefly in Edgeworthstown and practised what they preached. 'This town': the word is used for 'townland', a village, hamlet or farm.

    The parents of T.E. Lawrence (1888–1935) eloped from South Hill, near Delvin.
38. Like Ennis, Co. Clare [6], the slender connection of Mullingar with James Joyce (in *Stephen Hero*) is recorded on a plaque. Uisneach is north of the road between Mullingar and Ballymore.
39. The 'stone of divisions' (*Aill na Mireann*) on the side of the hill is 'a large erratic boulder' (*SG*). Called 'umbilicus', 'the Navel of Ireland' by Gerald of Wales ('Giraldus Cambrensis') in his *History and Topography of Ireland* of 1135. There are deep traces of fire on the summit of the hill, indicating that it was the scene of Beltane (1 May) fire rituals. Michael Dames in *Mythic Ireland* (1992) explains the significance of ancient Uisneach as literally the centre of a wheel of fire beacons, whose sightlines could extend from horizon to horizon to the edges of the island, marking significant points in the solar year. The hill is mentioned in Ptolemy's Geography; it has associations with the 'Cattle Raid of Cooley'; with St Patrick; with Brian Boru; with an early (legendary) 'festive hall of literature'; and with later (Norman) persecutions of bards (who had great influence on their hereditary rulers).
40. *Annals of Westmeath Ancient and Modern* by James Woods (Dublin, 1907).
41. He was born (probably) at Pallas, near Ballymahon, Co. Longford; moved to Lissoy (Auburn, The Pigeons) aged two; his father's church near there was at Kilkenny West. Later he also went to school in Elphin (Co. Roscommon) and to Trinity College, Dublin (a statue of him is outside the entrance); he left Ireland in 1749. There is a memorial at Forgeney church (on the Ballymahon-Mullingar road).
42. Goldsmith's long poem 'The Deserted Village' (1770) is 'ostensibly an English village ruined by the Industrial Revolution, but quite clearly based on his memories of some village in Longford or Roscommon in the 1740s, ruined by the Penal Laws or a grasping landlord' (Brian Cleeve, *Dictionary of Irish Writers*, 1966).
43. 'There is scarcely a book of tunes published in the eighteenth century which doesn't contain something of his, and even when anonymous it is nearly always possible to identify his peculiar blend of masculinity and grace.' (Frank O'Connor, *LMC*).

'Leo' Casey (1846–70), author of popular 'Fenian' ballads such as 'The Rising of the Moon', was born near Ballymahon. One of the articles in *Annals of Westmeath* is by a journalist from Buenos Aires, who had heard Leo Casey recited by 'suntanned sheepshearers on the Pampas'.

At Longford Charlotte Brooke died (see below); also Isola Wilde, aged 9, sister of Oscar, whose poem 'Requiescat' was written for her.

44. Edgeworth's other 'Irish novels' are *Ennui* (1809), *The Absentee* (1812), and *Ormond* (1817). Quotations from *The Life and Letters of Maria Edgeworth*, ed. Augustus Hare (1894).

45. Quoted by Hare, as above.

46. William Wordsworth (1770–1850) made an extensive Irish tour in 1829. He is taking a gloomy view of the feared effects of the recent Catholic Emancipation. Scott ('the Spaniard in Mexico'): letter to Joanna Baillie, 1825.

47. T.W. Rolleston (1857–1920), *Myths and Legends of the Celtic Race* (1911). Another of the 'sorrowful tales' is that of Deirdre. The outline of Lough Derravaragh is supposed to be the shape of a swan in flight.

Between Lough Derravaragh and Mullingar is Lough Owel, site of the 9th-century story of the Drowning of Turgesius (a Viking who demanded the daughter of the local king: she came with fifty beardless youths disguised as handmaidens, who took revenge); also of a house called Lilliput, said to be the origin of the name in *Gulliver's Travels*. The ruin of Tristernagh, Sir John Piers's house (see below, Betjeman's poem) by the smaller Lough Iron nearby, is said to have inspired *Rackrent*.

48. *Letters*, ed. Hare, as above.

49. John Betjeman: the poems on Sir John Piers in 'Old Lights for New Chancels' (1940); 'Ireland with Emily' ('Bells are blooming down the bohereens . . .') in 'New Bats for Old Belfries' (1945); 'The Small Towns of Ireland': in 'High and Low' (1966). When young he stayed frequently in Ireland, among other places at Clandeboye and Ballinahinch (reluctantly, fishing with his father). During the Second World War he was a press attaché in Dublin.

50. They produced mainly classic plays at the Gate theatre from 1936. Longford's *Yahoo* (on Swift and his 'ladies') was a success in London in 1934. His translations from Irish included Merriman's *The Midnight Court*. Christine Longford's novels (e.g. *Country Places*, 1932) have been called 'an Irish version of Evelyn Waugh' (*DIL*).

51. 'People used to say that Sheridan's wit and sweet gaiety was the harp of David, that could play the evil spirit out of Saul' (i.e. the Dean) (Lord Dufferin in his biography of his mother, a descendant of this Sheridan). *Portrait of a Parish* by the Mullagh (Cavan) Historical Committee (1988) gives contemporary accounts of the sale: Quilca House was described as long, single-story and thatched, with a painted canvas ceiling in the hall. Swift's 'Brobdingnag' is said to have been inspired by a local giant who performed feats, carrying a pony.

Thomas Sheridan the Younger was an actor in London and Dublin, and manager of the Smock Alley Theatre in Dublin; he was Swift's godson and wrote a memoir of him, with anecdotes of Quilca. His wife was the playwright and novelist Frances (Chamberlaine) Sheridan (1724–66).

52. Comments by Wesley and Kingsley in *FDA*. Brooke's other successful works were the poem 'Universal Beauty' (1735) and the play 'Gustavus Vasa' (1739). He lived at Corfoddy/'Longfield' from the 1770s, after he lost money. *Brookiana*: anon., 2 vols, 1804.

53. 'She will excuse us' quoted in 2nd ed. of the *Reliques* (1816), with a memoir by Aaron Crossley Seymour, who says that in Dublin 'she could scarce meet with any person that could read a word of the originals'; also that in reduced circumstances after her father died, she tried unsuccessfully to get a job in the Royal Irish Academy.

Chapter 3: The North-West

1. Cloonyquin (north of Tulsk – Rathcrogan road) has a monument at the birthplace of Percy French (1854–1920), writer and performer of popular songs ('The Mountains of Mourne', 'Phil the Fluter's Ball', etc.).

2. 'Cattle Raid': unpub. trans.

3. James Stephens, *In the Land of Youth* (1924), the Tale of Nera.

4. *Annals of the Kingdom of Ireland, by the Four Masters, from the Earliest Period to the Year 1616*, ed. John O'Donovan, 1851. Michael O'Clery (chief of the Four) in his introduction says: 'It is a thing general and plain throughout the whole world, in every place where nobility or honour has prevailed in each successive period, that nothing is more glorious, more respectable, or more honourable (for many reasons) than to bring to light the knowledge of the antiquity of ancient authors, and a knowledge of the chieftains and nobles that existed in preceding times; in order that each successive generation might possess knowledge and information as to how their ancestors spent their time and life, how long they were successively in the lordship of their countries, in dignity or in honour, and what sort of death they met.'

5. *FDA*. The Gaelic League was founded in 1893; Hyde resigned from it in 1915 when it became politicized. Fenianism: Irish nationalism, called after the *Fianna*, the band of warriors led by Finn MacCool.

6. Austin Clarke, *Twice Around the Black Church* (1962), his first autobiography; a second is *A Penny in the Clouds* (1968).

7. 'Bán $=$ 'white' (as in Pangur Ban the scholar's cat; also 'fair' as in 'colleen bawn', 'fair maid'). Mary O'Hara, the singer and harpist, considers this among the most perfect of the Gaelic 'high songs', ranking them among the greatest of the *chansons* and *Lieder*. (*A Song for Ireland*, 1982).

8. O'Connor, *KLC*.

9. W.B. Yeats (1865–1939), *Autobiographies* (1926). He met Douglas Hyde and other figures of the Gaelic Revival when he was an art student in Dublin. His first collection of verse (*The Wanderings of Oisín*) was published in 1889.

10. A concrete viewing-tower now replaces the house. A few outbuildings and some service tunnels (see below) have been preserved.
11. Thomson lived at the house 1932–44, and last describes it in 1968.
12. Turlough (O') Carolan (1670–1738): *Carolan: The Life and Times of an Irish Harper* by Donal O'Sullivan (1958); see also Goldsmith's 'Life' of Carolan [2].
13. Anthony Trollope, *An Autobiography* (1883). Trollope's other books set in Ireland are: *The Kellys and the O'Kellys* (1848); *Castle Richmond* (1860, set around Mallow); *The Conors of Castle Conor* (story); *An Eye for an Eye* (1879); *The Landleaguers* (1883). In Ireland he lived in Dublin (1841 and 1855, in Donnybrook); at Banagher (Offaly); Clonmel (Tipp.); Milltown Malbay (Clare, near the Cliffs of Moher); Mallow (Cork); and Belfast. He was invited to Coole Park (he had been at school with Sir William Gregory). He planned and wrote part of a guidebook to Ireland, but failed to interest the publisher (John Murray), who returned it unopened. (Victoria Glendinning, *Trollope* (1992).)
14. *Dublin Review* quoted in Stephen J. Brown, S.J., *Ireland in Fiction* (1919).
15. *Woodbrook* also has a section on this almost legendary landlord.
16. John McGahern (b. 1934) sets novels in Co. Leitrim. An ancient frontier of Ulster is the earthwork ridge between the present counties Fermanagh and Leitrim – Cavan. The play *At the Black Pig's Dyke* (1992) by Vincent Woods (b. 1960) deals with the folklore and tensions of this border country. Lough Macnean (Cavan) is the lake associated with the 'Yellow Bittern' [2].
17. Robin Flower, *The Irish Tradition*. See Moira [1].
18. i.e. Celts, Irish: see note on *Tuatha* at Tara [2].
19. Stephen Gwynn (1864–1950), *Highways and Byways in Donegal and Antrim* (1899).
20. John Montague, 'A Lost Tradition' in *The Rough Field* (1972). He lived in Fivemiletown (Tyrone/Fermanagh, above Lough Erne).
21. Pearse Hutchinson, from the book of the same name (1975). He lives in Dublin; also a broadcaster in Irish and co-editor of the magazine *Cyphers*.
22. William Carleton, from his unfinished autobiography (pub. 1896).
23. Thomas Flanagan, *The Irish Novelists 1800–1850*, quoted by James Kilroy in *DIL*.
24. Anthony Cronin: poet, author of biography (*No Laughing Matter*, of Flann O'Brien) and memoirs (*Dead as Doornails*); from his introduction to Carleton's *The Courtship of Phelim O'Toole: Six Irish Tales* (1962).
25. Patrick Kavanagh (1906–67), from introduction (1968) to Carleton's *Autobiography*.
26. Carleton, *Autobiography*.
27. At Enniskillen on Lough Erne, the Portora Royal School includes among past pupils Oscar Wilde, Samuel Beckett (who excelled at cricket) and H.F. Lyte, the hymnwriter ('Abide with me').
28. There are many accounts of the traditions and mythology of the lake and the pilgrimage: e.g. by the early 16th-century Italian Papal Nuncio Francesco Chiericati; and by (Sir) Shane Leslie (1885–1971), *Lough Derg in Ulster* (1909) and *St Patrick's Purgatory: A Record from History and Literature* (ed., 1932).

29. William Carleton, *Traits and Stories of the Irish Peasantry* (1830–33).
30. Rev. Caesar Otway (1760–1842): he wrote short stories and travel journalism.
31. Shuler: 'traveller'.
32. Seamus Heaney (b. 1939), 'Station Island': poem in twelve sections from book of the same name (1984). Ribbonmen, Orange: Catholic and Protestant secret societies.
33. Patrick Kavanagh (1906–67), 'Lough Derg' and notes from *Complete Poems* (1972).
34. Douglas Hyde, in *The Religious Songs of Connacht* (1906). This translation unpub.
35. A film has been made of the story.
36. A modern friary near Kilbarron exhibits stones from the ruins and houses the Masters took refuge in. De Cuellar, one of the few survivors from the wrecked Spanish Armada who lived to tell the tale, came to shore near here (Evelyn Hardy, *Survivors of the Armada*, 1966).
37. Allingham went to school in Ballyshannon, worked in the bank there, left in 1849 to train as a customs officer; after 1870 lived in England and edited *Fraser's Magazine*. He wrote 'Up the airy mountain' in Killibegs (Donegal), in 1849; and 'Laurence Bloomfield in Ireland' (pub. 1864) in Lymington, England – Gladstone quoted it in the House of Commons, and Turgenev (quoted in *IJ*) remarked after reading it that he never understood Ireland till now. In Ballyshannon there are memorials to Allingham on the house where he was born, on the bridge, and opposite the bank.
38. John Hewitt, ed., *Poems of William Allingham* (1967).
39. Allingham's *Diary* (1907), rev. ed. (1967) by Geoffrey Grigson. Tennyson (1809–92) in Ireland: see Curragh Chase, Limerick [4]. Thomas Carlyle (1795–1881) toured Ireland, angrily, in 1849, at the end of the Famine; *Reminiscences of my Irish Journey in 1849* (an impressionistic diary), pub. 1882.
40. Quoted by Hewitt.
41. These 'falls' (like the Shannon Rapids [6]) are now reduced by hydroelectric works.
42. From 'Under the Grass' (1st line, 'Where these green mounds o'erlook the mingling Erne . . .').
43. *Mythic Ireland*.
44. Mangan lived in poverty, worked as a lawyer's clerk and for the Ordnance Survey, died of cholera. See Killaloe [4]; Dublin [7].
45. The 'Cathach' is now in the Irish National Academy; its precious cover in the National Museum.
46. *Early Irish Lyrics*, ed. Gerard Murphy (1956).
47. Geoffrey Grigson (1905–85), English poet, editor and anthologist. 'High on the hill-top . . .': 3rd verse of Allingham's 'The Fairies'. 'Slieve League': the immense cliff at the end of the Glencolumkille peninsula. 'The Rosses': the moorland above the Gweebarra River. 'Donegal: The Glen' in *Country Writings* (1984).

48. MacGill wrote popular poems (*Songs of a Navvy*, etc.); *Children of the Dead End* sold 10,000 copies in two weeks. He wrote equally savagely about life in the ranks in the First World War.

49. The road taken by most tourists from Glenties to Kilmacrenan passed through The Rosses: Carlyle (in 1849) said, 'I never drove, or walked, or rode, in any region, such a black, dismal twenty-two miles of road'. Tory Island (8 miles off north Donegal) is the site of many legends concerning the Formorians, primeval sea-creatures/pirates, and their leader Balor of the Evil Eye. Further up the coast is Sheephaven; AE (George Russell) had a summer studio here at Marble Hill.

50. Stephen Gwynn (1864–1950), *Highways and Byways in Donegal and Antrim* (1899).

51. Dinah Craik (1826–87): *An Unknown Country* (1887).

52. Giraldus Cambrensis (Gerald of Wales, 1146?–1220?): *Topographia Hibernica, History and Topography of Ireland* (Penguin Classics).

53. Geoffrey Keating (Seathrún Céitinn, *c.* 1580–1650): he wrote his *History* (which includes much legendary material) to refute English misrepresentations. It is considered a masterpiece of Gaelic prose.

54. Edmund Spenser (1552–99), *A View of the Present State of Ireland* (written 1596, in the form of a classical dialogue). He was possibly describing similar ceremonies at less remote crowning-stones (e.g. the O'Neills' at Tullyhogue, near Lough Neagh).

55. Gogarty quoted in *DIL*. Gwynn's account of meeting James Kelly from 'The Shanachy' in *Irish Books and Irish People* (1921).

56. The Irish-language writers Seosamh MacGrianna (1901–90) and his brothers came from Rannafast near Letterkenny (translations in *FDA*). Much of Donegal is 'Gaeltacht' (official Irish-speaking areas); satirized by Flann O'Brien (or Myles na Gopaleen) in his novel translated as *The Poor Mouth* (1941, trans. 1973).

57. Charlotte Brooke (*c.* 1740–93): see Mullagh (Cavan) [1].

58. Eleanor Alexander (ed.), *Primate Alexander: A Memoir* (1913).

59. John Colgan (1592–1658): *Acta Sanctorum ... Hiberniae* (Deeds of the Saints of Ireland, 1645), 'an immensely valuable source of material' – *FDA*. Wallace Collection (London): Sir Richard Wallace (1818–90) owned the town of Lisburn (Co. Antrim).

60. William Alexander, preface to his Poems, *St Augustine's Holiday* (1886). He was born of a clerical family, and spent most of his life in Derry. He married Cecil Frances (Humphreys, 1818–95) in 1850; they lived at Fahan 1855–60. He became Bishop of Derry in 1867.

61. Ed. (1897) George Sigerson (1836–1925). Sir John Davies quoted in Preface to the *Annals*.

62. Two books by Joyce Cary (1888–1957) are set on the Lough Foyle side of Inishowen: the novel *Castle Corner* (1938), and an account of his childhood at the family house (Castle Cary, now 'tossed'): *House of Children* (1941). He was educated and lived mostly in England, with some years in Africa. Forrest Reid's *The Retreat* (1934) is set at Greencastle.

John Toland (1670–1722), controversial writer on politics, religion and history (*Christianity Not Mysterious*, 1696), was born near Muff. He left Ireland in 1687; returned briefly to Derry ten years later, when his books were burned. His *History of the Druids*, on Irish customs, was published posthumously.

Sir Walter Scott (1771–1832) sailed down Lough Foyle on his cruise from Scotland in September 1814: 'We have had our guns shotted all this day for fear of the Yankees – a privateer having been seen. . . .' They were unable to reach Derry because of unfavourable winds and had to be towed out; Scott admired the Donegal shore, with its 'beautiful variety of cultivated slopes, intermixed with banks of wood . . . studded by a succession of villas and gentleman's seats, good farm-houses, and neat white-washed cabins. . . .'

63. Anon. (12th century), in *Early Irish Lyrics*.
64. Trans. George Sigerson, in *Bards of the Gael and the Gall*.
65. Thomas Babington Macaulay (1800–59), historian and politician: his immensely popular *History of England* (up to 1697) came out in 1849–55.
66. Mrs C.F. Alexander, 'The Siege of Derry'. Mrs Craik on her visit to Derry (1886) quotes this then new poem, predicting that it will take its place with Macaulay in popular imagination. (She also heard Dr Alexander preach, finding him a bit ornate).
67. Grianan Aileach ['Gree-anaun Ailach']: 'Grianán' = 'sun-house', a home of gods in many myths.
68. Seamus Deane: general editor of *FDA*. 'Derry' in *Penguin*.
69. Red Hand of Ulster: a boatload of chieftains from Scotland agreed that whoever touched land first would own it: the MacDonnell (O'Donnell) cut his hand off and threw it to the shore.

A full selection of Ulster writing can be found in the anthologies *Poets from the North of Ireland* (1979, new ed. 1990), *A Rage for Order*, Poetry of the Northern Ireland Troubles (1992), and *Northern Windows* (autobiographies, 1987), all ed. Frank Ormsby; and *The Rattle of the North: An anthology of Ulster prose*, ed. Patricia Craig (1992).

Chapter 4: The South and Centre

1. Moore's journals and letters quoted in L.A.G. Strong, *The Minstrel Boy* (1937). His fame was due to the *Irish Melodies* which came out from 1808 to 1834, and his 'oriental' narrative poem 'Lalla Rookh' (1817). He grew up in Dublin where his father kept a shop; went to Trinity College; then lived mainly in England. He wrote on satirical themes as well as the romantically patriotic 'Melodies', but despised the 'demagoguery' of Daniel O'Connell. He attempted a History of Ireland, wrote memoirs of Byron, Sheridan and the revolutionary Lord Edward Fitzgerald; and defended Catholicism in *Travels of an Irish Gentleman in Search of a Religion* (1834).

2. The novelist John Banville was born in Wexford (1945). Molly Keane/M.J. Farrell grew up in Co. Wexford; the Slaney valley calls itself 'Molly Keane country' (but see Blackwater valley, below).

3. She married (Sir) William Wilde in 1851 and held a salon in Merrion Square, Dublin; after he died she moved to London, and died during Oscar's (b. 1854) imprisonment. She had another son and a daughter (Isola) who died as a child. *The Parents of Oscar Wilde* by Terence de Vere White (1967).

4. *Ireland*. The three illustrated volumes (dedicated to Prince Albert) came out in 1841. Mrs Hall (Anna Maria Fielding, 1800–1889) spent her first fifteen years at Bannow; married Samuel Hall (b. Waterford 1800) in England; published many 'Irish' stories in magazines he edited.

5. Newtown is north of the main road from Waterford; Ballylaneen on the Waterford-Bunmahon road. Latin epitaph (trans. Sigerson) and newspaper obituary quoted by Daniel Corkery, *THI*.

6. Stephen Gwynn, *The Fair Hills of Ireland* (1906).

7. Brendan Behan (1923–64) quoted by Seamus O'Neill: section on Gaelic Literature in *DIL*.

8. Last verse of "Christ's-Heart Castle' by Tadhg Gaelach Ó Súilleabháin, trans. David Marcus, in *Taisce Duan*.

9. (Sir) Walter Ralegh (1554?–1618): biography by John Winton (1975).

10. The Midleton episode described in *The Ancient and Present State of the County and City of Cork* (1750) by Charles Smith (1715?–62). He is quoting from Holinshed's *Chronicles* (1577, 1587), a compilation by various writers, including a *History* and *Description* of Ireland (also quoted below, at Lismore).

11. Corkery, *THI*.

12. Elizabeth (Boyle) Spenser's family home was at Kilcoran, south of Youghal; she probably married Spenser in Cork. Sir Robert Tynte held land at Castlemartyr and Ballycrenane, along the coast of this peninsula. A grandson of Spenser (a Catholic) was excused confiscation of his lands by Cromwell in the next century, on account of his ancestry.

13. Quoted in *THI*; also Fitzgerald's 'Litany'.

14. Robin Flower, *The Irish Tradition*.

15. Quoted by Flower, as above.

16. *THI*.

17. Francis MacManus (1909–65): *Men Withering* (1939); the other parts are *Stand and Give Challenge* (1934) and *Candle for the Proud* (1936).

18. O'Connor, introduction to *KLC*.

19. Thomas Kinsella: as in *Poems of the Dispossessed*.

20. Berkeley attended the Royal College, Kilkenny, and Trinity College Dublin; went to England in 1713, travelled in Europe and returned to Ireland 1723. He received a legacy from Esther Vanhomrigh (friend of Swift; see Celbridge [7]) in 1723, and spent three years in Newport, Rhode Island, trying to establish a college in the Bermudas.

21. Quoted in Colum, *RRI*.

22. *The Querist* (1753) (*FDA*).

23. Quoted in J.M. Hone, *Bishop Berkeley* (1931).
24. George O'Brien, from his memoir of Lismore in the 1950s, *The Village of Longing* (1987); published with its sequel, *Dancehall Days* (1989).
25. Molly Keane/M.J. Farrell: *Two Days in Aragon* (1941). The house in the book, above a tidal river, resembles Dromana.
26. *FDA*. Daniel O'Connell: the 'Liberator', champion of Catholic Emancipation, lawyer and politician, Lord Mayor of Dublin, etc. *Florence Macarthy: An Irish Tale* (1818) by Lady Morgan (Sydney Owenson, 1775?–1859); Dromana figures as an abandoned mansion in the complicated but entertaining plot, characteristically pro-Gael. *Lady Morgan* by Mary Campbell, 1988.
27. Standish Hayes O'Grady (1832–1915), from *Silva Gadelica* (1892) (tales from ancient MSS), which was a strongly influential source of Irish material for the Literary Revival. (Not to be confused with Standish O'Grady (1846–1928), popular historian and novelist.)
28. 'Colloquy of the Ancients' (*Acallam na Senórach*): the tales in the 'Fenian Cycle' are one of the main groups from the ancient manuscripts.
29. (St) Edmund Campion was in Ireland 1569–71, and contributed *A History and Description of Ireland* to Hollinshed's *Chronicles* (1577–87). He became a Jesuit, and in 1580 was sent to England, arrested and executed. Evelyn Waugh wrote a *Life* of him (1935).
30. George Moore (1852–1933): *A Story-Teller's Holiday* (1918) is a collection of romances based on ancient poems, mostly set in Moore's home county, Mayo. Moore's story is about the religious women said to live with the early hermits as a test of chastity.
31. Elizabeth Bowen, *Bowen's Court* (1942/64); see below.
32. Thomas Davis (1814–1845): son of an army surgeon; left for Dublin as a child, went to Trinity College, worked with O'Connell, whom he later disagreed with. *The Nation* newspaper founded 1842. It published nationalist poems, among them Davis's 'A Nation Once Again'.

    Anthony Trollope also lived at Mallow, 1848–51, in a Georgian house on the High Street. From here he hunted with the Duhallow (described in a scene in *Castle Richmond*), which often met at Bowen's Court. Elizabeth Bowen wrote a dialogue for radio (in 1946) between the ghost of Trollope and a soldier (Victoria Glendinning, *Trollope*).
33. Hone, *Bishop Berkeley* (1931).
34. Edmund Spenser, *A View of the Present State of Ireland* (written *c.* 1596, pub. 1633). Spenser first published poems from Cambridge; was employed in the household of the earl of Leicester where he met Sir Philip Sidney, and in 1580 as secretary to Lord Deputy Grey in Ireland. He revisited London in 1589 and 1596; married Elizabeth Boyle in 1594, probably in Cork.
35. Ralegh may have read parts of his long (incomplete) lament addressed to the Queen, *The Ocean to Cynthia*, which uses pastoral images for lost delight: ('No feeding flocks, no shepherd's company, That might renew my dolorous

conceit . . .'); Spenser says 'His song was all a lamentable lay/Of Cynthia the Lady of the Sea/ Which from her pleasure faultless him debarred . . .'

36. O'Faolain, *IJ*.
37. Quoted in R.W. Church, *Spenser* (1880).
38. Spenser, *A View* (as above).
39. As above.
40. Flower, *The Irish Tradition*.
41. R.W. Church, *Spenser*.
42. All following quotations from Elizabeth Bowen, *Bowen's Court*. She left Ireland as a child and lived in England; inherited the house in 1928, lived there permanently 1952–9. *Seven Winters* (1942) describes her childhood in Dublin; *The Last September* (1929) is a classic 'Big House' novel of the time of the Troubles; *The Heat of the Day*, set in wartime London, has Irish interludes. *Elizabeth Bowen: Portrait of a Writer* (1977) by Victoria Glendinning.
43. Robert Hogan in *DIL*: '. . . one longs for him to have been better, and if his literary excellence had not sometimes been in opposition to his clerical goodness, he might have been. . . .' Another literary priest at Doneraile was Tadhg O Duinnín (d. 1726), last official head of the bardic school at Blarney [5].
44. Quoted in Glendinning biography; also below.
45. Peter Somerville-Large in *The Grand Irish Tour* (1982).
46. Arthur Young (1741–1820): writer on agriculture ('the magic of property turns sand into gold') and travel. He was agent to Lord Kingsborough 1777–9; *Tour in Ireland* pub. 1780.
47. Claire Tomalin, *The Life and Death of Mary Wollstonecraft* (1974). Margaret Mountcashel was living in Pisa (as Mrs Morgan) when the Shelleys went there in 1820. She wrote *Advice to Grandparents*.
48. Cyril Connolly (1903–74), *Enemies of Promise* (1938).
49. Spenser, *Faerie Queene*, Book VII, canto 6.
50. *FDA*.
51. Stephen Gwynn, *The Fair Hills of Ireland* (1906).
52. Trans. Douglas Hyde, in *The Hidden Ireland*.
53. See below, at Mullinahone.
54. John O'Leary (1830–1907): a revolutionary journalist, arrested in 1865, imprisoned and exiled, returned to Ireland 1885 and lived in Dublin; wrote memoirs.
55. Earl Gerald: 'Ireland was full of the fame of his wisdom', according to the *Annals*. Lough Gur was at the centre of the earldom of Desmond (which means 'south Munster'). The seven-yearly apparition on the silver-shod white horse is also told of other Irish lost leaders; a symbol of hope after the failed rebellion of a later, 16th-century, Earl Gerald had led to the devastation of Munster. Many of the tales attached to Gerald are widespread in Europe.
56. Version by the Earl of Longford, in *Faber*.

57. Mary Carbery, *The Farm by Lough Gur: The Story of Mary Fogarty (Sissy O'Brien)* (1937; reprint 1986). In her preface she says that she wrote from the reminiscences of the aged Mrs Fogarty (b. 1858), 'filling inevitable gaps'.

58. Griffin wrote romantic historical novels and stories containing much folklore, and lyrical poems ('Aileen Aroon'). He went to London in 1823, helped by John Banim, and lived in poverty doing literary work (he was a friend of Keats's sister Fanny and her Spanish husband). Three years later, after an illness, he returned to live at Pallaskenry and started *The Collegians*. Much of the book is set around Killarney [5]; one of the minor characters is a pony-seller from the Kerry mountains, 'Myles na Coppalleen' ('of the little horses'), the name taken by Brian O'Nolan (Flann O'Brien) in his famous newspaper column.

59. William MacLysaght and Sigerson Clifford, *The Colleen Bawn – the facts and the fiction* (1953/82). Dion Boucicault (1820–60): actor, writer and producer of plays, with sensational stage effects, in Europe, America and Australia; many plays adapted from novels, and *The Colleen Bawn* (1860, with water scenes) one of his greatest successes.

60. Aubrey de Vere, Curragh Chase: see below.

61. O'Twomey: comments and quotation from *THI*. A revisionist view of Corkery is *The Hidden Ireland: Reassessment of a Concept* by Louis Cullen (1988).

62. Trans. Tomás O Canainn in *Taisce Duan*.

63. O'Connor also describes his Civil War experiences around here in his autobiography *An Only Child*.

64. Wordsworth missed the de Veres on his Irish tour in 1829.

65. Aubrey de Vere (the younger): *Recollections* (1897).

66. O'Connor, *LMC*.

67. Heinrich Böll (1917–85, German novelist and Nobel Prize winner), *Irish Journal* (1957, trans. 1967).

68. Kate O'Brien (1897–1974), *MI*. She went to Spain in the 1920s, then lived in England, returned to live in Ireland in 1965 (at Roundstone, Connemara). Her early success, *Without My Cloak* (1931), is based on her early life.

69. O'Connor, *LMC*. Merriman (see below, at Feakle) now figures in the Limerick tourist leaflets.

70. Roger Chatterton Newman, *Brian Boru* (1983).

71. Stephen Gwynn, *The Fair Hills of Ireland* (1906). Brian was king of Thomond = north Munster: a kingdom covering Clare, with parts of neighbouring Limerick, Offaly, Tipperary.

72. Edna O'Brien (b. 1930) moved to London in 1959; *The Country Girls* trilogy (1960–4) and other stories have Co. Clare settings. *Mother Ireland*, a 'personalized history' (1976).

73. Brian Merriman: 'The Midnight Court' composed 1780. Trans. O'Connor in *KLC*; comments from *DIL*. An Irish-language Merriman summer school is held yearly in Co. Clare.

Between Feakle and Portumna (Co. Galway) is Woodford, scene of the arrest in 1887, at a protest meeting of tenants he organized, of the English poet Wilfred Scawen Blunt (1840–1922). He was a friend of Lady Gregory; was convicted at Loughrea and imprisoned for two months in Galway and Dublin; his poems *In Vinculis* (1889) describe this.

74. Robin Flower, *The Irish Tradition*. Southern Half: an ancient division of Ireland was along a geological line (the Esker Ridge) from Dublin to Galway Bay.

75. Letter quoted in Winifred Gérin, *Charlotte Bronte: The Evolution of Genius* (1967).

76. Arthur Bell Nicholls (1818–1906) was born in south Antrim, and had been brought up in the family of his uncle, Dr Bell, rector of Banagher. He went to Haworth in 1845; Charlotte married him in June 1854; she died in March 1855. After his return (1861) he was also rector of Birr, Offaly. The portrait by Branwell Bronte of Charlotte, Emily and Anne was found in the Nicholls house; the photograph of Charlotte in the National Portrait Gallery (London) is thought to have been taken while they were in Ireland.

77. Offaly: formerly 'King's County', named after Philip of Spain, husband of Mary Tudor; Laois was 'Queen's County' after Mary, in whose (Catholic) reign (1553–8) these counties were 'planted'.

78. Another more ancient 'centre' at Uisneach in Westmeath [2] is a little further north, between Athlone and Mullingar.

79. T.W. Rolleston: this poem (headed 'From the Irish of Enoch [Angus] O'Gillan') was his one lasting poetic success. With Yeats, he was a disciple of O'Leary in Dublin in the 1880s, and an active cultural nationalist (co-founder of the Irish Literary Society) in London. He wrote on German and on Irish literature; lived in London from 1908.

80. O'Connor, *LMC* (*c*.1945).

81. *MI*.

82. Devenish Island: near Cloonburren. *At Swim-Two-Birds* quoted at Dublin [7]. Tullamore is the background to Flann's O'Brien's novel *The Third Policeman*, written 1940, pub. 1967 – said (by Aidan Higgins, quoted by Cronin) to be a 'portrait of Hell'. Anthony Cronin, *No Laughing Matter: The Life and Times of Flann O'Brien* (1989).

83. O'Faolain, *IJ* (1940). 'Slievenamon': a song of defiant defeat with a 'magical tune' (trans. in *KLC*).

84. James Warren Doyle (1786–1834), 'Pastoral Address to the Deluded and Illegal Association of Ribbonmen' (1822), in *The Cabinet of Irish Literature* (1897, vol. 2). He studied in Portugal; returned in 1808, became bishop of Kildare and Leighlin in 1819, using these initials as a pen-name. In the 1830s he gave evidence on the state of Ireland to parliament in London; he advocated national education and the union of Christian Churches.

85. Melosina Lenox-Conyngham in *The Kilkenny Anthology*, ed. Macdara Woods (1991); also below. Lady Eleanor Butler (1739?–1829); Sarah Ponsonby (1735?–1831). *The Hamwood Papers . . .*, ed. Mrs G.H. Bell (1930).

86. Lockhart, *Life of Scott*.

87. Lenox-Conyngham, as above.

88. Heaney: see [1], at Moira (note 51).
89. O'Connor, *Irish Miles*.
90. Thomas Moore (1779–1852) quoted in L.A.G. Strong, *The Minstrel Boy* (1937). The theatre closed in 1819.
91. Ghostly scenes in *The Fetches* by the Banim brothers are set in the College grounds.
92. *Ireland*, vol. II.
93. Alexis de Tocqueville (1805–59), *Journeys to England and Ireland* (his unpublished notes), trans. Lawrence and Meyer (1958). His classic works are on democracy in America (1835–40) and France (1856).
94. They (or rather, John) also published historical novels, e.g. *The Boyne Water* (1826) – 'hamstrung by a wish to be fair to all sides' (Brian Cleeve, *Dictionary of Irish Writers*); written 'with maturity and insight' (Mark Hawthorne, *DIL*). There is a classical bust of John Banim in the municipal offices. Several stories have local settings: *Peter of the Castle* at the ruin of Kells Priory (south of Kilkenny); *The Peep o' Day* on Slievenamon. *The Kilkenny Anthology*, ed. Macdara Woods (1991), has extracts from the Banims and other writers.
95. Mary Tighe (1772–1810) was celebrated as the author of 'Psyche, or the Legend of Love' (1795), a narrative in Spenserian stanzas. A white marble effigy of her on the sofa she died on at Woodstock is shut in a mausoleum in the churchyard at Inistioge.
96. Black and Tans: the paramilitary forces sent from England to quell the nationalist guerrillas, following the 1916 Rising and before the 1921 Treaty. The name came from a pack of hounds (see above, at Limerick).
97. Hubert Butler, *The Sub-Prefect Should Have Held His Tongue* (collected essays, 1990). Standish O'Grady (1846–1928): popular historian and historical novelist.
98. Iris Origo, *Images and Shadows* (1970).
99. Butler, *The Sub-Prefect* . . . (as above).
100. O'Connor, in *KLC*.
101. Sterne's mother's family came from here. As a child he moved around Ireland; one of the few incidents he recalls is falling into the millrace at Annamoe, Co. Wicklow [7, note].
102. Borrow was in Clonmel in 1815; *Lavengro* (1851) is a 'fictionalized autobiography'.
103. O'Connor, *LMC*.
104. Trollope lived at Clonmel 1844–5. Elizabeth Bowen's *The Shelbourne* (1951) describes the Bianconi coaches and their effect on Irish life.

      Lady Blessington (Marguerite Power, 1789–1846), famous beauty and hostess, friend of Thomas Moore, author of *A Journal of Conversations with Lord Byron* (1832) etc., was born at Knockbrit (east of Cashel) and lived at Clonmel as a child.

      Peter Somerville-Large in *The Grand Irish Tour* (1982) gives an account of the lively *Retrospections of an Outcast* by Dorothea Herbert (1770–1829;

published 1919/1930), daughter of a 'well-connected clergyman' at Carrick-on-Suir (east of Clonmel).

105. Unpub. trans.

106. Stephen Gwynn, *Fair Hills of Ireland*, also above. Price had earlier been a suitor for Swift's 'Vanessa'; he was her local clergyman, and she is supposed to have given deathbed instructions, 'no Price, no prayers'.

107. Sir Aubrey de Vere, 'Cashel' in *Penguin*.

Chapter 5: The South-West

1. O'Connor, *LMC* (*c*. 1945).
2. Mr and Mrs S.C. Hall, *Ireland* (1841), vol. i.
3. H.V. Morton, *In Search of Ireland* (1930).
4. Mitchel was sent to Bermuda and then Van Diemen's Land (Tasmania) where his family joined him; escaped in 1853 to America. He died on his return to Ireland, having been elected as a member of parliament.
5. Trans. Kuno Meyer, in *FDA* and *A Celtic Miscellany*. The 'Vision' was of a world made of food.
6. Böll, *Irish Journal*.
7. O'Connor (1903–66), *LMC*. He was a librarian in Cork and director of the Abbey Theatre; lived in America in the 1950s. *An Only Child* (1961) is his autobiography.
8. O'Faolain (born John Whelan, 1900–91), *IJ*. He was a teacher in England and America; editor of *The Bell* literary magazine from 1940; biographer. His autobiography is *Vive Moi!* (1964).
9. Alexis de Tocqueville (1805–59), *Journey to England and Ireland*.
10. Thackeray, *The Irish Sketchbook* (1842); all quotations from this.
11. Daniel Corkery (1878–1964), described in O'Connor, *LMC*.
12. Hyde and Raftery: see Ballylee, Galway [6]. O'Connor's translation in *KLC*.
13. Unpub. trans. James Stephens quoted in *FDA*.
14. O'Connor, trans. ('A Grey Eye Weeping'), and comment below in *KLC*.
15. Arthur Young (1741–1820), *Tour in Ireland* (1780). This is the style of garden Bishop Percy was contriving (Dromore, [1]).
16. Colum, comment on Milliken in *A Treasury of Irish Folklore* (1967, reprinted). *Memoir* (1823) quoted in *FDA*. The catchy metre of 'The Groves' was also used in the popular humorous pieces by Cork-born 'Father Prout' (Francis Mahony, 1804–66); e.g. 'The Bells of Shandon' ('That sound so grand on / The pleasant waters / Of the River Lee . . .'). An example from Irish quoted at Belmullet [6].
17. Colum was an original member of and playwright for the Abbey Theatre; taught at St Enda's (Patrick Pearse's Irish-speaking school); went to America in 1914.
18. Kelly: anecdote in *LMC*.

19. Eibhlín Ní Chonaill, known as Eilín Dubh (= 'dark'). Keened: *caoineadh* ['keen'] = 'lament'.
20. Translation by Eilis Dillon. Comments on the poem by Peter Levi in Inaugural Lecture, Oxford, 1984.
21. *FDA*.
22. Poem trans. Seán Dunne in *Taisce Duan*. Ó Coileáin ['O Cuilloyn'] (anglicized 'John Collins') is buried at Kilmeen, north of Rosscarbery.
23. Charles Smith (1715–62), *The Antient and Present State of the County and City of Cork* (1750). Others claim that Swift's excursions went further down the coast, to Roaringwater Bay.
24. In Lady Gregory's version (*GFM*), the King of Ulster's son elopes with Cliodhna of the Fair Hair; he leaves her in the boat on the shore (at 'Teite's Strand') while he goes hunting; she falls asleep and is swept back to the sea. Tidal waves occur on this coast; 'Cliodhna's Wave' is claimed both by Glandore Harbour and Rosscarbery Bay. Glandore is a deep inlet, a likely site for the story; whereas the legendary roaring, revenging 'Great Waves' are usually placed on wide strands, like the one at Owenahincha by Rosscarbery (where there is also a 'Cliodhna's Rock').
25. Swift was 56 in 1723, Shaw 50 in 1906. Shaw had married in 1898. The previous year, he had stayed for three months at his wife's family home, Derry House near Rosscarbery, writing *Man and Superman* ('it will be TREMENDOUS, simply'). Shaw's Irish play, *John Bull's Other Island* (1904), was his first real success.
26. *Irish Memories* (1917); also anecdote about the Gregorys (below). Gifford Lewis, *Somerville and Ross: The world of the Irish R.M.* (Penguin ed., 1987) is an illustrated account of their lives.
27. From 'Trinket's Colt', in *Some Experiences of an Irish R.M.*
28. *LMC*.
29. The settings of the Somerville and Ross books are generally composite, with made-up names. *The Big House at Inver* (1925, inspired by Tyrone House on Galway Bay), written by Somerville after Ross's death, was dedicated 'To Our Intention, 1912–25', with an Author's Note: 'An established Firm does not change its style and title when, for any reason, one of its partners may be compelled to leave it. The partner who shared all things with me has left me, but the Firm has not yet put up the shutters. . . .'
30. *LMC*. O'Connor, like O'Faolain, lived at the south end of Dublin Bay, not far from Dun Laoghaire, the ferry port.
31. This story, and O'Connor's 'Guests of the Nation', in *FDA*.
32. *Ireland* (1841), vol. I.
33. Callanan made a collection of legends and ballads which was lost. Most of his poems were published posthumously. See below, at Killarney.
34. Said to be the second on the left going up from the main road to Gougane Barra.
35. O'Connor, *LMC*.
36. O'Connor, introduction to *The Tailor* (1964 edition).

37. Corkery, *THI*.
38. *The Irish Sketchbook* (1842).
39. *Hungry Hill*, the family-saga novel by Daphne du Maurier (1943), is based on the ruined mansion at Dunboy, opposite Beare Island.
40. Translations in order quoted: 'Ebb tide . . .' and 'Where once . . .', John Montague (*Faber*); other lines from *A Golden Treasury of Irish Poetry AD 600–1200*, ed. David Greene and Frank O'Connor. The Hag also personifies Ireland in subjection (the 'Shan Van Vocht': 'old poor woman'); and in ancient mythology as a disguise (hag, *cailleach*, literally 'veiled') of the Great Goddess.
41. Another famous hotel is Parknasilla on the south-east coast, along the road from Kenmare. It was the home of the bishop of Limerick, father of Alfred Perceval Graves (1846–1931), who wrote light verse and popular songs ('Father O'Flynn'), and was father of the poet Robert Graves.
42. Sean O'Faolain, *King of the Beggars* (1938).
43. Tennyson and de Vere: see [4] at Curragh Chase (Limerick). 'So dark . . .' in 'Merlin and Vivien'. 'Tomorrow' printed 1885.
44. Grigson, 'Skellig Michael', in *Country Writings* (1984).
45. From 'After the Irish of Egan O'Rahilly' by Eavan Boland, in *Penguin Contemp.*
46. Version by Eiléan Ní Chuilleanáin, 'Against Blame of Women', in Faber. Comment by Kinsella (below) in *Poems of the Dispossessed*.
47. Synge, *In West Kerry* (1907). Sybil Ferriter: a runaway bride, drowned in a cave below the castle.
    Also near Ballyferriter is the Oratory of Gallarus, 'the most perfect piece of early Irish building' (subject of a poem by Seamus Heaney). Below Mount Brandon, St Brendan (the Voyager, the Navigator, 484–577) is supposed to have set out on the Atlantic expedition related in the 9th-century Latin *Voyage of St Brendan* – the pagan *Voyage of Bran* is also connected with these shores. On the south coast, Ventry (Finntraigh) is the 'White Strand' of Finn's battle with the 'King of the World'.
48. Flower, *The Western Island; or, the Great Blasket* (1944). The islanders called him 'Blaheen', 'little flower'.
49. Sayers, *An Old Woman's Reflections* (1939), trans. S. Ennis (1952).
50. Synge, *In West Kerry* (1907); also below.
51. O'Sullivan, *Twenty Years A-Growing* (1933), trans. Moya Llewellyn Davies and George Thompson, with introduction by E.M. Forster (also 1933).
52. The quatrain from unpub. trans.
53. O'Crohan, *The Islandman* (1929, written 1926), trans. Robin Flower (1937).
54. Opposite the entrance to Muckross Abbey, at Killeghy, the creator of 'Baron Munchausen' is buried: Rudolf Raspe (1737–94), a Hanoverian adventurer who was visiting Killarney as a geological adviser.
55. *Irish Sketchbook*.
56. See note at Dublin [7] on their first visit, in 1812. This time they had reached Dublin in early March, after an attack in Wales by masked intruders. When their books arrived they headed west, to a secret address; before the end of

March they heard that Hogg had arrived, rushed back to Dublin, missed him, and went straight on to London. Harriet's sister and their Irish servant Dan Healy were left in Killarney to pack up the books and sail home from Cork to Bristol (*The Pursuit* by Richard Holmes, 1974).

57. Thomas Hogg (1792–1862), *Life of Shelley* (1858). They were friends at Oxford, and had been in Scotland together the previous year. Hogg had been told the Shelleys were in Killarney, but decided that pursuing them any further might be a wild-goose chase. He did not think much of Dublin ('I never once met a woman in the street with silk stockings . . .') but was gratified to hear Shelley spoken of 'with uniform, unvarying kindness and respect'.

58. Tennyson's lyric 'The splendour falls . . . set the wild echoes flying' is supposed to be inspired by the echoes at the 'Eagle's Nest', where a bugle was blown for tourists.

59. Charlotte Bronte (1816–55), letters quoted in biography by Gérin.

60. O'Connor's translation ('Last Lines'), and comment, in *KLC*. The line is in 'The Curse of Cromwell', one of Yeats's last poems.

61. Owen Roe (Eoghan Rua, 'red-head') O'Sullivan; from 'To the Blacksmith with a Spade', trans. O'Connor in *KLC*.

62. Michael Hartnett, 'Chef Yeats . . .', from *A Farewell to English* (1975–8). 'The Last Vision', poem in both languages, in *Penguin Contemp.*

In north Kerry, near the Limerick border, Listowel is a modern literary centre, with a writers' festival. Bryan MacMahon, author of *The Honey Spike* (play and novel, about the life of tinkers), was born there (in 1909); also the playwrights George Fitzmaurice (1877–1963) and John B. Keane (b. 1928).

Chapter 6: The West

1. William Wordsworth (1770–1850), letter (18 Sept. 1829).
2. Charlotte Bronte, letter (27 July 1851), and Arthur Nicholls letter, quoted in biography by Winifred Gérin.
3. Opening lines from 'Farewell to Ireland', quoted in *DIL*.
4. Iris Murdoch (b. 1919, Dublin), *The Unicorn* (1963).
5. Another novel by Lawless is set in the Aran islands: *Grania* (1892), which Swinburne called 'just one of the most perfect and exquisite works of genius in the language'.
6. Grigson, 'The Melancholia of Burren' in *Country Writings*.
7. W.B. Yeats, *Autobiographies* (1955; this volume is a collection of separate books of Yeats's memoirs). Synge's *Riders to the Sea* (1902) is set on Aran ('an Island off the West of Ireland'); *The Playboy* (1907) 'on a wild coast of Mayo'. His visits to the Blasket islands [5] came a few years later.
8. O'Flaherty, 'Going into exile', from *Spring Sowing* (1924) in *FDA*, which also quotes 'holding a robin'. 'Patsa' in *Stories* (Wolfhound Press 1991).

9. de Basterot: a cousin of Edward Martyn; wrote travel memoirs, d. 1904 and has a handsome tomb by the ruined church beside Durrus. French literary celebrities are said to have stayed at Durrus; it seems unlikely that Maupassant actually went there, but Paul Bourget (1852–1935), also a traveller and writer, called the Burren 'royaume de pierres', Kingdom of Stones.

   At Kinvar(r)a, the castle-house by the sea, Donogory, belonged to Oliver St John Gogarty, who restored it with the help of Yeats. 'Irish feasts' are held there, with readings.

10. She had decided to learn Irish through meeting Douglas Hyde. When she met Yeats she 'dragged him in and out of cottages where she took down stories and tried to learn her Irish. Yeats listened, and half listened . . .' (Kate O'Brien, *MI*). Yeats did not learn Irish.

11. Yeats, *The Trembling of the Veil* (part of *Autobiographies*); also following quotations.

12. O'Connor, *LMC* (*c.* 1950); also following quotations.

13. Yeats, as above. In 1910 Wilfred Scawen Blunt (1840–1922), the English poet and traveller, old friend of Lady Gregory and agitator for Irish rights, noted after having dinner with them both: 'Yeats . . . is an extremely pleasant fellow, and has a more prosperous look, and is fatter and rosier, than formerly. Lady Gregory has been the making of him' (*Interviews with Lady Gregory*, ed. E.H. Mickail [1977]).

14. Last line of Prologue 'To Lady Gregory' of a play, *The Shadowy Waters* (1900).

15. O'Connor, *LMC*, also below.

16. Sir Horace Plunkett (1854–1932) was a Unionist MP (1892) and a Senator of the Free State (1922). He left Ireland after his house was burnt by extremists, but worked for agricultural cooperatives all his life.

17. Ulick O'Connor (b. 1929), *Celtic Dawn: A Portrait of the Irish Literary Renaissance* (1984).

18. Gregory, *GFM*.

19. *DIL*.

20. 'To be Carved on a Stone at Thoor Ballylee' (written 1918). He spent summers there until 1928.

21. In 'Blessed be this place . . .' (written 1927); part of 'Blood and the Moon' ('. . . I declare this tower is my symbol; I declare / This winding, gyring, spiring treadmill of a stair is my ancestral stair . . .').

22. From part II of 'The Tower' (written 1925).

23. 'The Road at my Door' (written 1922), part V of *Meditations in Time of Civil War*.

24. As above, part VII, 'I see Phantoms of Hatred and of the Heart's Fullness and of the Coming Emptiness'.

25. P.J. Kavanagh, 'Yeats's Tower' (written 1958): *Collected Poems* (1992).

26. Raftery is buried at Killineen, on the north bank of the river west of Craughwell (he has a statue in the village).

27. *Songs Ascribed to Raftery*, part of Hyde's *The Songs of Connacht* (1903).

28. Hyde, as above.

29. Yeats, from 'The Tower', as above.
30. O'Connor, quoted in *DIL*; also on O'Donovan, below.
31. Austin Clarke (1896–1974), 'The New Cathedral in Galway': *The Echo at Coole* (1968).
32. Harriet Martineau (1802–76), *Letters from Ireland* (1852); all quotations from this. A pioneering journalist; the previous year, she had published an 'agnostic rationale of moral obligation . . . an ideology of industry whose ideal is neatness' (Maxwell, *The English Traveller in Ireland*). An earlier and even more intrepid single female traveller (on foot), who actually stayed in such cabins and took a more sympathetic view of them, was the American Asenath Nicholson (*The Bible in Ireland: Excursions . . . 1844–5*). Peter Somerville-Large follows her tracks, and other travellers', in *The Grand Irish Tour* (1982)
33. Sir William Wilde (1815–76), *Lough Corrib: Its Shores and Islands* (1867). An enthusiastic interpreter of ancient sites; his house 'Moytura' was near Cong.
34. Colum, *RRI* (1926).
35. O'Faolain, *IJ* (1940).
36. Kate O'Brien, *MI* (1962; all quotations from this).
37. Plays and novels by Walter Macken (1915–67; actor, and manager of the Gaelic theatre) are set in Galway. Nora Barnacle (Mrs James Joyce) came from Galway; her family's house is now a tourist attraction. The Joyces visited in 1912.

    North of Galway, on the east side of Lower Lough Corrib, is Annaghdown, where in 1828 nineteen people were drowned in the sinking of a boat taking them (and their sheep) to the fair of Galway; subject of a lament by Raftery.
38. O Conaire, 'My Little Black Ass': trans. Eoghan O Tuairisc in *The Finest Stories of Padraic O Conaire* (1991).
39. Pearse and O Conaire quoted in *FDA* (introduction to 'Irish Writing 1900–1981').
40. O'Faolain, *IJ*.
41. O Cadhain, *The Road to Brightcity*: trans. Eoghan O Tuairisc (1981).
42. 'The Death of Irish' in *Penguin Contemp.*
43. 'I am Ireland . . .' (trans. Pearse) and 'Naked I saw thee . . .' (trans. Mac-Donagh, title 'Ideal', in *Taisce Duan* – this poem was also translated by Pearse, with title 'Renunciation'). Pearse is said to have brought Gaelic poetry into the twentieth century.
44. *Irish Memories* (1917). Letters (below) quoted in Lewis, *Somerville and Ross: The world of the Irish RM*.
45. Chevalier de Latocnaye, *A Frenchman's Walk through Ireland*, trans. John Stevenson, 1984.
46. 'I know my job as a queen'.
47. Maria Edgeworth (1767–1849): *The Life and Letters*, ed. Augustus Hare (1894); and *Tour in Connemara and the Martins of Ballinahinch*, ed. Harold Edgeworth Butler (1950). She was 67 at the time of the tour; she describes it in letters (1834) to her young half-brother in India.
48. Somerville and Ross, *Through Connemara*.

49. Richard Murphy (b. 1927), 'Slate' in *Penguin Contemp.*
50. 'The Battle of Aughrim' (1968).
51. *Through Connemara.*
52. Gogarty, Sackville Street (1937). Yeats, Shaw, Augustus John, and many others stayed at Renvyle.
53. Proudly described by the young Oscar: '. . . in every way magnificent . . . teeming with sport of all kinds. . . .'
54. *A Celtic Miscellany.*
55. *Ulick and Soracha*, included in *A Story-Teller's Holiday* (1918), is also set on the lake.
56. *HF.*
57. *LMC.*
58. Gogarty, *I Follow St Patrick* (1938).
59. Moore, *A Storyteller's Holiday*: this begins with Moore staying at 'Westport Lodge' above the town; he there meets the fern-gatherer 'Alec Trusselby' and they exchange stories, mostly of ancient Ireland.
60. T.H. White (1906–64), *The Godstone and the Blackymor* (1959).
61. Thomas De Quincey (1785–1859), 'Autobiographic Sketches'; quoted in *A Flame in Sunlight* by Edward Sackville-West (1936). De Quincey devotes several chapters to this visit, two to the 1798 Rebellion. He is returning to Dublin by canal when he is rescued from the snubs of a snobbish fellow-traveller by this ideal companion.
62. *Journal of the Westport Historical Society* (1992).
63. Martineau, *Letters from Ireland.*
64. Louis MacNeice, from 'Western Landscape'.
65. Heinrich Böll (1917–85), *Irish Journal.*
66. MacNeice, from 'The Strand' (1945).
67. T.H. White, *The Godstone and the Blackymor.*
68. MacNeice, from 'Sligo and Mayo', part III of *The Closing Album* (1939).
69. Gregory, *GFM.*
70. Richard Barrett, 'Another Round', in *FDA*, trans. Donal O'Sullivan.
71. Yeats's play *Cathleen ni Houlihan* is set in 'a cottage close to Killala, in 1798'.
72. Benedict Kiely, *All the Way to Bantry Bay* (1978).
73. 'Cathleen ni Houlihan': i.e. the spirit of Ireland; disguised as an old woman, she inspires the young men of a family to rebellion (at Killala, see above; see also the 'old Woman of Beare' [5]).
74. Yeats, *Autobiographies. Walden, or Life in the Woods*: by H.D. Thoreau (1854).
75. Sheelah Kirby, *The Yeats Country* (1985 ed.).
76. From 'Three Songs to One Burden'.
77. Robin Flower, *The Irish Tradition* (1947).
78. O'Connor's version in *Faber.*
79. O'Connor, *LMC.*
80. Yeats, from 'In Memory of Eva Gore-Booth and Con Markiewicz' (1927). Eva Gore-Booth (1870–1926); Constance (Gore-Booth) Markiewicz (1868–1927).

81. Gregory, *GFM*. The hunting scenes in the ancient stories are, of course, set in an Ireland covered with forest.
82. 'Cathach': see Donegal [3].
83. See above, at Coole.
84. Quoted in Kirby, *The Yeats Country*, as above; also Lily Yeats's remark, below.

Chapter 7: *Around Dublin*

1. The 'Fenian cycle' of stories with Finn as hero, with many satellite tales, were collected by Lady Gregory as *Gods and Fighting Men* (1904); quotations here are from this. Among other retellings is James Stephens's *Irish Fairy Tales* (1920). Many hills etc. are associated with Finn.
2. O'Faolain, *IJ* (1940).
3. The tower was put up by Sir Gerald Aylmer.
4. W.B. Yeats, preface to *GFM*.
5. *GFM*.
6. *GFM*.
7. W.B. Yeats, preface to *GFM*.
8. Line from 'All Things Can Tempt Me' (1909).
9. Brigit (or Brigid; also 'St Bride') was born at Faughart near Dundalk [2], where there is a shrine to her. One of the 'Blessed Trinity of Ireland', with Sts Patrick and Columcille. In *GFM*, when the Tuatha Dé Danann, the ancient gods, come to Ireland, they bring among the greatest of their women 'Brigit, that was a woman of poetry. . . . And one side of her face was ugly, but the other side was very comely. And the meaning of her name was "Breo-saighit", a fiery arrow.'
10. R.A.S. Macalister, *Tara* (1931).
11. The Irish festivals came at the turn of the seasons, between solstice and equinox. Imbolc (1 Feb.) is thought to mark the lactation of ewes, and first signs of spring. There are many 'Bridie' folk customs at this time.
12. *Faber*.
13. Quoted by O'Faolain, *IJ*.
14. 'Culdee': anglicization of *Céle Dé*, lit. 'a companion of God's', a name given to anchorites (solitary holy men); part of an 8th–9th-century religious reform movement.
15. From 'The Downfall of Heathendom' in *A Golden Treasury of Irish Poetry AD 600–1200*, ed. Greene and O'Connor.
16. J.G. Lockhart (1794–1854), *Memoirs of the Life of Sir Walter Scott* (1837–8). Scott (1771–1832) was 53 at the time.
17. Colum, *RRI* (1926).
18. Robin Flower, *The Irish Tradition*: lines in Irish from a Latin grammar, followed by an explanation: 'That is, the wind is keen when men go to church at Glendalough for vespers and nocturnes.'

19. Terence de Vere White, *The Parents of Oscar Wilde* (1967), quoting Wilde's book on the antiquarian Béranger. The Wildes spent holidays in Co. Wicklow, the young Wildes helping with sketches for their father's books. The curious name 'Sebastian Melmoth' adopted by Oscar in his exile in France derives from *Melmoth the Wanderer* by Charles Maturin (a great-uncle of Lady Wilde's), a famous 'gothic' novel (1820) set chiefly in the dungeons of the Spanish Inquisition, but beginning and ending in a crumbling mansion in Co. Wicklow.

20. 'Stream and Sun' in *The Winding Stair*, 1933.

21. Quoted in Geoffrey Ellsom, *Francis Stuart: A Life* (1990).

22. *The Shadow of the Glen* was first produced in 1903. Synge's *The Well of the Saints* (1905) and *The Tinker's Wedding* (1907) are also set in Wicklow. John Millington Synge (1871–1909) was born in Rathfarnham, on this side of Dublin, and stayed many summers in Wicklow, at Greystones on the coast, and in houses rented by his family in the hills. Tiglin, Ashford, now a Youth Hostel, was a farm belonging to an aunt. At Tomriland House he listened through the floor to the rhythms of the servant girls' talk in the kitchen (see Clogher [3]). He started visiting the West in 1898. Synge also stayed at Castle Kevin above Annamoe, where Laurence Sterne (1713–68) had a 'wonderful escape' as a child, after 'falling through a mill-race whilst the mill was going, and of being taken up unhurt. . . . Hundreds of the common people flocked to see me'.

    Avoca, where the river Avonmore (from Laragh) joins the Avonbeg from Glenmalure valley, is the 'Meeting of the Waters' of Thomas Moore's famous song.

23. From *Nepenthe*, in *Penguin*. Darley was born in Dublin; left Ireland after attending Trinity College, but the Dublin hills remained his poetic ideal ('one green spot far o'er the waves of Time. . .' '. . . And where the valley slopes down to the sky / With nought beyond but the blue gulf of air . . .' – from his last sonnets).

24. From 'Anna Livia Plurabelle', part of *Finnegans Wake*, in *Oxford 1958*.

25. The final chapter in *Sackville Street* (1937).

26. O'Connor, *LMC*. 'Da Dearga's Hostel' (or 'The Destruction of the Hall of Da Derga') is a 9th-century tale of magic and monsters; 'and its firelight . . .' from *GFM*.

27. Eoin O'Brien, *The Beckett Country* (1986); Beckett's early home was at Foxrock, inland from Dun Laoghaire below these mountains.

28. George Moore, *HF*.

29. V.S. Pritchett, *Dublin* (1967, 1991).

30. In O'Brien's book a mad scientist conjures up the spirit of St Augustine, in an underwater cave by a bathing-place below the hill at Dalkey.

    George Bernard Shaw lived (1866–74) at 'Torca Cottage', his mother's house at Dalkey, with a view over the bay.

31. Robert Nicholson, *The* Ulysses *Guide: tours through Joyce's Dublin* (1991).

32. Thackeray is describing a boat-race.

33. Böll, *Irish Journal*.
34. Gogarty, *Sackville Street*; also on Merrion Sands (below).
35. Quoted by Ulick O'Connor, *Oliver St John Gogarty* (1964).
36. The incident happened in 1715. Irvin Ehrenpreis, Swift (vol. iii).
37. Robert Bernard Martin, *Gerard Manley Hopkins: A very private life* (1991). The Prospect cemetery at Glasnevin is mainly Catholic; Mount Jerome at Harold's Cross in south Dublin is the Protestant equivalent.
38. Mary Moorman, *William Wordsworth* (1965; vol ii), quoting *Life* of Hamilton by R.P. Graves (1889).
39. Colum, *RRI*. Sean O'Casey, *Autobiographies* (1963).
40. Gogarty, *Sackville Street*.
41. 'Vanessa''s letters were published by degrees, many by Scott. An example of the legend at its extreme is Sybil Le Brocquy's *Cadenus* (1962). Denis Johnson's *In Search of Swift* (1959) sifts the evidence. Biographers such as Irvin Ehrenpreis see no need for much mystery. Swift's summer tour had been planned for some time before the death of Vanessa, who was already fatally ill. Swift used also to visit her and her sister in Dublin. There is no evidence she changed her will; Swift would have wished her to leave money to charity, which Berkeley could perform (he used it for a scheme to found a college in America).
42. 'Jealousy' printed with Swift's *Poems*. 'Stella' (Esther Johnson, 1681–1728) moved to Ireland with a friend and chaperone, Rebecca Dingley, in 1701. They lived in lodgings, and occupied Swift's houses when he was away. Swift wrote his 'Journal to Stella' from London in 1710–13. They also stayed in the houses of mutual friends: e.g. at Quilca, Co. Cavan [2].
43. The old road into Dublin passes below Phoenix Park; Samuel Ferguson's monologue in the style of Browning, 'At the Polo-Ground' (on the Phoenix Park murders) in *New Oxford*. G.K. Chesterton wrote *Christendom in Dublin* on the enormous Eucharistic Congress held there in 1932.
44. Attributed to James Stephens in Cronin, *No Laughing Matter* (1989).
45. Patrick Pearse: see Rosmuck, Galway [6]; and below. Thomas MacDonagh (b. 1878): also a playwright, associate of Pearse at St Enda's, and university lecturer. Joseph Mary Plunkett (b. 1887): associated with Edward Martyn's Irish Theatre; he drew up the detailed plans for the Rising. There are poems by MacDonagh and Plunkett in *Penguin*. Descriptions of MacDonagh and Plunkett from Austin Clarke, *A Penny in the Clouds* (1965).
46. Patrick Pearse, *The Murder Machine* [i.e. English education]: extracts in *FDA*.
47. From extract from Sean O'Casey, *Drums Under the Window*, and introduction, in *FDA*. Jimmy O'Dea: perhaps best known for his song in drag, as 'Biddy Mulligan the Pride of the Coombe'. Tommy Handley: star of the BBC war-time radio show 'ITMA', written by Ted Kavanagh; famous for its puns. The rebuilt Post Office in O'Connell Street contains a Christ-like memorial bronze of the dying Cuchulainn.
48. James Stephens, *The Insurrection in Dublin* (1916, reprint 1992). Stephens's *The Charwoman's Daughter* (1912) is a fantasy set realistically in Dublin slums.

49. From a radio broadcast, 1946; in *James, Seumas and Jacques: Unpublished Writings of James Stephens*, ed. Lloyd Frankenburg (1964); also in *A Book of Ireland*, ed. Frank O'Connor (1959, 1991).

50. Letters quoted in biography of Hopkins by Robert Martin (see above, Dunsink).

51. James Joyce (1882–1941), *Portrait of the Artist* (1916). Robert Nicolson's *Ulysses Guide*, and others, have plotted the Joyce connections with Dublin in books and life. The university building is also described in Flann O'Brien's *At Swim-Two-Birds* (1939; its narrator is a student there).

52. St Stephen's Green and the Shelbourne Hotel figure in many memoirs. George Moore described escaping from his nurse-maid in the gardens and taking off his clothes; later he stayed at the Shelbourne, and wrote there. *A Drama in Muslin* (1887), about the stultifying effects of wealthy 1880s society on two girls, is largely set in the Shelbourne: it contains a famous description of the families in their finery driving from the hotel through the slums to a ball at Dublin Castle. Elizabeth Bowen's *The Shelbourne* (1951) is a social history of middle-class Dublin; her autobiography of her childhood in Dublin is *Seven Winters* (1942). G.K. Chesterton has a chapter on the Stephen's Green statues in *Irish Impressions* (1919) (see below, on Mangan).

53. George Moore, *HF*. He also describes the house and former garden in Upper Ely Place in *A Storyteller's Holiday* (1918). Irish Revival plays were acted in the garden. Stories of AE and Moore in *A Memoir of AE* by 'John Eglinton' (1937); Gogarty's stories in *Sackville Street* and its sequels.

54. *MI*.

55. V.S. Pritchett, *Dublin* (1991).

56. *Ulysses*: from the scene in the National Library ('Scylla and Charybdis') in which 'AE' and other writers appear. 'Mulligan' is on his way to a party at Moore's.

57. Denis Johnston, 'A Short View of the Progress of Joyceanity', in *A Bash in the Tunnel: James Joyce by the Irish*, ed. John Ryan (1970). *The Old Lady Says 'No!'* was produced at the Gate Theatre in 1928.

58. From 'The Siege of Mullingar' by John Montague (1963, about a folk festival).

59. O'Connor, *LMC*. The theatre was reopened in 1966.

60. *MI*.

61. *LMC*.

62. Austin Clarke, *A Penny in the Clouds*.

63. See Inniskeen [2]. 'Leafy-with-love banks' from 'Canal Bank Walk'; 'O commemorate' from 'Lines Written on a Seat on the Grand Canal'.

64. Flann O'Brien (Brian O'Nolan, 1911–66) and Sweeney: see also notes at Moira, Co. Down [1], and Shannonbridge [4].

65. Sean O'Faolain, 'Discord', in *Collected Stories*.

66. James Joyce, lecture in Italian on 'Giacomo Clarenzio Mangan' given at the Università Popolare in Trieste; quoted in *FDA*. See also note on Mangan at Donegal [3].

67. G.K. Chesterton, *Irish Impressions* (1919).

68. From 'Twenty Golden Years Ago' (1840), in *FDA*. 'Speranza': quoted at Wexford [4].
69. John Mitchel, introduction to his edition of Mangan.
70. Laetitia Pilkington (1712–50): extracts from her *Memoirs* (pub. 1748–54) in *FDA* (vol I). She had an adventurous life including a divorce, keeping a bookshop in London and being jailed for debt.
71. Esther Johnson ('Stella'): see note above, at Celbridge.
72. Swift's Hospital (on the old road from Kilmainham to the centre) is still used as a psychiatric unit (He gave the little wealth he had / To build a house for fools and mad; / To show by one satiric touch / No nation wanted it so much – 'Verses on the Death of Dr Swift', written in 1731).
73. Böll, *Irish Journal*.
74. Muriel McCarthy, *All Graduates and Gentlemen: Marsh's Library* (1980).
75. On their first visit to Ireland (February–April 1812) Shelley, aged 19, and his first wife Harriet (17) lodged at the lower end of Sackville/O'Connell Street (no. 7, with a balcony; they also stayed at 17 Grafton St). Shelley had written an *Address to the Irish People*, which he hoped to distribute among the true 'people', converting them to rationalist virtue. He addressed another pamphlet, *Proposals for an Association of Philanthropists*, to the young gentlemen of Trinity College, and spoke for an hour at a meeting in the Fishamble Street Theatre (reported by government spies). Shelley admitted that his mission was a failure; he was appalled by the degree of poverty in Dublin, and realized that the politically educated were locked into local realities, rather than progressive ideals. He wrote several early poems to Ireland, including one on Robert Emmet. D.F. MacCarthy, *Shelley's Early Life from Unpublished Sources* (1870); Holmes, *The Pursuit* (1974). See also Killarney [5].
76. Scott was visiting his son, an army officer, newly married and living in St Stephen's Green. Thomas Moore (see Wexford [4]) went to see the house where he was born, over a shop in Aungier Street (on site of no. 12).
77. Yeats: from 'The Municipal Gallery Revisited'.
78. On the 'Cathach' (see Donegal [3]) and the painters of Kells: Bernard Meehan, 'Irish Manuscripts in the Early Middle Ages', essay in *Treasures of Ireland* (Irish National Academy, Dublin, 1983).
79. Mangan, from 'Dark Rosaleen' (to which he wrote historical footnotes).
80. Patrick Kavanagh, 'In Memory of Brother Michael' – that is, Michael O'Clery; written for a celebration of the Four Masters in 1944 (see notes at Rathcrogan and Donegal [3]). Kavanagh 'was ashamed of the rhetoric in this verse: "Anger has no place in poetry" ' – note in *Collected Poems*.

ACKNOWLEDGEMENTS

The author and publishers would like to thank all those responsible for giving permission to reproduce copyright material.

Sam Hanna Bell, *December Bride*, 1951. Reprinted by permission of The Blackstaff Press, Belfast. *Erin's Orange Lily*, 1956. Reprinted by permission of Fergus Hanna Bell, c/o Fisher & Fisher Solicitors, Newry, Co. Down.

John Betjeman, 'The Return' and 'Ireland with Emily' from *Collected Poems*, 1958. Reprinted by permission of John Murray (Publishers) Ltd., London.

Eavan Boland, 'From the Irish of Egan O'Rahilly'. Reprinted by permission of Carcanet Press Ltd, Manchester.

Heinrich Böll, *Irish Journal*, Secker, London, 1983. Reprinted by permission of Verlag Kiepeheuer and Witsch, Koln.

Elizabeth Bowen, *Bowen's Court*, 1942. Reprinted by permission of Curtis Brown, London.

Eiléan Ní Chuilleanain, 'Lay Your Arms Aside', by Pierce Ferriter, translated by Eiléan Ní Chuilleanain. Reprinted by permission of the author.

Austin Clarke, *Twice Around the Black Church*, 1962; 'The New Cathedral in Galway', in *The Echo at Coole*, 1968; *A Penny in the Clouds*, 1968. Reprinted by permission of R. Dardis Clarke, 21 Pleasants Street, Dublin 8.

Padraic Colum, *The Road Round Ireland*, 1926; 'She Moved Through the Fair'. Reprinted by permission of The Estate of Padraic Colum.

Daniel Corkery, *The Hidden Ireland*, 1925. Reprinted by permission of Gill & Macmillan, Dublin.

Seamus Deane, 'Derry', from *Selected Poems*, 1988. Reprinted by kind permission of the author and The Gallery Press, Dublin.

Robin Flower, *The Irish Tradition*, 1947; *Western Island*, 1944. Reprinted by permission of Oxford University Press.

E.M. Forster, *Selected Letters* (ed. Iago and Furbank). Reprinted by permission of King's College, Cambridge, and The Society of Authors as the literary representative of the Estate of E.M. Forster.

Brian Friel, *Translations*. Reprinted by permission of Curtis Brown, London.

Oliver St John Gogarty, *As I Was Going Down Sackville Street*, 1937; 'The Chronicles Say' in omnibus edition, *Sackville Street*, 1988. Reprinted by permission of Oliver Gogarty, S.C., Dublin.

Geoffrey Grigson, *Country Writings*, Century, 1984. Reprinted by permission of David Higham Associates Limited.

Stephen Gwynn, *Highways and Byways in Donegal and Antrim*, 1899; *The Fair Hills of Ireland*, 1906. Reprinted by kind permission of the Irish Jesuit Community.

Michael Hartnett, 'The Last Vision of Eoghan Rua O Suilleaghain', from *A Necklace of Wrens*, 1987; 'Chef Yeats', from *A Farewell to English*, 1978. Reprinted by kind permission of the author and The Gallery Press, Dublin.

Seamus Heaney, 'A Lough Neagh Sequence', from *Door into the Dark*, 1969; *Sweeney Astray*, 1983; *Sweeney's Flight*, 1992; 'Station Island', from *Station Island*, 1984. Reprinted by permission of Faber and Faber Ltd., London.

John Hewitt, *Poems of William Allingham*, 1967. Reprinted by permission of Keith Millar, Belvedere Lodge, Gatehouse of Fleet, Castle Douglas, Kirkcudbrightshire DG7 2DJ, on behalf of the Hewitt Archive. 'Ulsterman'; 'Freehold'; 'An Ulsterman'; 'Planter's Gothic'; 'At Each Hail Mary' and 'An Irishman in Coventry', from *The Collected Poems of John Hewitt*, 1991. Reprinted by permission of The Blackstaff Press, Belfast.

Pearse Hutchinson, 'The Frost is All Over', from *Selected Poems*, 1982. Reprinted by kind permission of the author and The Gallery Press, Dublin.

Douglas Hyde, 'The Necessity for De-Anglicizing Ireland'; 'Ringleted Youth of My Love', *Love Songs of Connacht*; *The Religious Songs of Connacht*, 1906. Reprinted by permission of Douglas Sealy, Ruloch, Thormanby Road, Howth, Co. Dublin.

Patrick Kavanagh, *The Green Fool*, 'Shancoduff'; *Kerr's Ass*; 'Lough Derg'; 'Leafy-with-love'; 'In Memory of Brother Michael'. Reprinted by kind permission of the trustees of the Estate of Patrick Kavanagh, c/o Peter Fallon, Literary Agent, Loughcrew, Oldcastle, Co. Meath, Ireland.

Benedict Kiely, *All the Way to Bantry Bay*, 1978. Reprinted by permission of the author.

C.S. Lewis, *Surprised by Joy*, Reprinted by permission of HarperCollins Publishers Limited.

Earl of Longford, 'Against Blame of Women'. Reprinted by permission of Thomas Pakenham.

Thomas MacIntyre, 'I Bailed out at Ardee', *The Yellow Bittern*. Reprinted by permission of the author and The Dedalus Press, Dublin.

Francis MacManus, *Men Withering*, 1939. Reprinted by permission of The Mercier Press, Co. Cork.

Louis MacNeice, *The Strings Are False*, 1966. Reprinted by permission of David Higham Associates Limited, London. 'Carrickfergus'; 'Belfast'; *Autumn Journal*, 1938; 'Western Landscape'; 'The Strand'; 'Sligo and Mayo', 1939, from *The Collected Poems of Louis MacNeice*. Reprinted by permission of Faber and Faber Ltd, London.

Derek Mahon, 'In Carrowdore Churchyard', from *Poems 1962–1978*, Oxford University Press, 1979. Reprinted by permission of Oxford University Press.

David Marcus, 'Poem to the Heart of Jesus' by Teague O'Sullivan, translated by David Marcus in *Taisce Duan*. Reprinted by permission of David Marcus.

Aidan Carl Mathews, 'The Death of Irish', from *Minding Ruth*, 1983. Reprinted by kind permission of the author and The Gallery Press, Dublin.

John Montague, 'A Lost Tradition'; 'Lament of the Old Woman of Beare', from *New Selected Poems*, 1989. Reprinted by kind permission of the author and The Gallery Press, Dublin.

Paul Muldoon, 'Ireland'. Reprinted by permission of Faber and Faber Ltd, London.

Iris Murdoch, *The Unicorn*, 1963; *The Red and the Green*. Reprinted by permission of Chatto and Windus, London.

Richard Murphy, 'Slate', from *The Battle of Aughrim*. 1968, in *New Selected Poems*. Reprinted by permission of Faber and Faber Ltd, London.

Flann O'Brien, *At Swim-Two-Birds*. Reprinted by permission of HarperCollins Publishers Limited, London.

Kate O'Brien, *My Ireland*, Batsford, 1962. Reprinted by permission of David Higham Associates Limited, London.

Tomás Ó Canainn, 'Sweeter for me' reprinted from *Taisce Duan* by kind permission of author.

Sean O'Casey, *Drums under the Window*. Reprinted by kind permission of Macnaughton Lowe Representation Ltd, London, and the Estate of Sean O'Casey.

Frank O'Connor, *Leinster, Munster and Connaught; Kings, Lords and Commons; Guests of the Nation*. Reprinted by permission of the Peters Fraser and Dunlop Group Ltd, London.

Sean O'Faolain, *An Irish Journey*, 1940; 'Lovers of the Lake'; 'The Silence of the Valley'; *King of the Beggars, Discord*. Reprinted by permission of the Estate of Sean O'Faolain and Julia Martines, c/o Rogers, Coleridge and White Ltd., London.

Liam O'Flaherty, from the story 'Patsa', or 'The Belly of Gold', by Liam O'Flaherty, in *Short Stories, The Pedlar's Revenge and Other Stories*, by Liam O'Flaherty, Wolfhound Press, Dublin, 1982.

Iris Origo, *Images and Shadows*. Reprinted by permission of John Murray (Publishers) Ltd., London.

V.S. Pritchett, *Midnight Oil*, 1971; *Dublin*, 1967. Reprinted by permission of the Peters, Fraser and Dunlop Group Ltd, London.

W.R. Rodgers, 'Armagh' in *Poems*, ed. Michael Longley, 1993. Reprinted by kind permission of the author and The Gallery Press, Dublin.

James Simmons, *The Cattle Rustling*, Reprinted by permission of Fortnight Educational Trust (FET), 7 Lower Crescent, Belfast BT7. 'Ulster Says Yes', from *Poems 1956 to 1986*, 1986. Reprinted by kind permission of the author and The Gallery Press, Dublin.

James Stephens, *In the Land of Youth*, 1924; 'The Ancient Elf', from *Collected Poems*, 1992; *The Insurrection at Dublin*, 1916. Reprinted by permission of The Society of Authors, on behalf of the copyright owner, Mrs Iris Wise.

Helen Waddell, *Life of St Brigit*, by Sedulius Scotus, translated by Helen Waddell. Reprinted by permission of Constable Publishers, London.

T.H. White, *The Elephant and the Kangaroo*, 1948; *The Godstone and the Blackymor*, Jonathan Cape, 1959. Reprinted by permission of David Higham Associates Limited, London.

While every effort has been made to secure permission, we may have failed in a few cases to trace the copyright holder. We apologize for any apparent negligence.

INDEX